Turner Publishing Company
4507 Charlotte Avenue • Suite 100
Nashville, Tennessee 37209
(615) 255-2665

www.turnerpublishing.com

Historic Photos of Theodore Roosevelt

Library of Congress Control Number: 2007923666

ISBN-13: 978-1-59652-336-4
ISBN: 1-59652-336-0

Printed in the United States of America

ISBN-13: 978-1-68336-950-9 (hc)

09 10 11 12 13 14—0 9 8 7 6 5 4 3

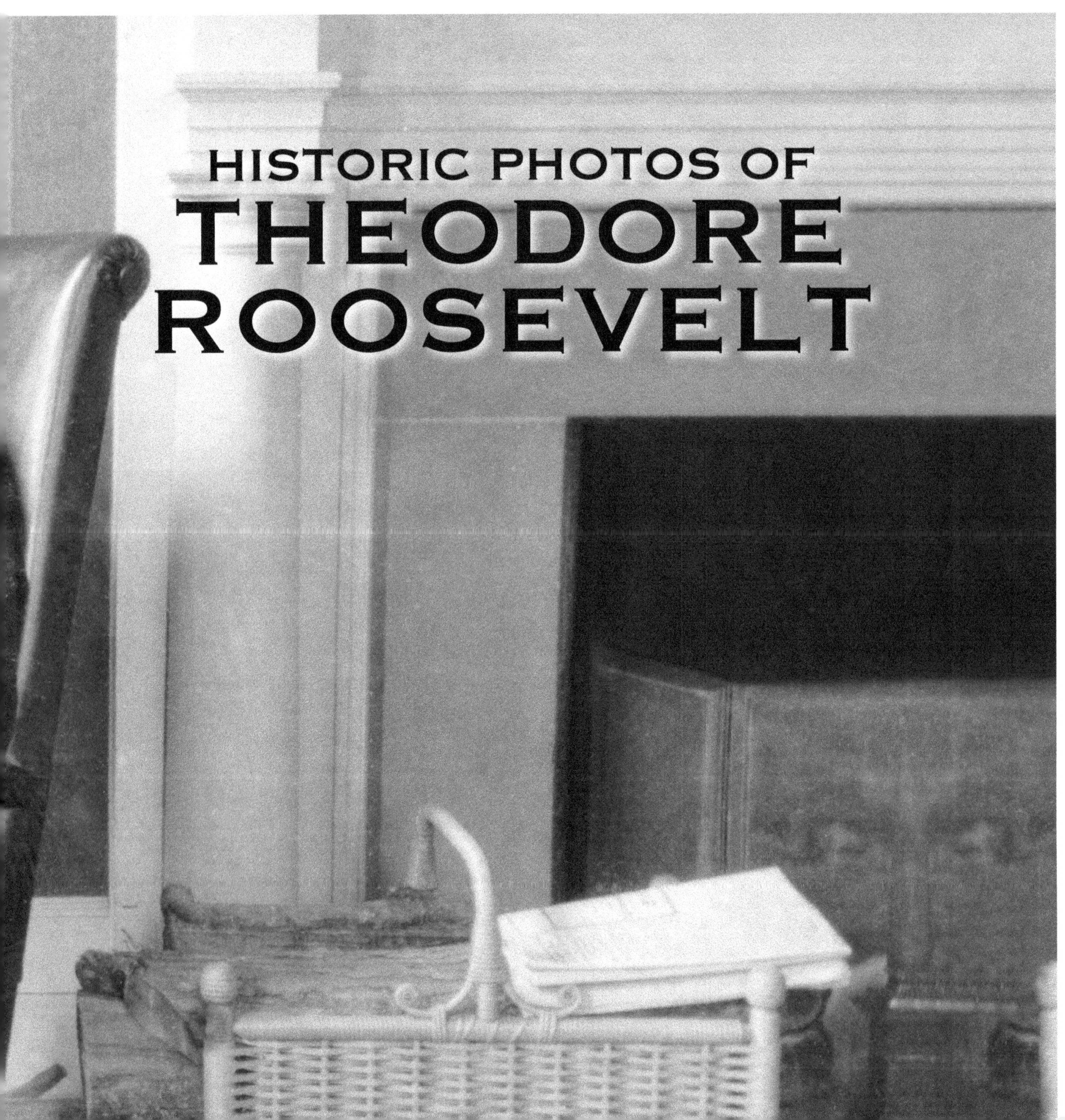
HISTORIC PHOTOS OF
THEODORE
ROOSEVELT

HISTORIC PHOTOS OF THEODORE ROOSEVELT

TEXT AND CAPTIONS BY STACY A. CORDERY

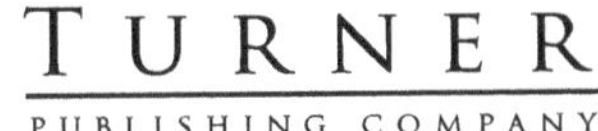

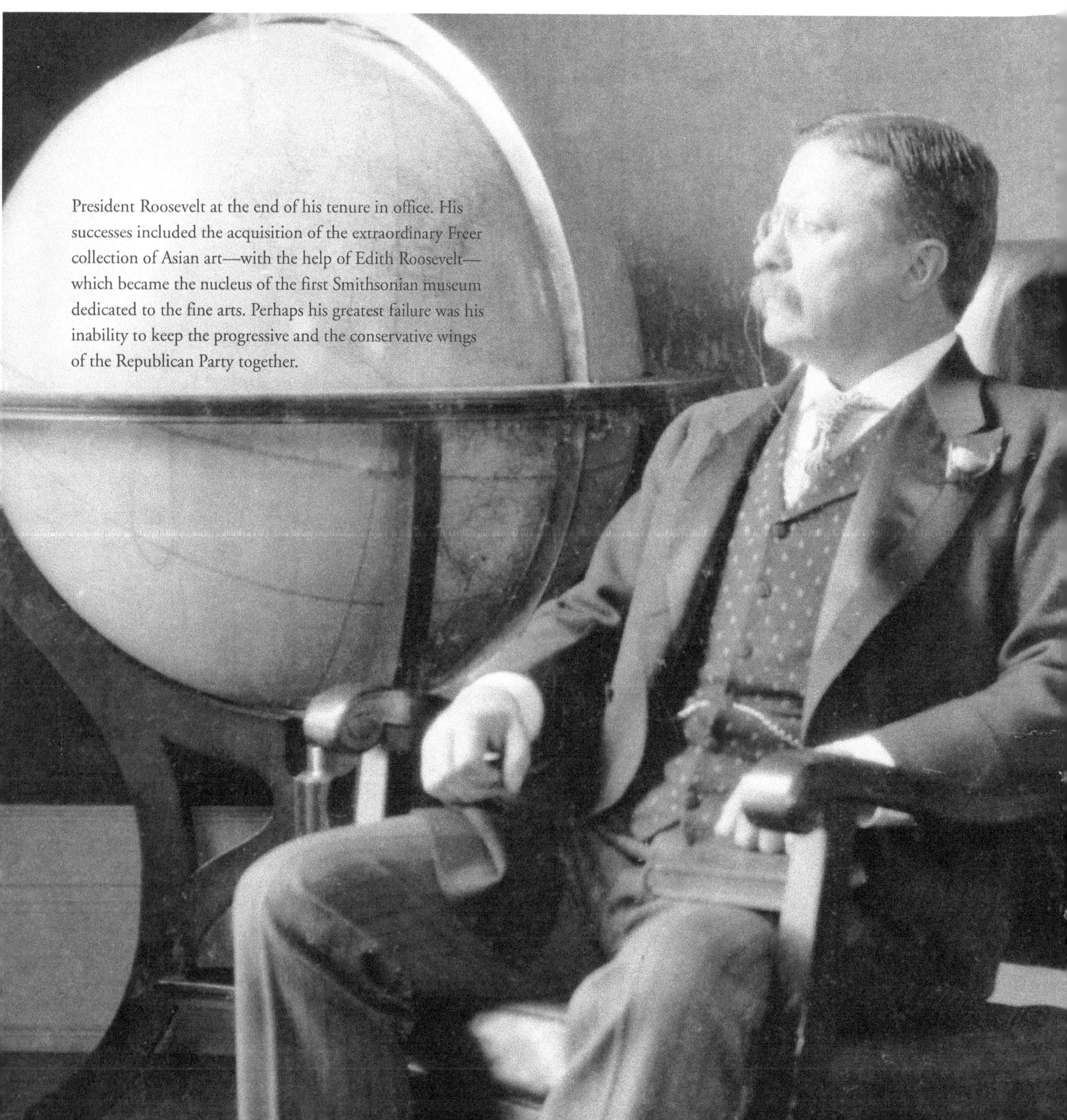

President Roosevelt at the end of his tenure in office. His successes included the acquisition of the extraordinary Freer collection of Asian art—with the help of Edith Roosevelt—which became the nucleus of the first Smithsonian museum dedicated to the fine arts. Perhaps his greatest failure was his inability to keep the progressive and the conservative wings of the Republican Party together.

Contents

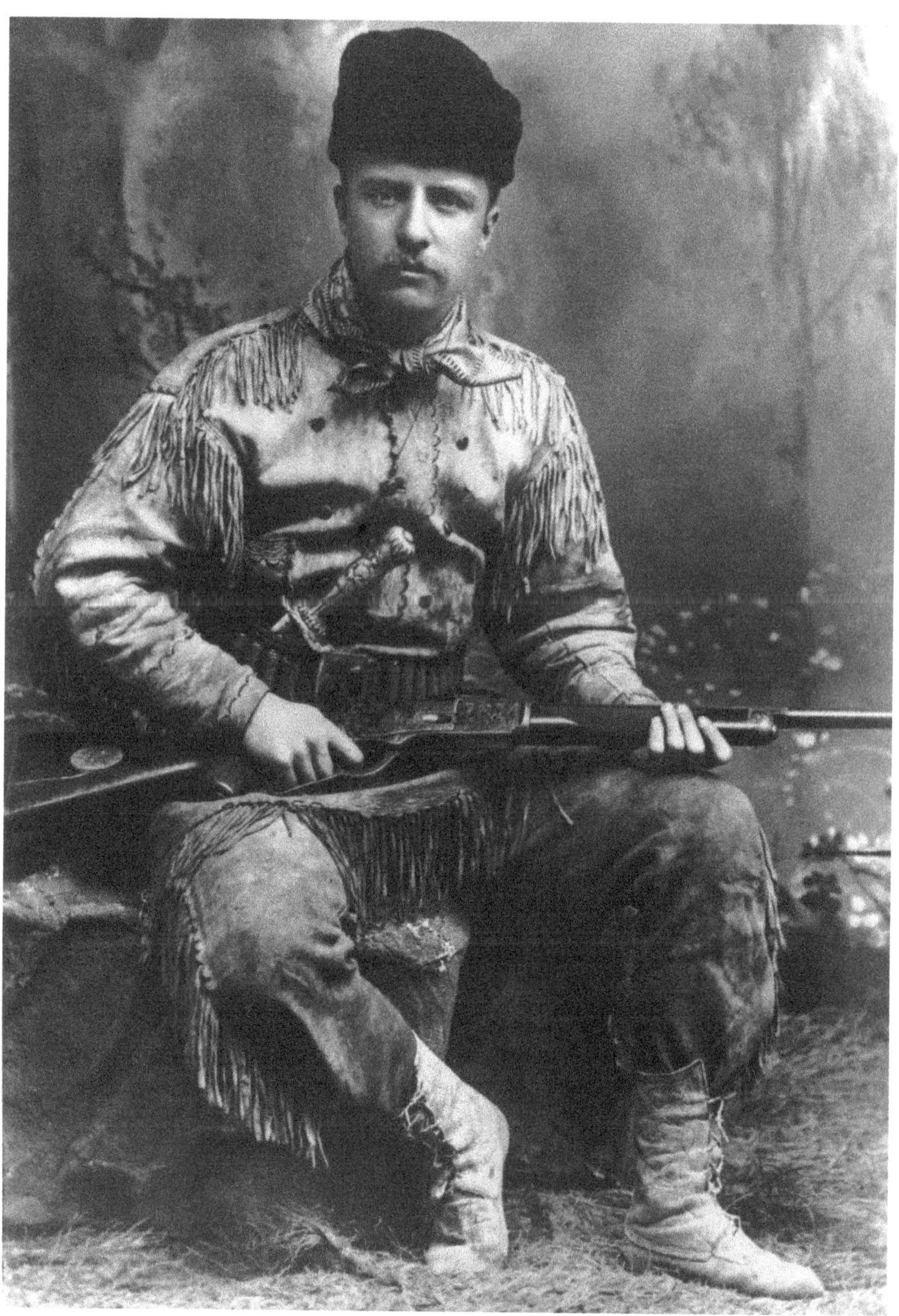

Theodore Roosevelt in buckskin, 1885.

Acknowledgments

This volume, *Historic Photos of Theodore Roosevelt,* is the result of the cooperation and efforts of a number of organizations and individuals.

We would like to thank in particular the Library of Congress and the Harvard College Library.

for

Wallace Finley Dailey

in partial repayment of the enormous debt owed him by all Roosevelt scholars and fans

—Stacy A. Cordery

PREFACE

A hundred years after his presidency Theodore Roosevelt continues to command our attention. Bigger than life in his own day, his presidency vigorously kick-started the twentieth century. His "Square Deal" used the power of the federal government to "bust" trusts and rein in corporate excesses. He demanded business serve the interests of consumers. Though not opposed to free-market capitalism, he insisted on a moral approach to the marketplace and ethical behavior from businessmen. He established a level playing field for labor and supported farmers' cooperatives. Roosevelt's conservation of natural resources and his dedication to preserving wild spaces were ahead of his time. Everyday Americans saw him as their champion.

The photographs reproduced in this collection, many of them rare and unusual, reveal the various dimensions of the man. We see TR as conservationist, big game hunter, rancher, reformer, ornithologist, writer, soldier, peacemaker, police commissioner, explorer, governor, vice president, president, husband, father, and grandfather. Roosevelt's interests ranged from naval power to pronghorn elk, from bird calls to Icelandic folk sagas, and from civil service reform to world history. Americans continue to find in Theodore Roosevelt a reflection of some of the best of the nation's ideals.

Theodore Roosevelt loved what he called the "bully pulpit." His actions helped the United States become a world power and, though he would "speak softly and carry a big stick," he was not above demonstrating the country's military might when he felt it was warranted. His Roosevelt Corollary extended the Monroe Doctrine by warning that the U.S. would act as a hemispheric policeman to keep European empire-builders at bay. He helped Panama secede from Colombia and subsequently purchased the right to construct the Panama Canal. But Roosevelt never took the United States to war. He worked through the International Court of Arbitration at the Hague, settled the Alaskan boundary dispute, won the Nobel Peace prize for mediating an end to the Russo-Japanese War, and played an important covert role at the Algeciras conference that helped avoid outright conflict in Europe in 1906.

We have many of the photographs in this book because Roosevelt adroitly used the press. He knew when to release good news to trump his adversaries and how to keep reporters on his side. He captivated the public imagination and honed his image, keeping his detractors off-balance and to a minimum. He allowed his two daughters and four sons to be photographed when it became clear they humanized his administration. His wife, Edith Kermit Roosevelt, created the First Ladies' portrait gallery, modernized the White House, met weekly with Cabinet wives, hired a social secretary, and was considered a better judge of character than her husband. While Edith loathed publicity, TR—his daughter Alice claimed—liked to be the bride at every wedding, the baby at every christening, and the corpse at every funeral. Americans adored the man they called "Teddy."

Yet Roosevelt was not perfect. Like others of his class and time he exercised a genteel racism which limited his presidential accomplishments. He appreciated some Native American cultures but his policies were not as enlightened as they might have been. He invited Booker T. Washington to dine with his family at the White House, and he appointed African Americans to patronage positions, but TR turned a blind eye to the 1906 Atlanta race riots and discharged 167 black soldiers after an incident in Brownsville, Texas, that same year without ever proving their guilt. His "Gentleman's Agreement" decreased discrimination against Japanese schoolchildren in California, but played to xenophobic fears by limiting Japanese immigration. He warned about Anglo-American "race suicide" should white, Protestant women fail in their procreative duties.

When Theodore Roosevelt left office in 1909, his standing with voters was high but his party was split. Conservative Republicans loathed him, and Roosevelt's legacy included dividing the party he loved. He tried to regain the presidency in 1912, but Republic regulars rejected him and his attempt to win as the Progressive party candidate turned the White House over to Woodrow Wilson and the Democrats. Though out of politics, he was never out of the limelight. Roosevelt remained active to the very end, exploring Brazil's River of Doubt, opposing the League of Nations, and trying to patch his party back together. When he died in 1919, TR had iconic status in the United States, which he has not relinquished. The photographs in this book help us to understand why.

—Stacy A. Cordery

This project represents countless hours of review and research. The researchers and writer have reviewed thousands of photographs. We greatly appreciate the generous assistance of the archives listed here, without whom this project could not have been completed.

The goal in publishing the work is to provide broader access to a set of extraordinary photographs. The aim is to inspire, provide perspective, and evoke insight. In addition, the book seeks to preserve the past with respect and reverence.

With the exception of touching up imperfections caused by the vicissitudes of time and cropping where necessary, no changes have been made. The focus and clarity of some images is limited to the technology of the day and the skill of the photographer who captured them.

—Todd Bottorff, Publisher

Theodore Roosevelt and his party on Bright Angel Trail toward the South Rim of the Grand Canyon.

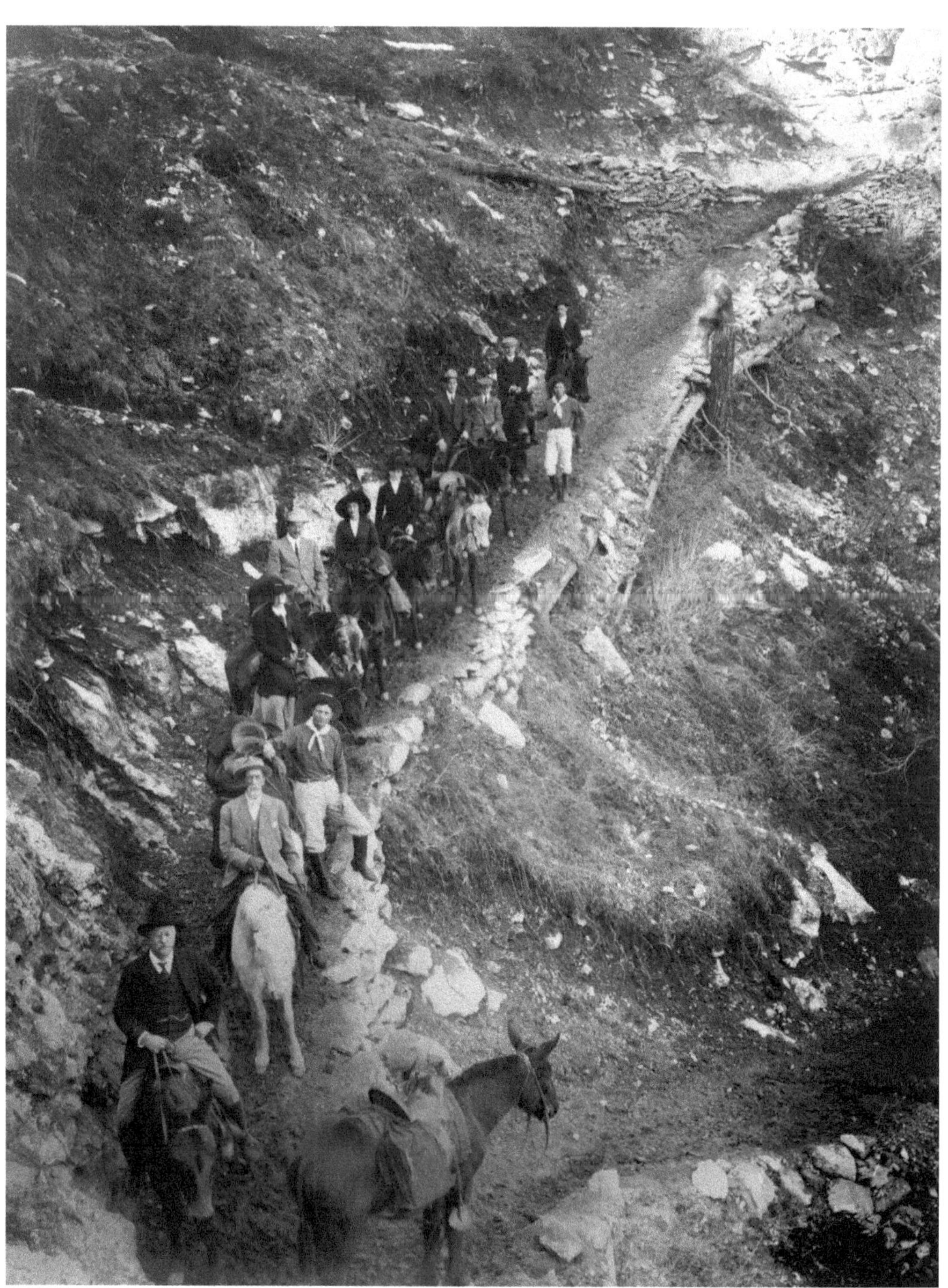

The Early Years (1858–1888)

Theodore Roosevelt was born just before the Civil War began and died shortly after the guns of the First World War fell silent. His life spanned barely sixty years, but they were full of "crowded hours," as he described them. His life began on October 27, 1858, in New York City. He was the first son and the second child of Martha ("Mittie") Bulloch Roosevelt of Georgia, and Theodore Roosevelt, Sr., of New York. Young "Teedie" had a joyful and privileged upbringing. Asthma attacks cast the only pall over his childhood, and when they occurred his father rushed to care for him. Thin and underdeveloped, he promised to "make his body" and devoted himself to strenuous exercise. But books were his real love: he read voraciously and wrote voluminously.

He graduated from Harvard College in 1880 and married Alice Hathaway Lee the same year. Theodore Roosevelt became New York's youngest Assemblyman two years later. Drawn west by the economic opportunities and the hunting, TR established ranches in the Dakota territory in 1883. Tragedy struck when both his wife and his mother died on St. Valentine's Day 1884. Roosevelt was left with his grief and his infant daughter Alice. Pushing aside sorrow, TR ran his cattle ranches until wooed back by the Republican Party to run—unsuccessfully—for mayor of New York City in 1886. That year he married Edith Kermit Carow, a dear childhood friend. He wrote several books, including the four-volume *Winning of the West,* and Edith gave birth to their five children, born between 1887 and 1897.

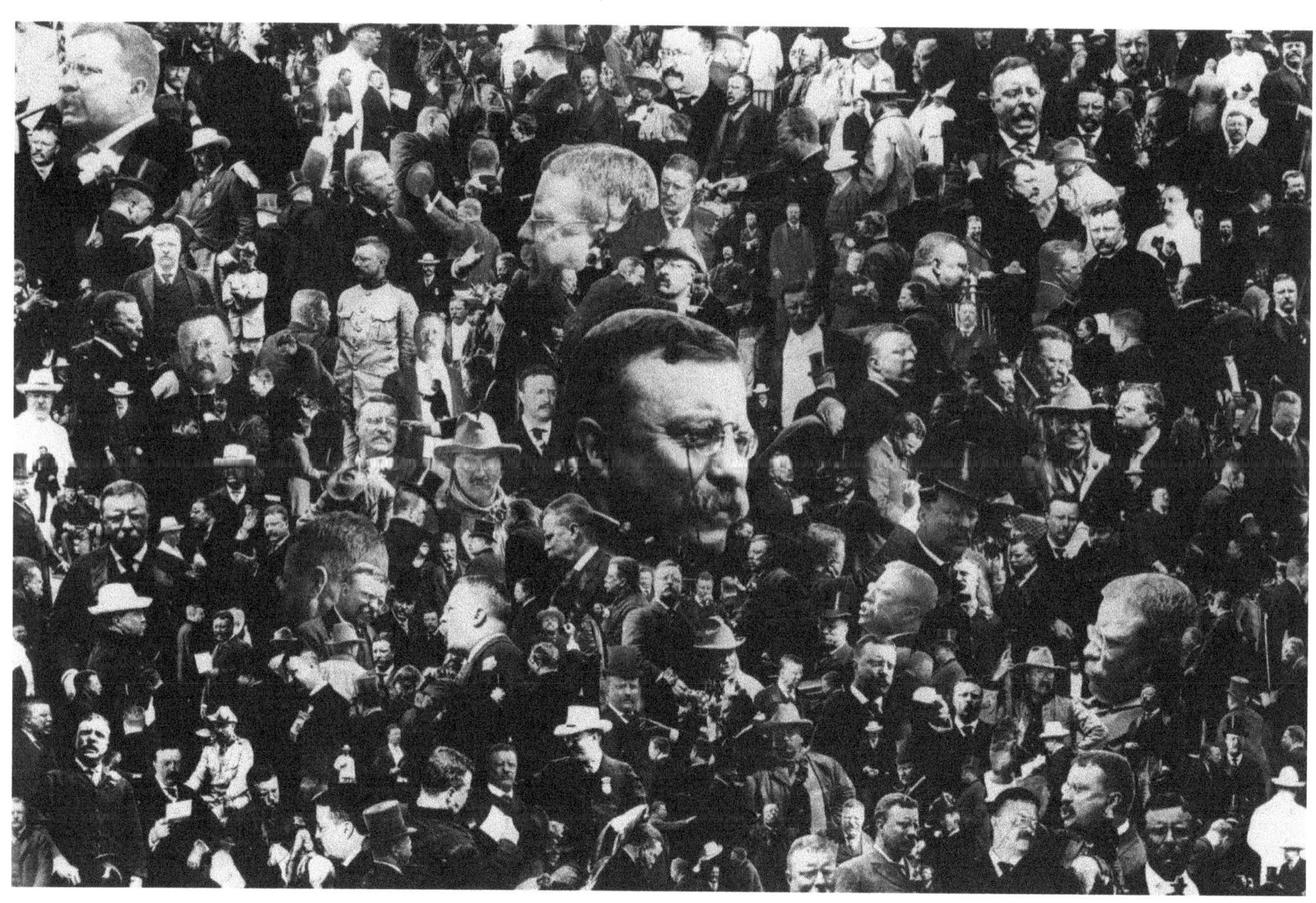

This collage of five hundred Theodore Roosevelt photographs attests to the president's enormous popularity. It was originally published in 1908 as a newspaper contest to spot the duplicate images. From Rough Rider to elected politician, his visage was instantly recognizable around the world.

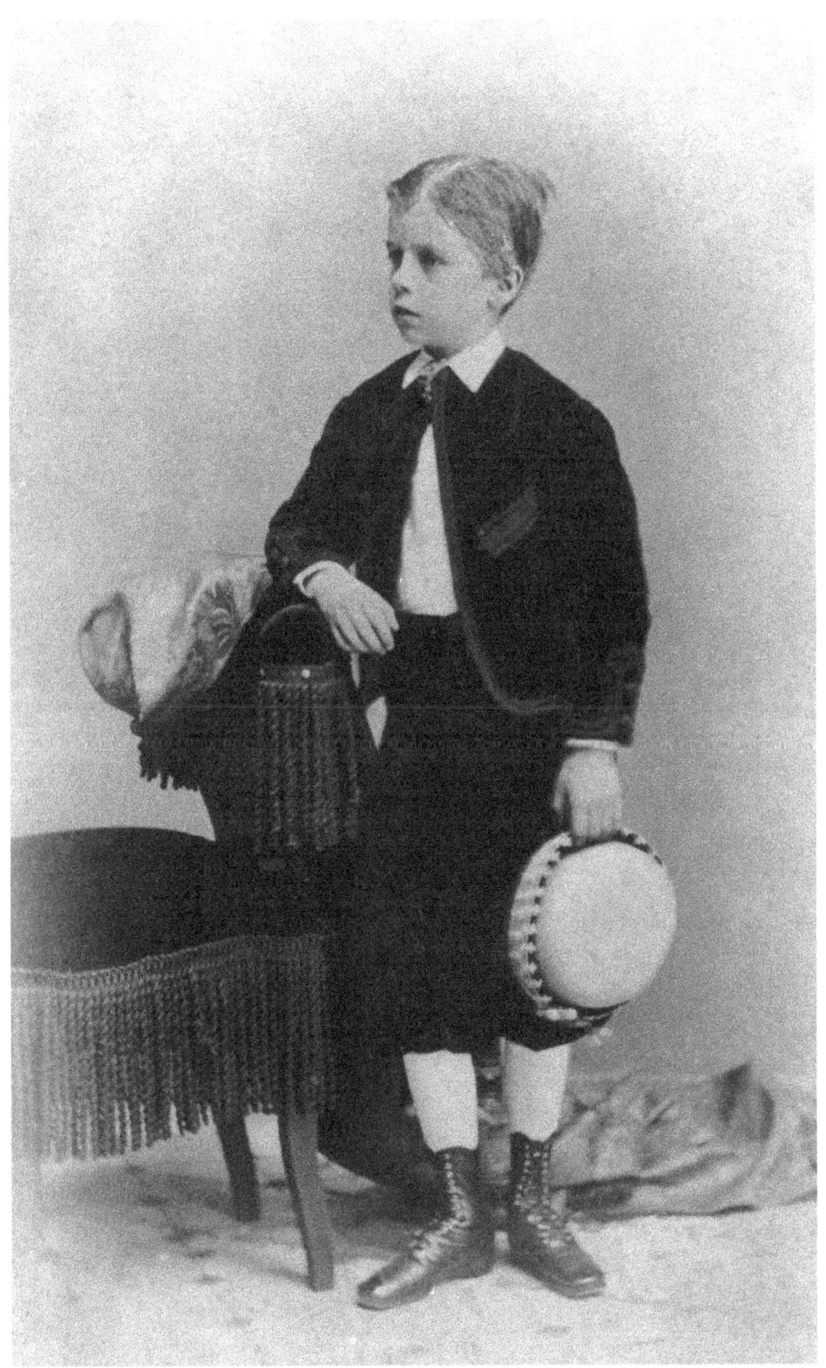

Born on October 27, 1858, in New York City, Theodore Roosevelt was the second of four children. Known affectionately in the family as "Teedie," he enjoyed all the privileges of wealth and long ancestry. Here at age seven, the traditional stance of his pose seems to convey the security and abundant love which infused his childhood.

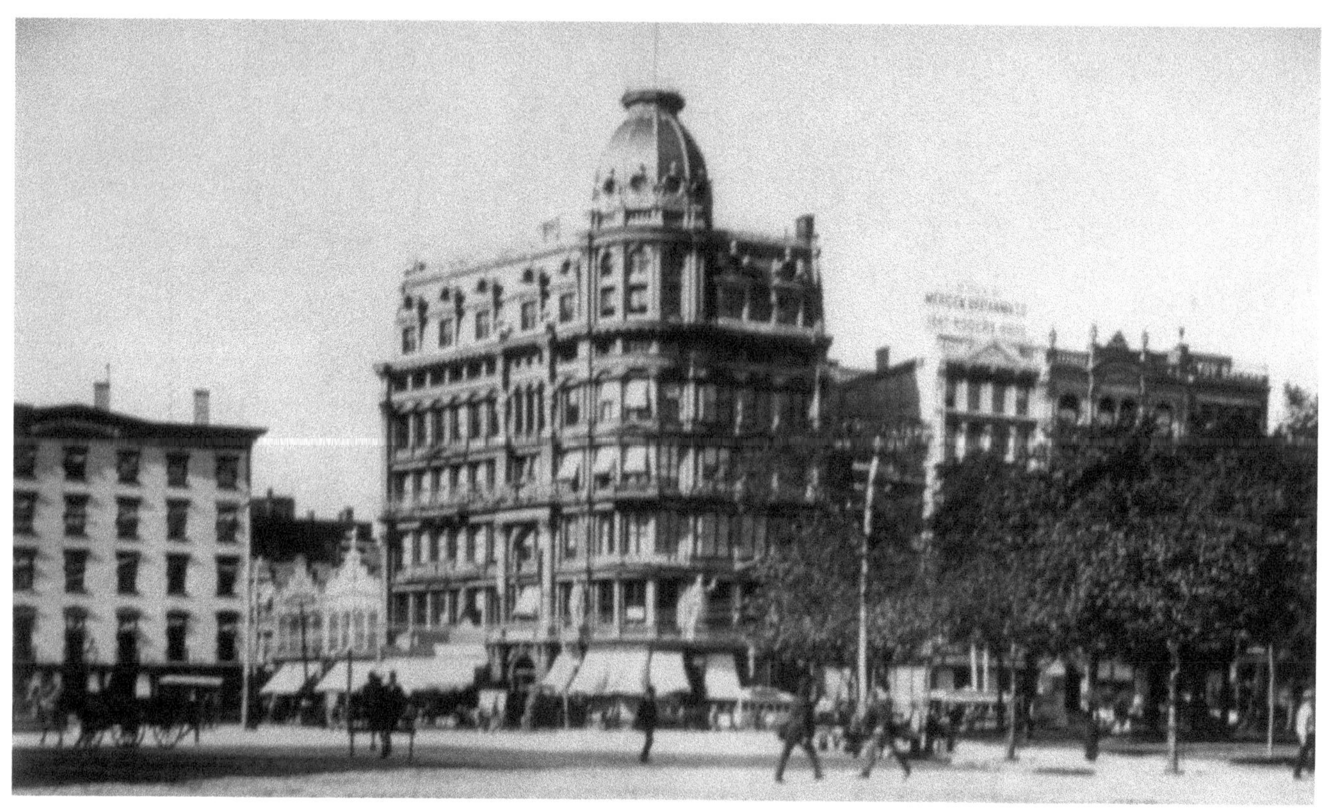

This was the site of Cornelius Van Schaak Roosevelt's home at the corner of 14th Street and Broadway in New York City. In this photo the Domestic Sewing Machine Company's building has taken the place of Theodore Roosevelt's grandfather's house, but it was from this vantage point that seven-year-old Theodore and his younger brother, Elliott, watched solemnly as Abraham Lincoln's funeral procession made its sad passage.

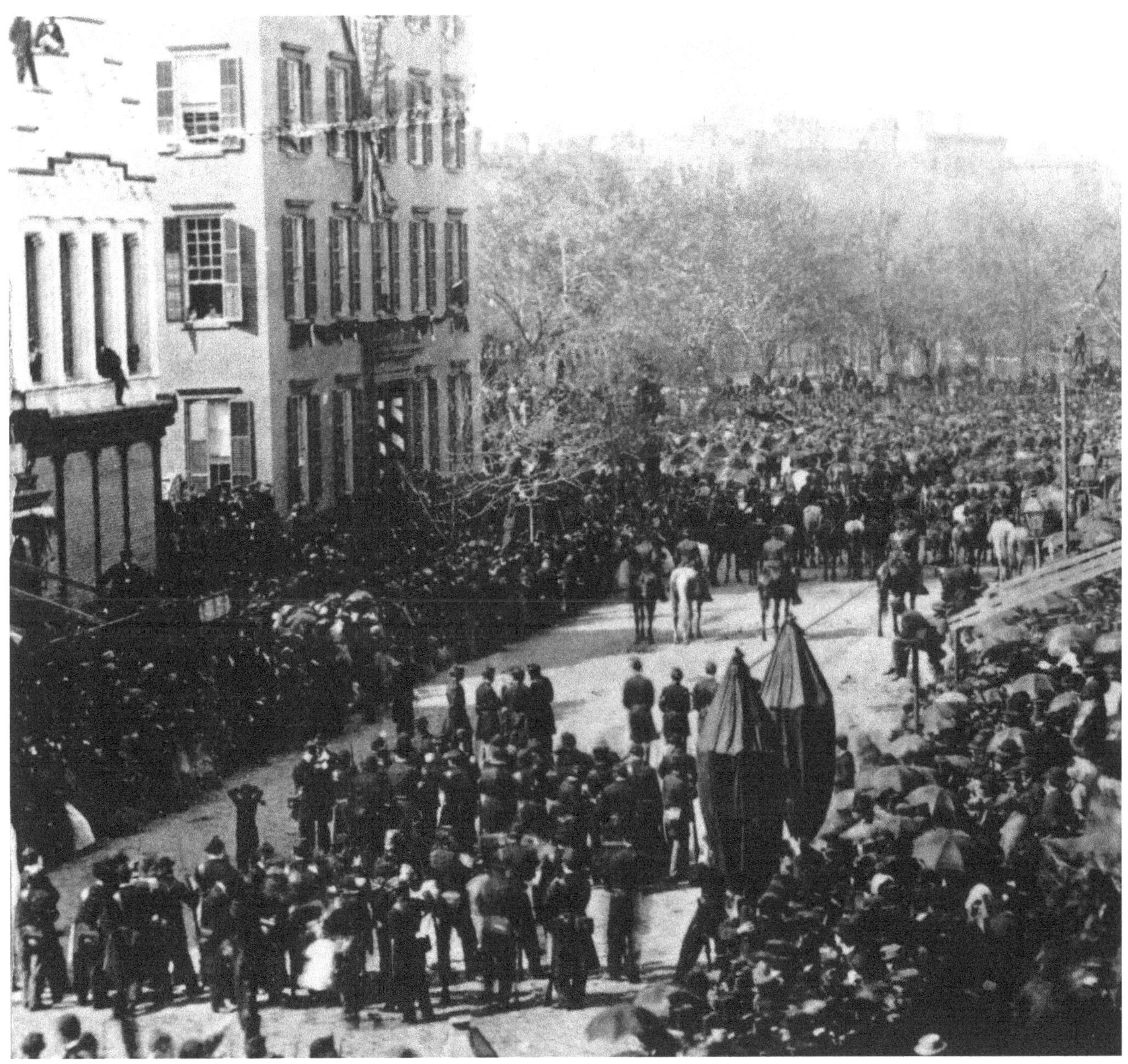

On April 25, 1865, President Abraham Lincoln's funeral cortege moves slowly past the window of their grandfather Cornelius Van Schaak Roosevelt's home as the young Theodore and his brother Elliott watch from the second-story window. Theodore, Sr., knew Lincoln, and the family grieved for their friend and fellow Republican.

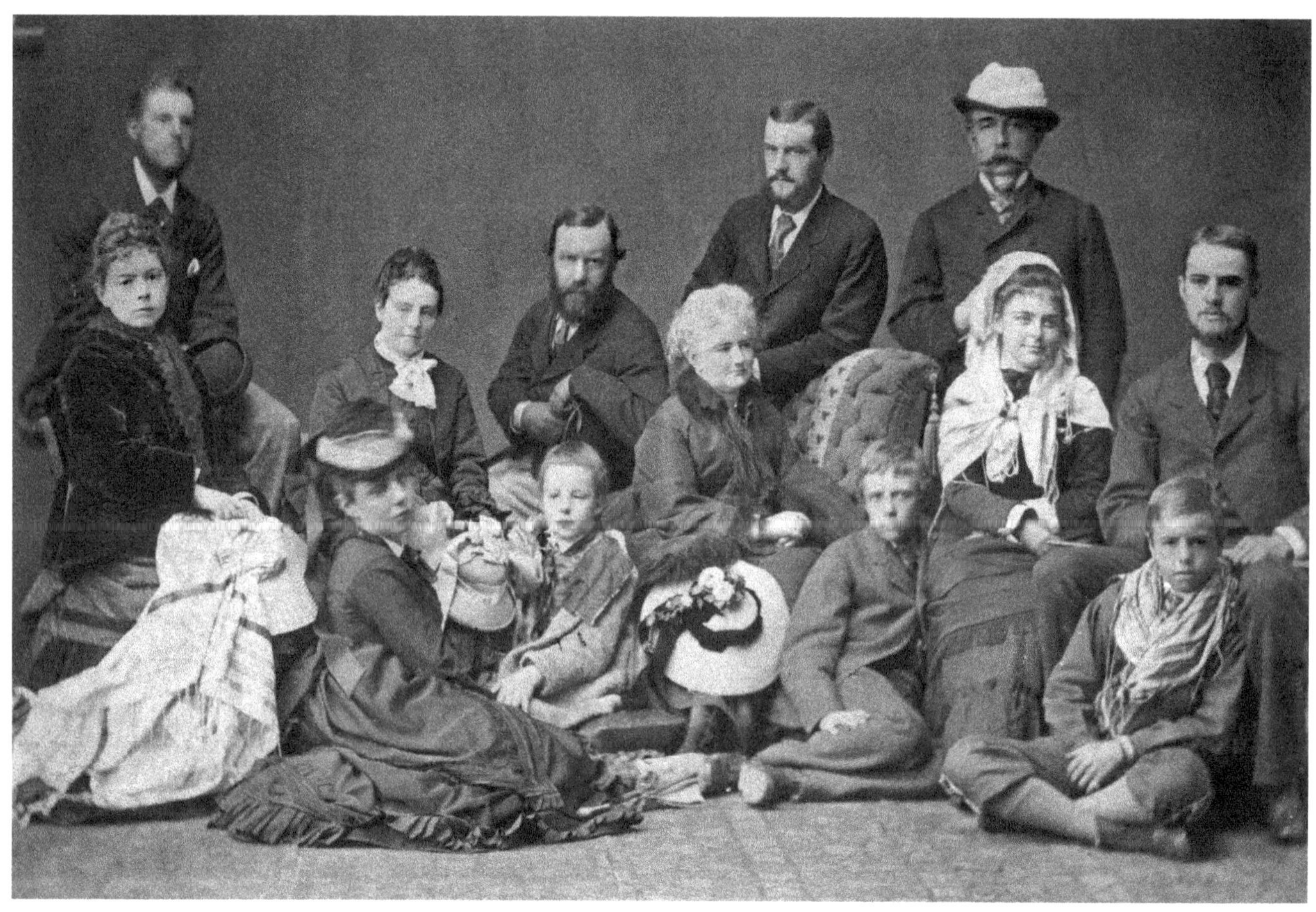

In 1872, when Teedie was 13, he traveled with family and friends to Egypt, Greece, and the Middle East. The budding scientist remembered particularly the birds he encountered—and after shooting, preserving, and systematically cataloging them (and learning their Latin names along the way), Theodore added them to his "Roosevelt Museum." In this photograph the four Roosevelt children are seated: Anna, Corinne, Theodore, and Elliott. Parents Martha ("Mittie") and Theodore, Sr., are behind the girls.

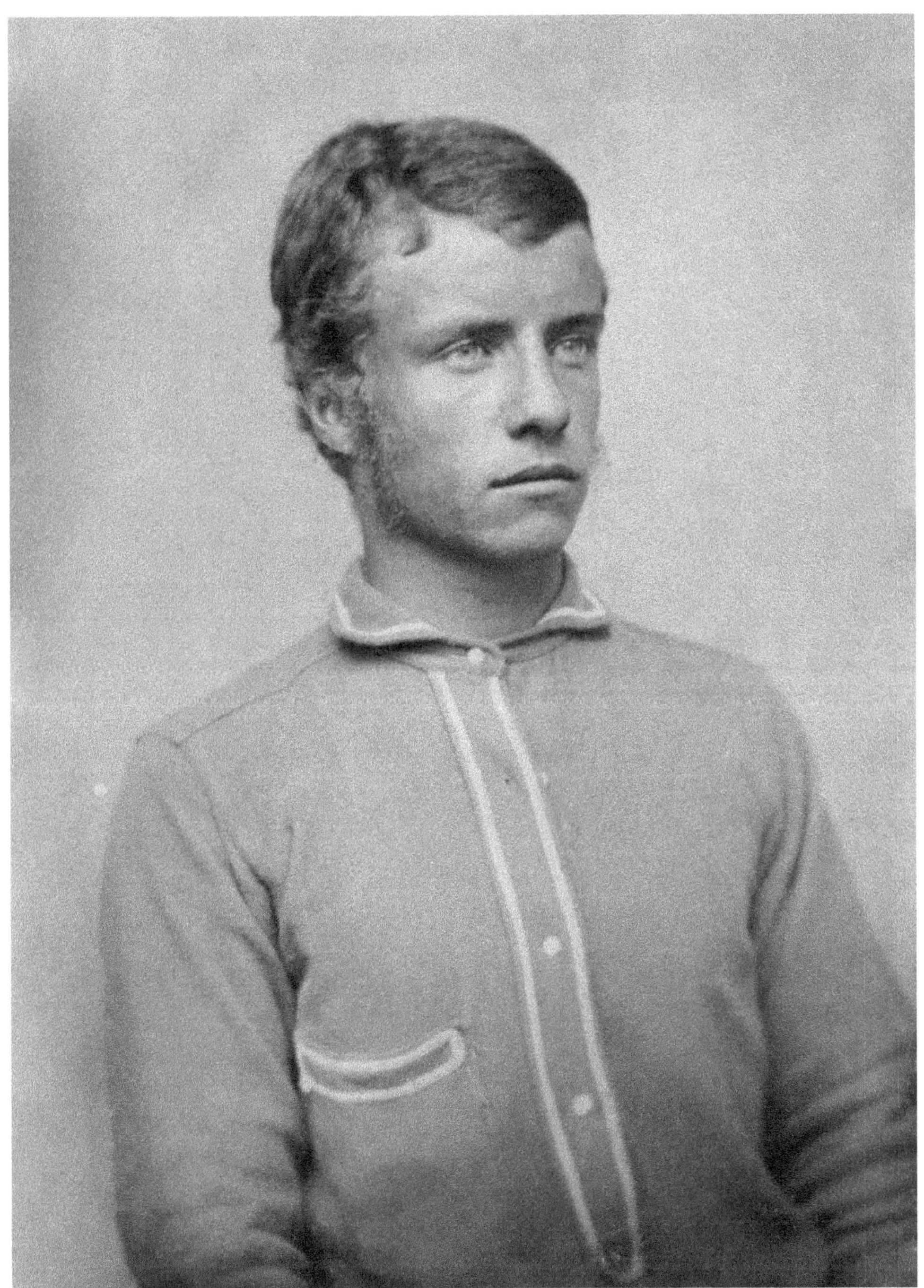

Roosevelt remembered himself as "a sickly, delicate boy." Asthma attacks occurred frequently, and as a result he was tutored at home. He loved natural history, especially zoology. Like all Roosevelts, he read widely—from poetry to novels, from folklore to science. By age seventeen, as he is here, Theodore was cataloging the birds of Long Island and preparing to enter Harvard College.

Theodore Roosevelt called his father "the best man I ever knew," and recalled the great joy he took in every aspect of life. A philanthropist with a brief career in Republican Party politics, Roosevelt, Sr., was by all accounts a kind and generous man. Known as "Greatheart," he combated cruelty to children and animals, gave of his time to orphans, and helped to found the Metropolitan Museum of Art, the American Museum of Natural History, and the New York Orthopedic Hospital before dying at age forty-six of stomach cancer.

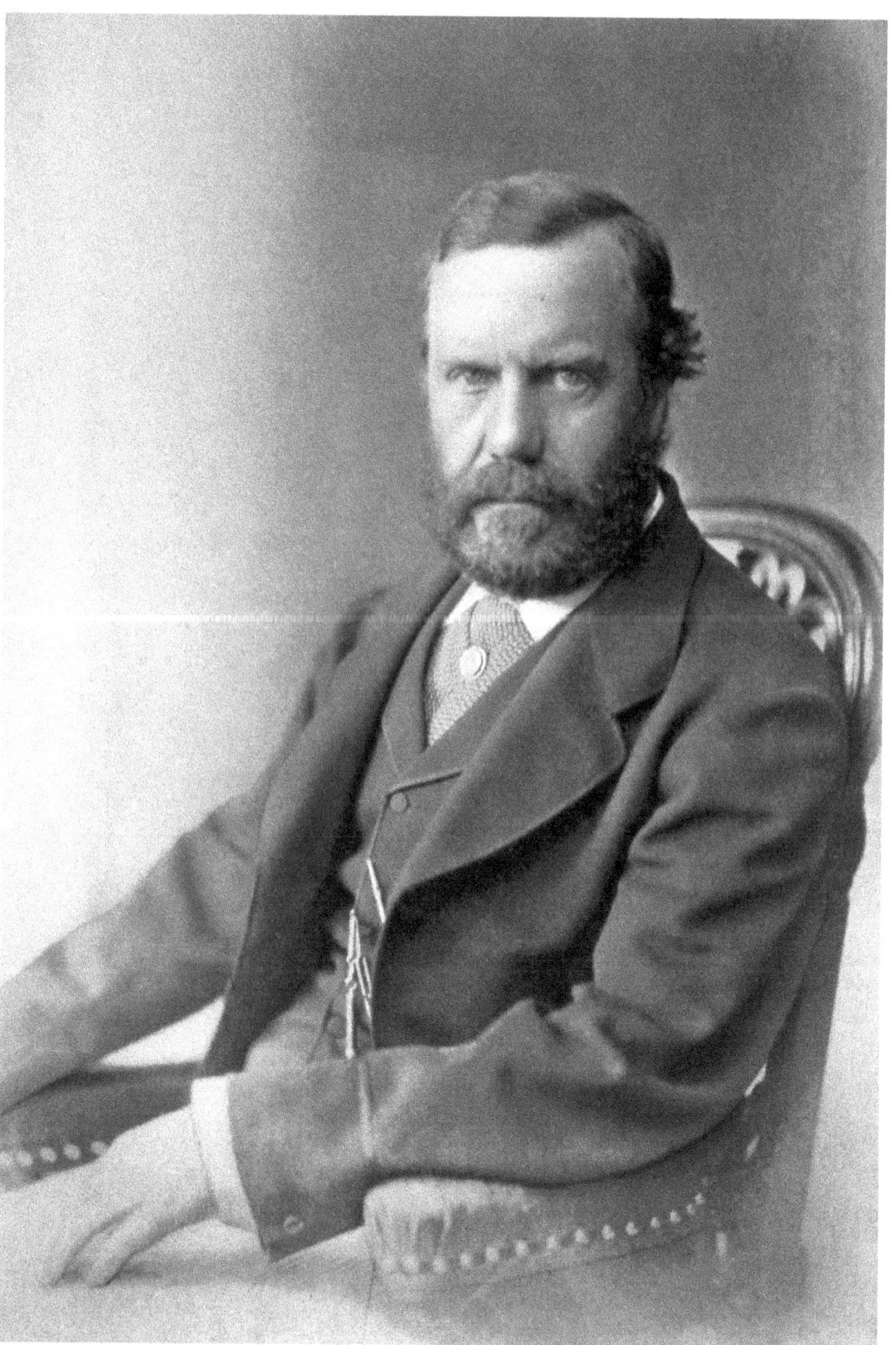

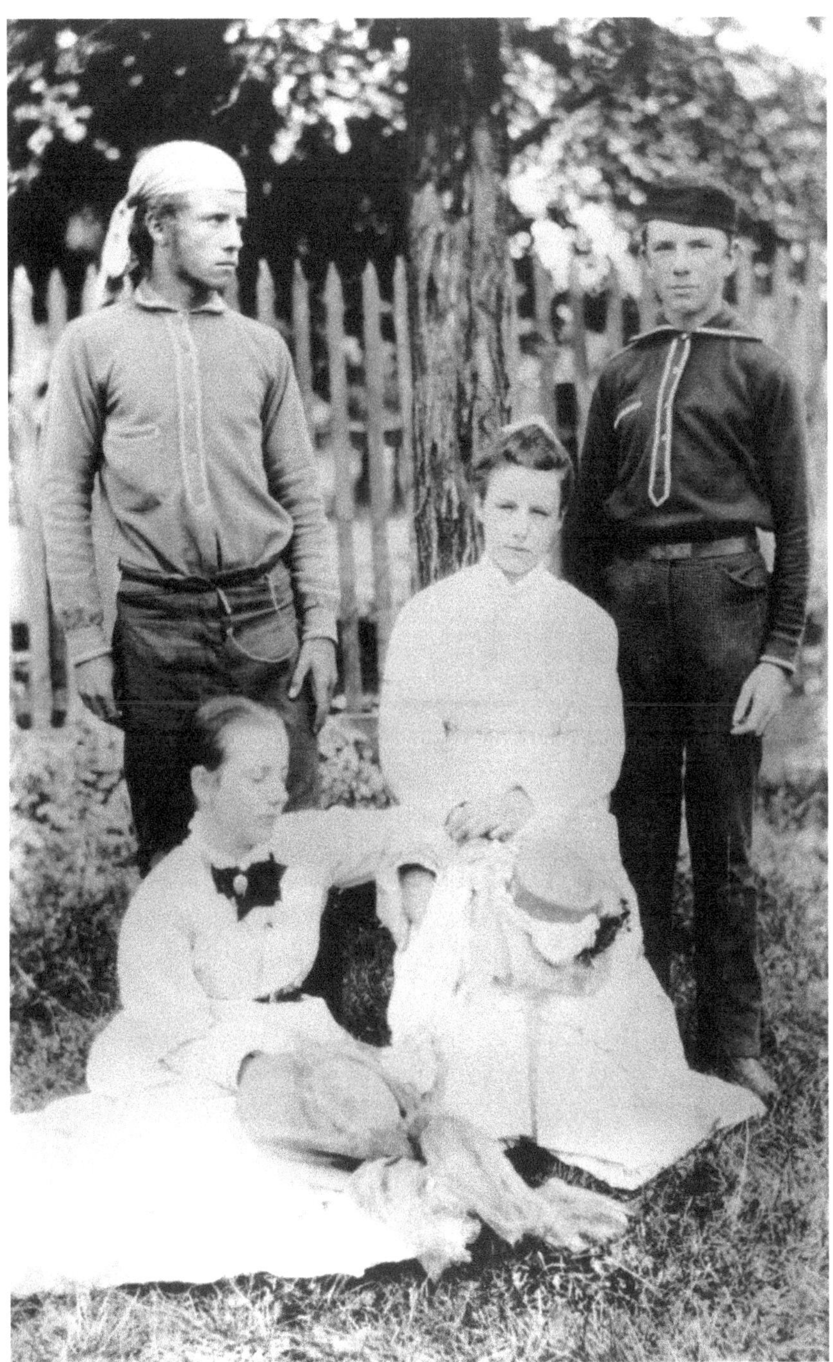

The three youngest Roosevelt children, Theodore, Elliott, and Corinne. Seated in the chair is family friend, the “bookish” Edith Kermit Carow. TR and Edith grew up together and were sweethearts until Roosevelt left for Harvard.

In 1876, TR entered Harvard where he intended to study the natural sciences. An expert ornithologist, Roosevelt became disillusioned by Harvard's focus on the laboratory at the expense of practical science outdoors. He took up history and political science instead, and graduated in 1880. TR loved the strenuous life and is in sculling costume here. At college he wrestled, boxed, rode, danced, and joined a number of social clubs, including the prestigious Porcellian.

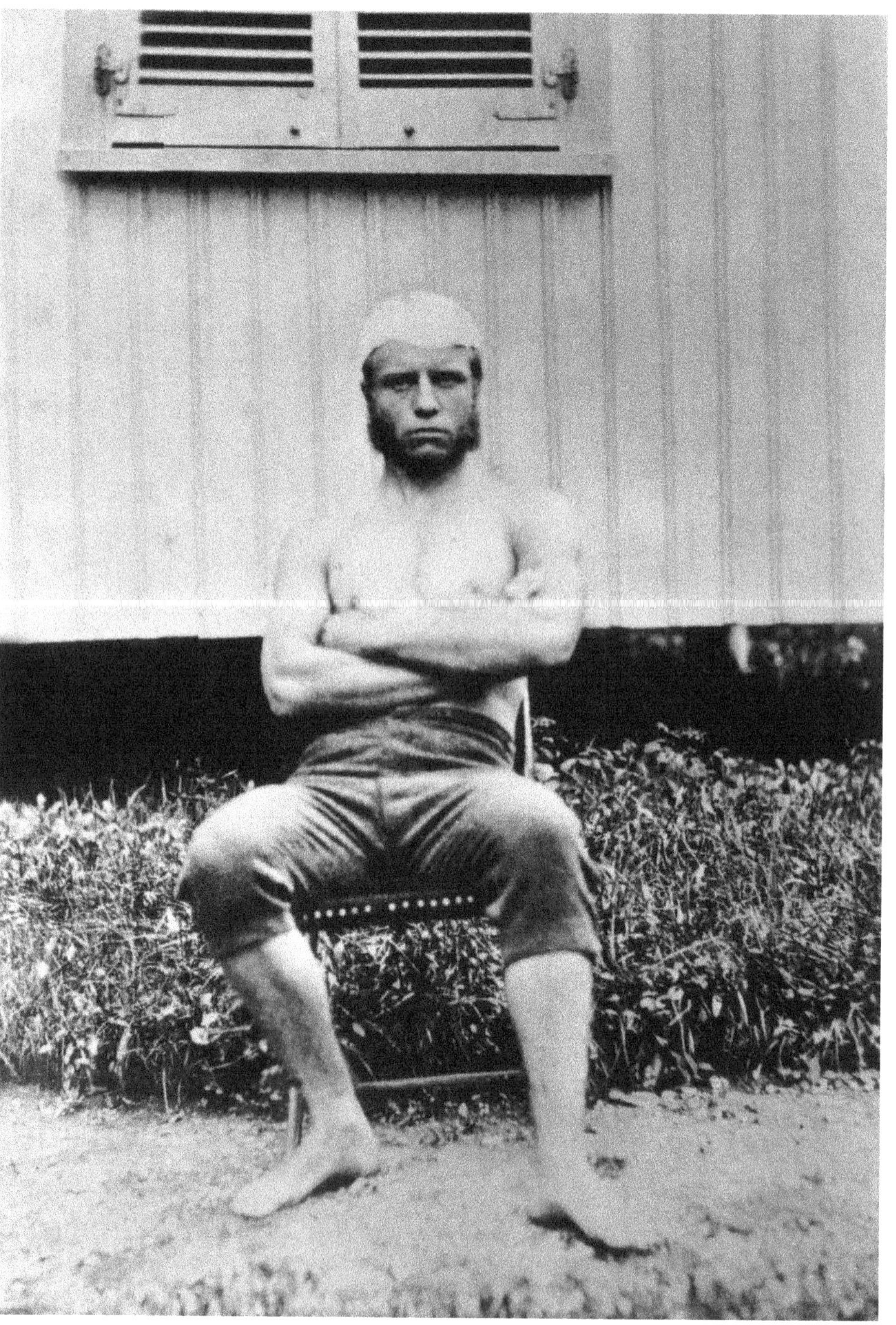

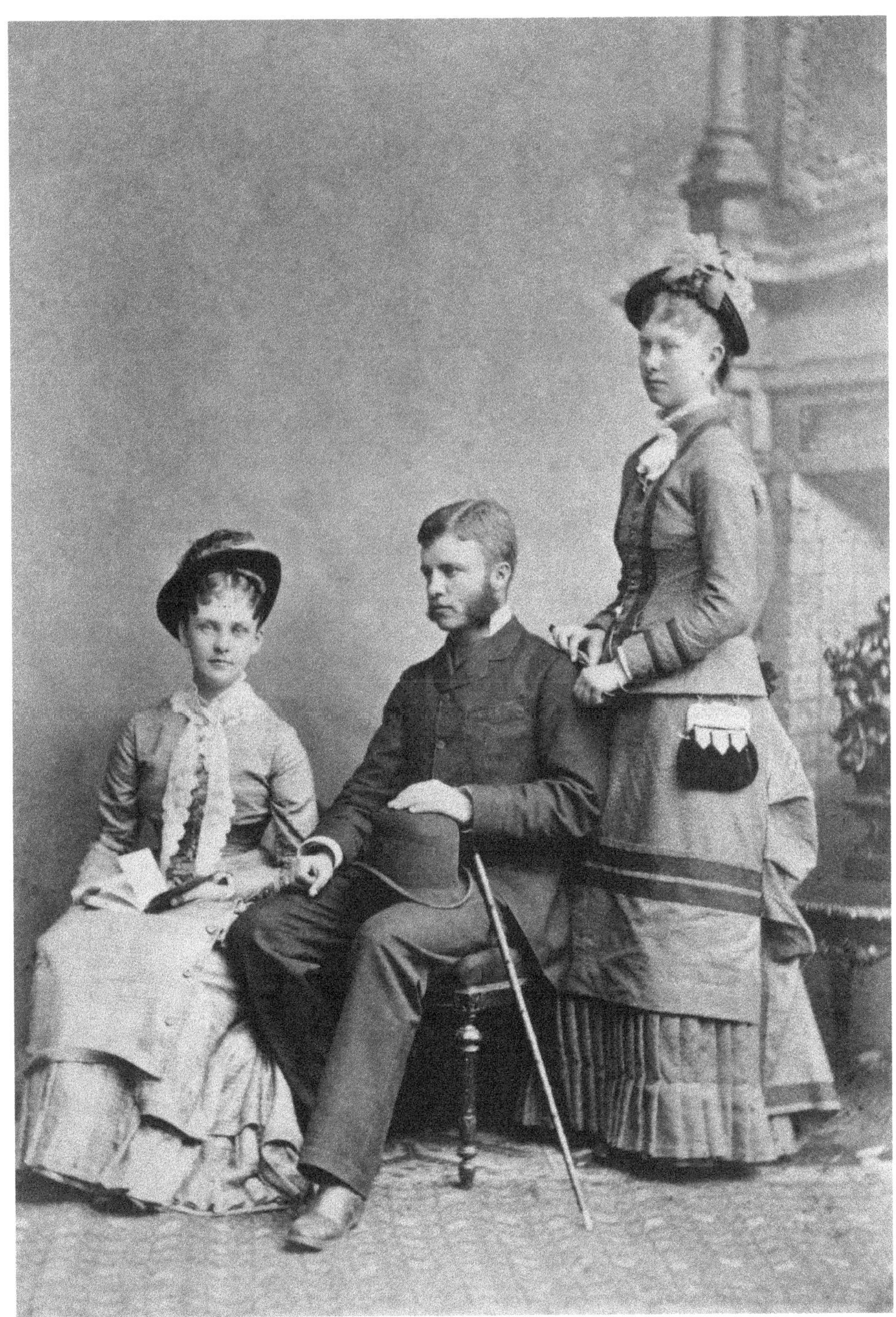

At Harvard, TR fell in love with the athletic Bostonian seated next to him, Alice Hathaway Lee. Their friend Rose Saltonstall stands behind TR. After an exhilarating courtship, Roosevelt married his "sweet, pretty queen" on his 22nd birthday. The pair became leaders of young New York society and Alice learned about politics as TR became a state assemblyman. Alice died on February 14, 1884, just after giving birth to their daughter, named Alice. Theodore's mother died the very same day.

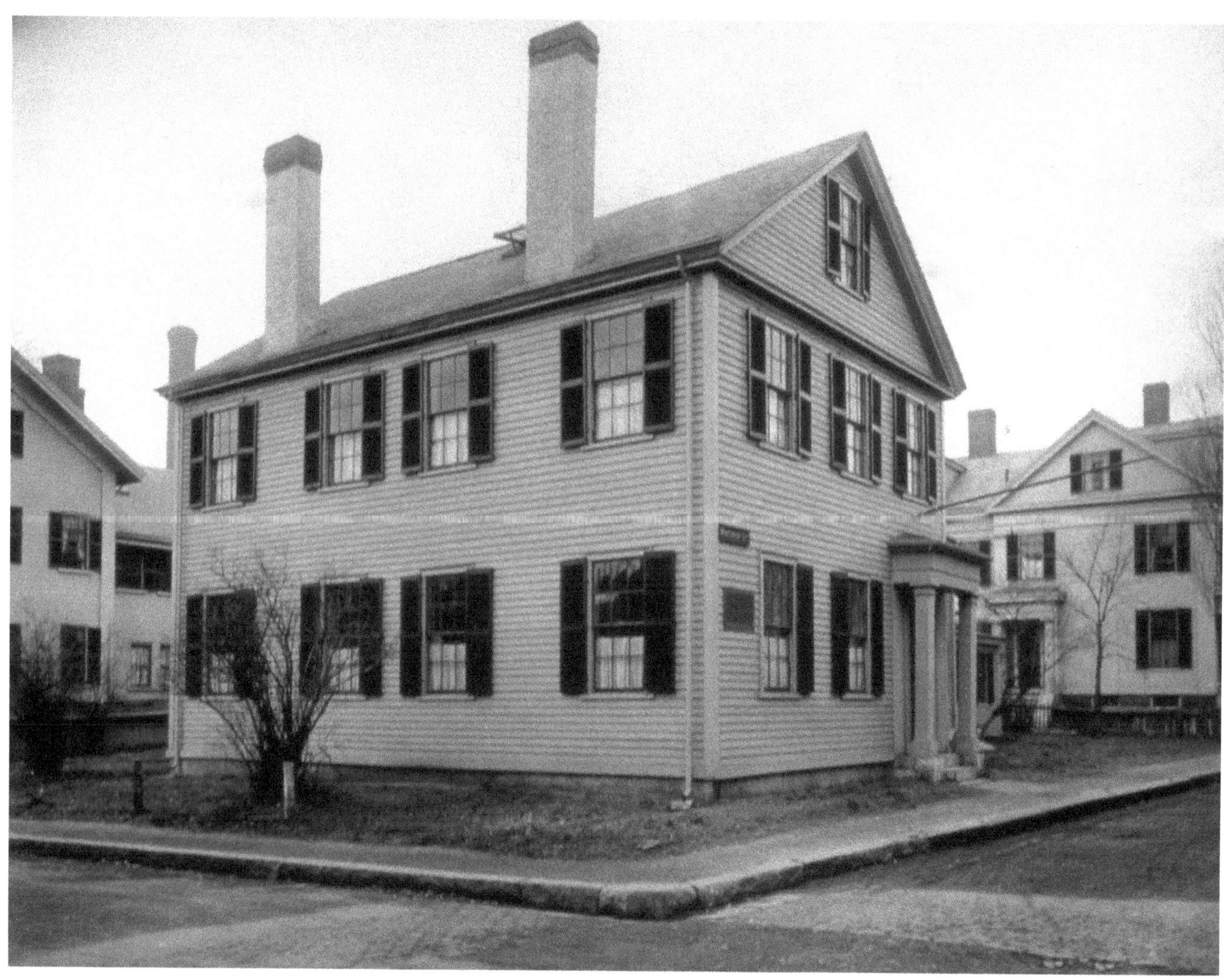

Theodore Roosevelt boarded upstairs in this house, on Winthrop Street in Cambridge, while he attended nearby Harvard College. His three rooms were furnished with the assistance of his sister Anna. She helped with the furniture and draperies and he stuffed the space full of taxidermy supplies, live animals, and his substantial library. Roosevelt studied and relaxed here, but the era's social strictures mandated that he call upon Boston's young women at their homes, not his.

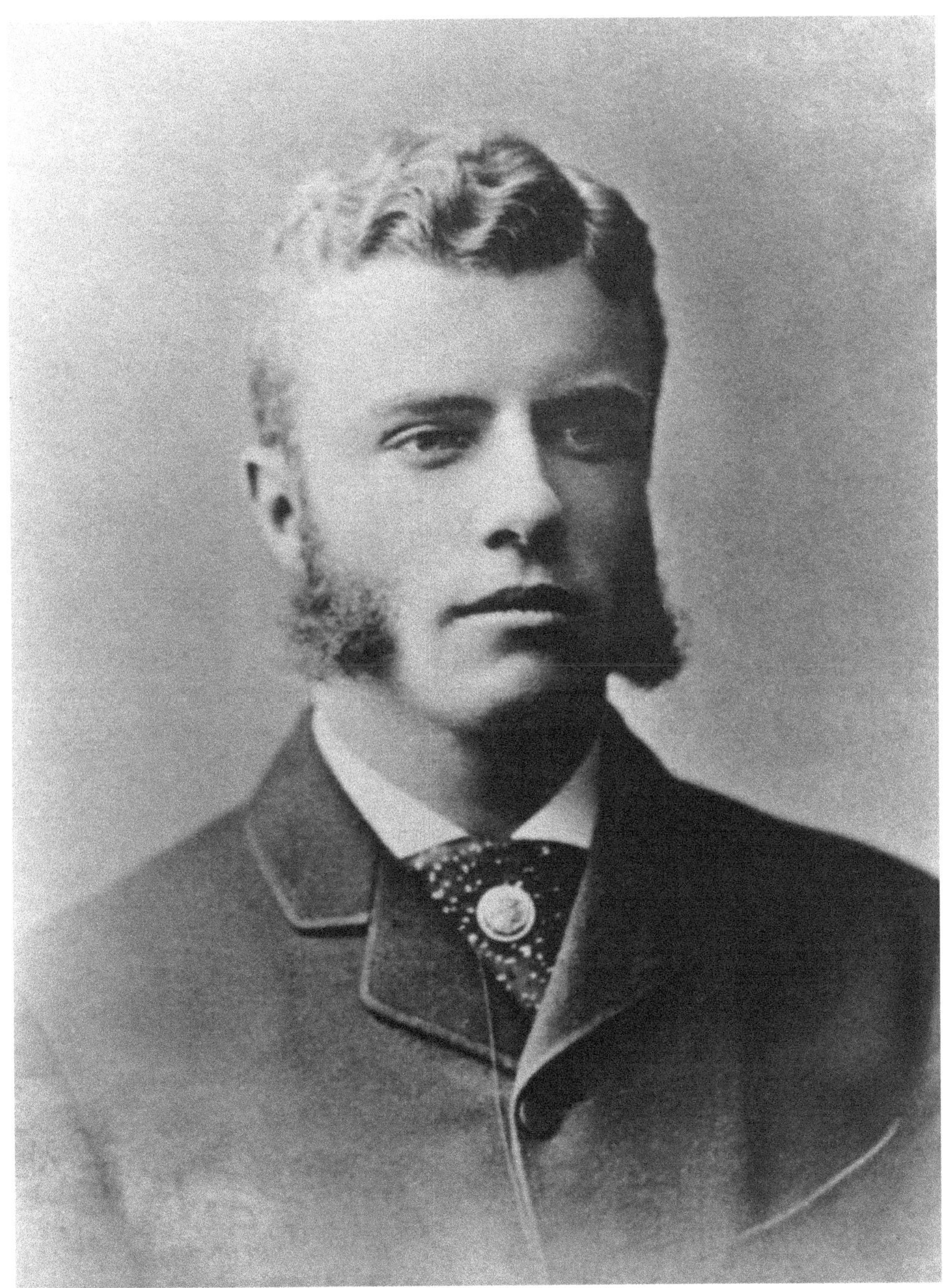

This photo of Theodore Roosevelt in 1880 comes from his class album. At Harvard TR's eccentric mannerisms, sumptuous dress, and devotion to physical exercise made him a standout. His time here was bounded by the terrible and lasting blow of his father's death and his fervent courtship of Alice Hathaway Lee.

In August 1880, two months before his wedding, Theodore and his brother Elliott left for a hunting trip across the Midwest. Roosevelt preferred the rifle to the shotgun and thought his marksmanship only "respectable," even after his aim improved substantially at age thirteen when he got his first pair of glasses. Roosevelt became an expert on the habits of several kinds of big game, and would write about his hunting adventures on three different continents.

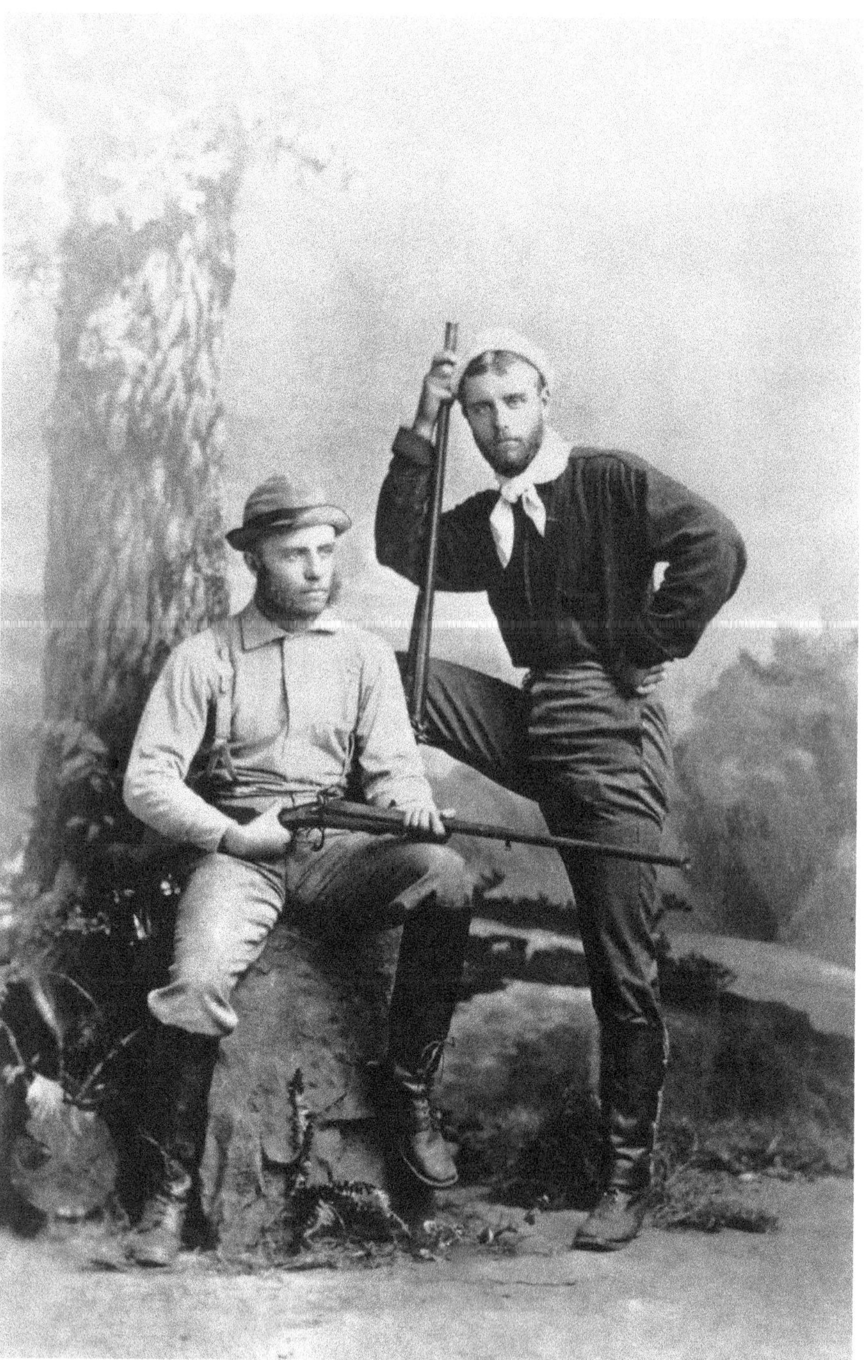

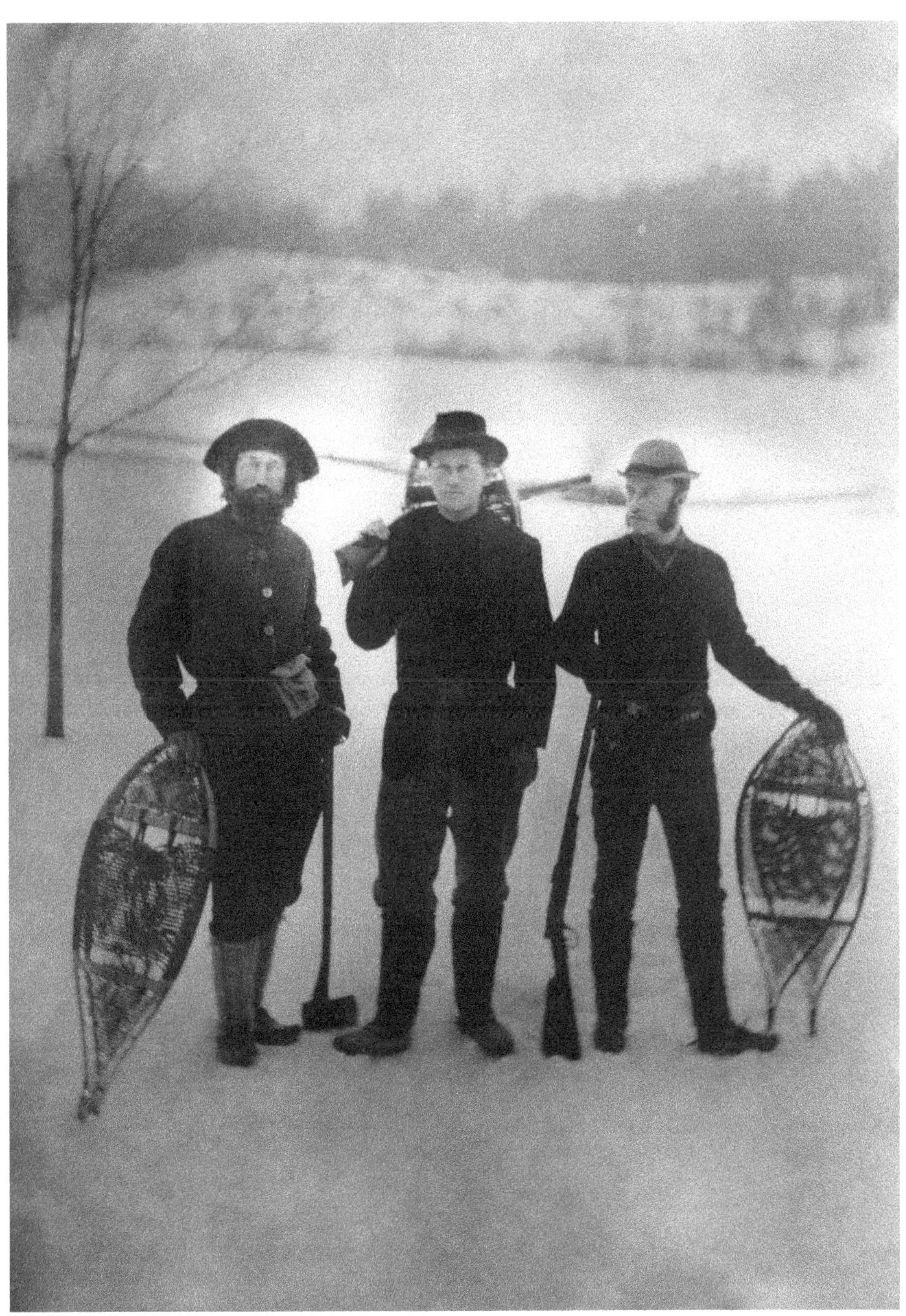

Wilderness guides Bill Sewall and Wilmot Dow stand beside TR in the frigid early spring of 1879. The trio had gone to Mattawaumkeag, Maine, so that Roosevelt could hunt, hike, and indulge his love of the outdoors. On such trips—like the time he climbed the 5,268-foot Mt. Katahdin—TR tested his stamina, kept the asthma at bay, and astounded the hardened guides with his energy.

Roosevelt joined the Republican Party in 1880 and became New York's youngest assemblyman a year later. This formal portrait was taken in 1883, just after he won a second term. Roosevelt became known as a reformer, finding common cause with society's powerless and exposing political corruption.

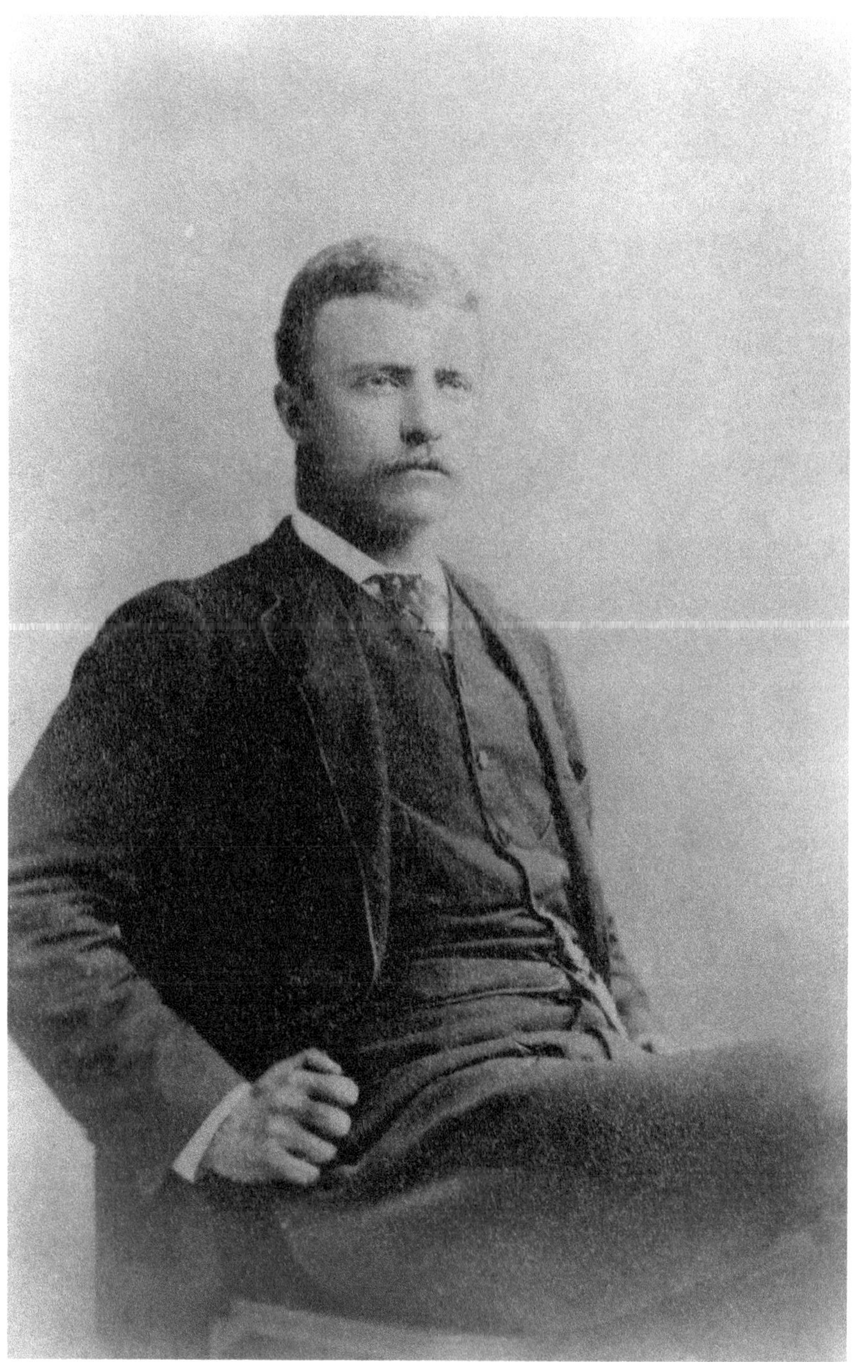

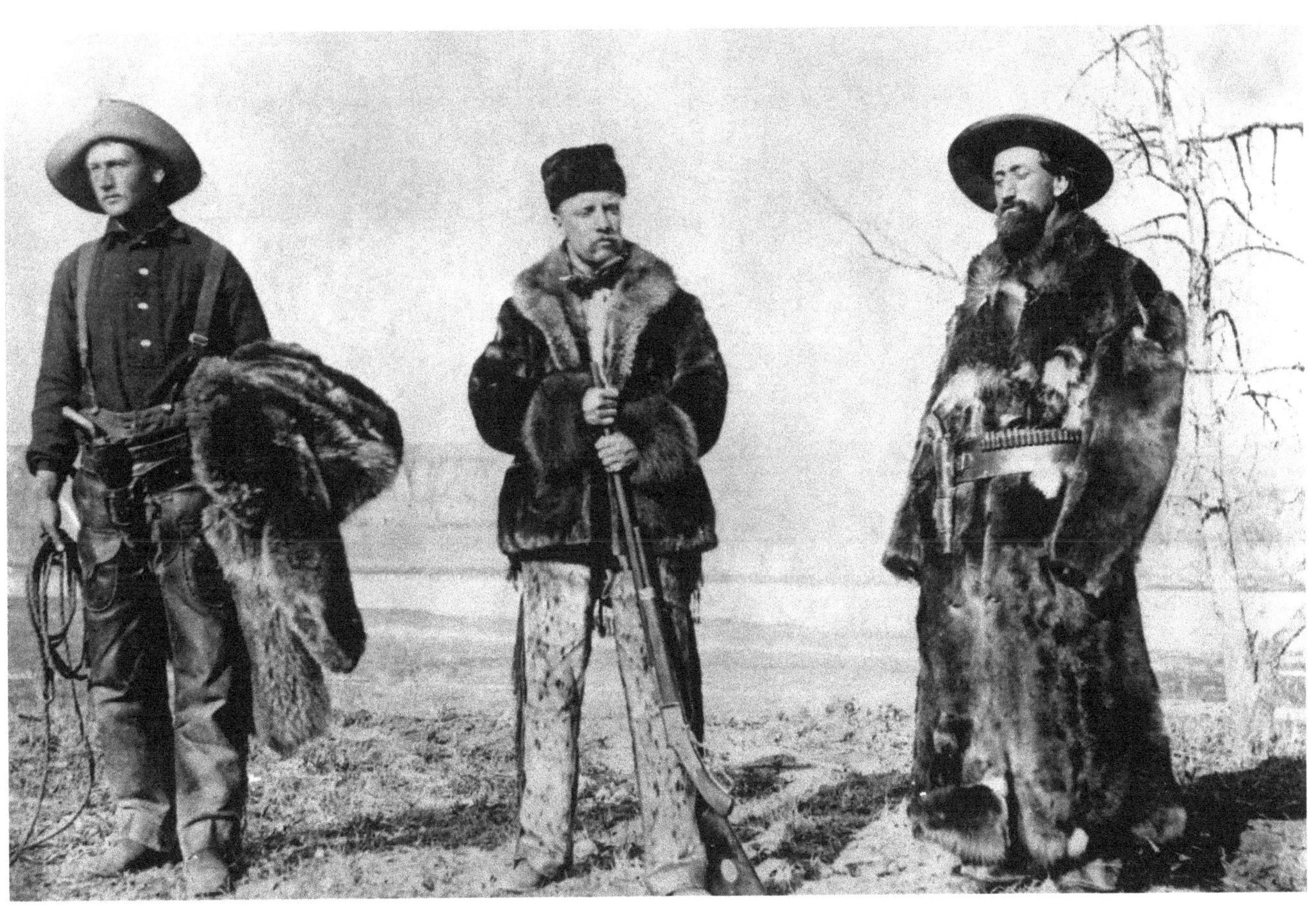

Roosevelt stands flanked by Bill Sewall and Wilmot Dow in the Dakota Territory. He had purchased land near Medora in 1882, and after the deaths of his wife and mother in 1884, threw himself into cattle ranching. He met Westerners of all sorts, tested his physical mettle on cattle drives, read, wrote, and let the big skies and the open vistas assuage his grief.

This intimate photo of Roosevelt was taken after his marriage to his childhood sweetheart, Edith Carow in 1886. He is sitting in his library in their rambling home, Sagamore Hill, in Oyster Bay, Long Island. Books were a constant companion in Roosevelt's life, which was happily enriched by his intelligent and commonsensical wife and the first of their five children. Theodore, Jr., born in 1887, joined his half-sister Alice in the cheerful nursery.

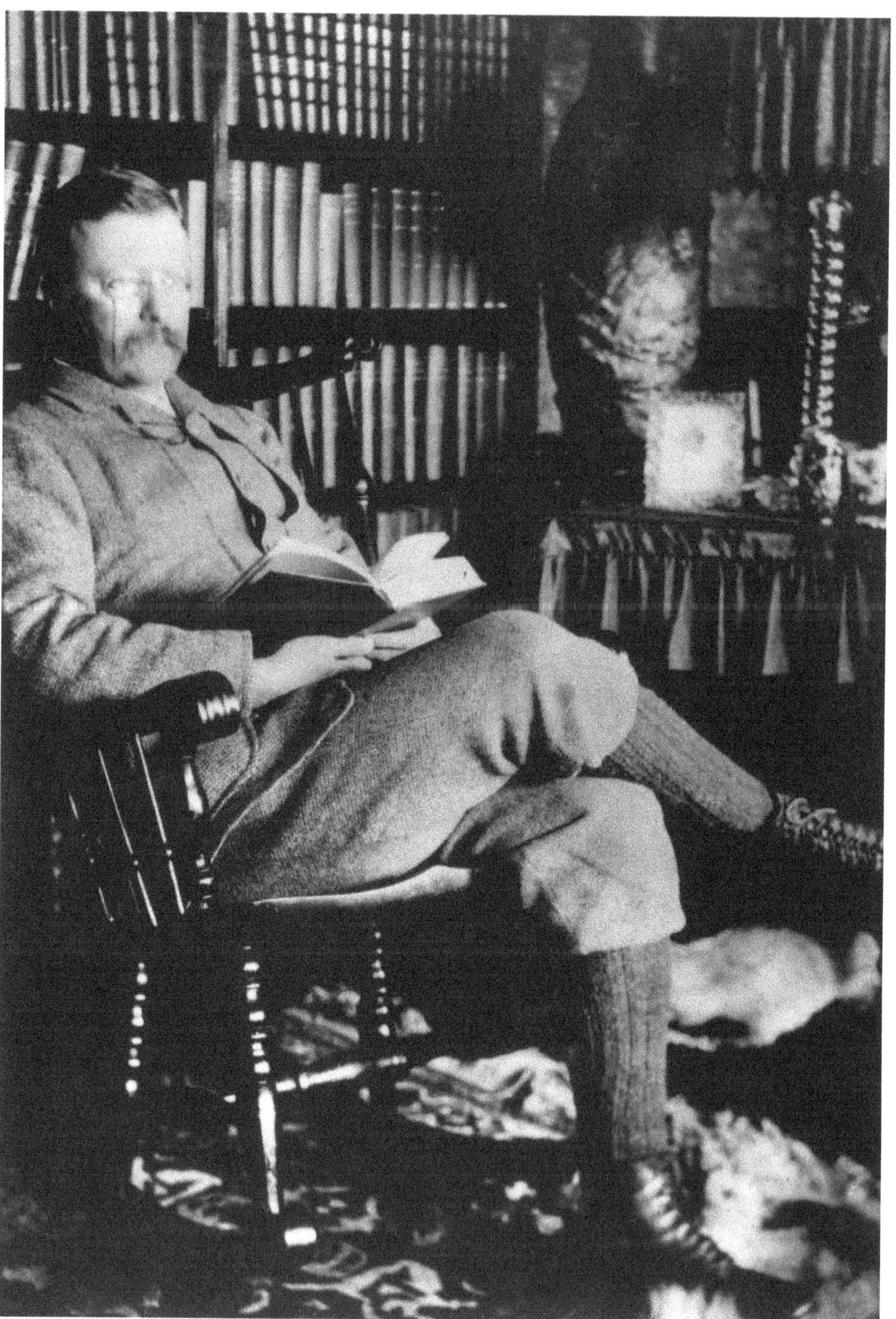

The Years of Preparation (1889–1900)

Republican president Benjamin Harrison chose former New York assemblyman Theodore Roosevelt to join the Civil Service Commission in 1889 because of his reputation as a reformer. Rationalizing federal service jobs and cleaning up the spoils system were lifelong missions for TR. In 1895 Roosevelt took on the leadership of the New York City Board of Police Commissioners. He applied Progressive Era notions of efficiency to the police force that had worked in the Civil Service. Enforcing the Sunday closing law on saloons, despite his personal dislike of the bill, earned him mixed reviews, and he gladly accepted the position of Assistant Secretary of the Navy in 1897 when offered him by newly inaugurated President William McKinley.

Roosevelt fervently believed in military preparedness. When war broke out in 1898 between the United States and Spain—over Spain's possession, Cuba—TR joyfully quit his desk job and formed the First United States Volunteer Cavalry. The colorful Rough Riders and their military fame propelled Colonel Roosevelt into the New York governor's mansion after the war. His brief stay in Albany reinforced his progressive reputation because of his environmental programs, his attempts to curb unfair corporate practices, and his actions on behalf of the poor. The Republican Party bosses, bowing to Roosevelt's popularity, made him the vice-presidential nominee in 1900. After a successful campaign, TR served in the second spot for less than seven months before President McKinley was assassinated, and Roosevelt assumed the presidency on September 14, 1901.

After writing seven books and serving in Washington, D.C., as one of President Benjamin Harrison's Civil Service Commissioners (1889–1895), Roosevelt returned to New York City as a member of the Board of Police Commissioners. There he fought corruption, standardized the police force, and implemented innovations such as the bicycle squad, regulation weapons, and firearms practice. He did not discriminate on religious grounds in hiring, and made the first appointment of a woman to an executive position.

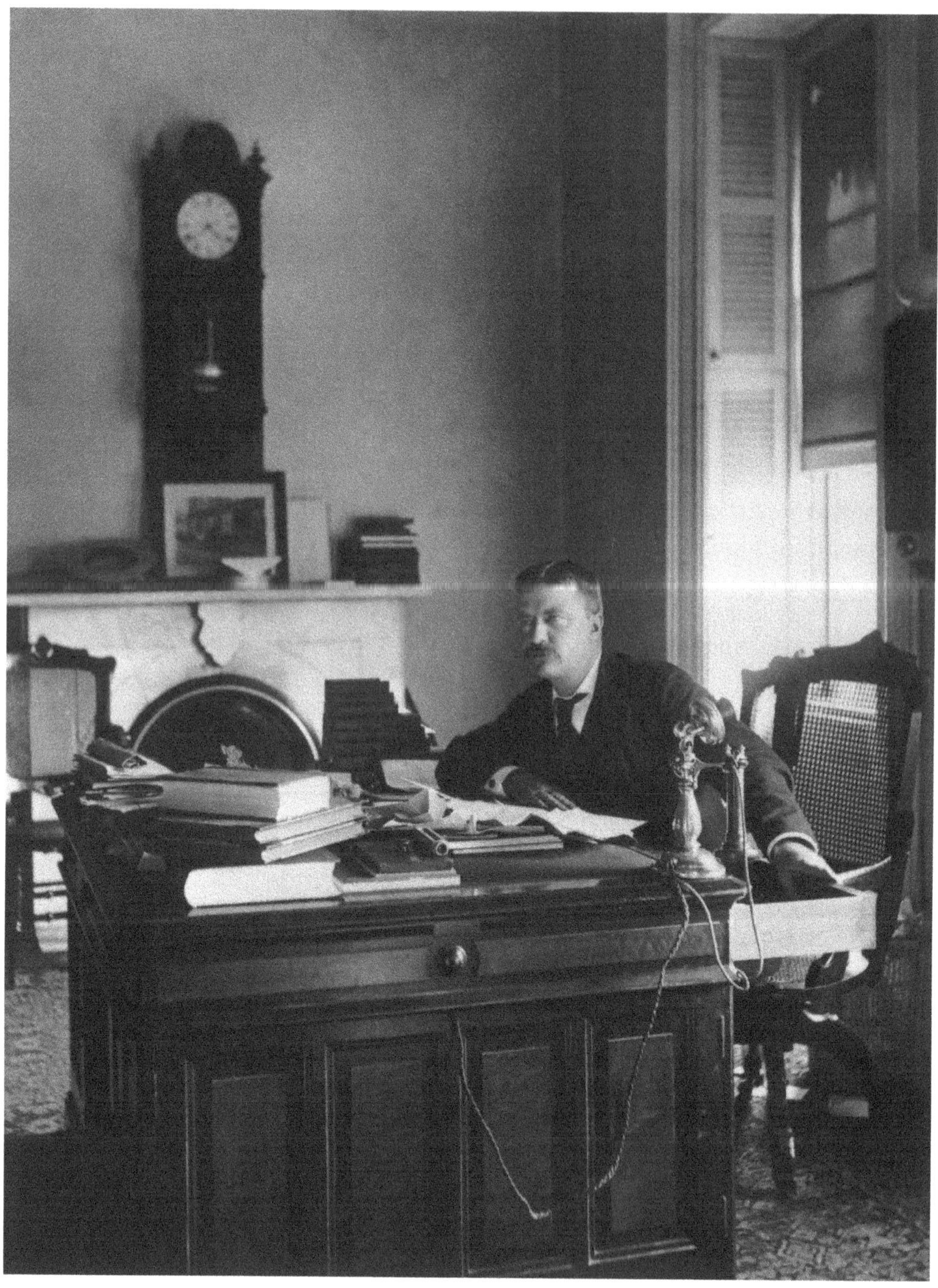

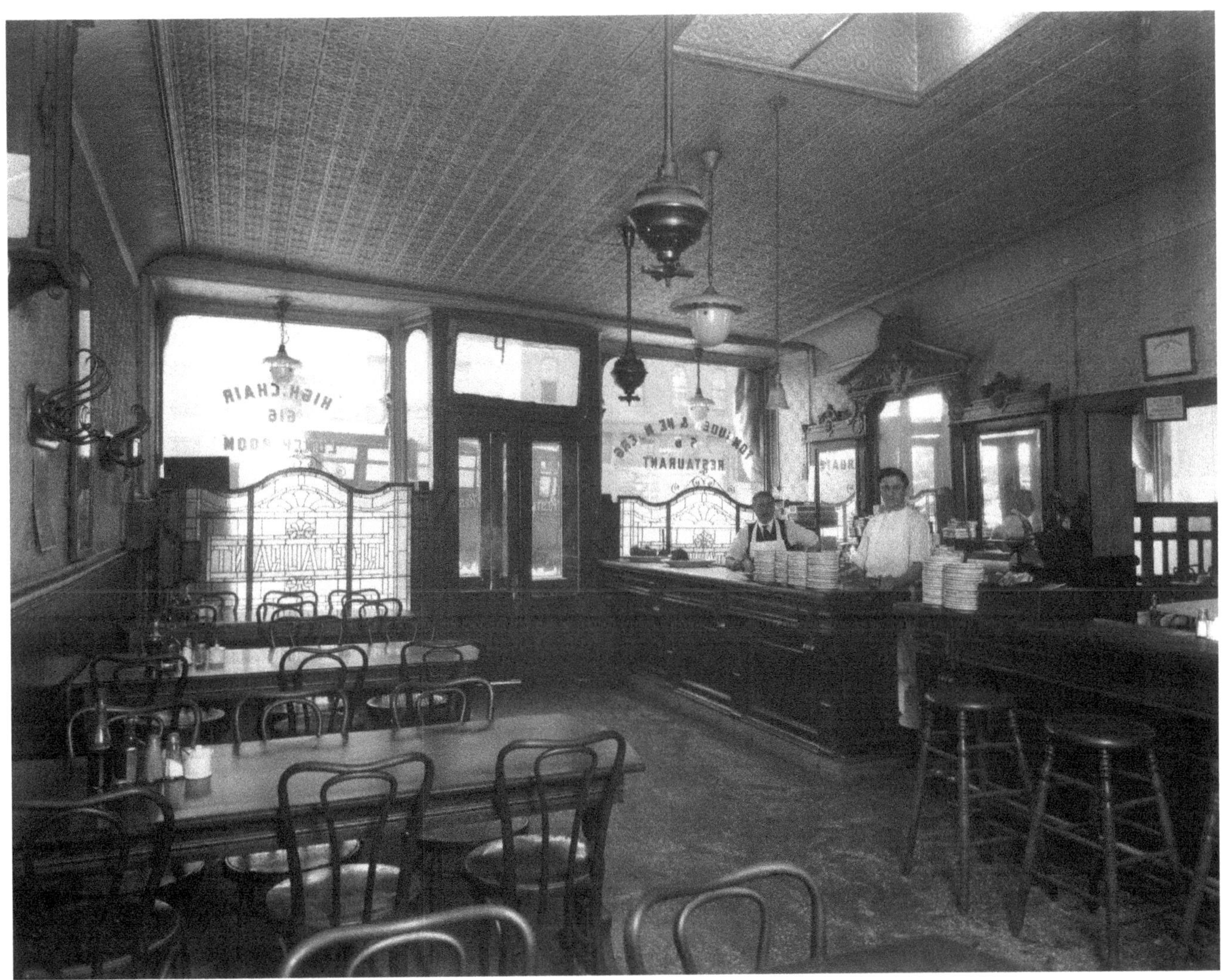

Police Commissioner Roosevelt frequently lunched at the High Chair Lunch Room on Grand Street. He would have heard the complaints of New Yorkers angry at the strict enforcement of the law that stated no liquor could be sold on Sunday—usually the only day working men had off. Although Roosevelt didn't like the law, he wrote they could either "instruct the police to allow all the saloon-keepers to become lawbreakers, or we could instruct them to stop all lawbreaking."

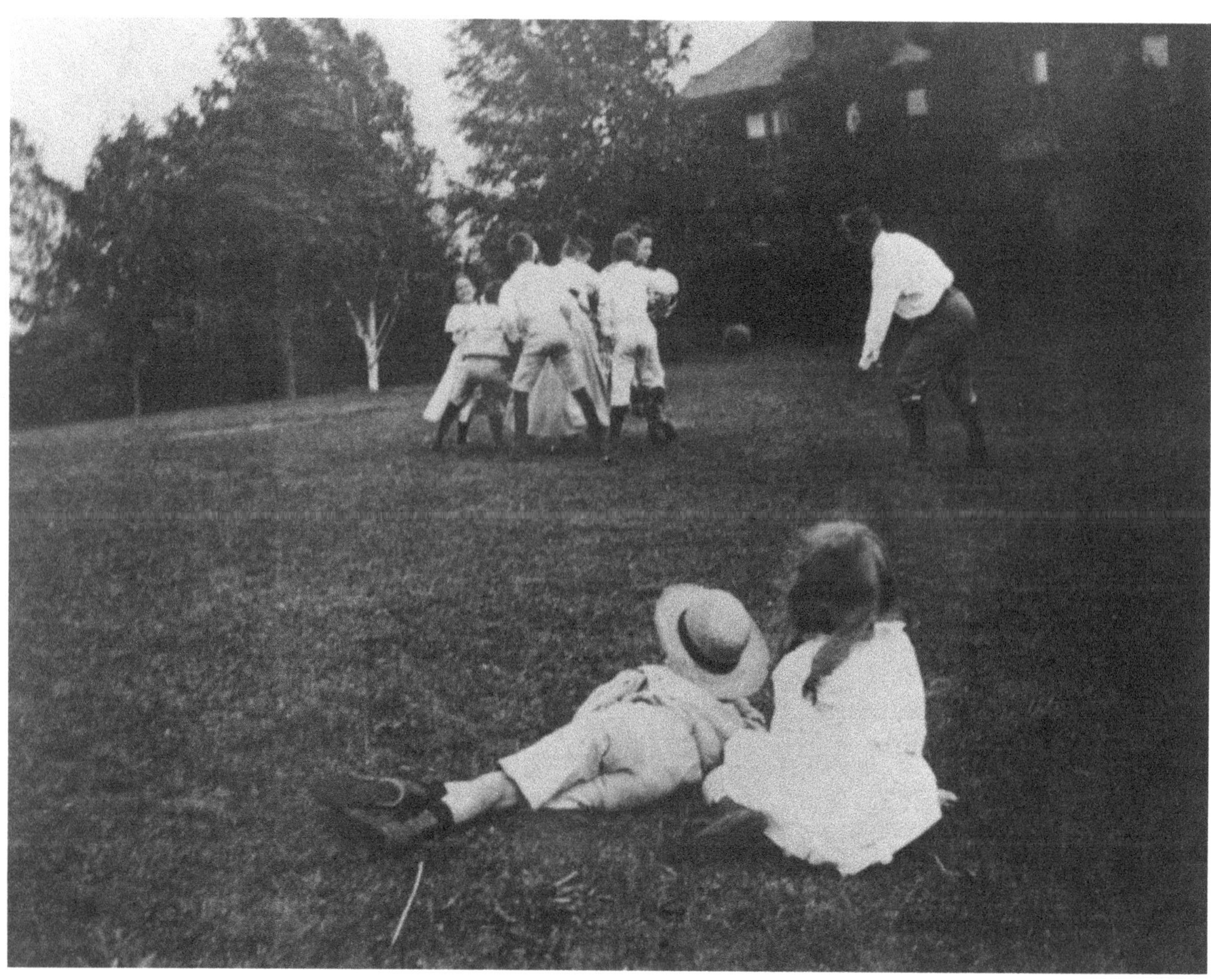

This photo shows Roosevelt doing one of the things he enjoyed most: playing with the children. Ted and Alice are in the foreground, while their older cousins tussle over the football. Roosevelt read to his children, scared them with ghost stories, had ferocious pillow fights, and led them on point-to-point walks where they could go over and through, but never around an obstacle. He inspired a tremendous love in all his children, who also inherited his commitment to public service.

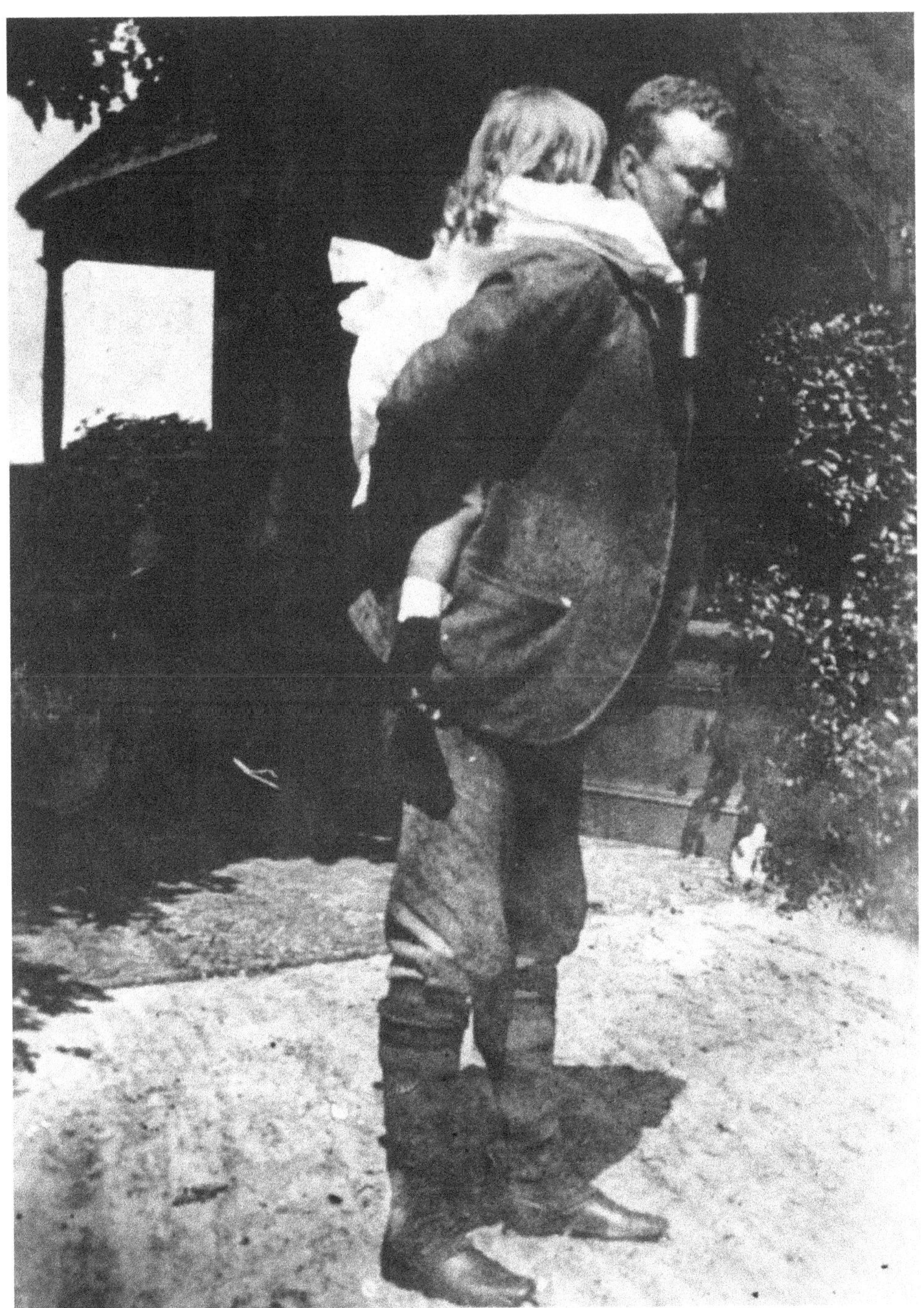

Edith and Theodore had five children: Theodore, Jr. (1887), Kermit (1889), Ethel (1891), Archibald (1894), and Quentin (1897). Ethel is riding piggyback on her father at the Roosevelt home, Sagamore Hill.

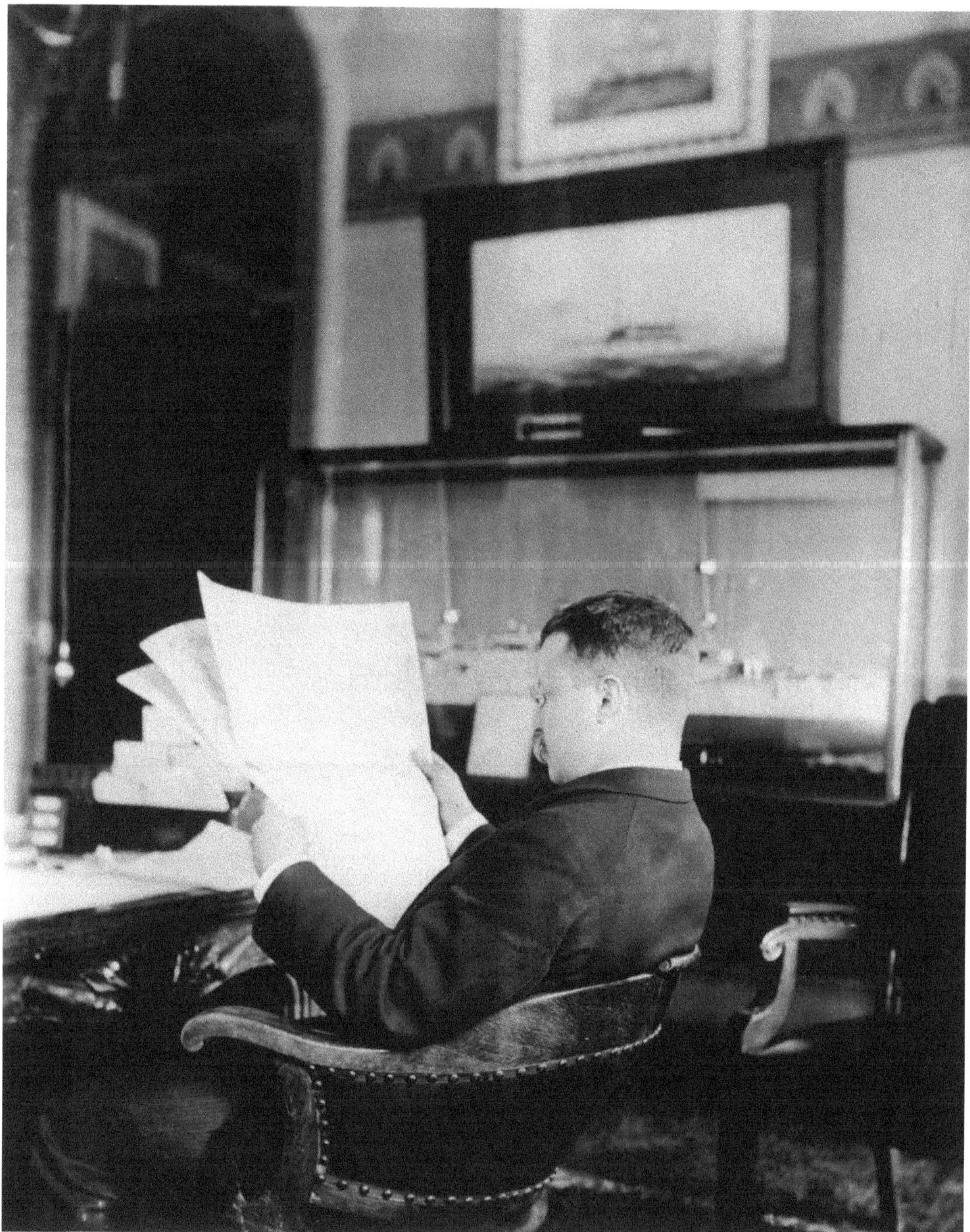

Roosevelt moved the family back to Washington, D.C., when he was appointed Assistant Secretary of the Navy by President William McKinley in 1897. He is shown here in his office at the State, War, and Navy Building (now the Old Executive Office Building). Roosevelt believed in U.S. naval preparedness and worked to increase the size and strength of the navy through his writings and his actions.

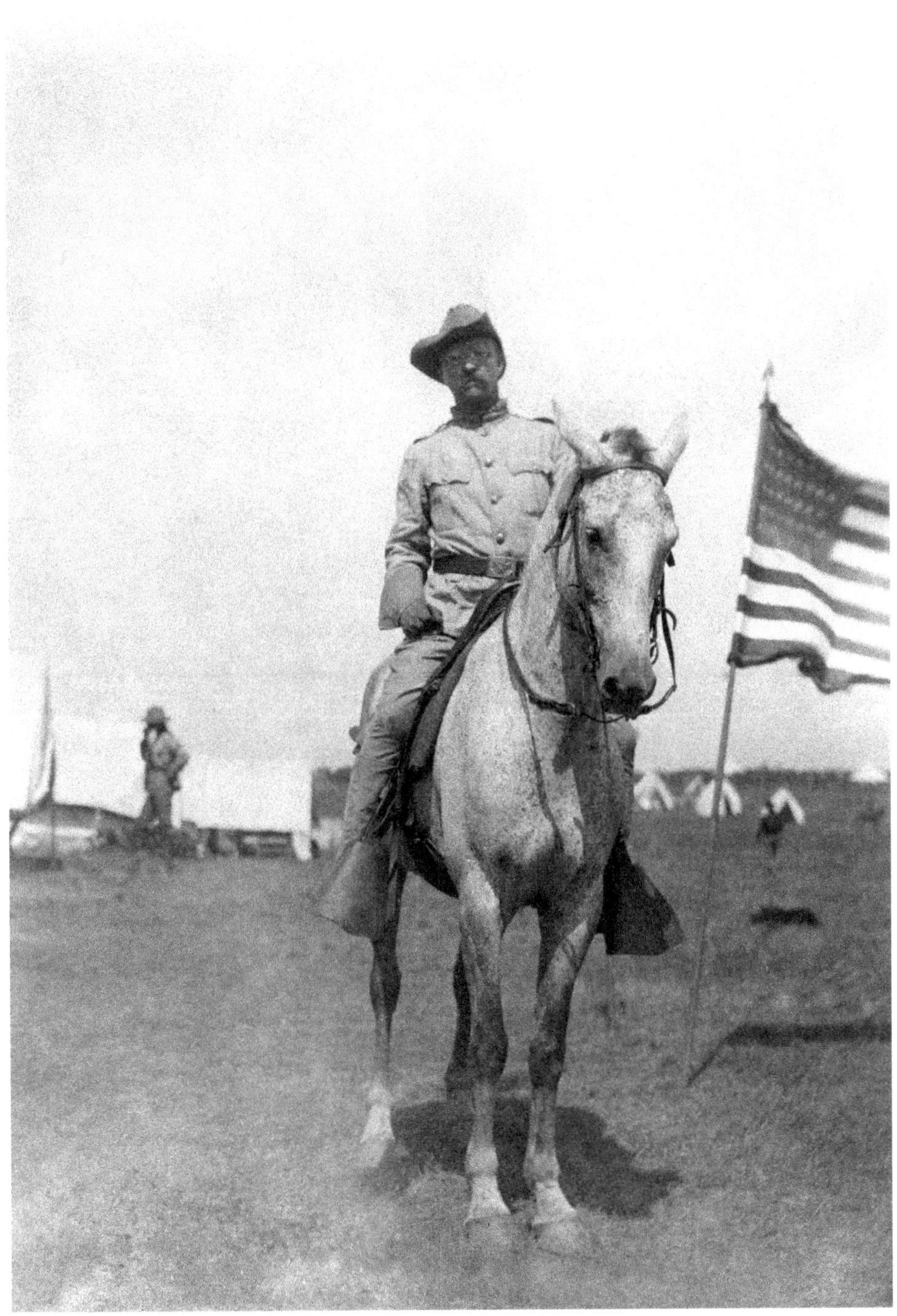

On February 15, 1898, the U.S. battleship *Maine* exploded in Havana harbor killing nearly 260 Americans. That was partly the impetus for the Spanish-American War, fought successfully in Cuba and the Philippines during the summer of 1898. Roosevelt left his position as Assistant Secretary of the Navy to join the fighting, and is shown here in his Rough Rider uniform.

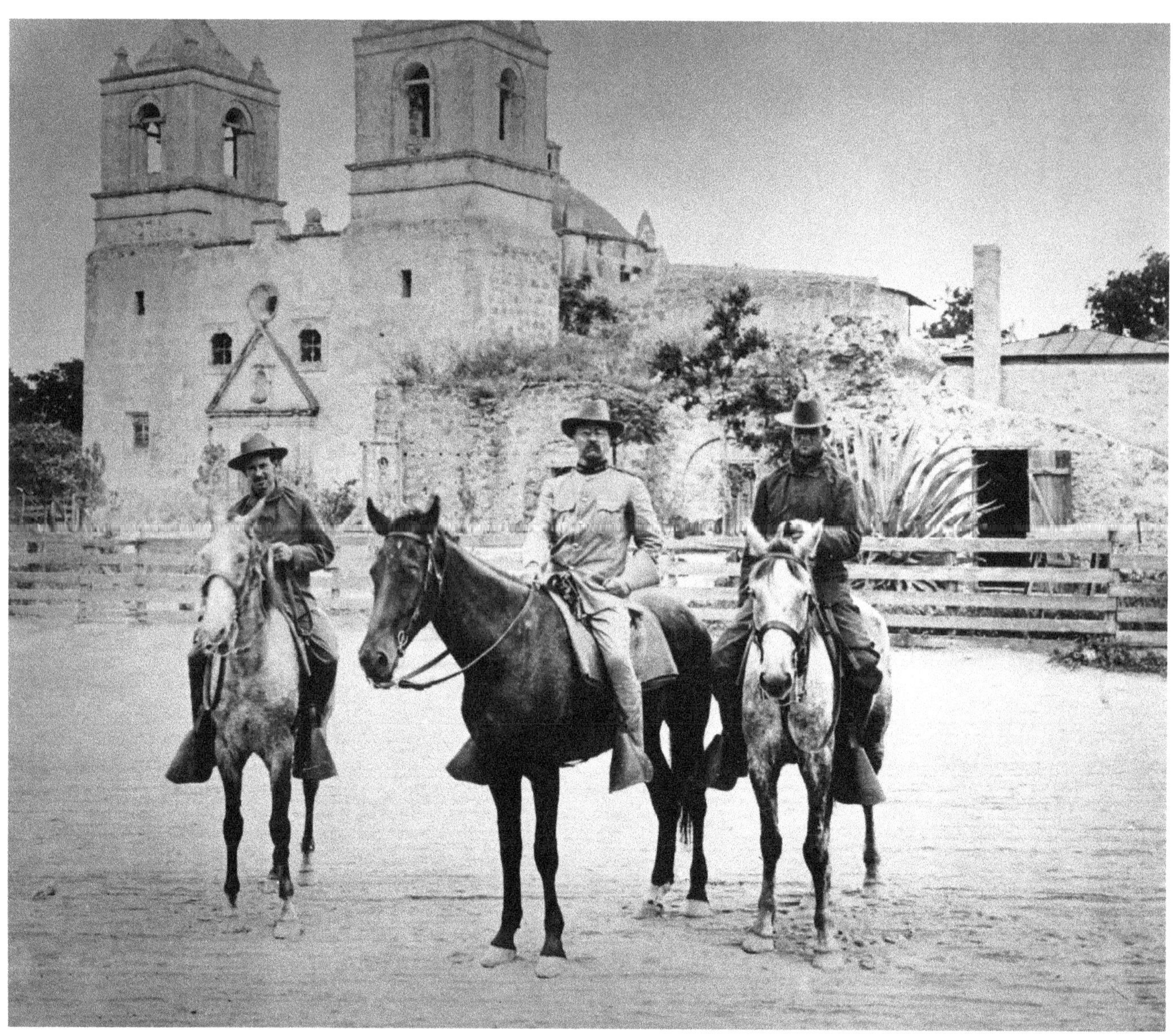

The First United States Volunteer Cavalry was one of three volunteer regiments authorized by Congress. Nicknamed the Rough Riders, the force of 1,250 men was led by TR's friend, army surgeon Col. Leonard Wood, with the assistance of the newly commissioned Lt. Col. Roosevelt. Roosevelt is on horseback here before being shipped to Cuba.

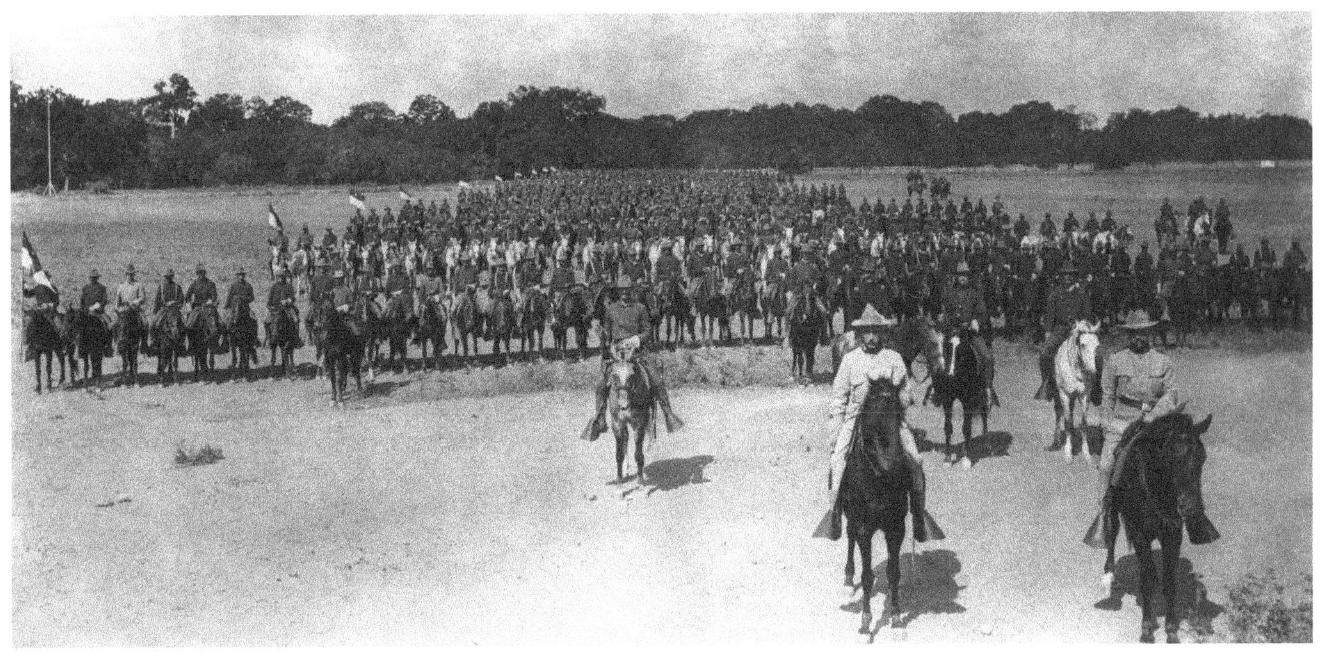

The Rough Riders in San Antonio, May 1898, readying to depart for Cuba. Col. Leonard Wood and Lt. Col. Theodore Roosevelt are in the foreground. The Rough Riders were an unusual mix of TR's Harvard friends, Native Americans, cowboys he met in the Dakotas, and politicians he knew from the East Coast.

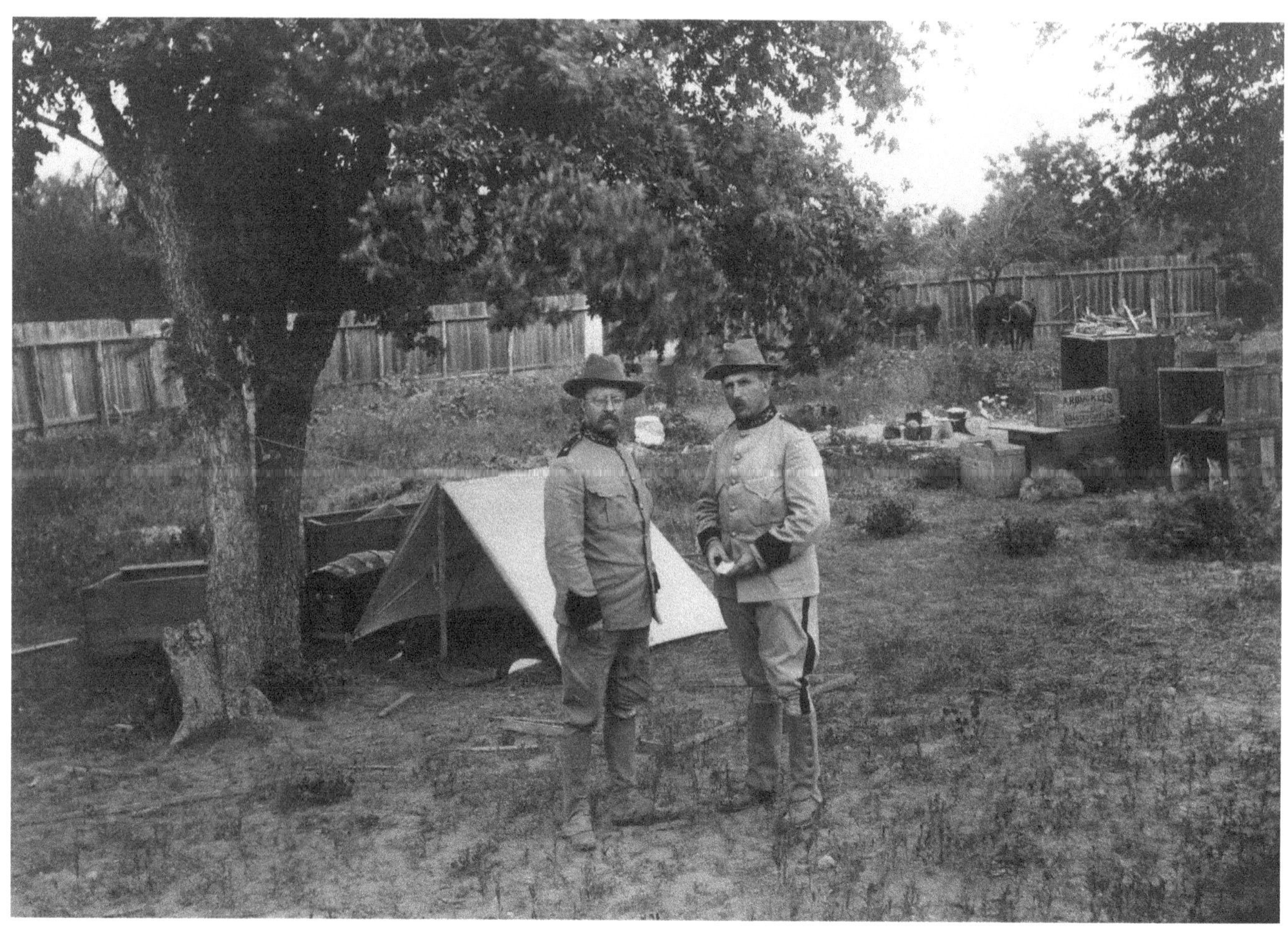

Theodore Roosevelt and Leonard Wood in San Antonio, in May 1898, where the troops assembled before embarking for the battlefields in Cuba. Wood readied the troops and TR drilled them. Roosevelt had been a captain in the New York National Guard for three years before his service in Cuba.

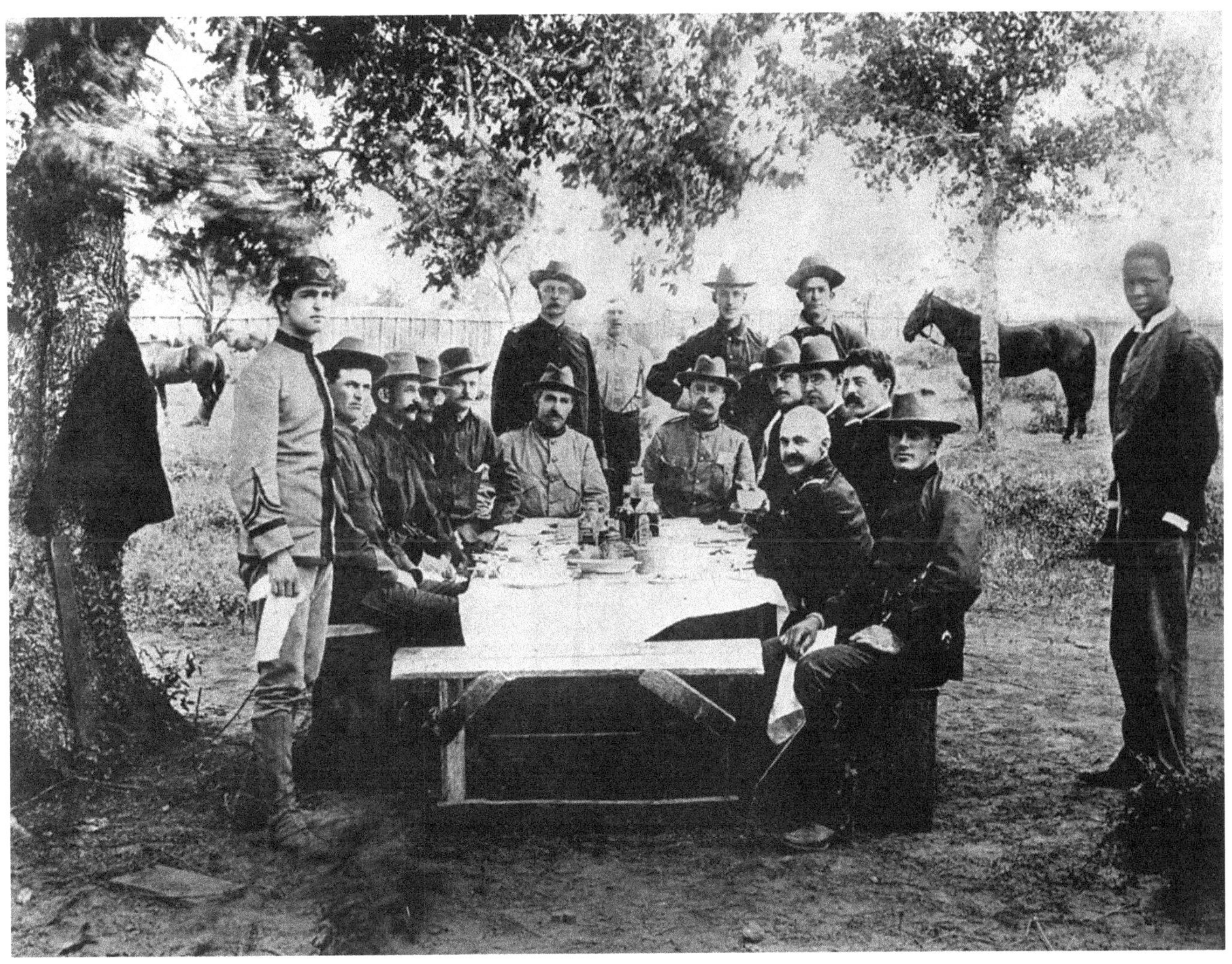

The Rough Riders' last dinner in San Antonio. These would have been the officers grouped around the table. From Texas they went to Tampa, Florida, and from there to Santiago.

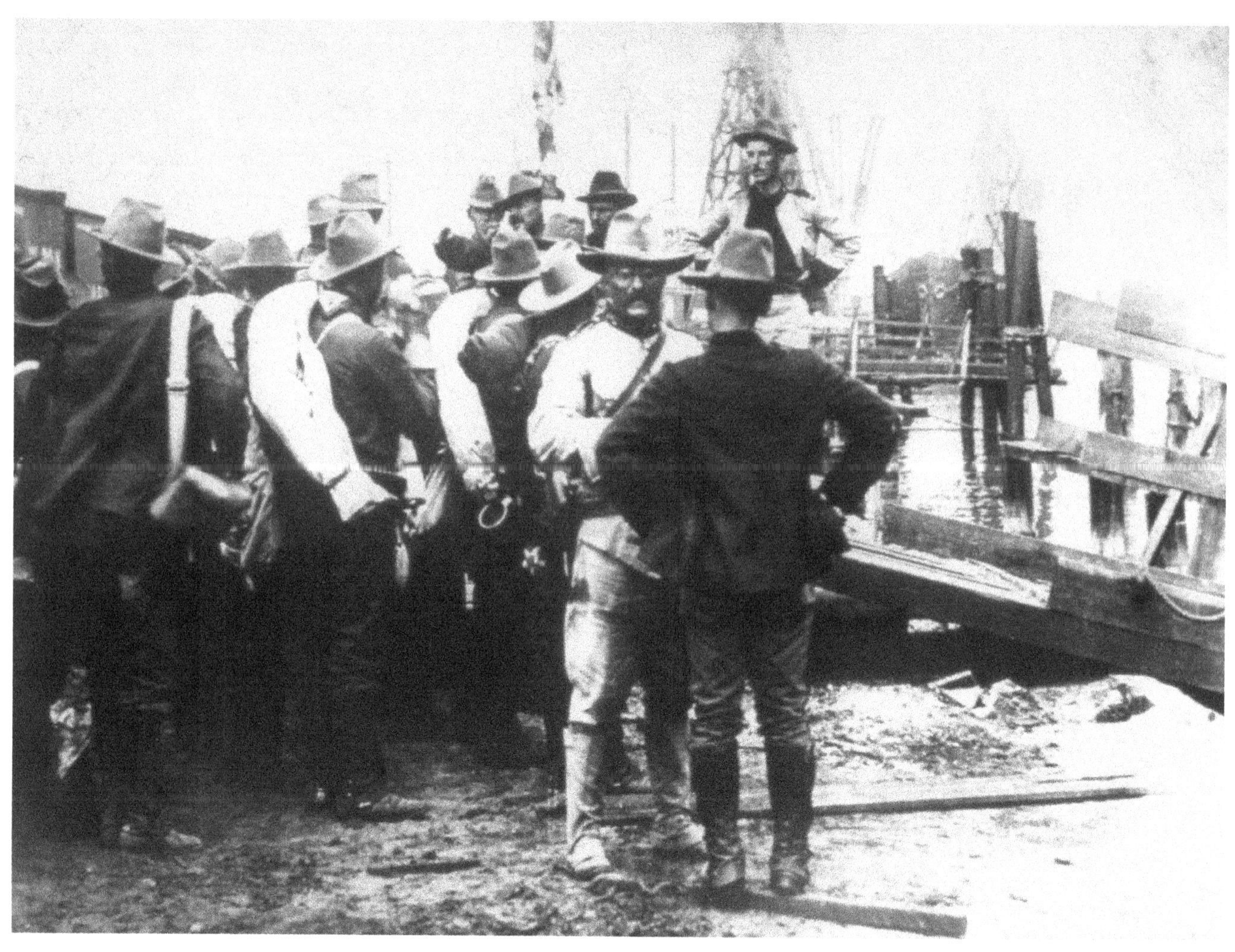

Embarkation at Tampa was chaotic. Roosevelt got his men there aboard coal cars; then, he and Colonel Wood commandeered a transport ship for their regiment.

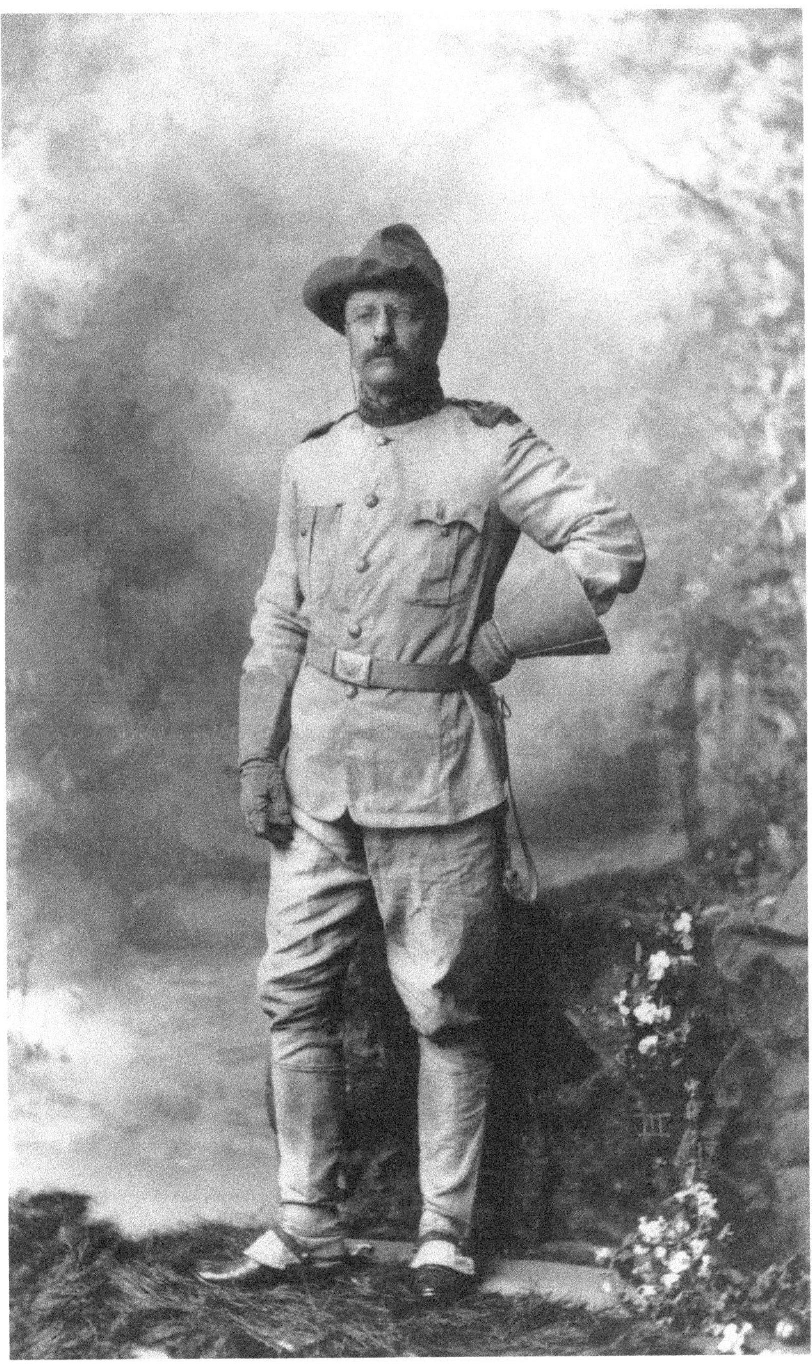

Theodore Roosevelt was promoted to colonel after the Battle of Las Guasimas, the battle that preceded the Rough Riders' charge up Kettle Hill and San Juan Heights. In this photo, TR wears his Rough Rider uniform, absent the blue polka-dotted scarf that became the emblem of the First U.S. Volunteer Cavalry—the insigne that his men could see as he rode horseback, a target for the Spaniards but an inspiration to his soldiers.

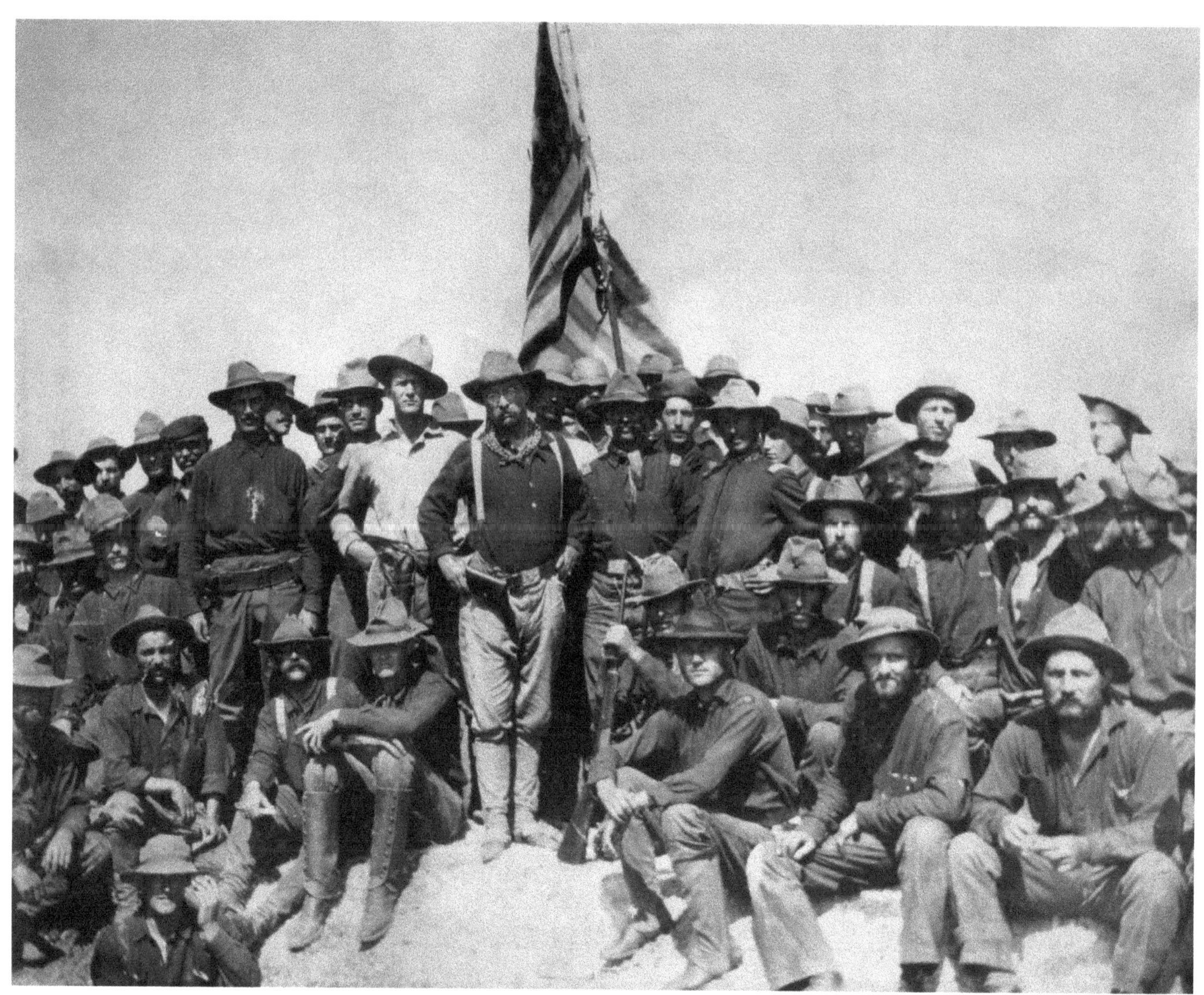

In 2001 Theodore Roosevelt was posthumously awarded the Congressional Medal of Honor for, as the citation reads, leading "a desperate and gallant charge up San Juan Hill, encouraging his troops to continue the assault through withering enemy fire." This was done "in total disregard for his personal safety, and accompanied by only four or five men." His actions "turned the tide" in the battle. This is TR and his Rough Riders at the top of San Juan Heights.

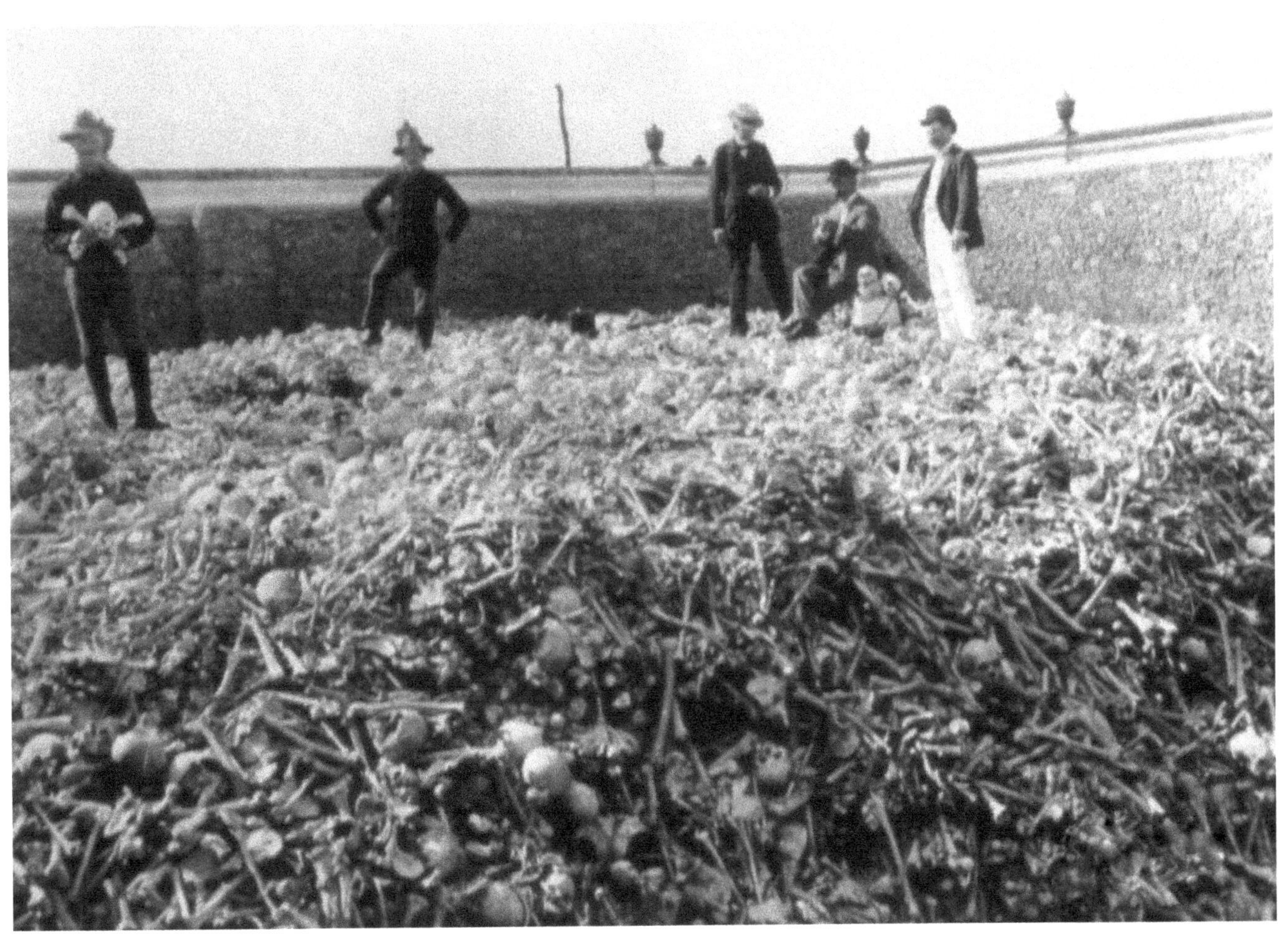

The boneyard of the Cabanas military prison, located at the mouth of the Havana harbor.

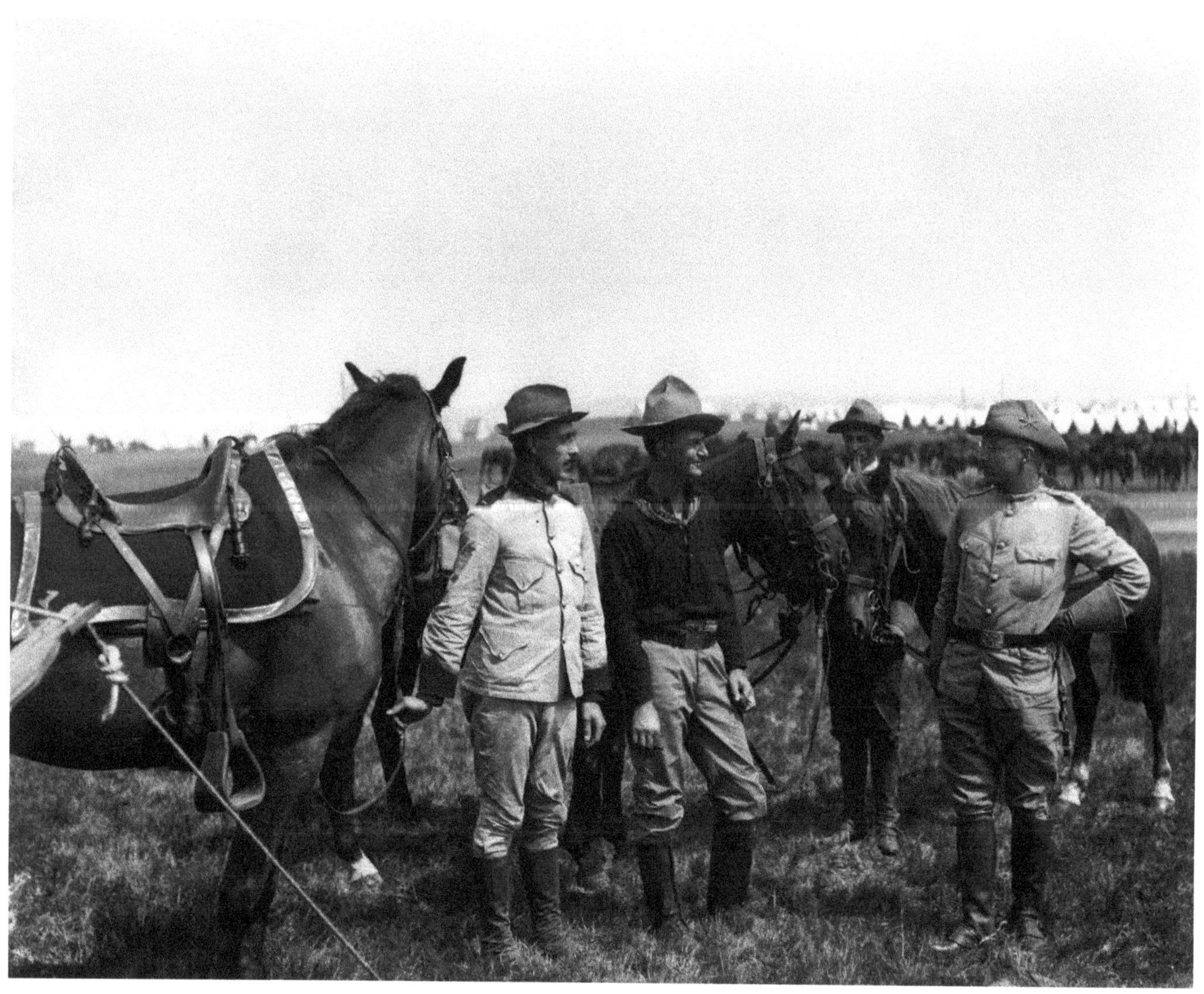

After the war ended in Spanish defeat, the Rough Riders were quarantined at Montauk, Long Island, before being mustered out in mid September. Rough Rider John Greenway is at center, and TR to the right in this photo. In his autobiography, Roosevelt remarked that there were "no four months of my life to which I look back with more pride and satisfaction."

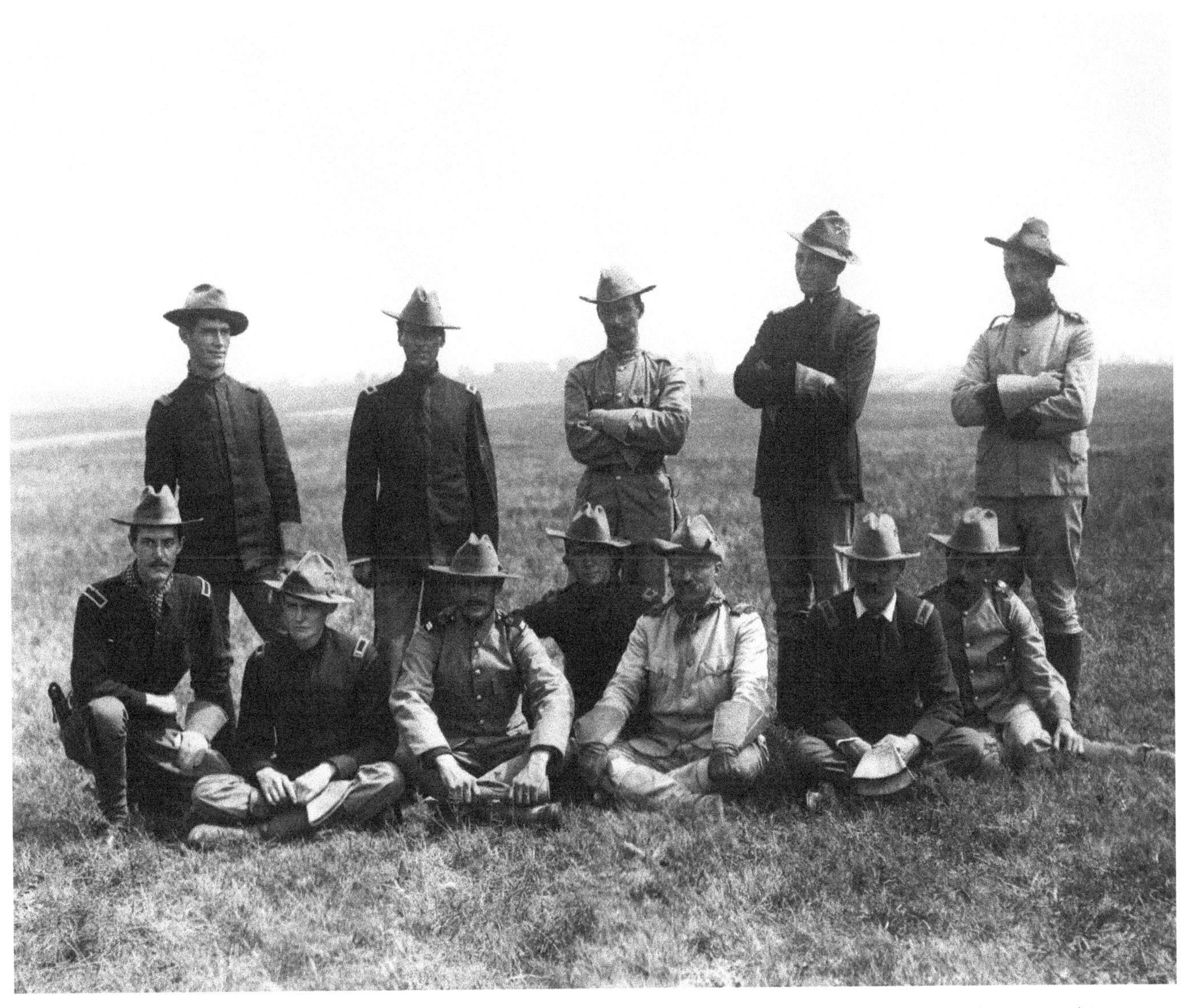

TR and some officers of the Rough Riders at Montauk in August or September 1898. The Roosevelt family remained in contact with the Rough Riders throughout all their lives.

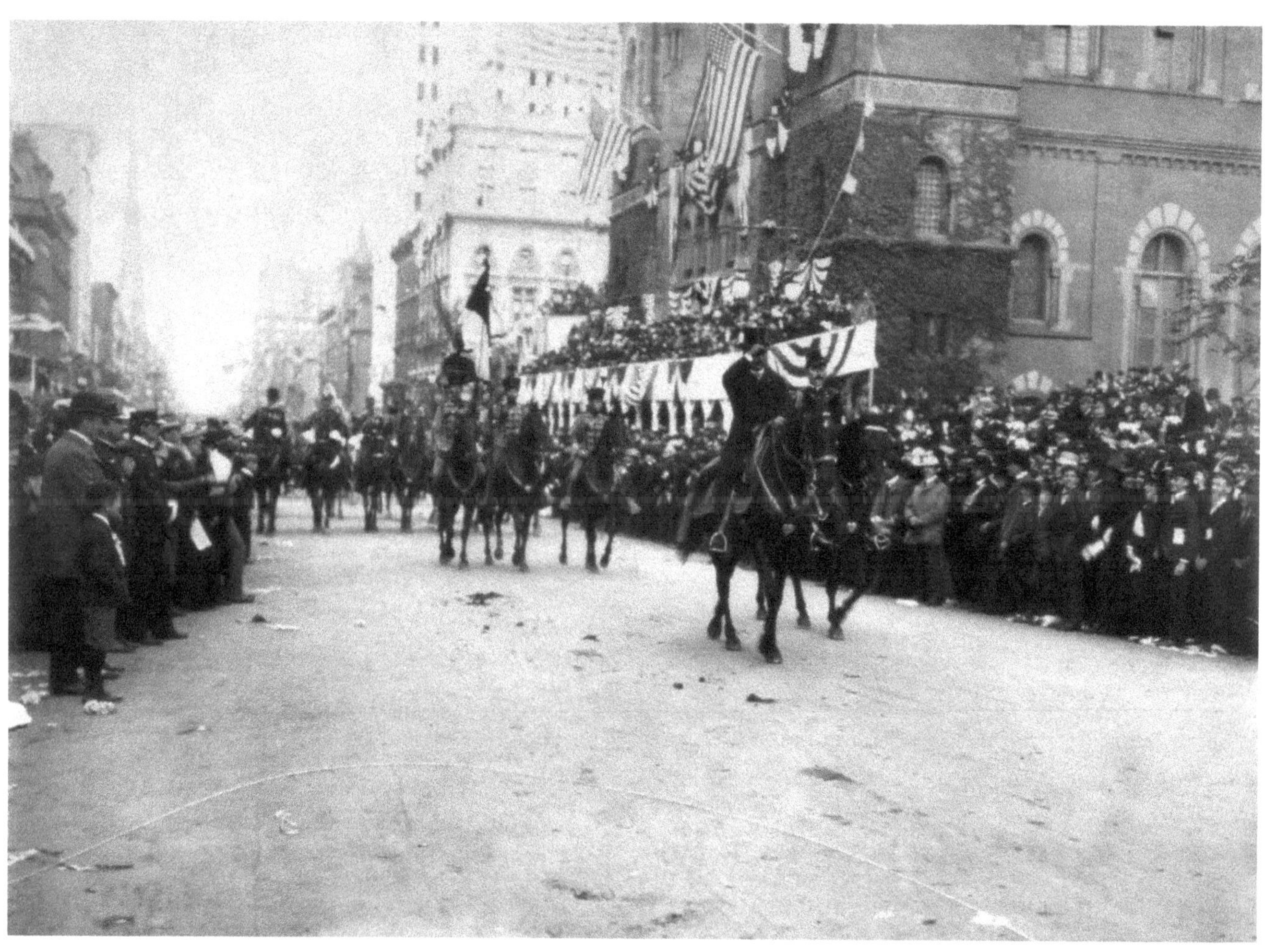

More hawkish than Secretary of the Navy, John D. Long, Roosevelt had been happy to assist with the preparations for war by sending a telegram to Commodore George Dewey laying out Dewey's duties in the Philippines. The actual order of war came from President McKinley two months later, on April 24, 1898. Dewey went on to fame at the Battle of Manila Bay, and many parades were subsequently held in his honor. This one featured the similarly celebrated Colonel Roosevelt, waving to his fans.

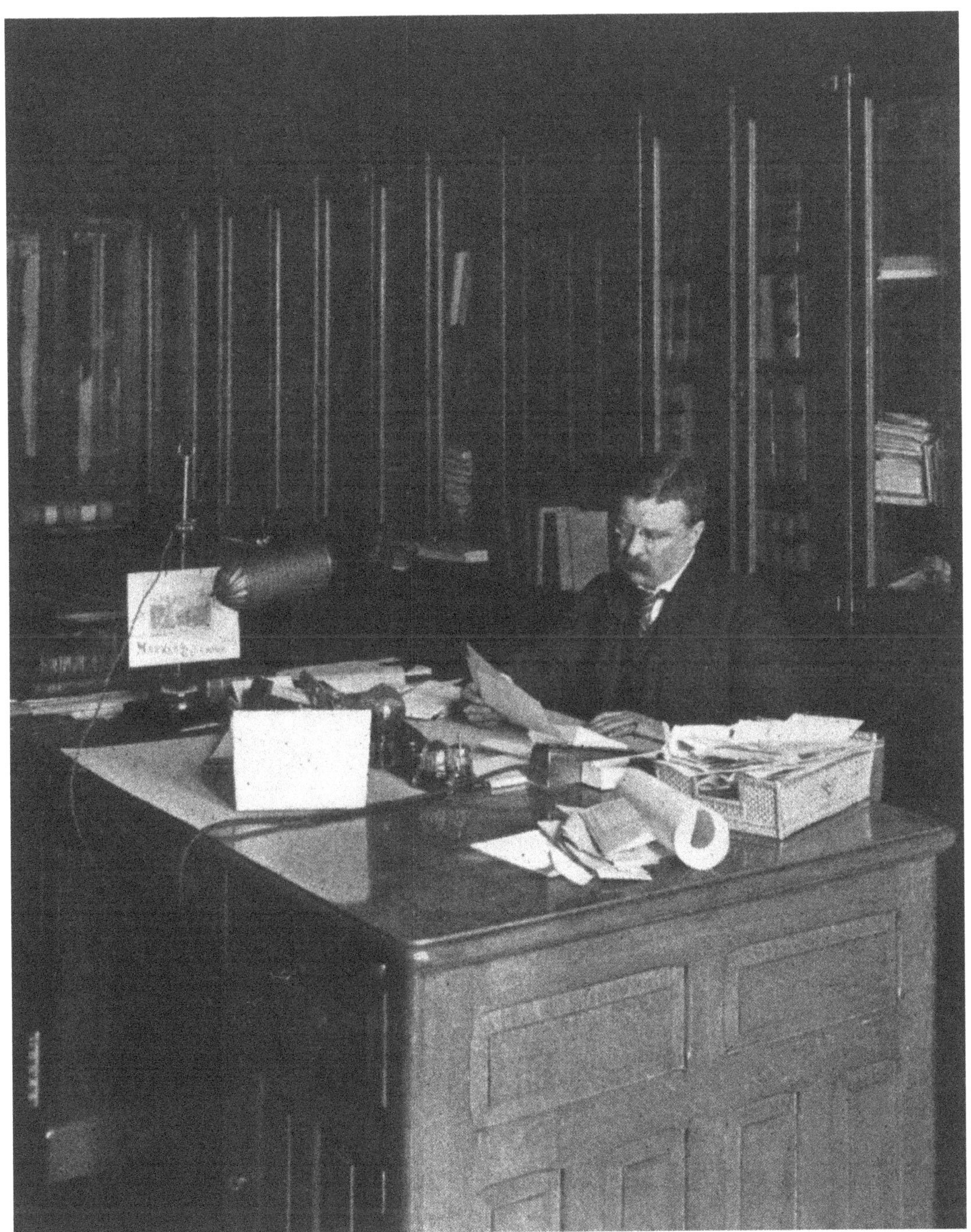

Propelled by his wartime fame and flanked by his Rough Riders, Theodore Roosevelt was elected governor of New York in 1898. Although New Yorkers were happy, the state's most prominent political boss, Thomas Platt, was furious to learn that he could not control TR. Roosevelt established his independence as he forced utility companies to pay taxes, rather than bribe Boss Platt.

Governor Roosevelt speaks to the New York State National Guard Association in early 1900. He wrote in his autobiography that he managed to get the critical reform bills passed in Albany "only by arousing the people, and riveting their attention on what was done." Roosevelt was a master communicator who knew how to manipulate the press and influence voters.

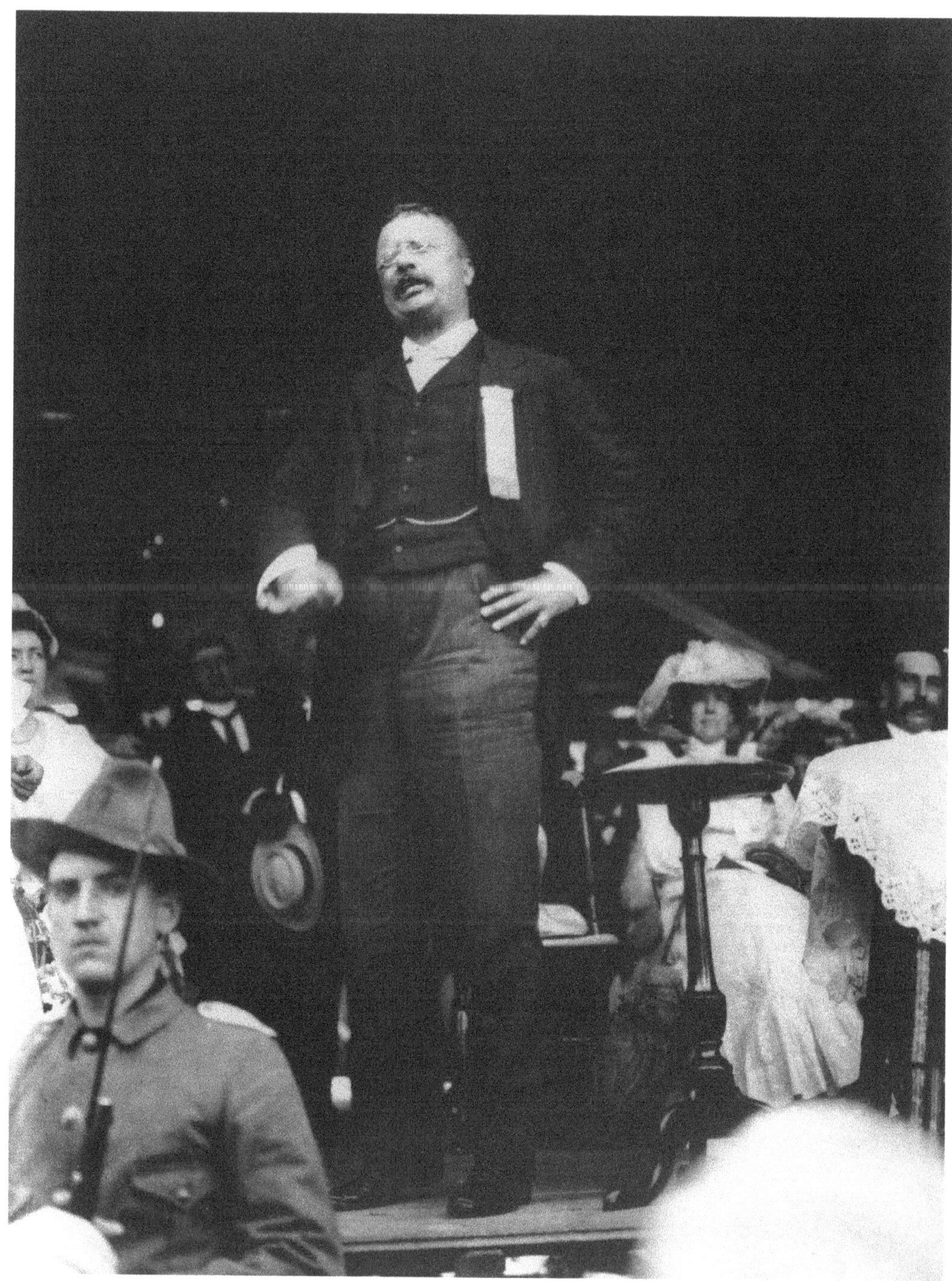

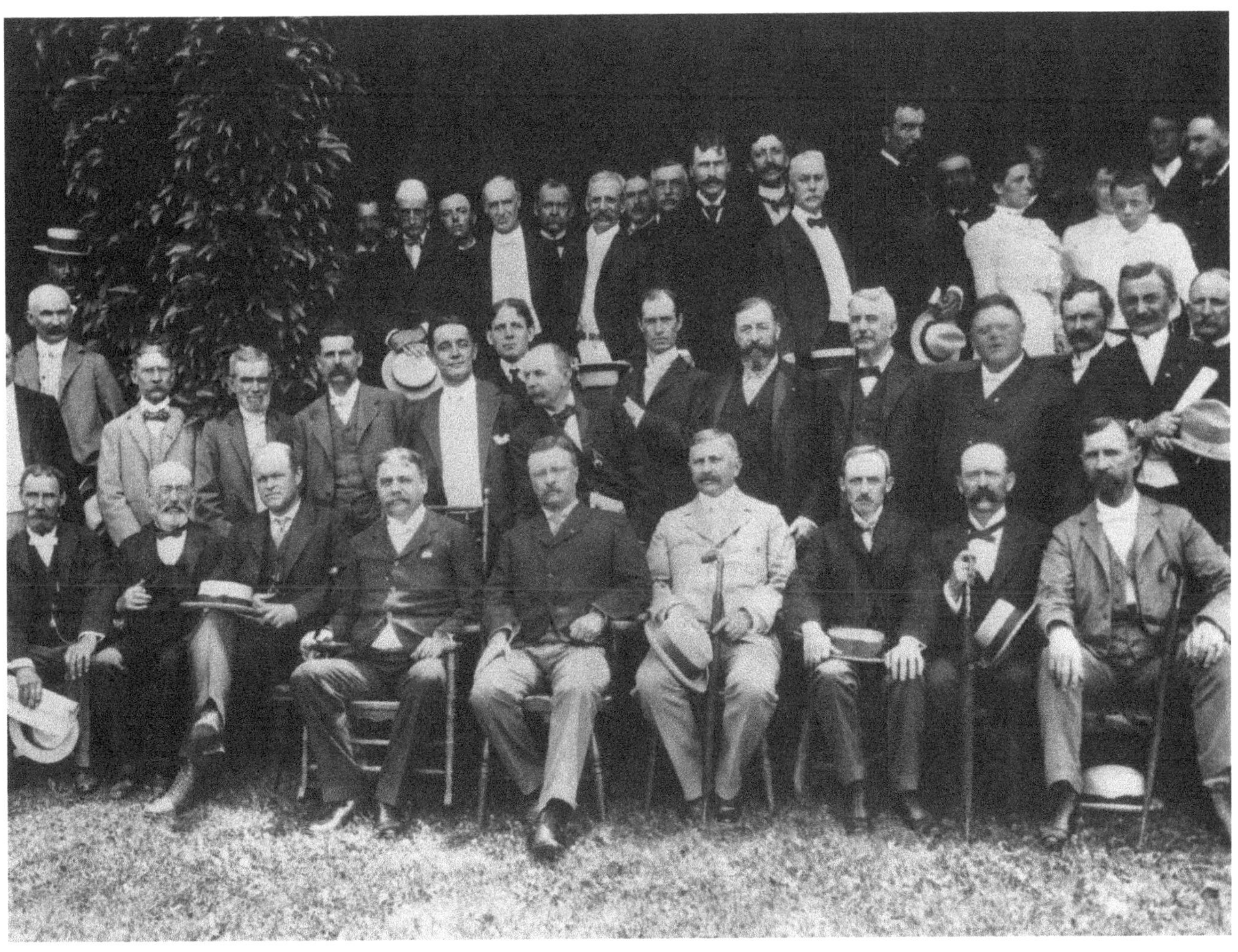

In the summer of 1900, this committee arrived at Sagamore Hill to notify the governor that he was the Republican Party's choice for vice-president. As governor, TR had increased teachers' salaries, supported environmental reforms, sent factory inspectors across the state to seek out shopfloor abuses, and instituted regulatory bills on topics from tenements to workers' hours to cities' water supplies. Governor Roosevelt had tangled with wealthy businessmen who disliked his antitrust legislation and his work on behalf of the rights of the laboring classes.

Roosevelt's official portrait as governor of New York, taken in June 1900, at the time he was deciding what to do about the Republican Party's tentative offer of the vice-presidential spot.

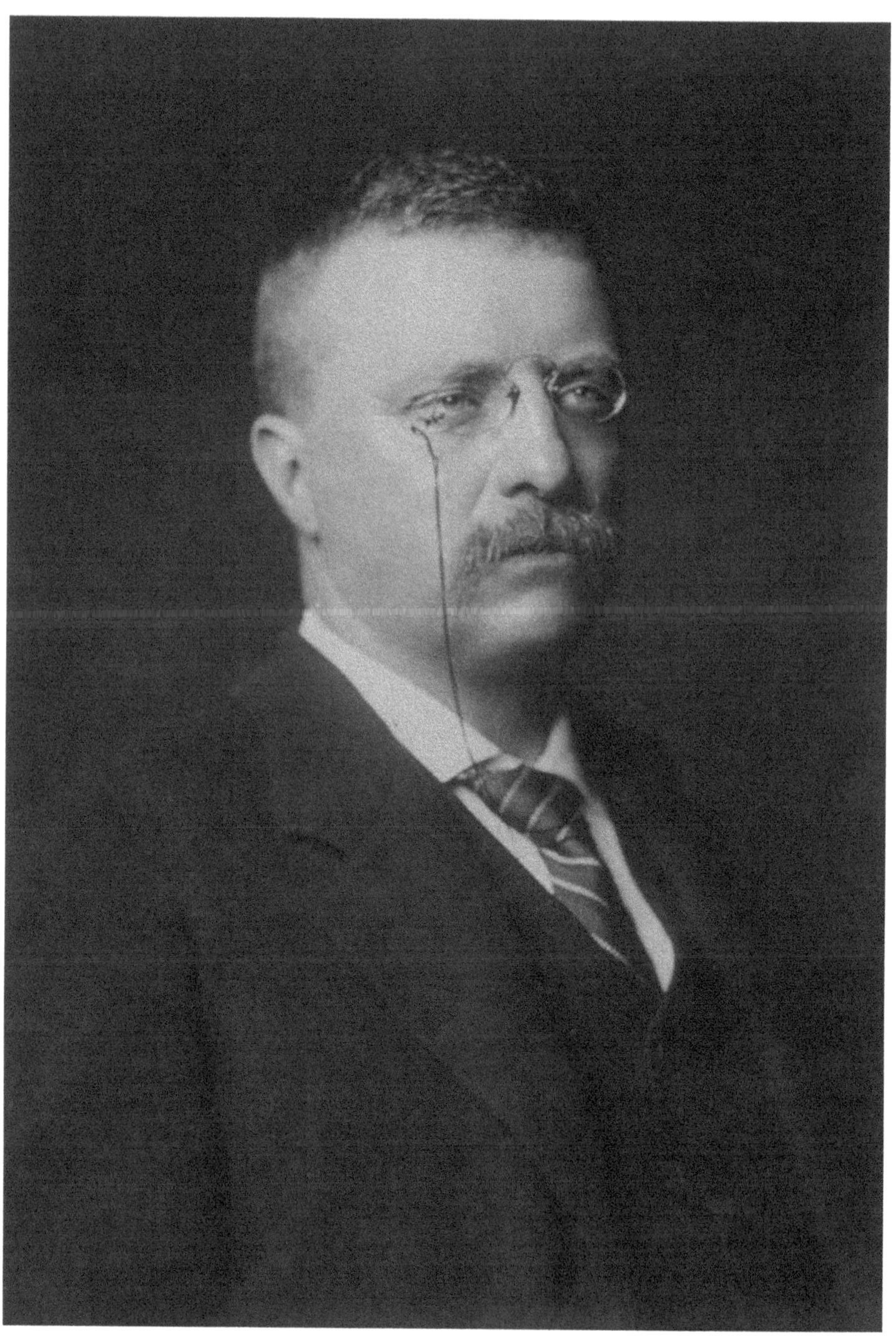

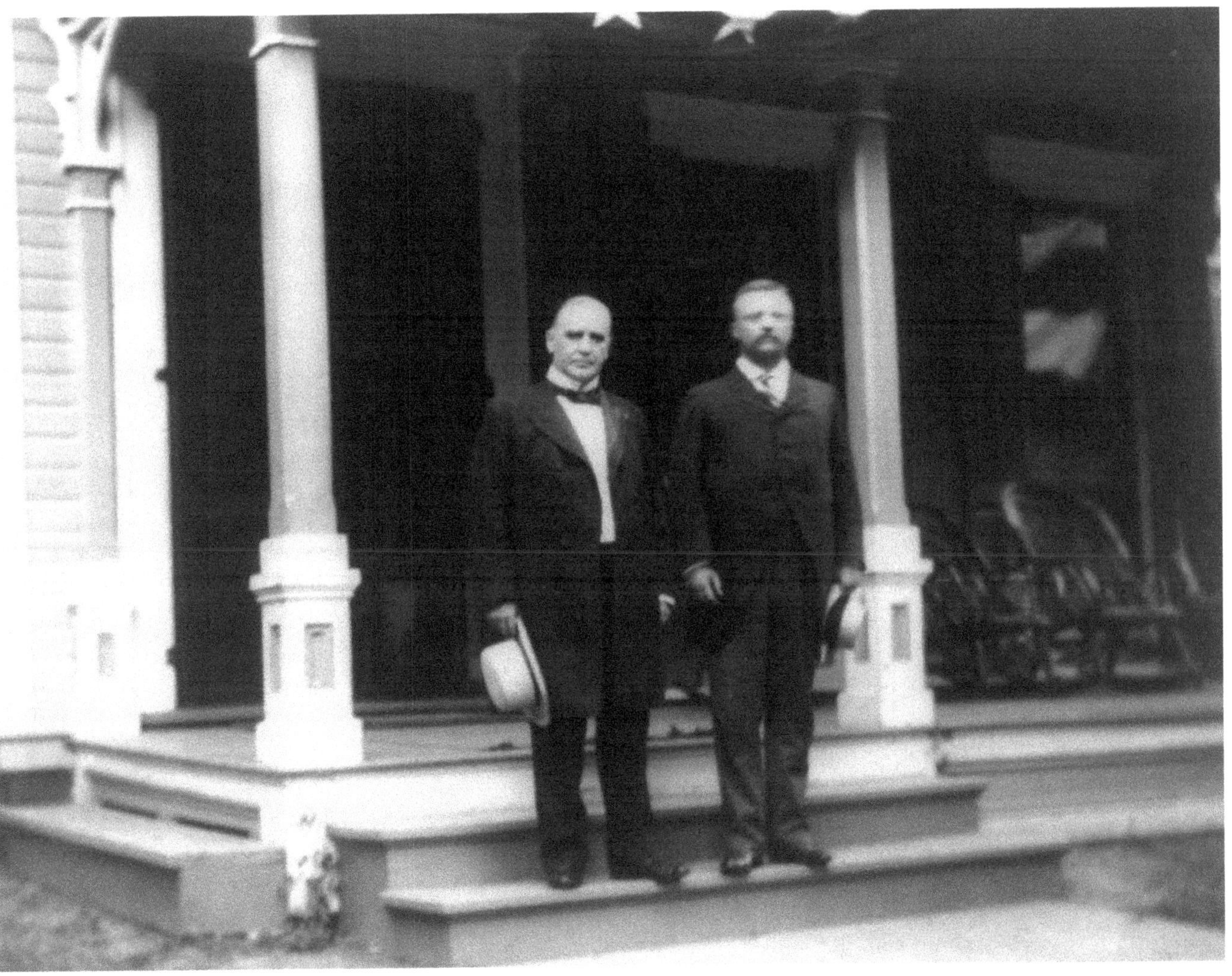

President William McKinley of Ohio, and Governor Theodore Roosevelt of New York, standing together for photographers as they embarked upon the 1900 presidential election.

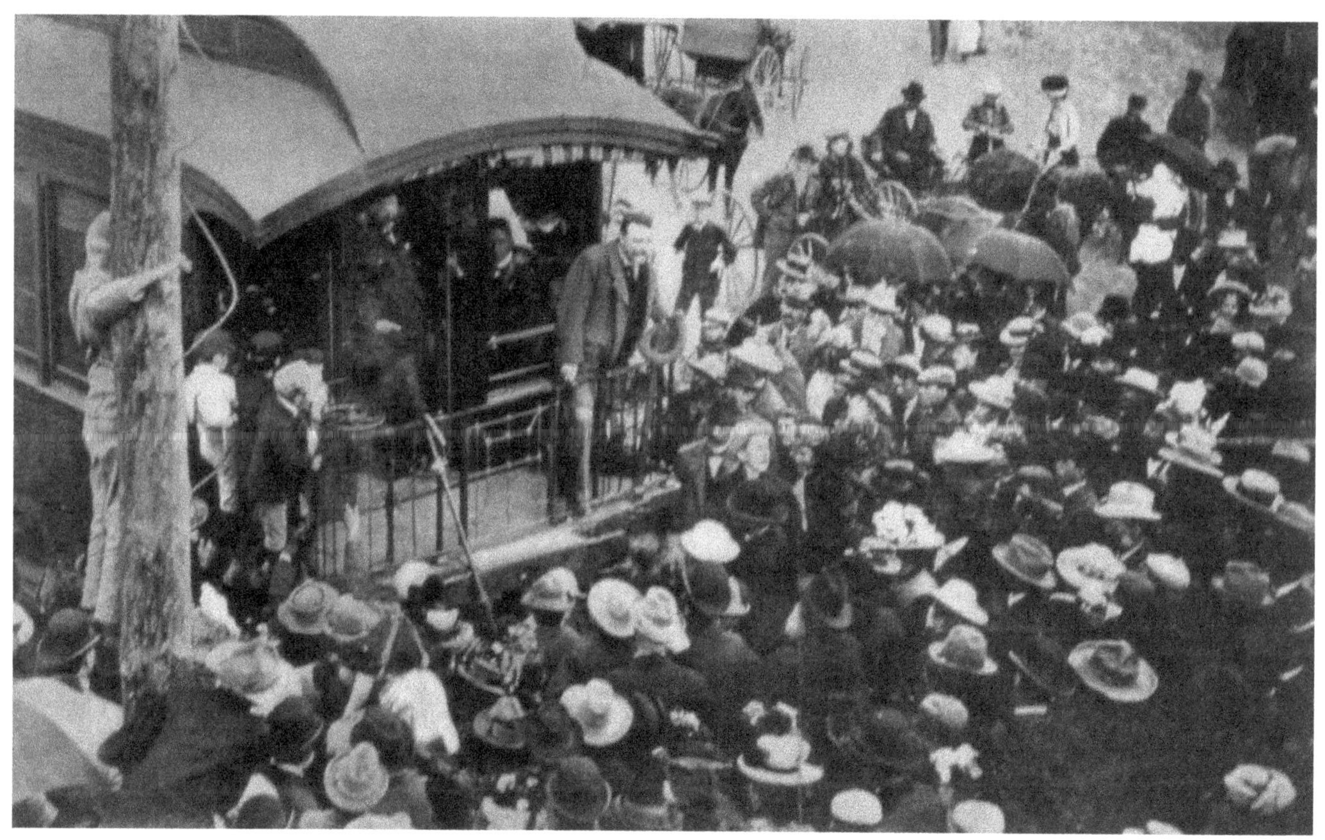

Theodore Roosevelt stumping the West during the 1900 vice-presidential campaign. Ever since his ranching days, Roosevelt had maintained special love for the land and the people of the western half of America. They returned the favor, and TR could count on their support for the 1900 and 1904 campaigns, as well as for most of his legislative initiatives.

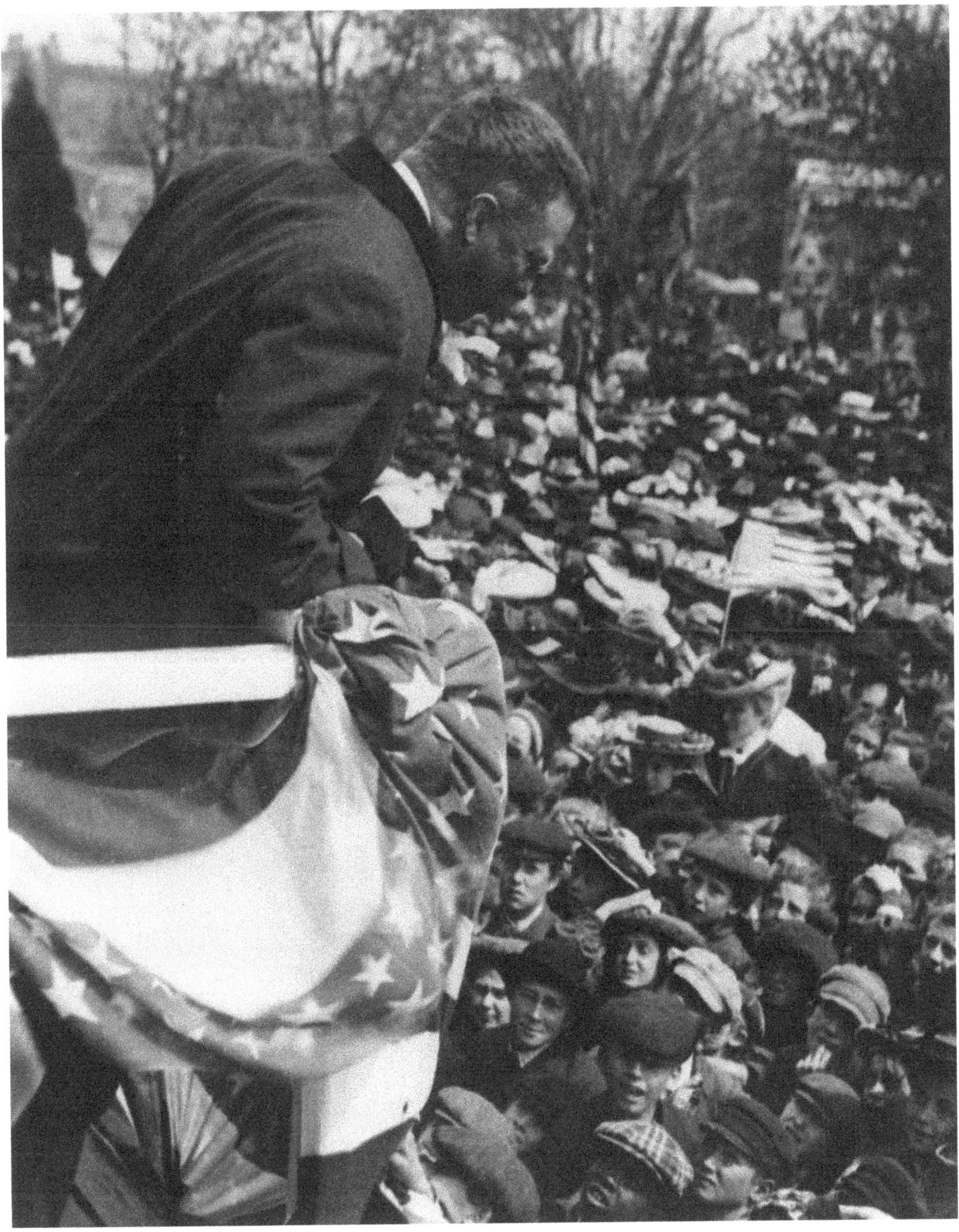

The well-known Irish-American political satirist, Mr. Dooley, created by Finley Peter Dunne, neatly captured the excitement of Roosevelt's vice-presidential campaign when he opined "'Tis Tiddy alone that's r-runnin', an' he ain't runnin', he's gallopin'." Here is TR galloping through Hastings, Nebraska, in October 1900.

Vice-presidential nominee Theodore Roosevelt campaigning in Freeport, Illinois, on behalf of President William McKinley, during the 1900 national election.

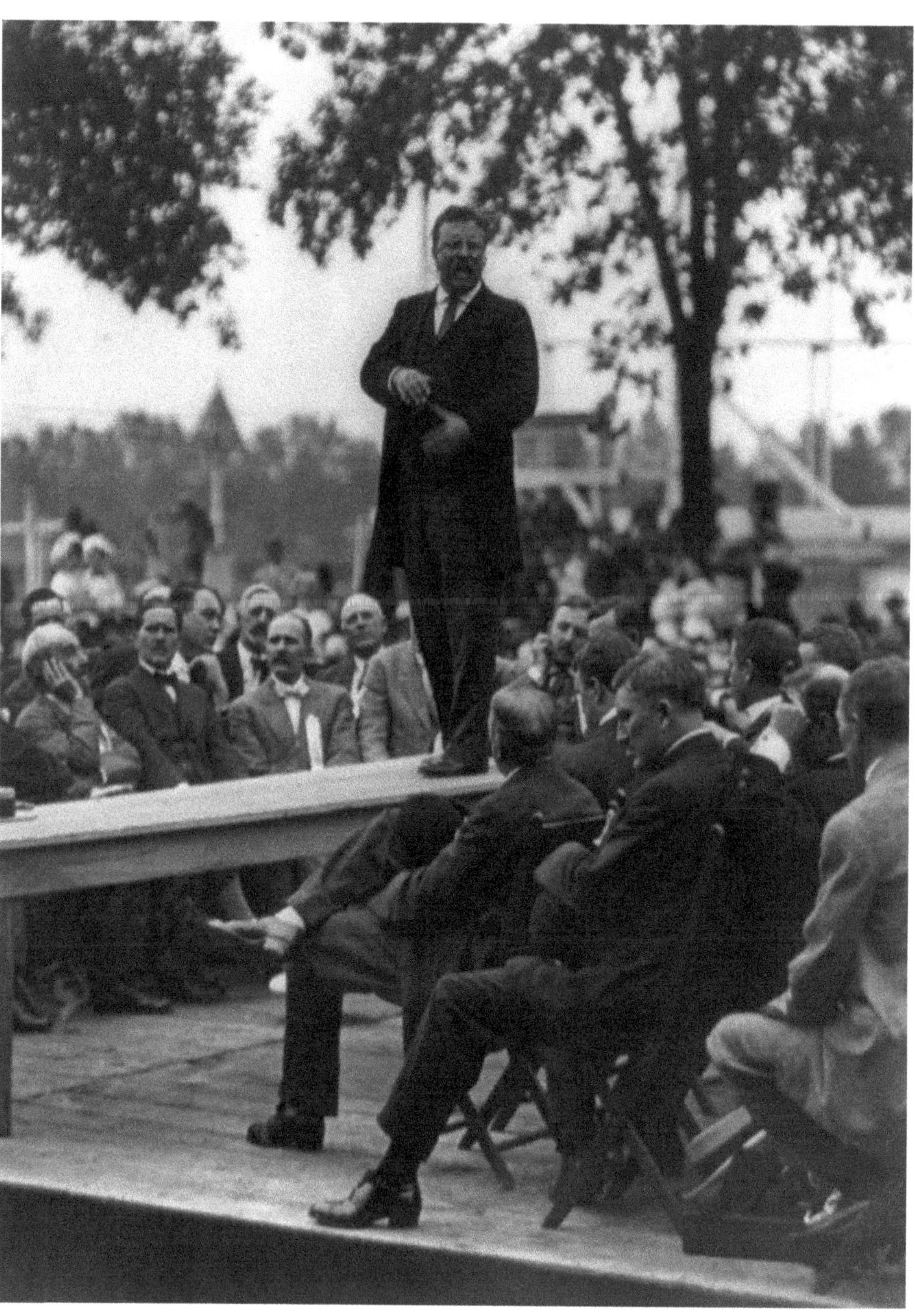

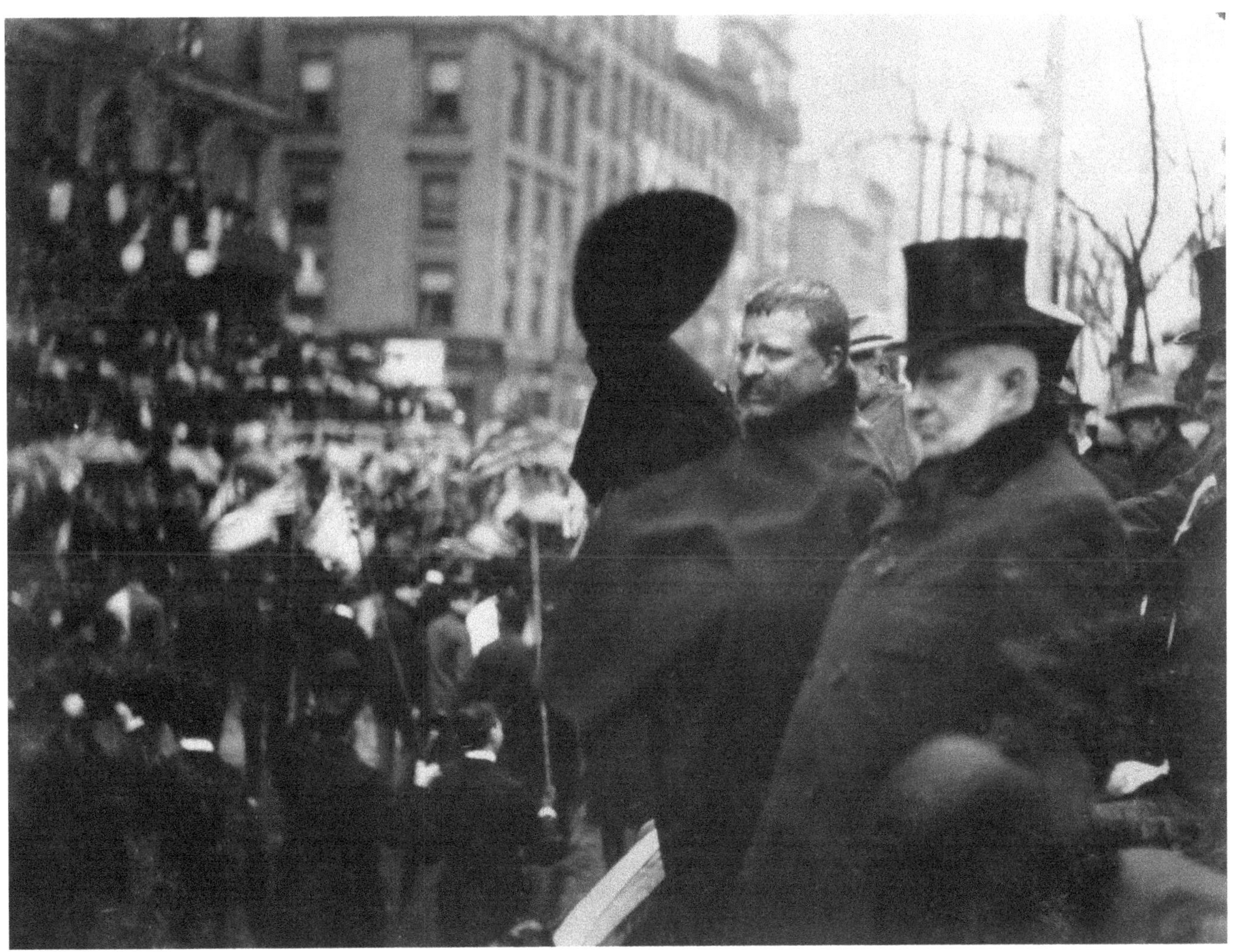

TR campaigned, as he did everything, vigorously. He toured more than half of America's 45 states speaking to millions of eager voters. This photograph shows him three days before the November 6 election, flashing his famous smile in a sound money parade in New York City.

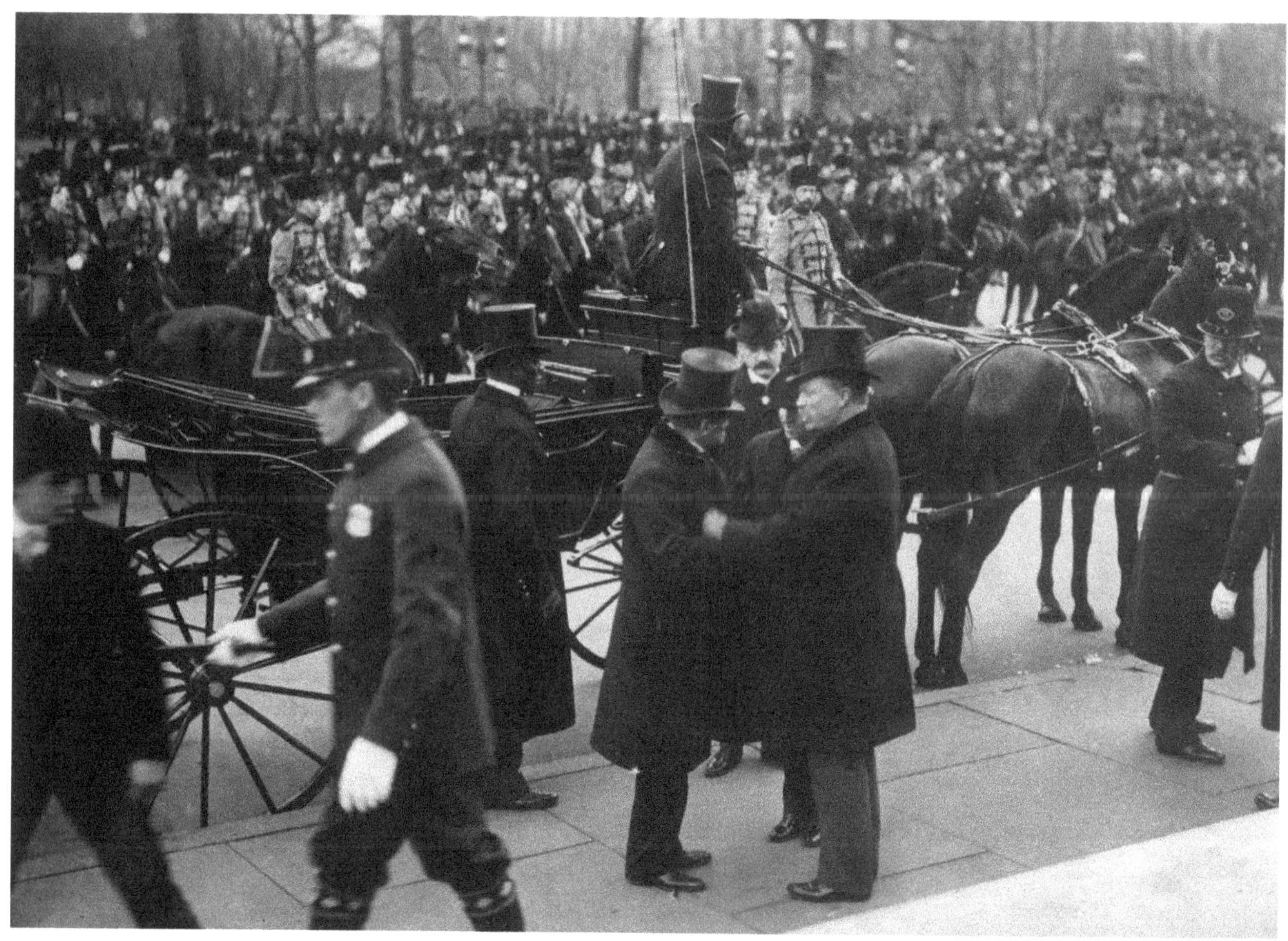

The election of 1900 was an easy victory for the Republican ticket of William McKinley and Theodore Roosevelt. Voters were pleased with the economic prosperity they attributed to McKinley's leadership and rejected the Democratic contenders, William Jennings Bryan and Adlai Stevenson. This photograph shows the triumphant Roosevelt arriving at the inauguration in Washington, D.C., on March 4, 1900.

The Presidency (1901–1909)

Theodore Roosevelt approached the presidency with his characteristic vigor. It was a "bully pulpit" and he wrote all his own sermons. A masterly communicator, TR's many speeches, articles, and books explained his view that the government must be used for the benefit of all Americans. The citizens' responsibility, he felt, was to work hard and honestly in return. President Roosevelt "busted" trusts that harmed everyday people, curbed the powerful railroads, promoted his "Square Deal" domestic legislation, set aside millions of acres of wilderness for future use and present enjoyment, and lent his prestige to progressive causes from good roads to workers' safety, from football reform to the abolition of child labor.

Roosevelt concluded the Philippine-American War that had begun after the close of hostilities with Spain. He backed the independence of Panama so the U.S. could build the canal, promulgated the Roosevelt Corollary warning European nations away from the western hemisphere, won the Nobel Peace Prize for assisting in the settlement of the Russo-Japanese War, flexed U.S. military might by sending out the Great White Fleet, and perhaps delayed the start of World War I with his behind-the-scenes diplomacy at the Algeciras Conference.

He could have used the bully pulpit more effectively on behalf of African Americans and Native Americans. He withstood cries of imperialism concerning Panama. His progressive actions alienated conservative lawmakers. But at the end of his seven years, President Roosevelt was an instantly recognizable icon in America, beloved of the citizenry who generally approved his message: that the U.S. had an international duty and the federal government must provide for the weakest citizens.

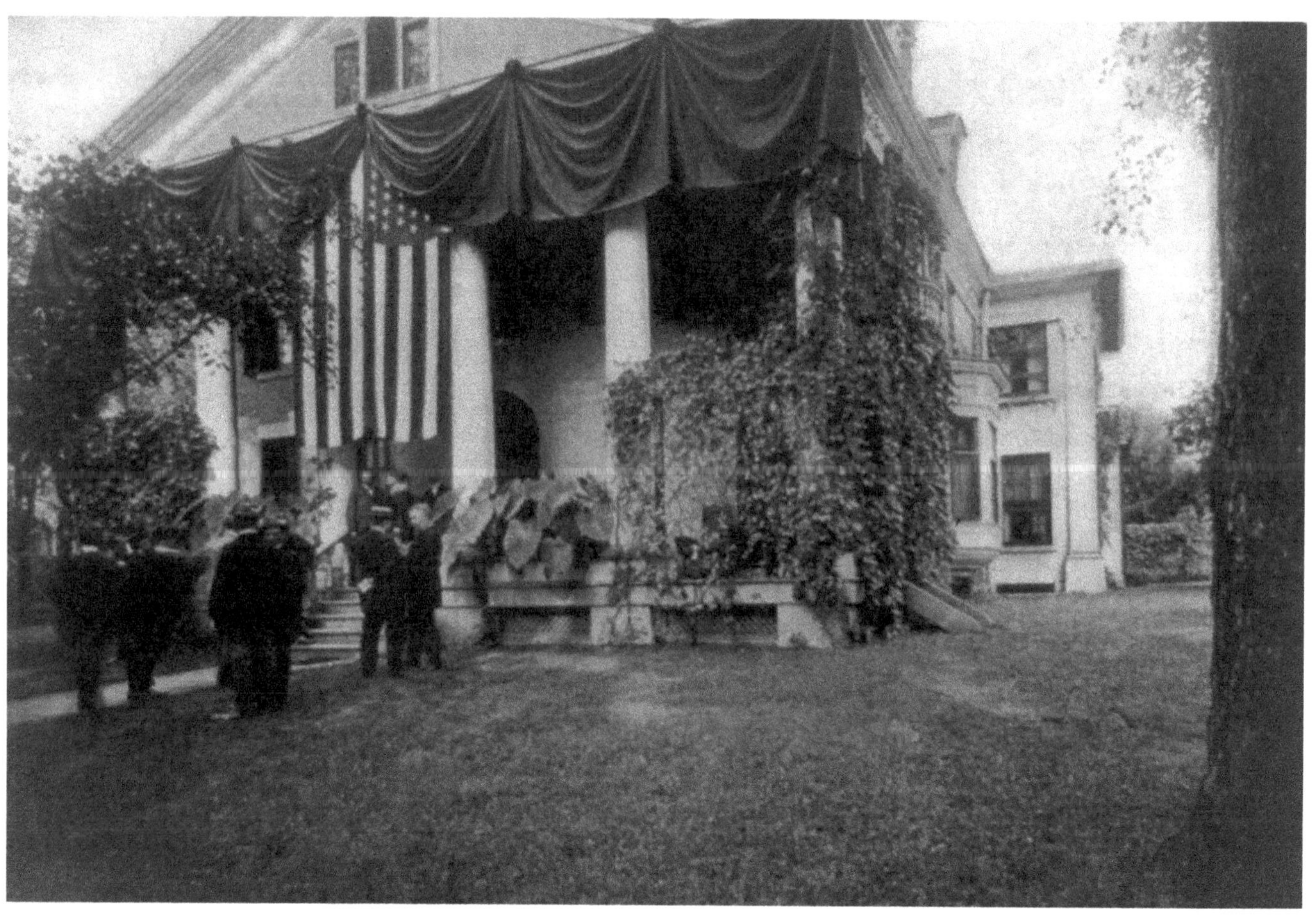

President McKinley was assassinated at the Pan-American Exposition and died September 14, 1901. The Roosevelt family was vacationing in the Adirondack mountains at the time, and TR was summoned to take the oath of office. He did so in the library at the home of Ansley Wilcox in Buffalo, New York. The black mourning bunting on the Wilcox mansion honors McKinley.

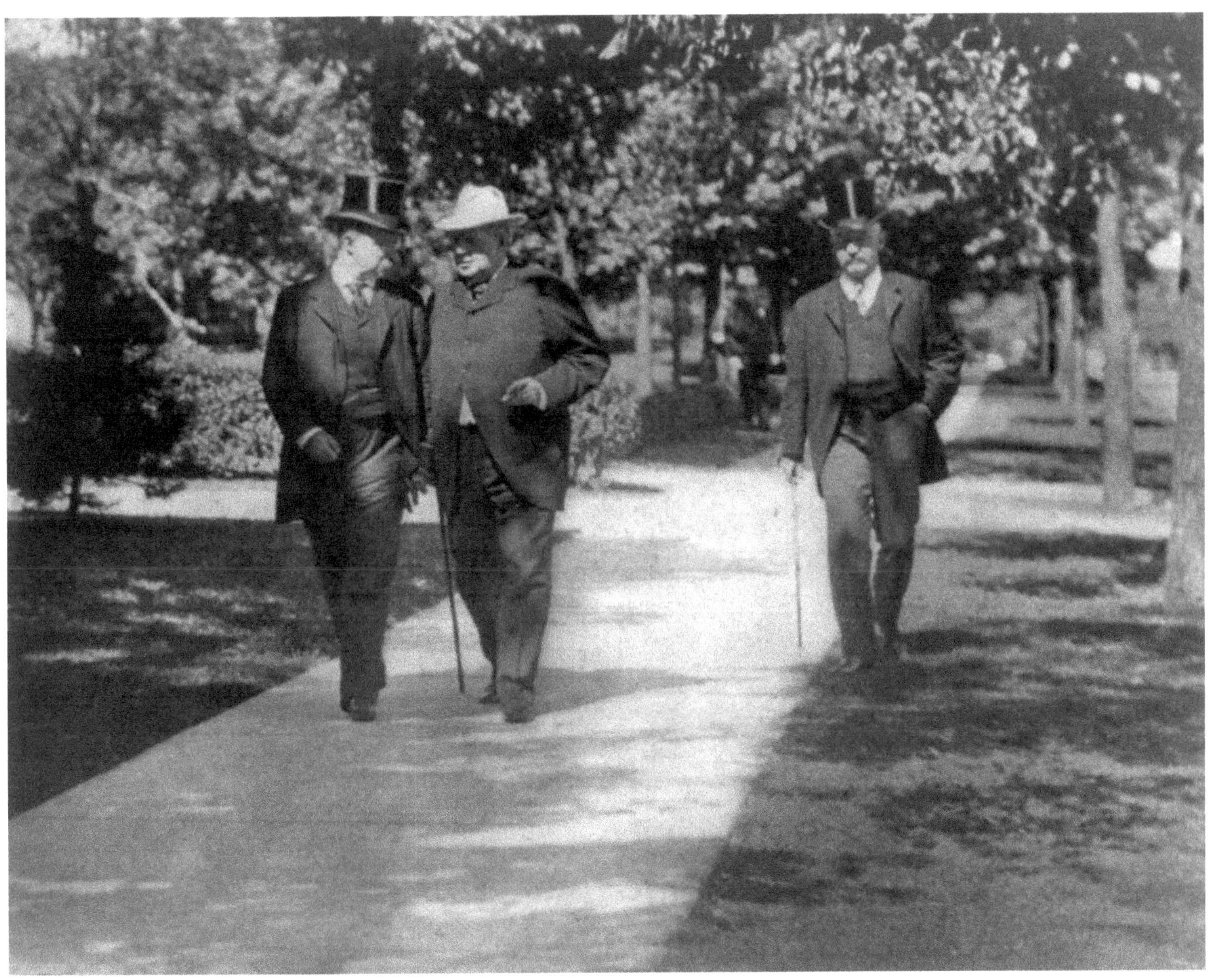

Senator Marcus Hanna's fear materialized when his good friend McKinley was killed. Now "that madman," Roosevelt, was president. Here, the two men confer on the way to the home of John Milburn in Buffalo, where McKinley died of the gunshot wounds he received from assassin Leon Czolgosz at the Pan-American Exposition.

"It is a dreadful thing to come into the Presidency this way," Roosevelt wrote to his old friend Henry Cabot Lodge just after taking office, "but it would be a far worse thing to be morbid about it." Roosevelt loved being president. The new First Lady, Edith Roosevelt, set about a much-needed renovation of the White House. The Roosevelt children captured the hearts of Americans with their games and menagerie of pets.

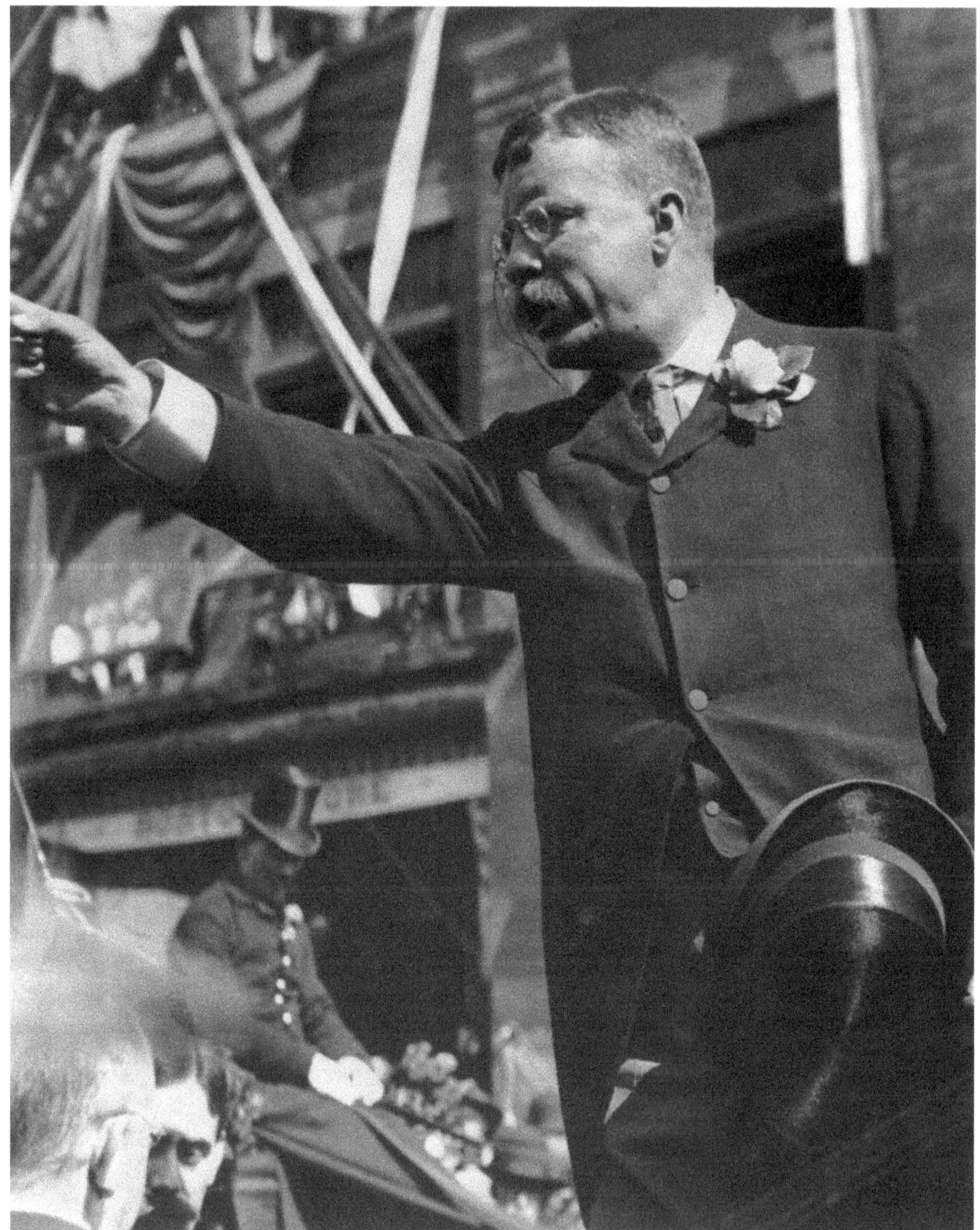

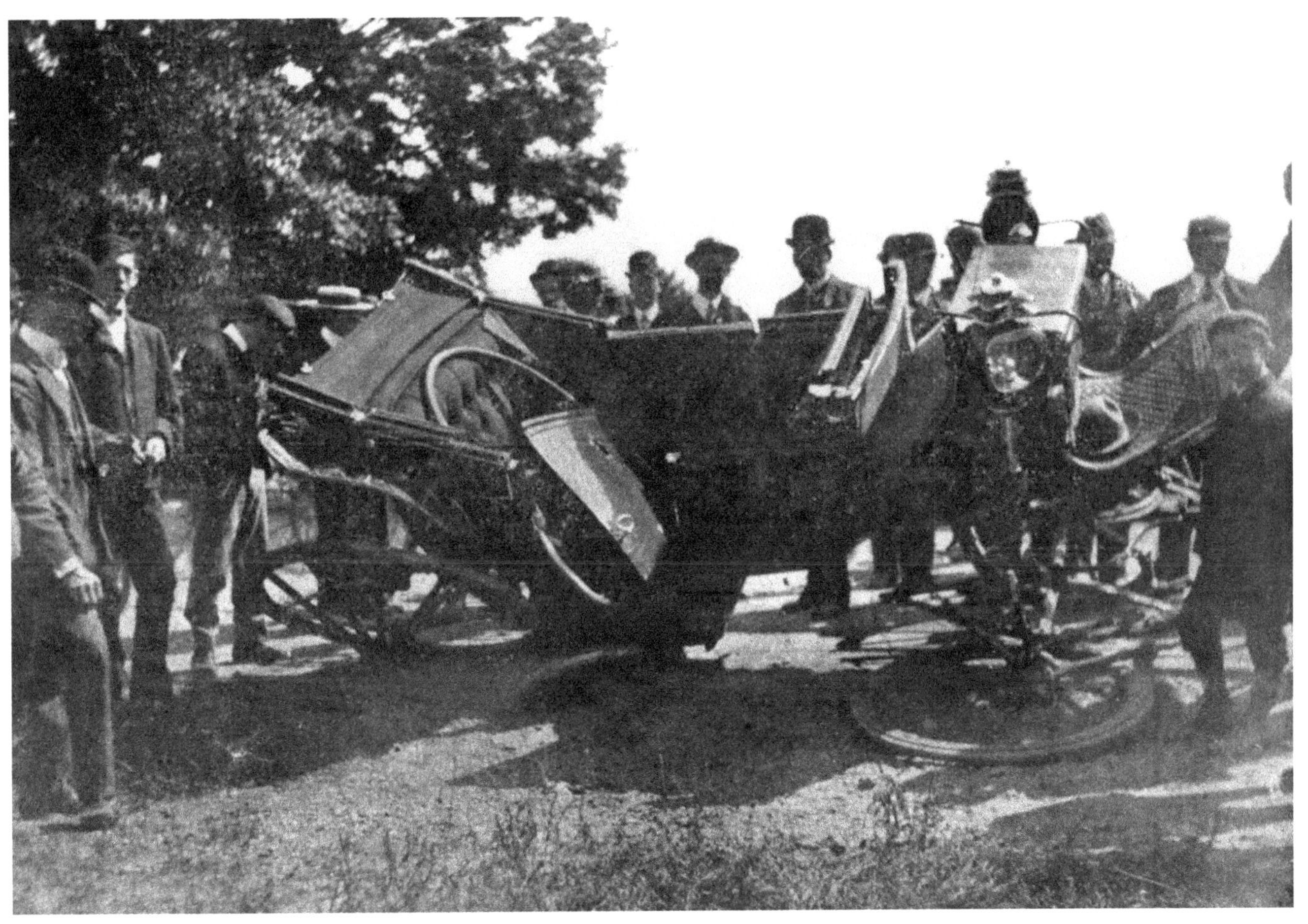

On a speaking tour of New England in September 1902, President Roosevelt was in a traffic accident. Massachusetts governor Murray Crane, presidential secretary George B. Cortelyou, and Secret Serviceman William Craig were riding in the horse-drawn carriage with Roosevelt when an electric trolley clipped the back of the carriage and tipped it over. Craig was killed. Cortelyou was injured. TR suffered most from a wound to his leg, which eventually required surgery.

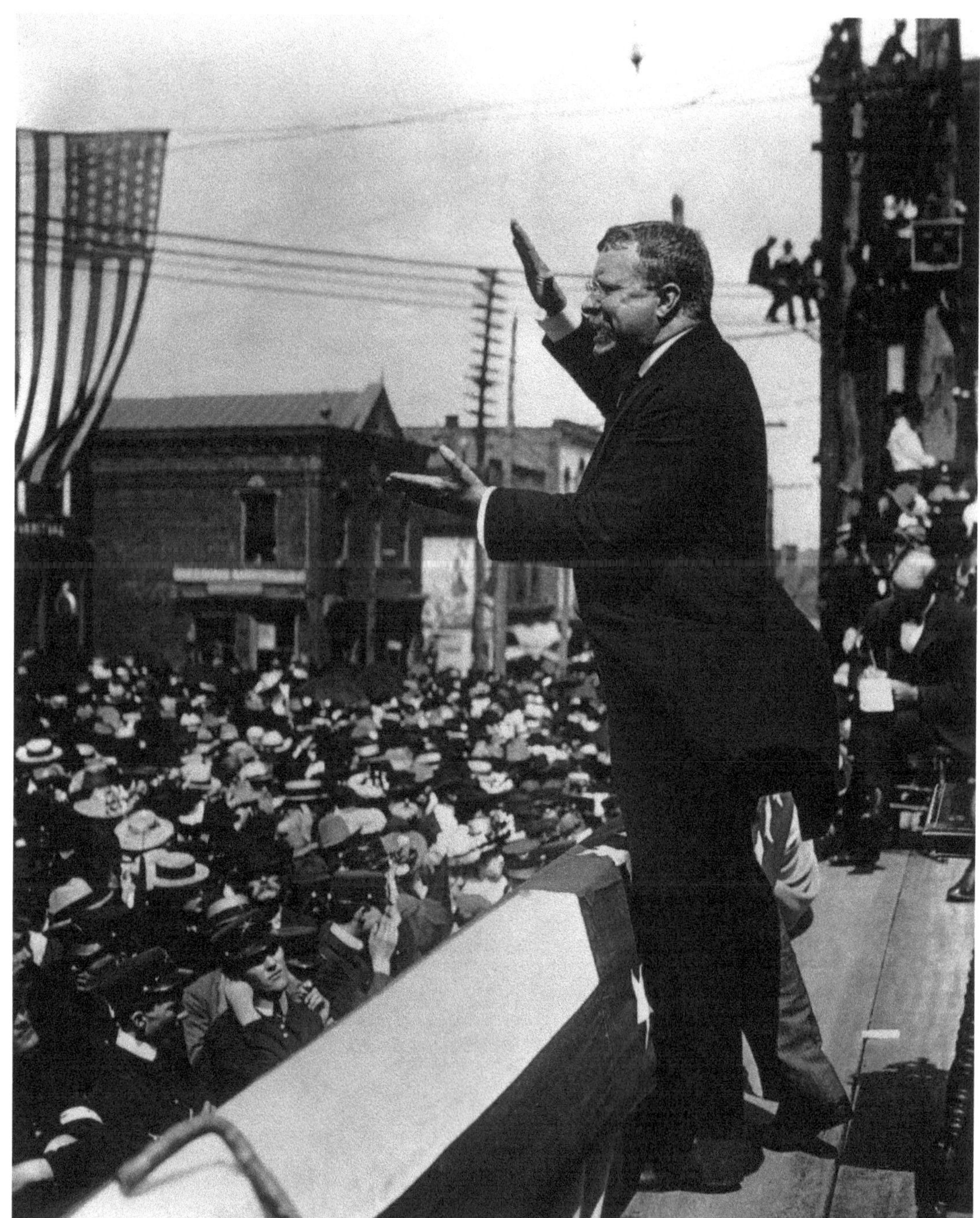

The distinctive hand gesture of President Roosevelt emphasizes the point he is making in this speech to a crowd of listeners in Asheville, North Carolina, in September 1902. TR angered white Southerners early in his presidency when he invited African American educator and author Booker T. Washington to dinner at the White House with his family. TR wanted to discuss politics with his fellow Republican. The outcry was such that Roosevelt never proffered a second invitation.

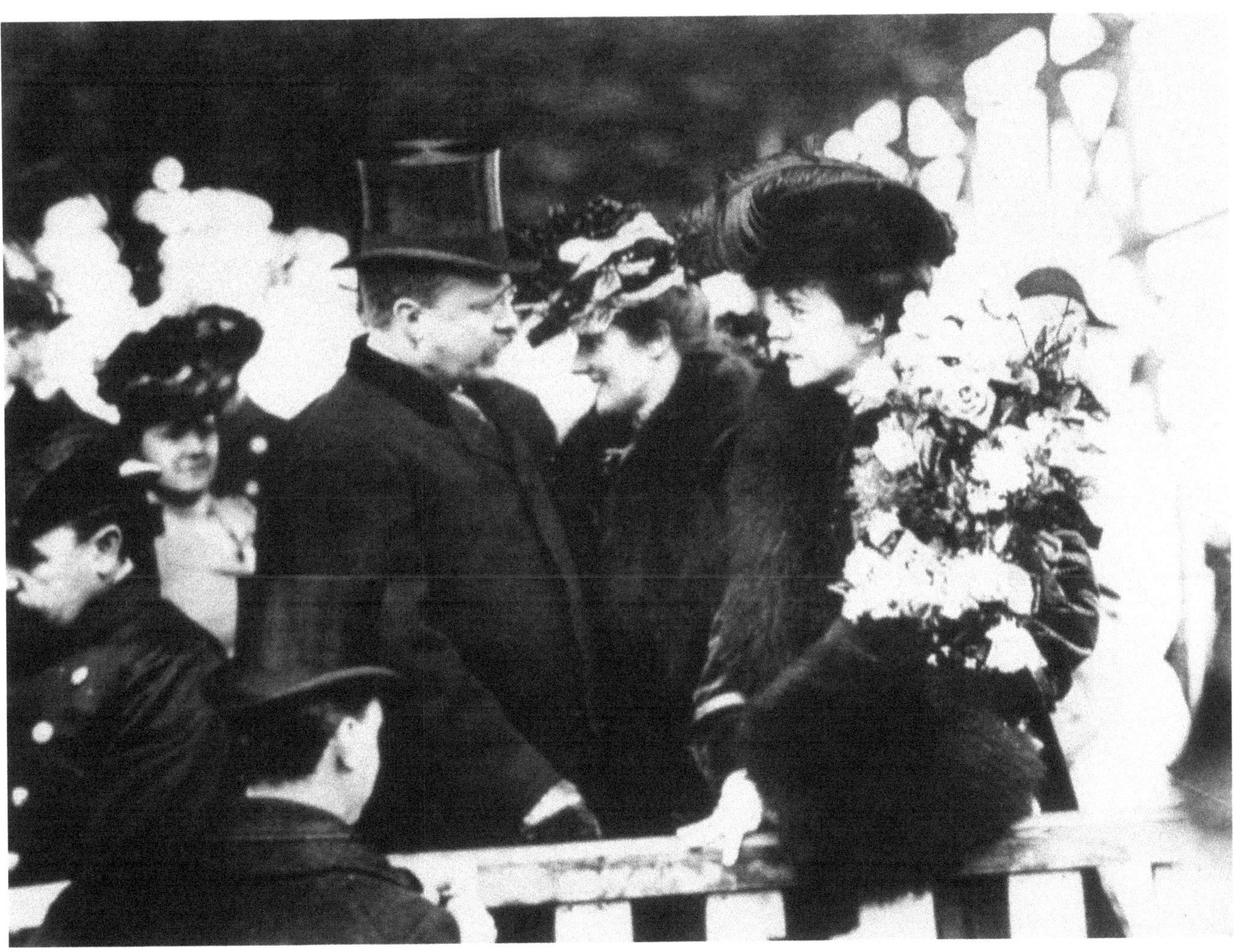

Eighteen-year-old Alice Roosevelt became an international celebrity after she launched Kaiser Wilhelm's American-made yacht, the *Meteor.* Huge crowds gathered wherever the feisty First Daughter went. Recalcitrant and unrepentant, Alice smoked in public, bet at the horse races, carried a green snake to enliven dull parties, drove her red roadster at excessive speeds, and kept a copy of the Constitution in her purse. Alice was a role model for young Americans, and her actions were copied by thousands of women.

Alice learned everything she ever knew about courting publicity from her father. This is a photograph of the president enjoying the limelight in Asheville, North Carolina, in 1902.

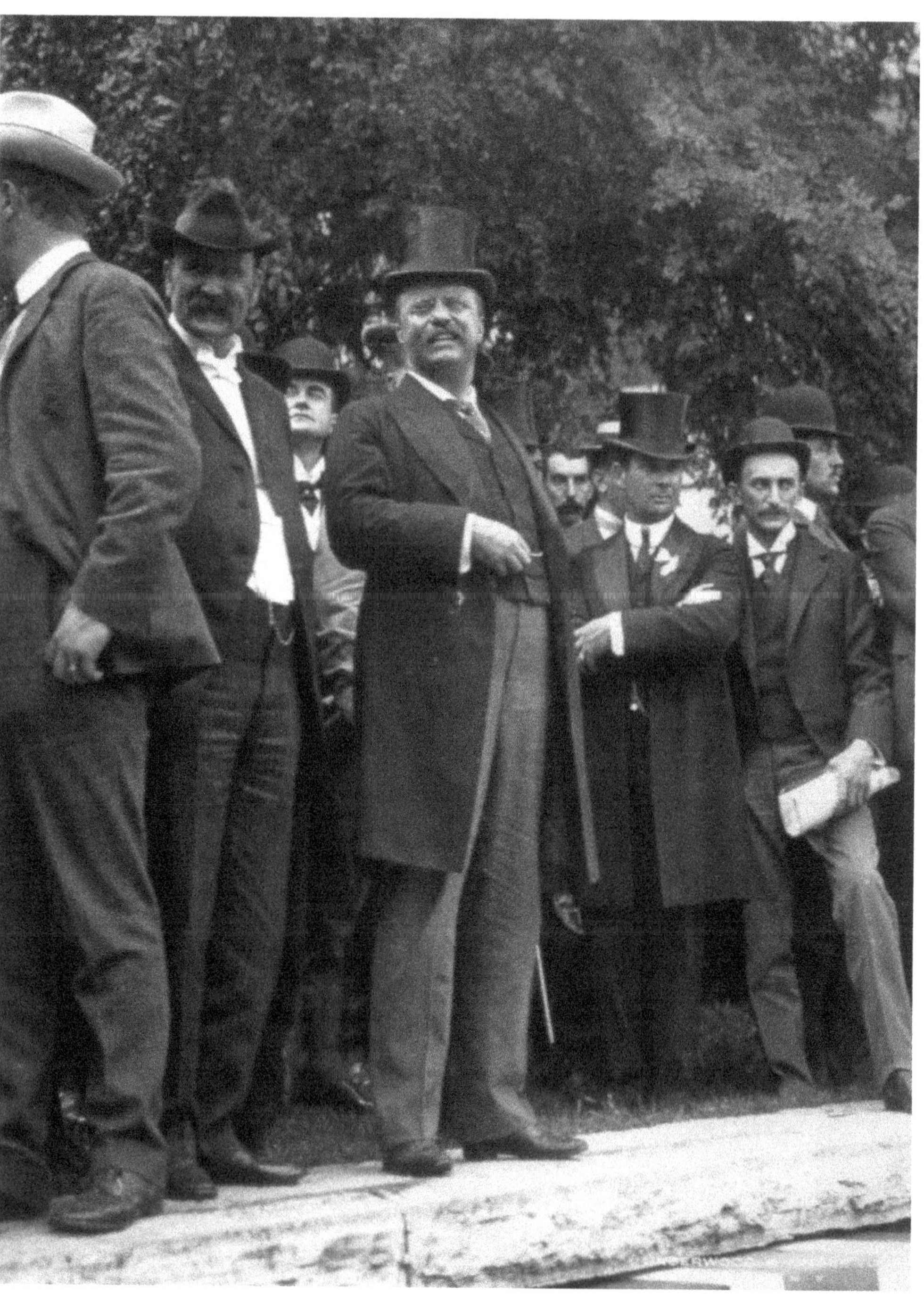

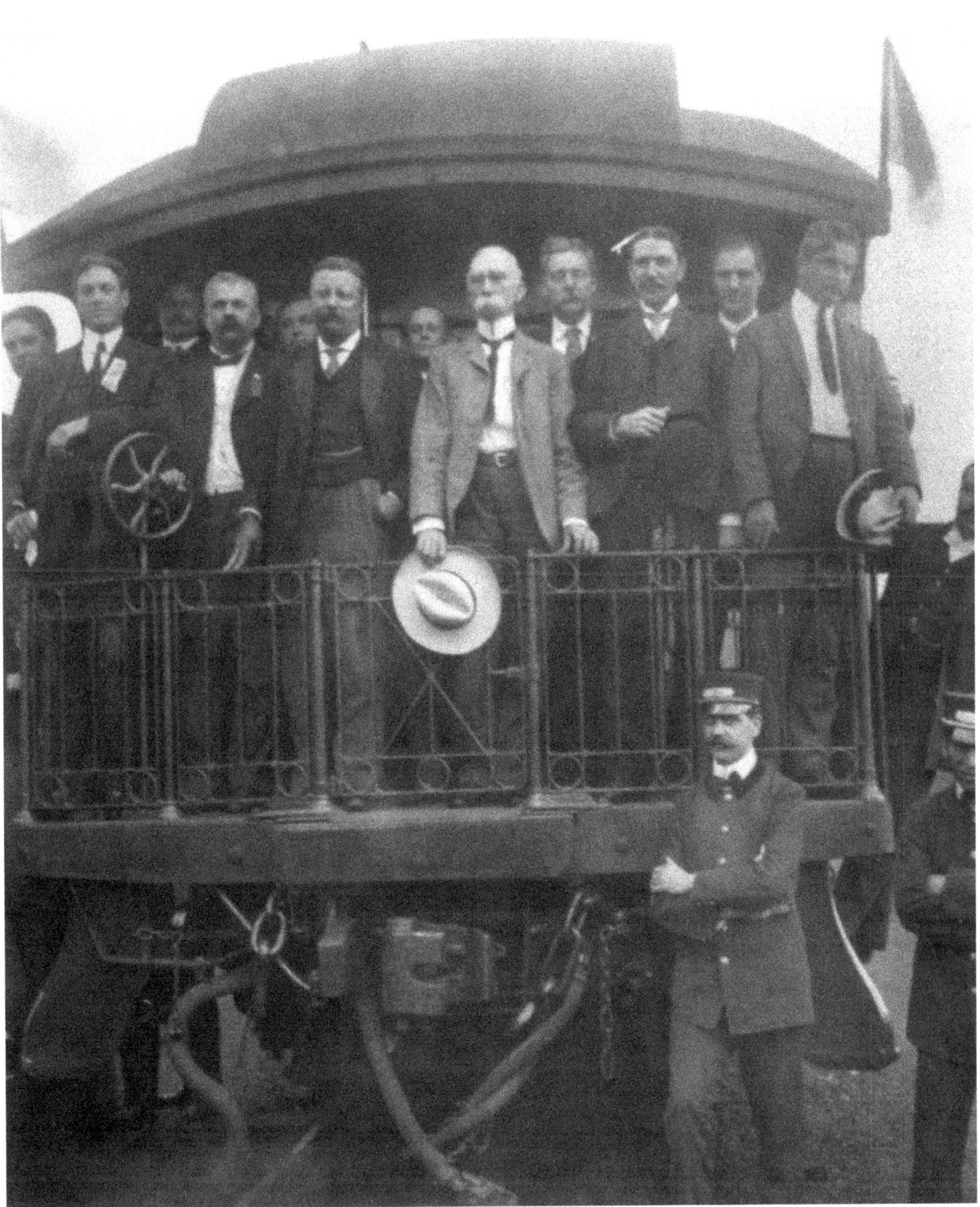

Roosevelt is surrounded by luminaries from Chattanooga, Tennessee, nearly one year into his presidency. Although the railroad's workers probably idolized TR, the railroad bosses did not. Railroads were America's first big business, and as president, Roosevelt tried to bring an end to their unfair practices by having the Justice Department file suit against the powerful Northern Securities Company, a railroad monopoly. Roosevelt won in 1904, his first act of "trust busting."

TR faces a group of students in Summerville, South Carolina. President Roosevelt had a mixed record concerning African Americans. He appointed African Americans to federal patronage jobs even in the South and spoke out against lynching, but he ignored the Atlanta race riots and dishonorably discharged a black regiment at Brownsville without proof of their guilt in the shooting of two white men in 1906.

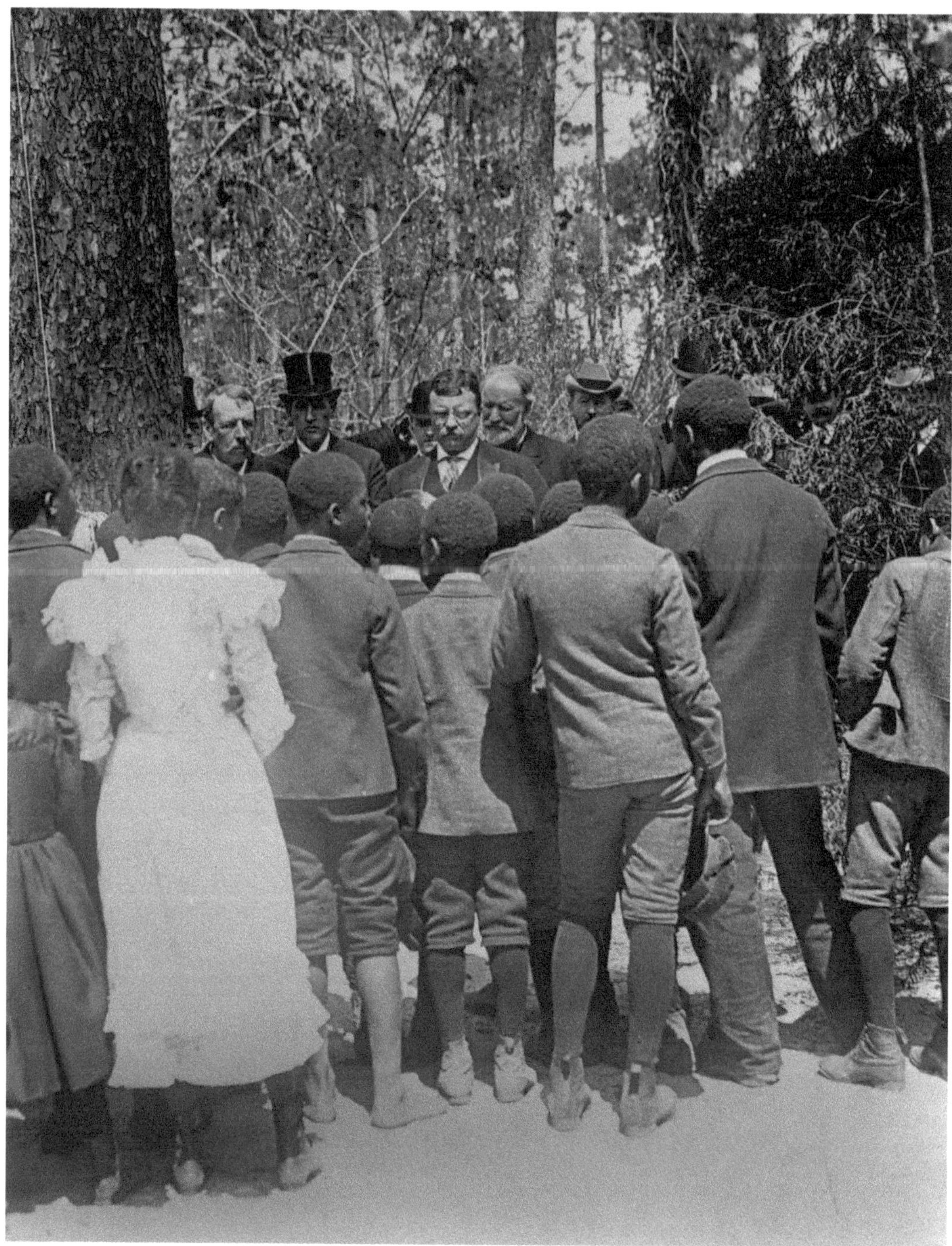

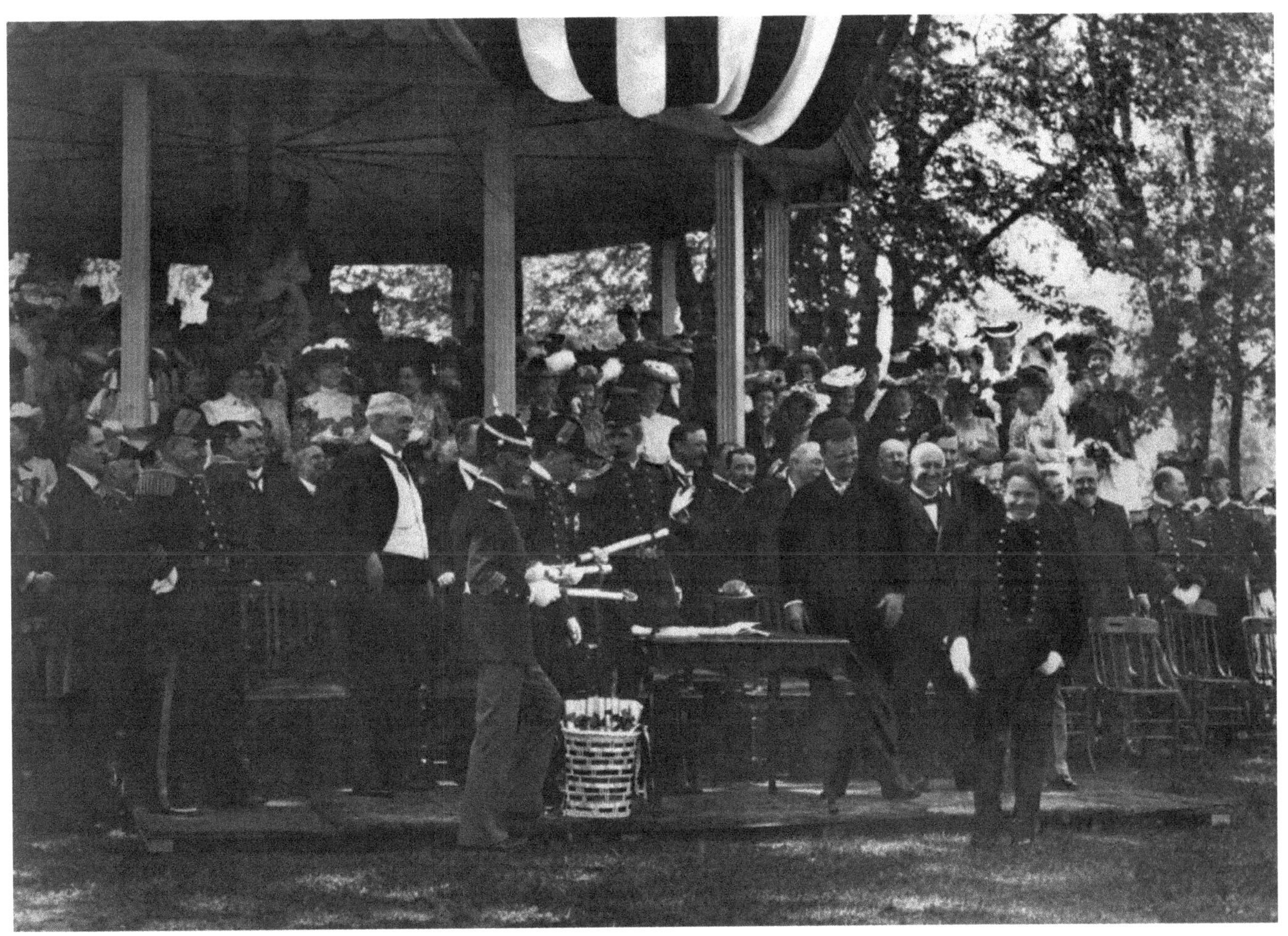

President Roosevelt took pleasure in all naval business, including awarding diplomas to these naval cadets at Annapolis. Always a firm believer in military preparedness, Roosevelt built the Great White Fleet of sixteen battleships and sent them first to the Atlantic and then the Pacific to demonstrate U.S. naval supremacy.

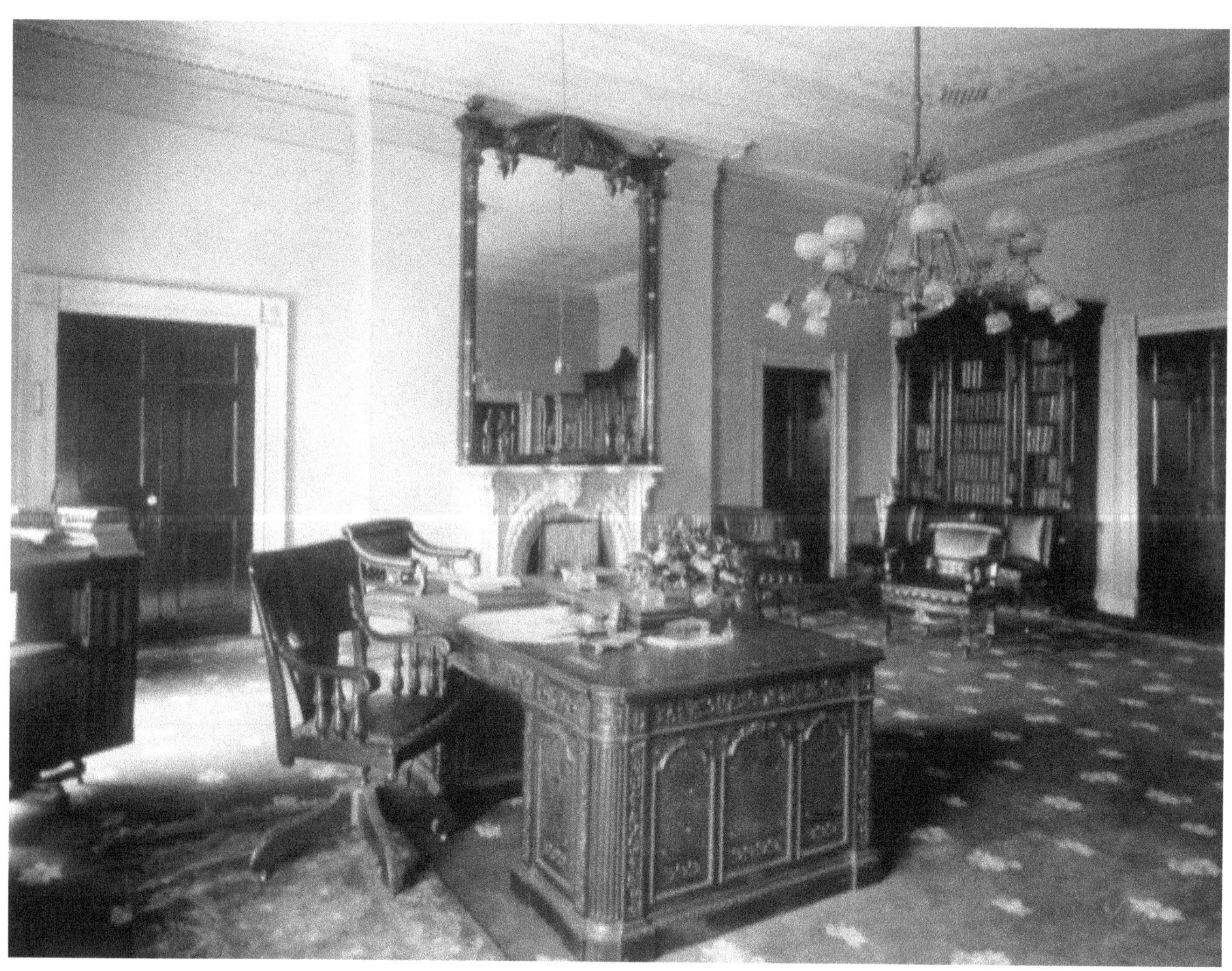

The office in the White House where much of President Roosevelt's workday occurred. TR worked long hours here, but sought the counsel of the thoughtful First Lady as they walked together each day. The Roosevelt children—their games, animals, friends, and questions—interrupted his work with impunity, and it was in this room TR exclaimed to a friend in mock desperation, "I can be President of the United States—or—I can attend to Alice. I cannot possibly do both!"

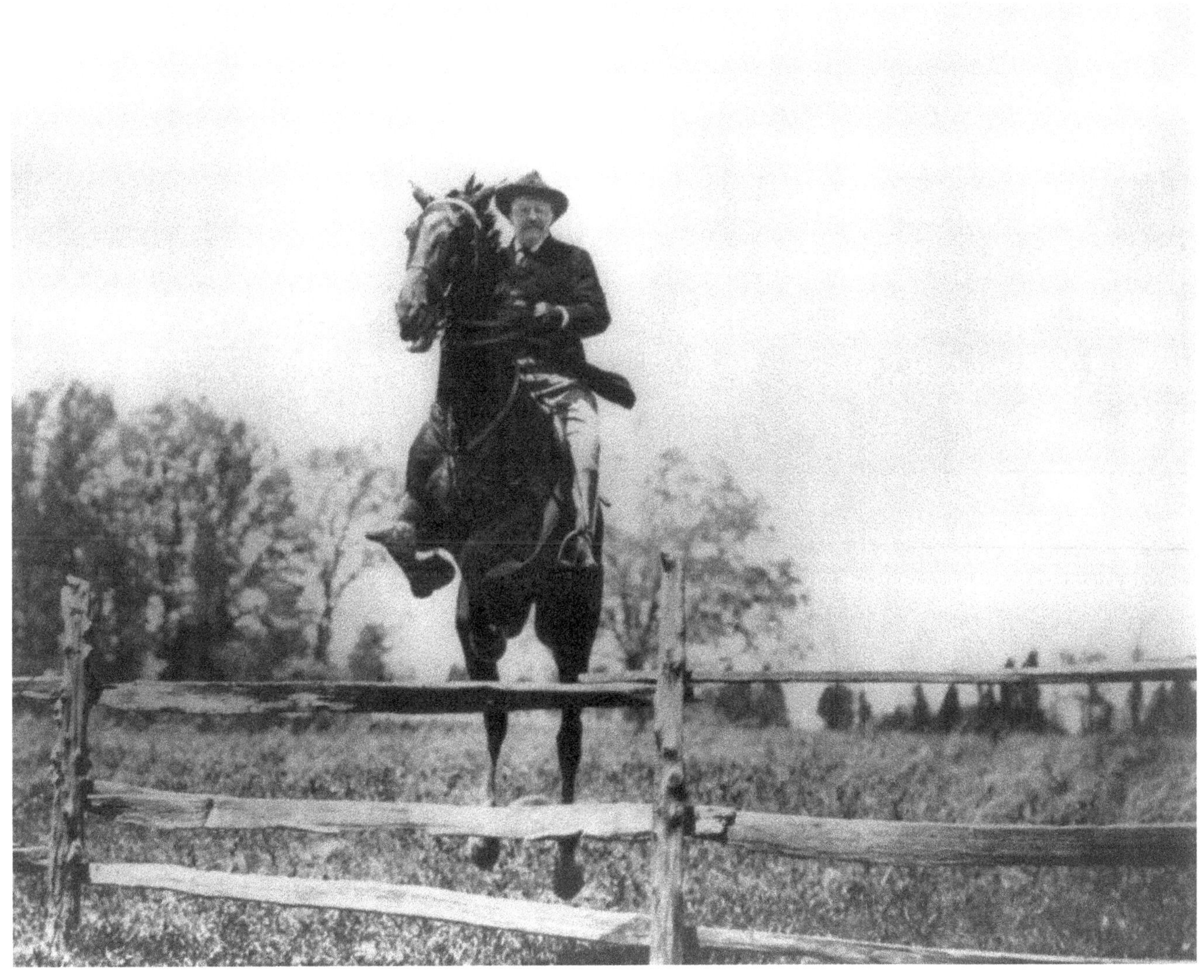

The entire Roosevelt family were excellent riders. As a young man, TR played polo and raced to the hounds. He and Edith rode regularly together around Oyster Bay. This photograph, taken in 1902, demonstrates TR's command of horseback riding.

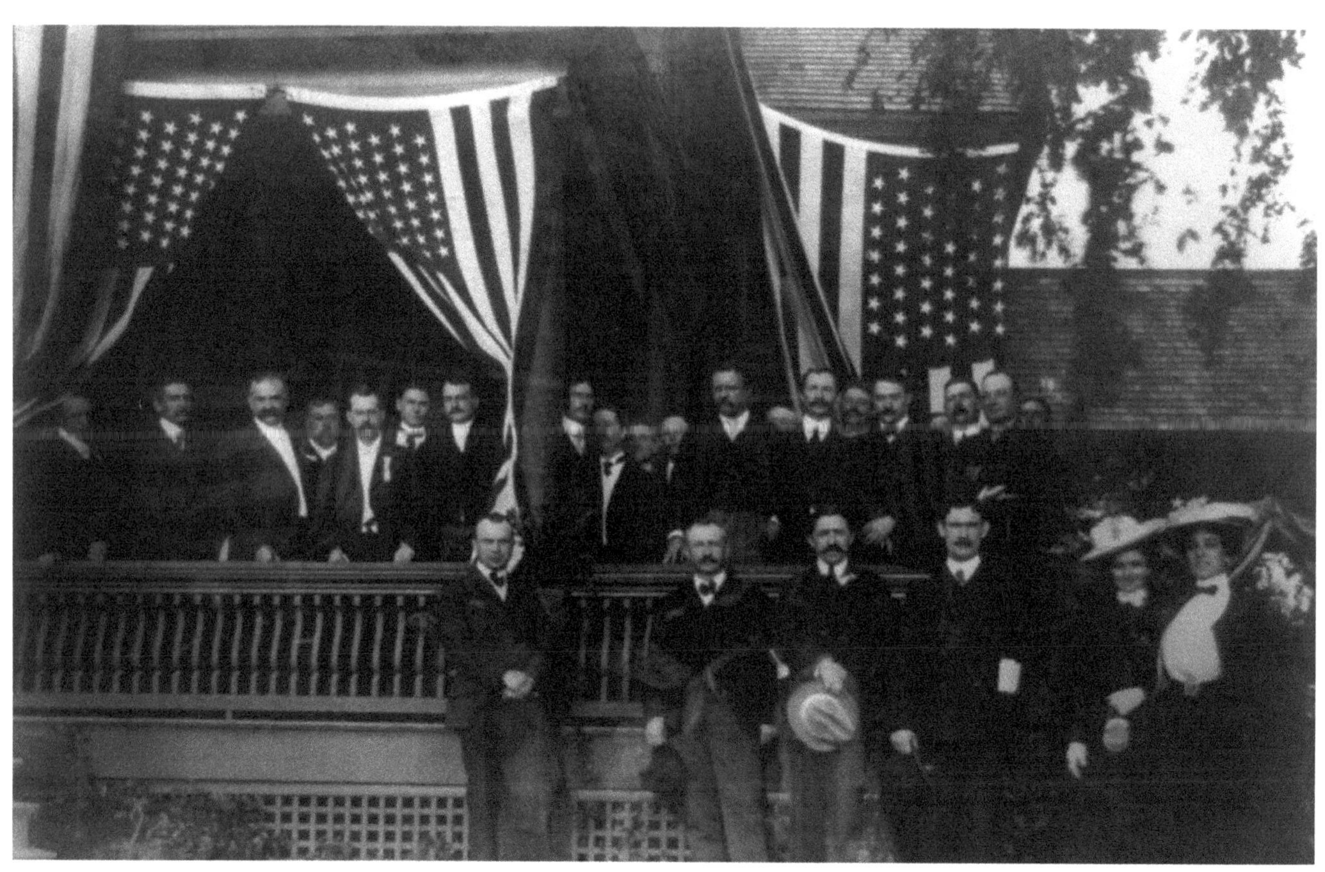

President Roosevelt at Sagamore Hill in 1902, posing with one of the many groups who came to lobby or to admire the charismatic TR.

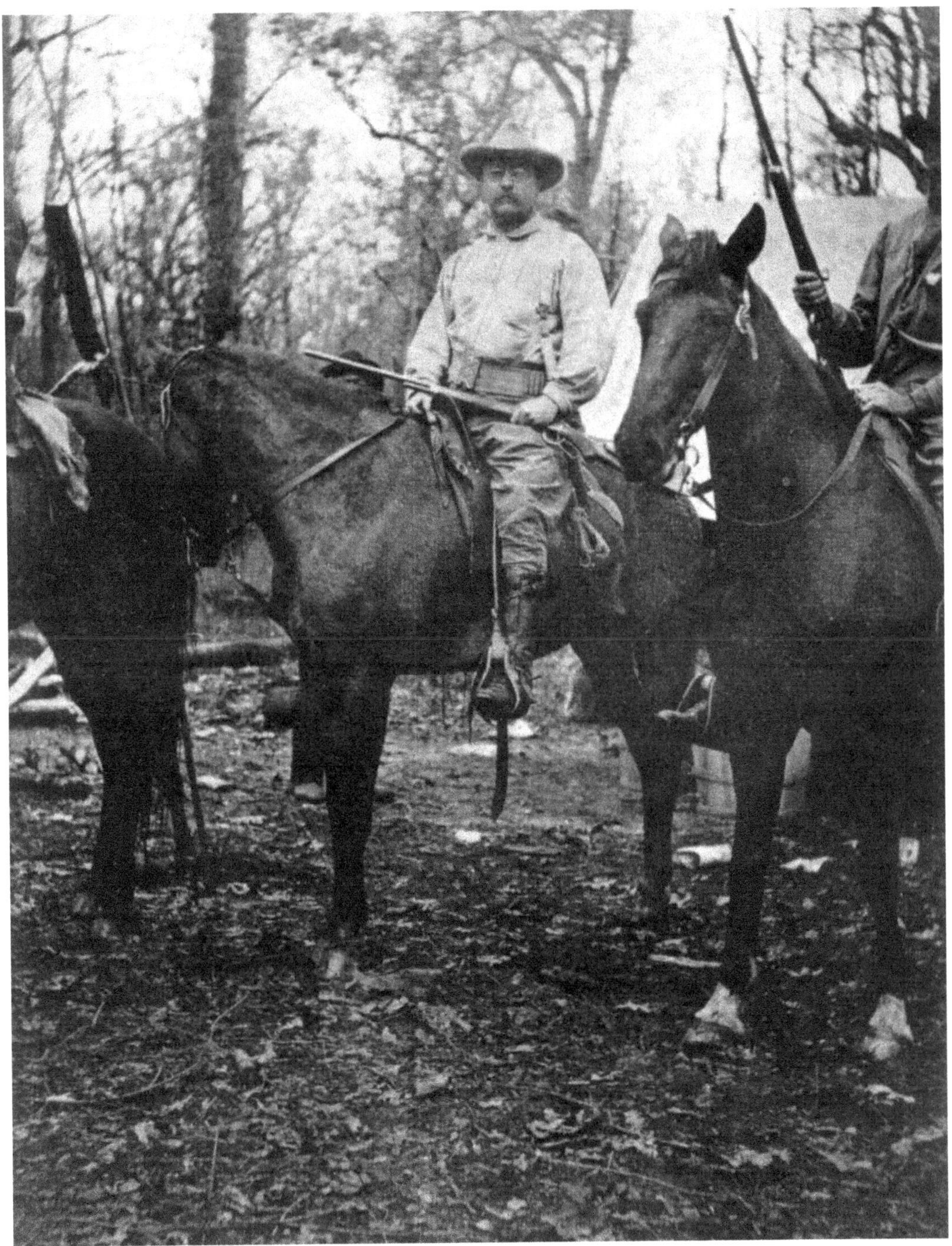

Theodore Roosevelt's reputation as a big game hunter preceded him to Mississippi, where local dignitaries wanted to be certain the president got his bear. Accordingly, they tied to a tree an aged bear—some stories say a cub—and presented it to Roosevelt for his trophy. He refused to shoot a defenseless animal. When Jewish immigrant toy makers Rose and Morris Mitchtom asked the president if they could call their toy bears "Teddy's bears," the president agreed. That was the birth of the teddy bear.

President Roosevelt, standing on the deck of the *Mayflower,* tipping his hat during the naval parade off Long Island. The president had the use of two yachts: the 2,690-ton *Mayflower,* and the smaller *Sylph.*

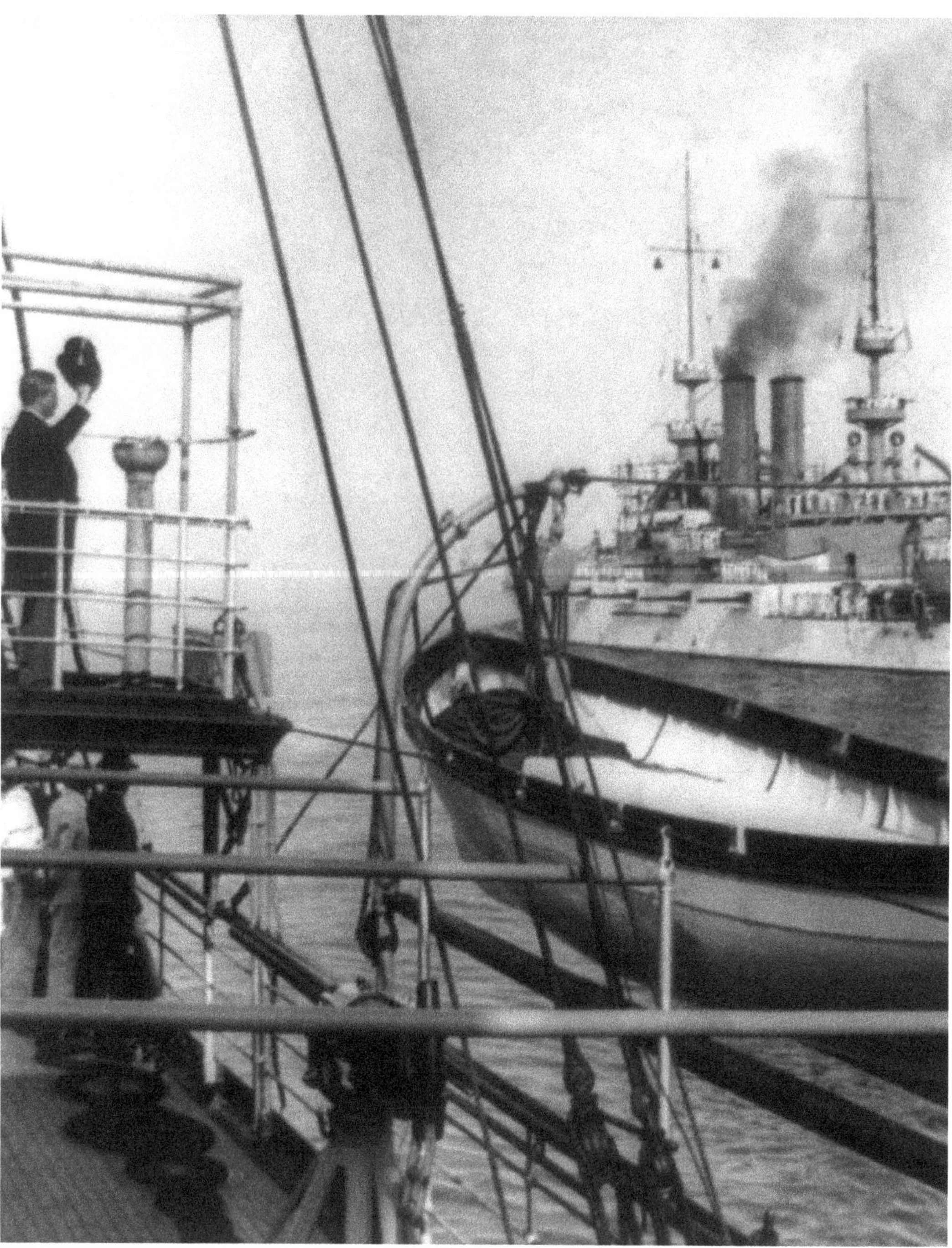

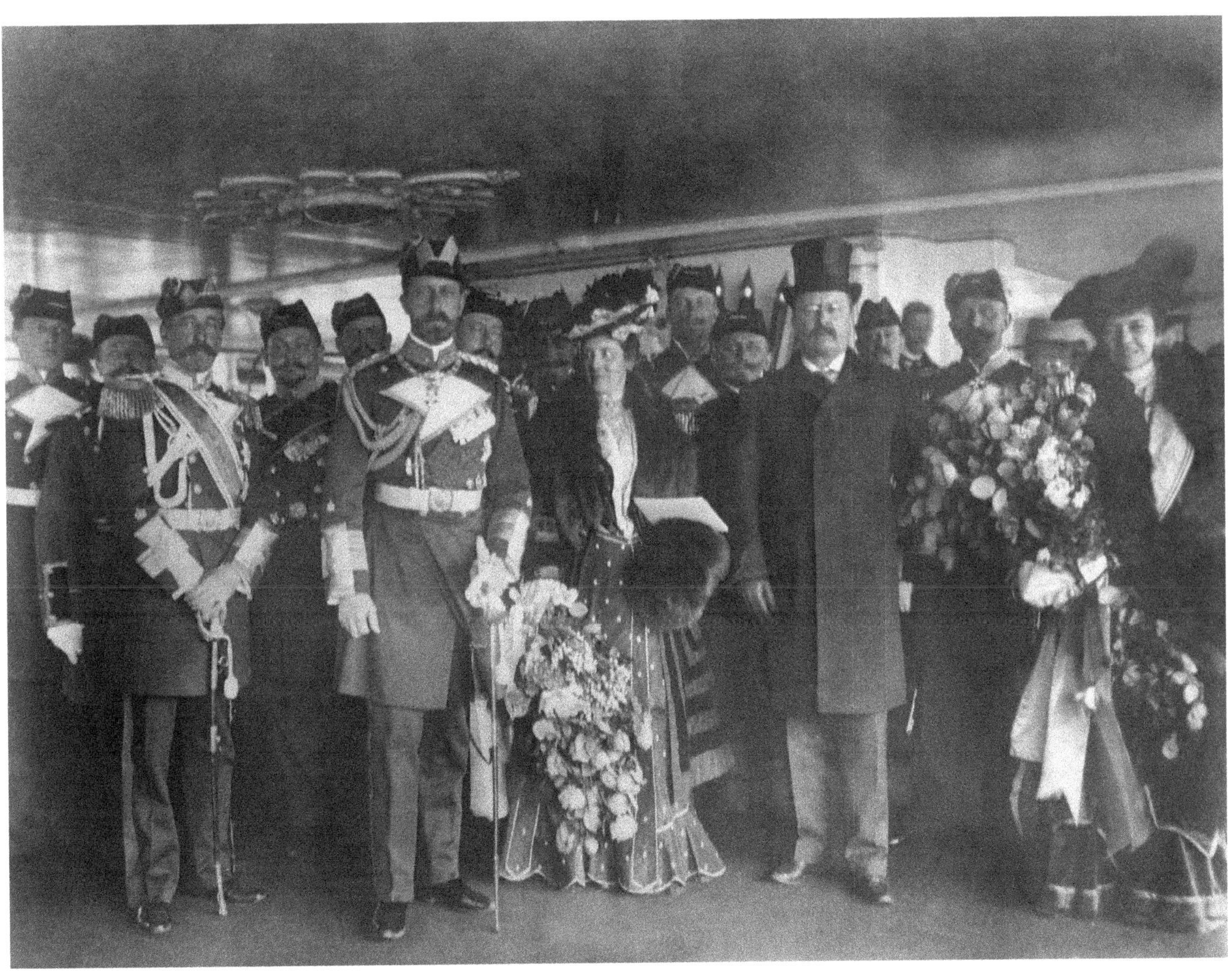

Prince Henry of Prussia, President Roosevelt, and their attendants and onlookers pose for a photograph. The prince was in Washington representing his brother, Kaiser Wilhelm, for the christening of the Kaiser's yacht, the *Meteor,* by First Daughter Alice, at far right. Roosevelt used the occasion to strengthen ties between Germany and the U.S., which worried the French and the Russians.

Evidence of Roosevelt's popularity with average Americans is clear from the crowd in Hannibal, Missouri, in the spring of 1903. They were standing on the rooftops and hanging out the windows to hear him. Hannibal's most famous citizen, Mark Twain, would write in 1908 that "our people have adored this showy charlatan as perhaps no impostor of his brood has been adored since the Golden Calf. . . ."

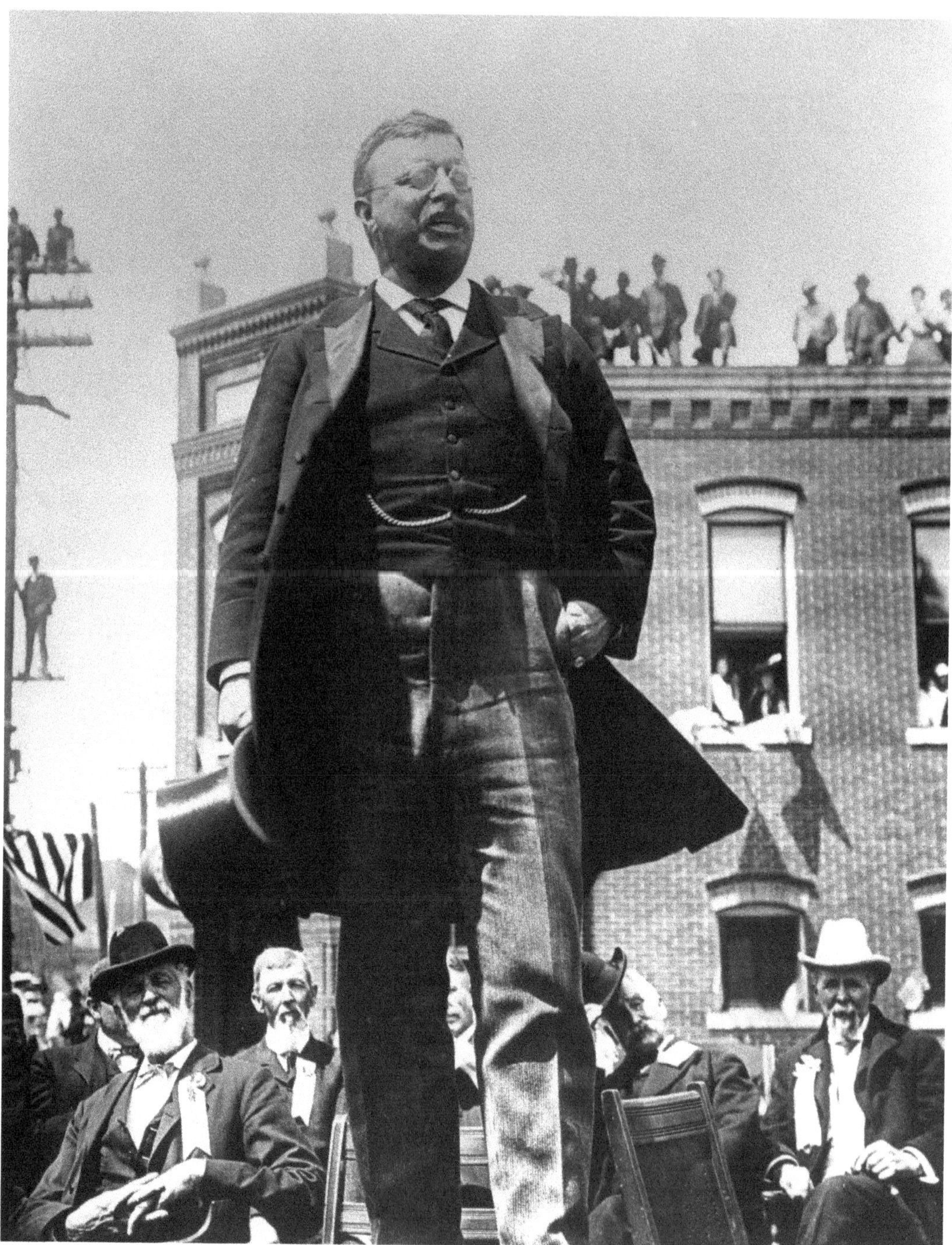

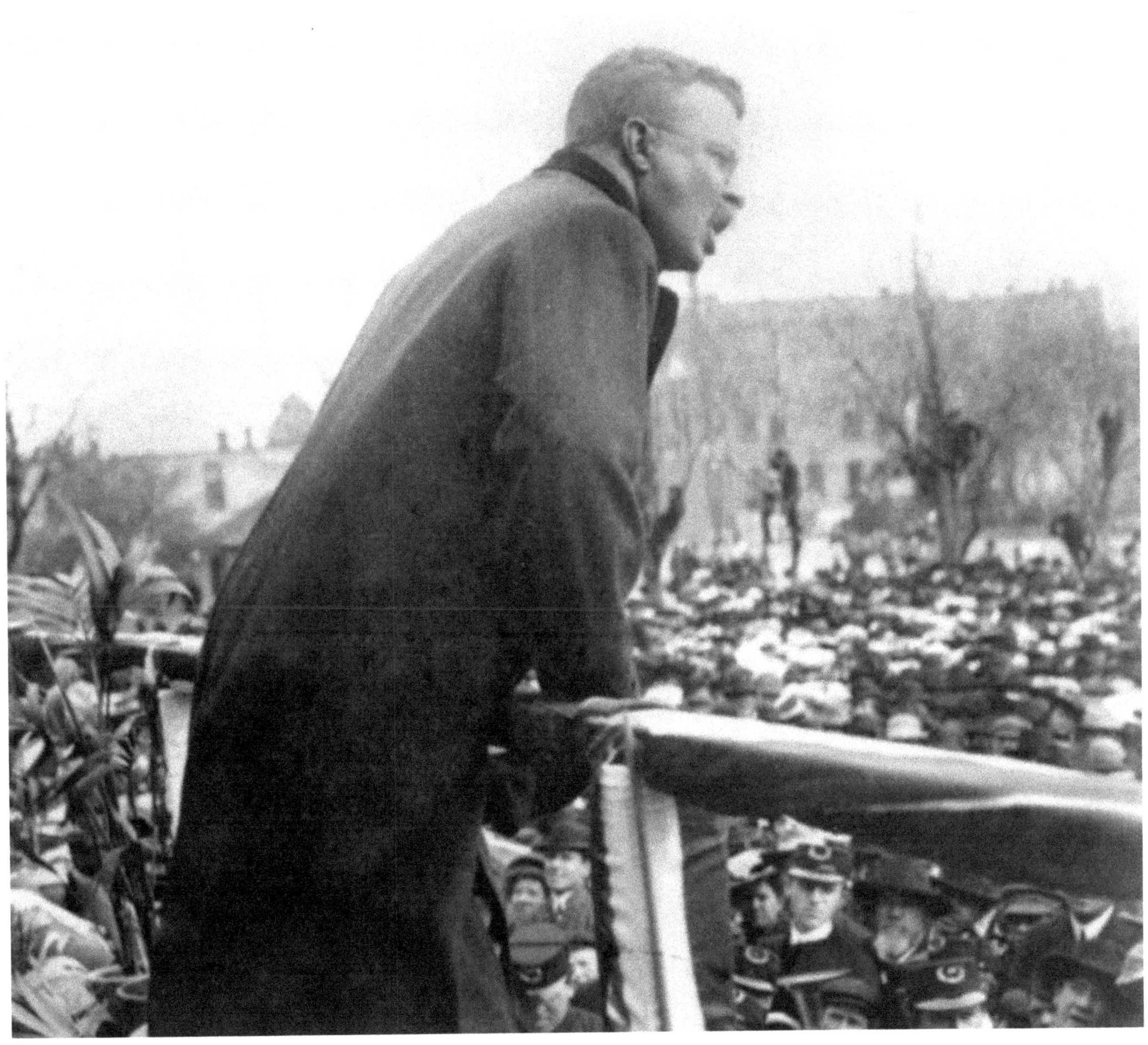

As president, Roosevelt used speaking engagements to make Americans aware of his concerns for the country. By 1903, when this photograph was taken in New York City, Roosevelt had settled the anthracite coal strike by calling both the workers and the bosses to the White House to negotiate. He promised that, unlike past presidents who sided with capital, he would function as an honest, impartial broker giving every citizen a "square deal."

President Roosevelt here stresses a point to an audience in Wyoming, in April 1903. Roosevelt was a conservationist influenced by his university-trained Chief Forester Gifford Pinchot. The two believed it necessary to conserve natural resources for the use of future generations.

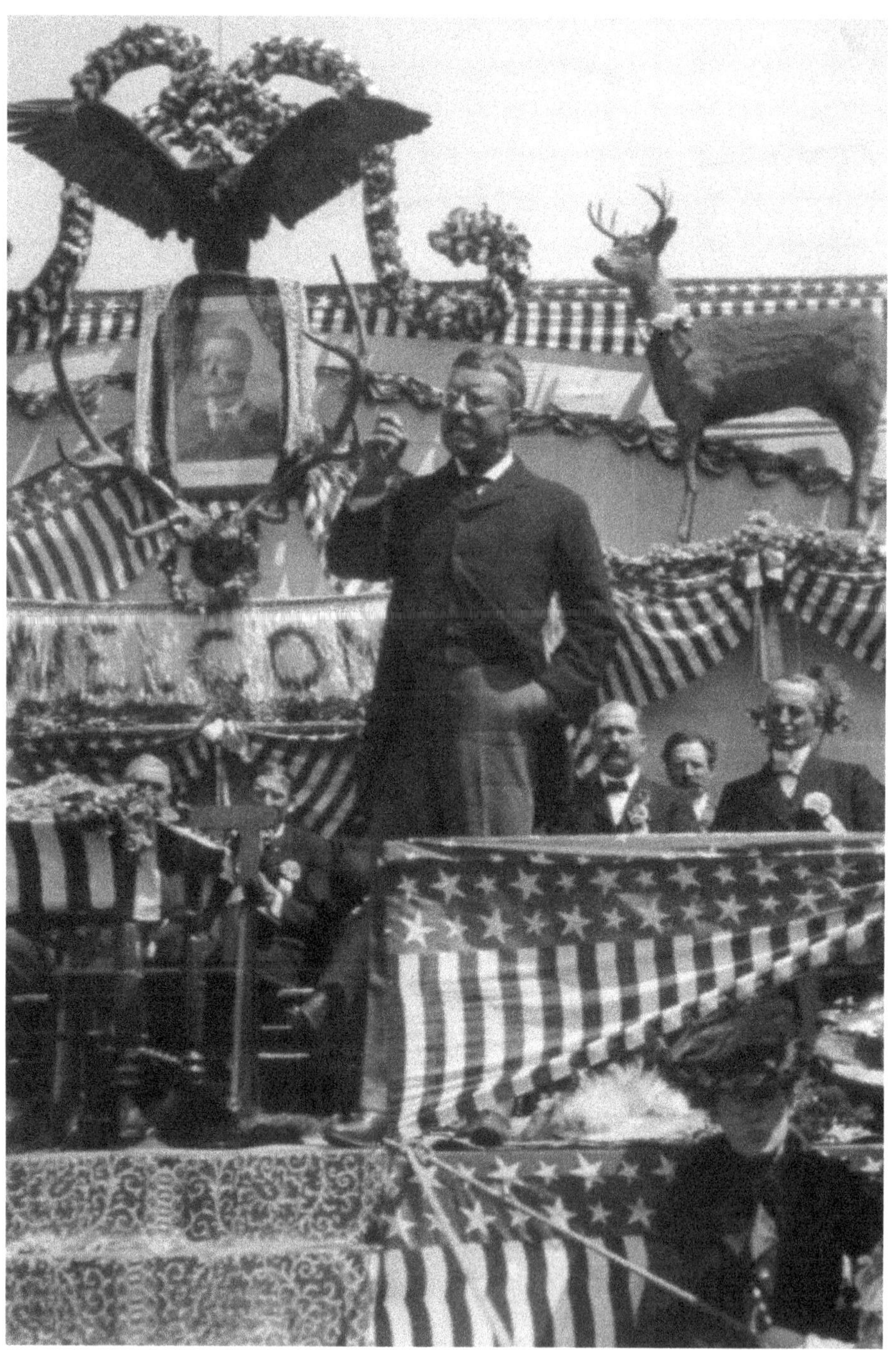

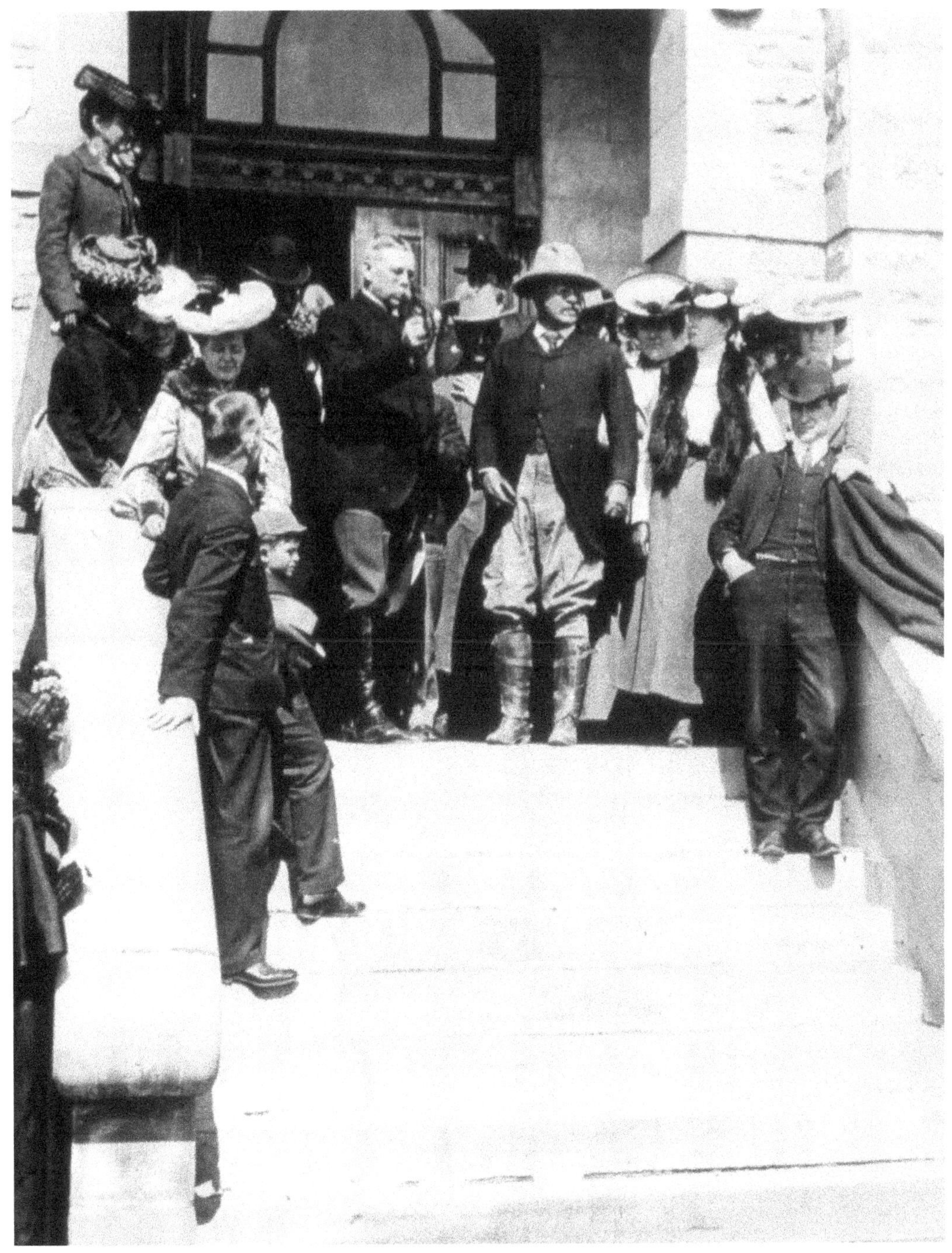

Republican Francis Warren of Wyoming, the chair of the Senate Committee on Irrigation and Reclamation of Arid Lands, presents President Roosevelt with spurs, likely in thanks for his support of the Newlands Reclamation Act. This legislation "reclaimed" dry, western lands by providing large-scale irrigation projects. The Newlands Act—for good or for ill—forever changed the face of the West by allowing for the construction of gigantic dams, which reshaped the landscape even as they permitted farming where none had been possible before.

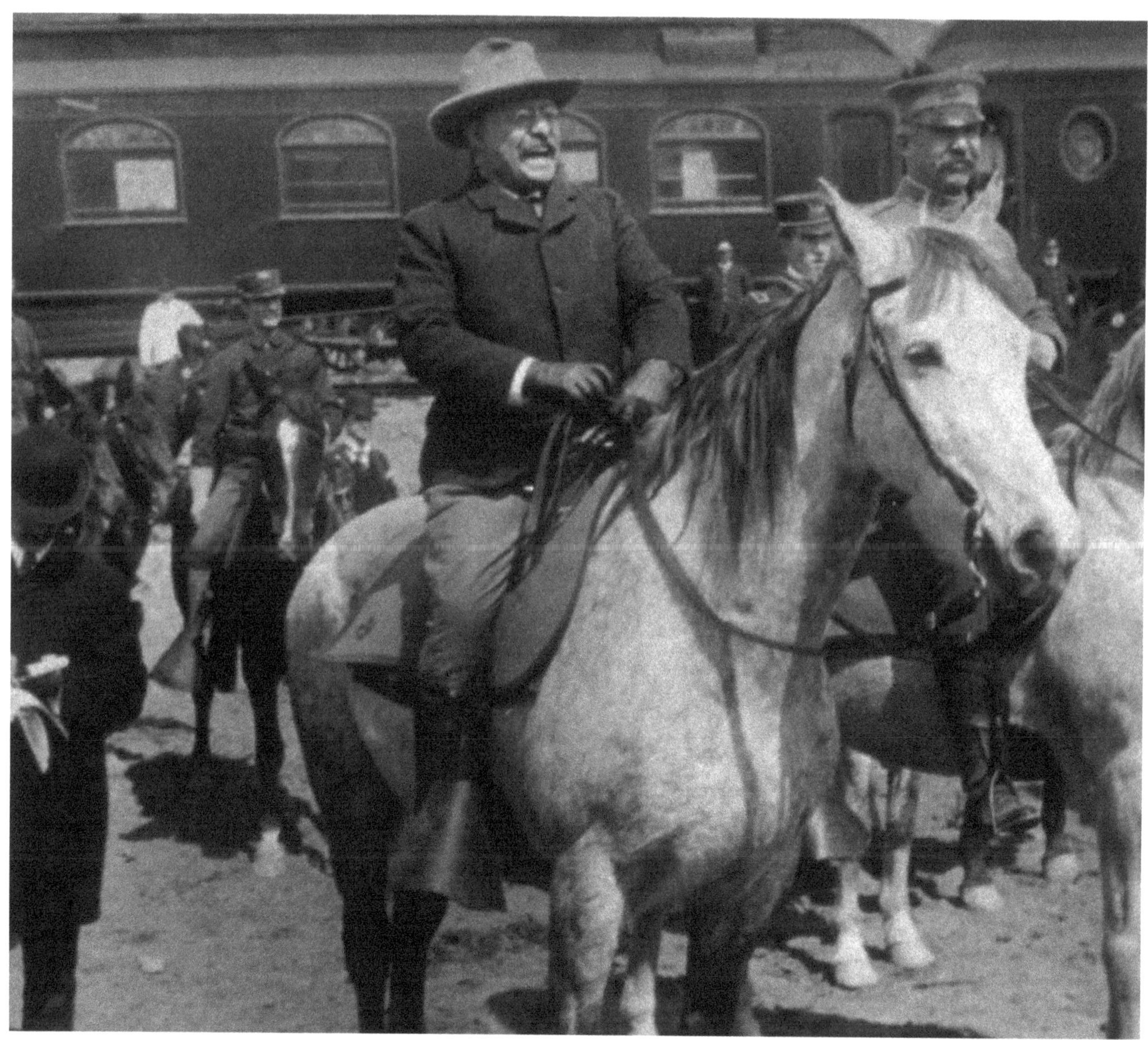

This photograph shows President Roosevelt on horseback, readying for a ride through the Grand Canyon in Arizona. The canyon, Roosevelt wrote his daughter Ethel, was "wonderful and beautiful beyond description." To preserve its beauty for future generations, he created the Grand Canyon Game Preserve in 1906 and the Grand Canyon National Monument two years later. President Woodrow Wilson turned the area into a national park in 1919.

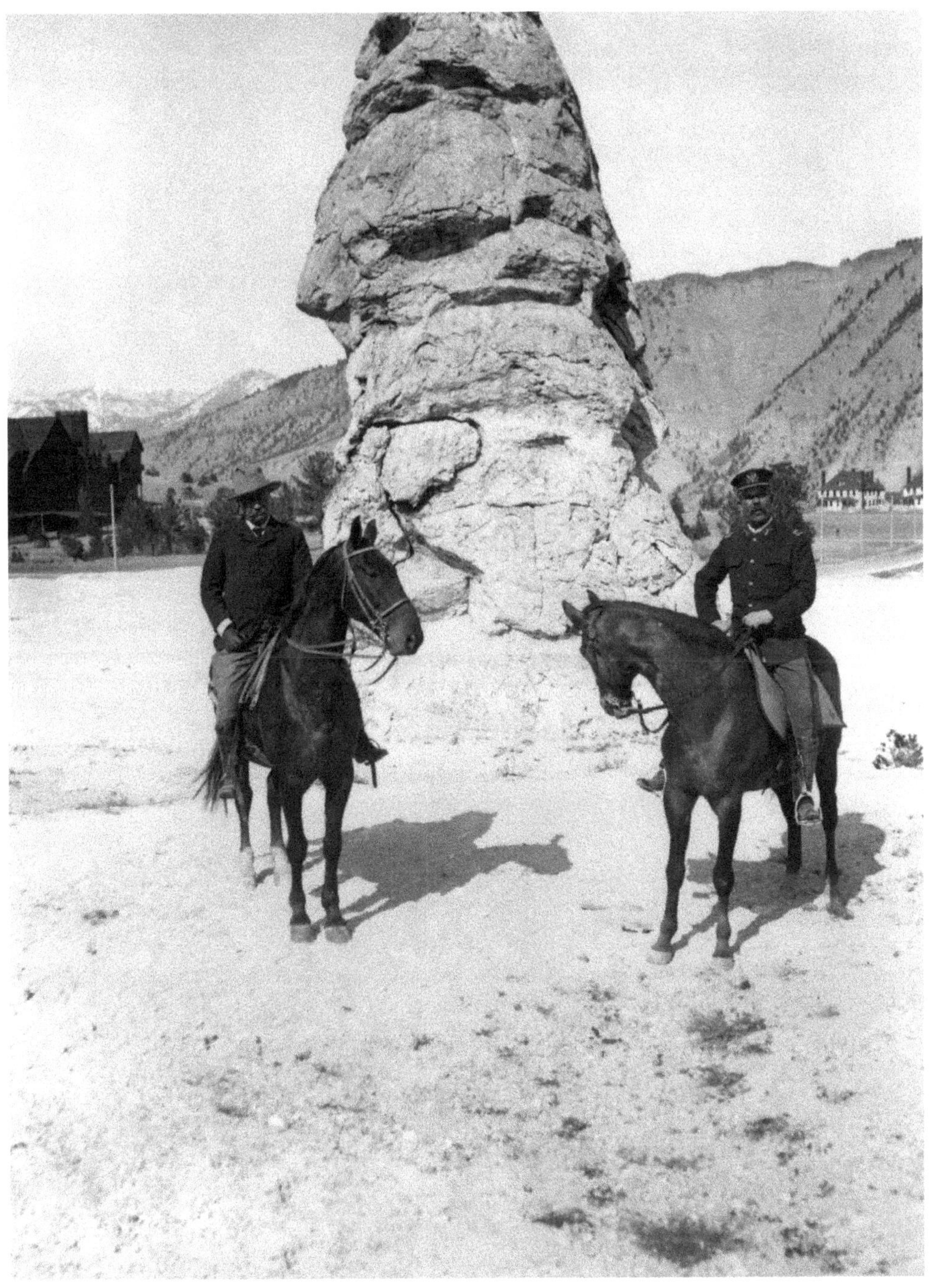

Roosevelt is seen here in Yellowstone National Park, which had been set aside in 1872. He was an advocate of conservationism, the planned management of natural resources, but he also understood the sentiments of preservationists like John Muir, who believed that nature must remain forever wild as an antidote to urban living. As president, TR straddled both camps.

Wilderness expert and nature essayist John Burroughs stands to TR's right. The president visited Burroughs at his home, Slabside, in 1903. The older man appreciated Roosevelt's efforts on behalf of the natural world. TR doubled the number of national parks, added almost 150 million acres of timberland to America's forest reserves, created 150 national forests, and established 18 national monuments, including Muir Woods and the Petrified Forest.

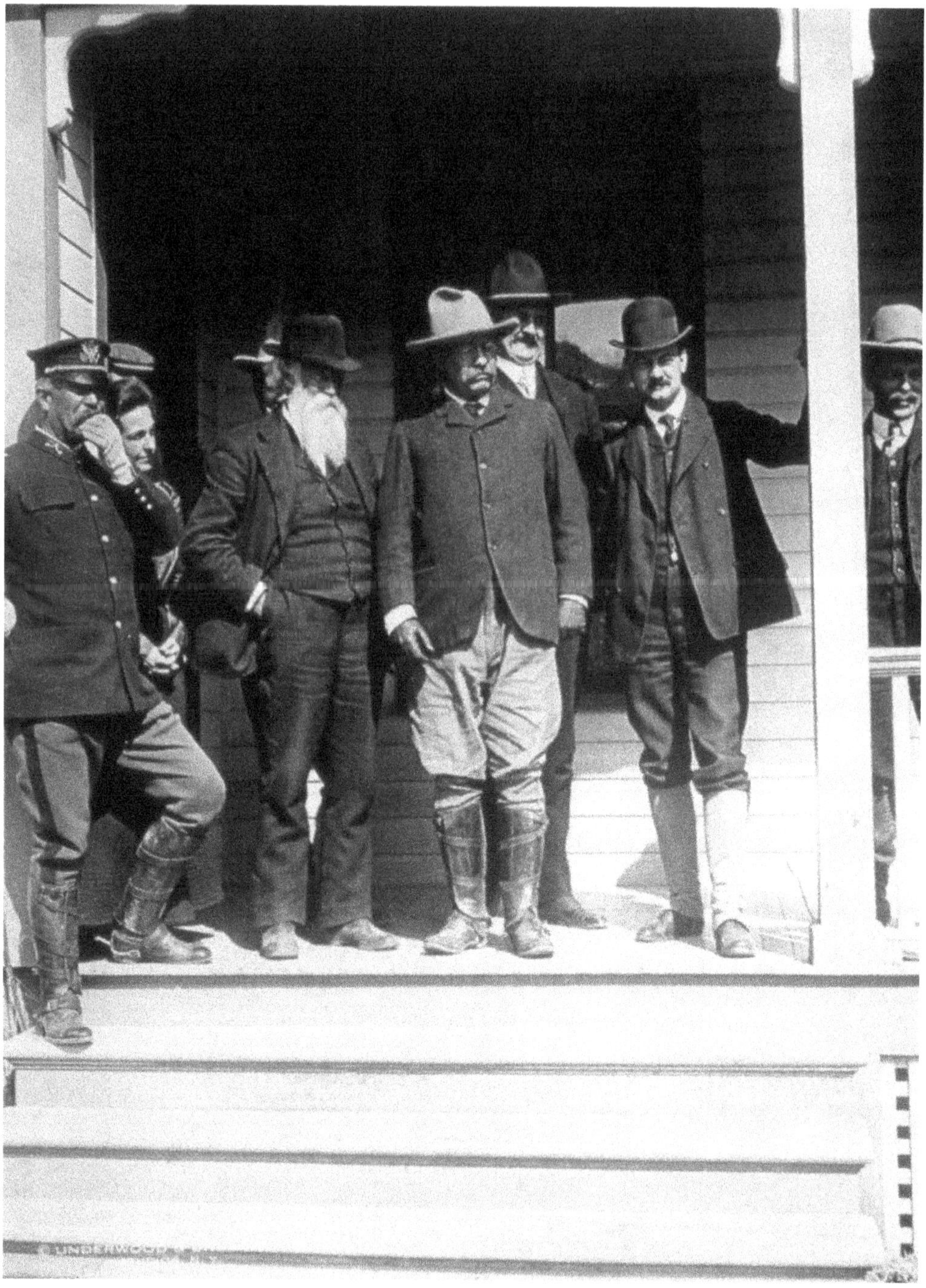

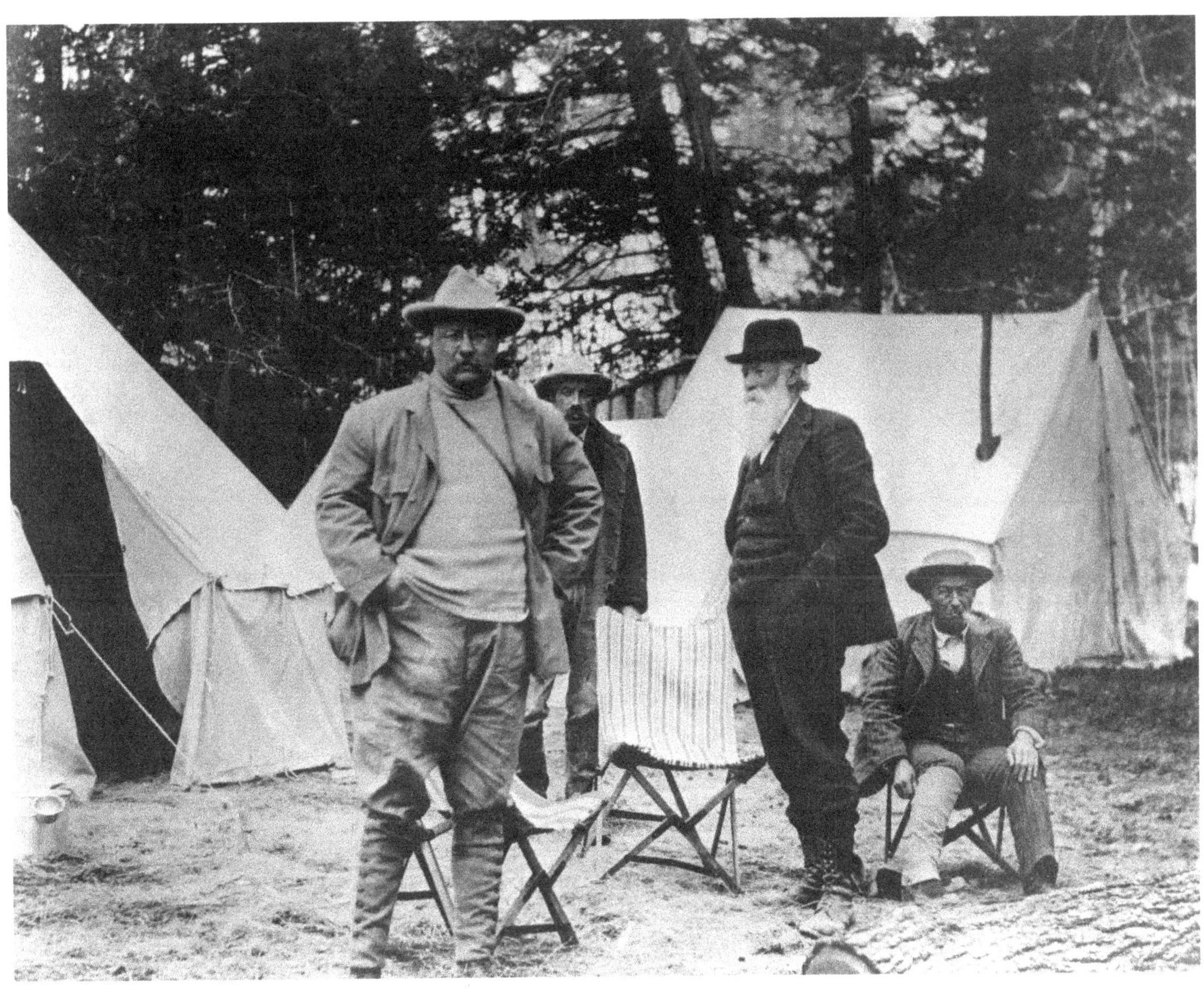

Roosevelt "camping and tramping" with John Burroughs. From his days as a founder of the Boone and Crockett Club in 1887, TR was part of a wide circle of scientists, explorers, hunters, and naturalists, all of whom shaped his thinking that the federal government must play an activist role in the conservation and preservation of the country's natural resources.

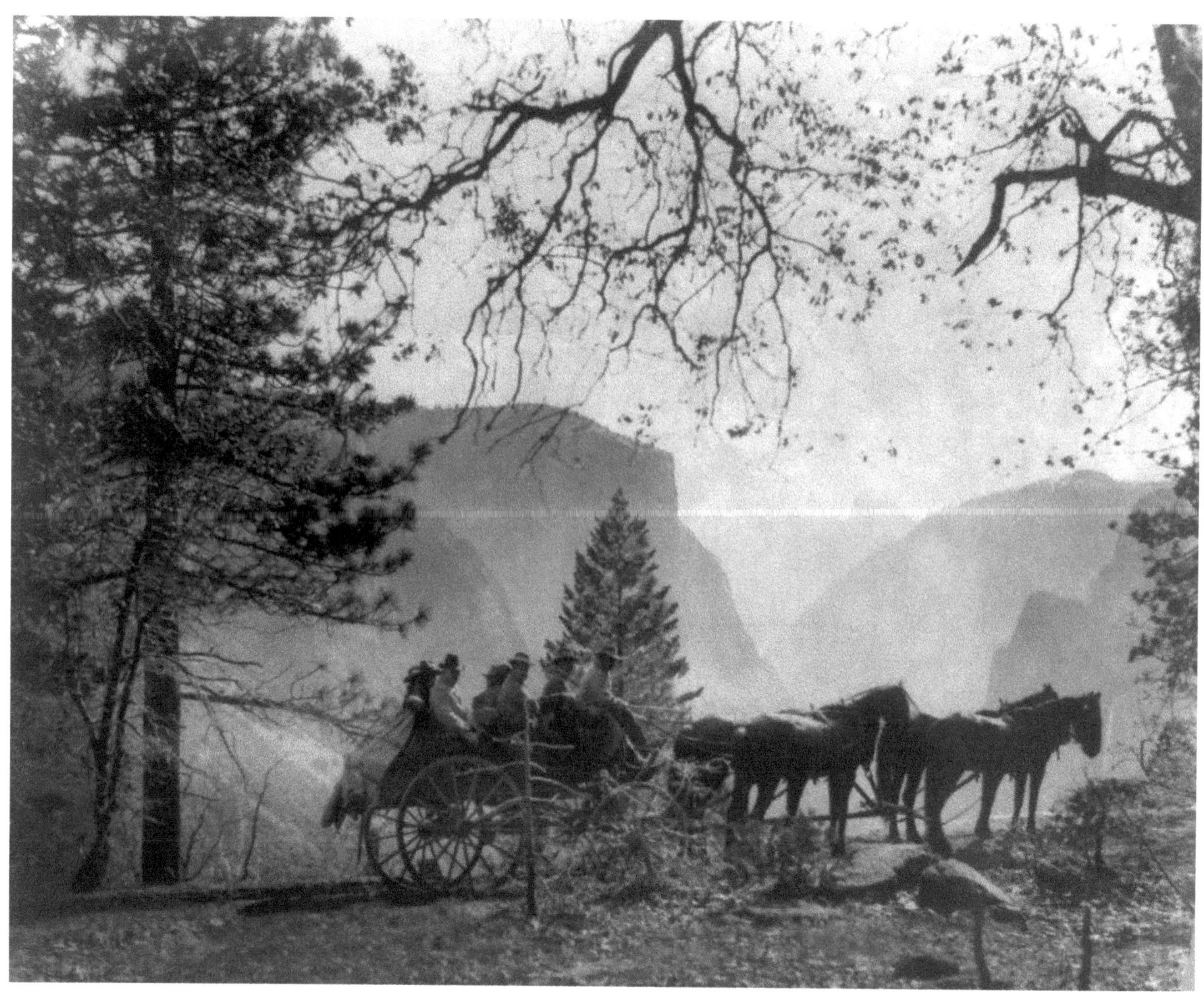

Roosevelt at Inspiration Point, in Yosemite Valley, California. In 1912, TR wrote in *The Outlook* magazine that "there can be no greater issue than that of Conservation in this country," and he thought that his efforts to that end were among his most important accomplishments as president.

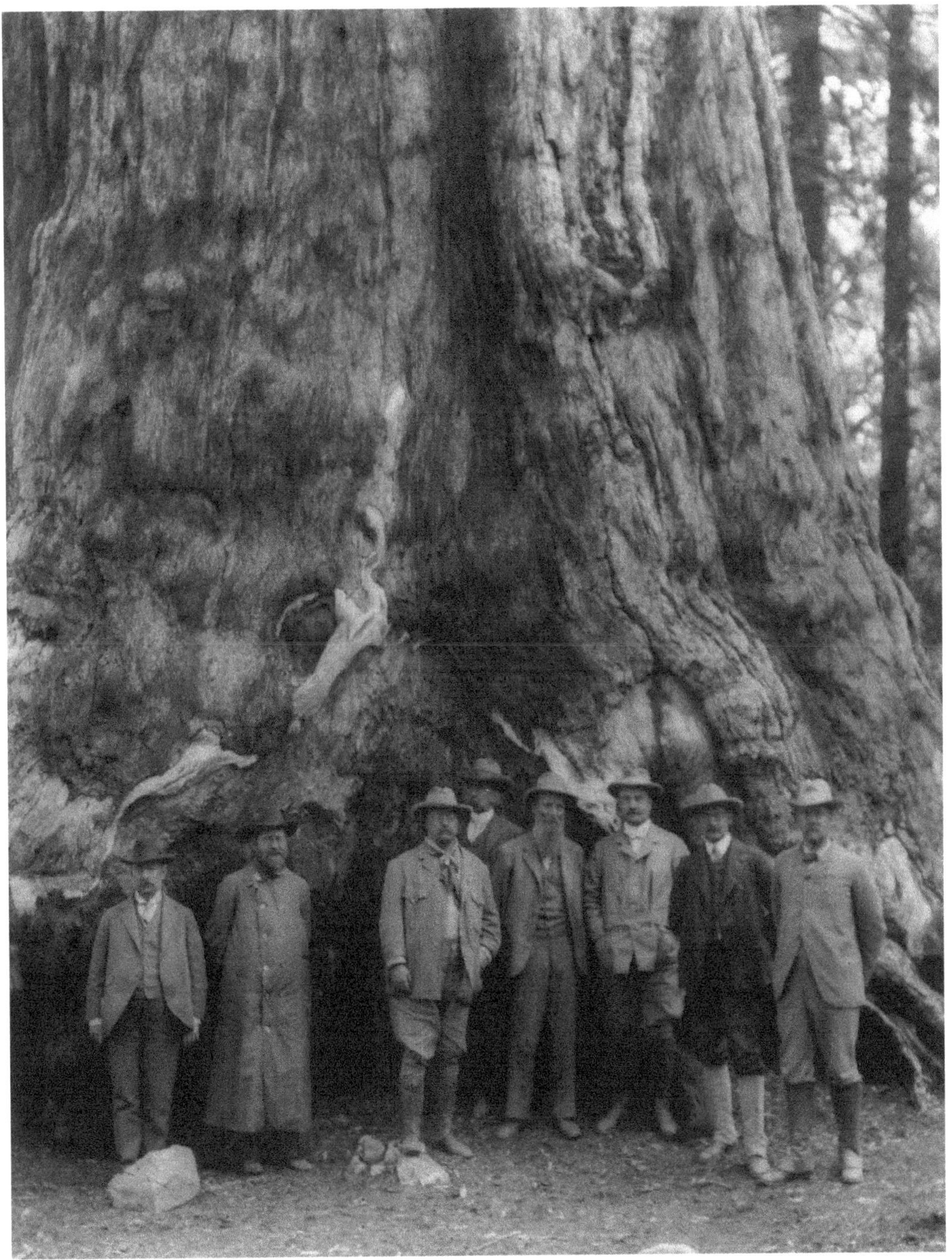

John Muir took Theodore Roosevelt wilderness hiking and camping through Yosemite Valley, California. Muir lobbied the president for the federal takeover of some state land—including the Mariposa Grove of Giant Sequoias—to be added to Yosemite National Park. TR concurred and in 1906 signed the necessary legislation. Like Pinchot and Burroughs, Muir's ideas influenced the president's actions.

Theodore Roosevelt at Glacier Point, Yosemite Valley, with Bridal Veil Falls in the background, May 1903. In a letter to George Bird Grinnell written at the time, TR noted that he and Burroughs had been "watching the game and the birds. We have been riding and walking and going on snowshoes." It was, he concluded, "a most pleasant holiday."

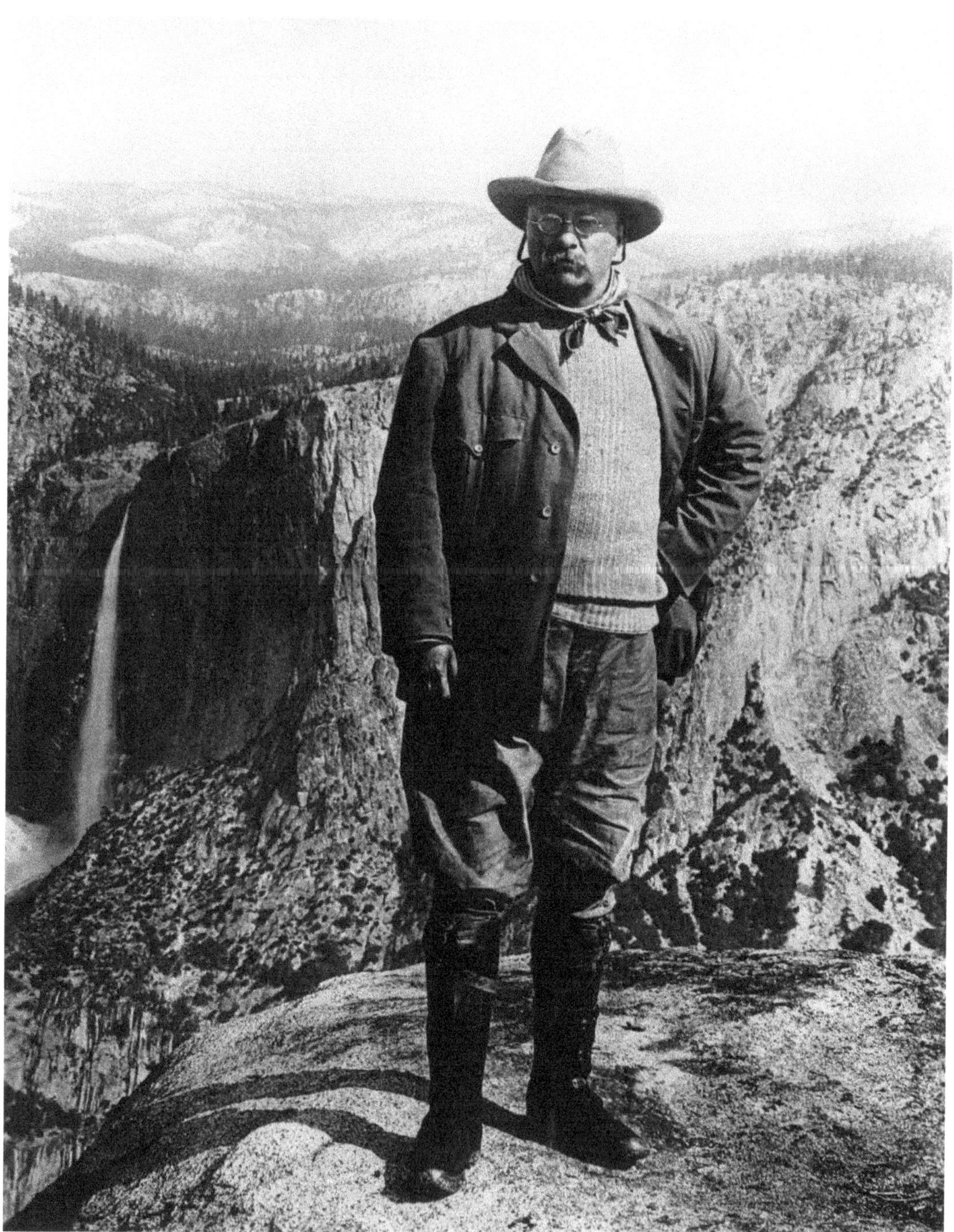

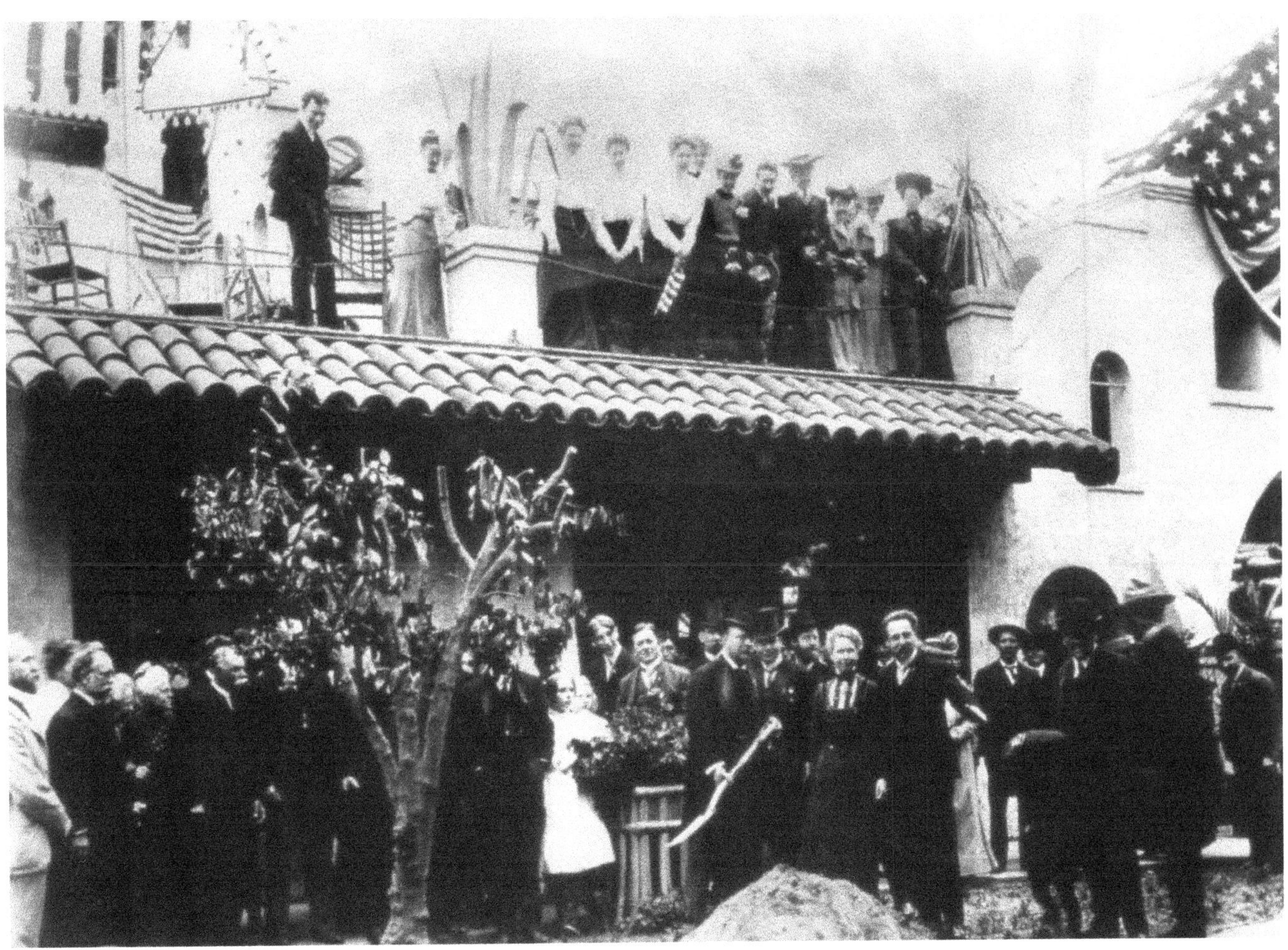

President Roosevelt wields a shovel in this photograph from his western trip in 1903. Here he was transplanting an orange tree in Riverside, California. A week later he was in San Francisco to dedicate the naval monument in Union Square. Wherever he went, Roosevelt made an impression on the crowds with his youth and vitality.

At the University of California, Berkeley, Theodore Roosevelt was awarded an honorary Doctor of Laws after giving the commencement address in May 1903. He had been invited there by his old friend Benjamin Ide Wheeler, president of the university. As the author of nearly thirty books in his lifetime, Roosevelt ranks among the most literate and learned of all American presidents.

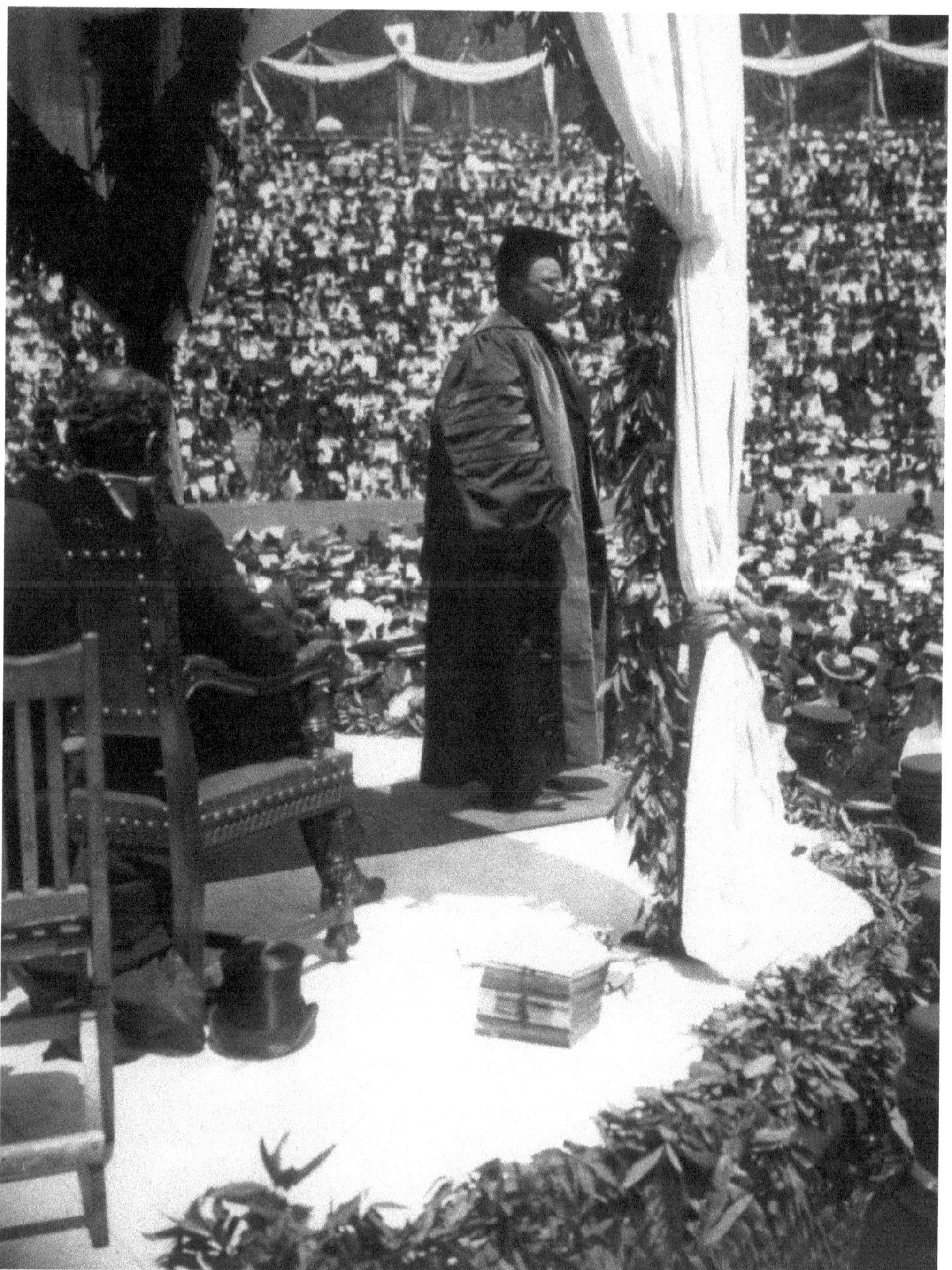

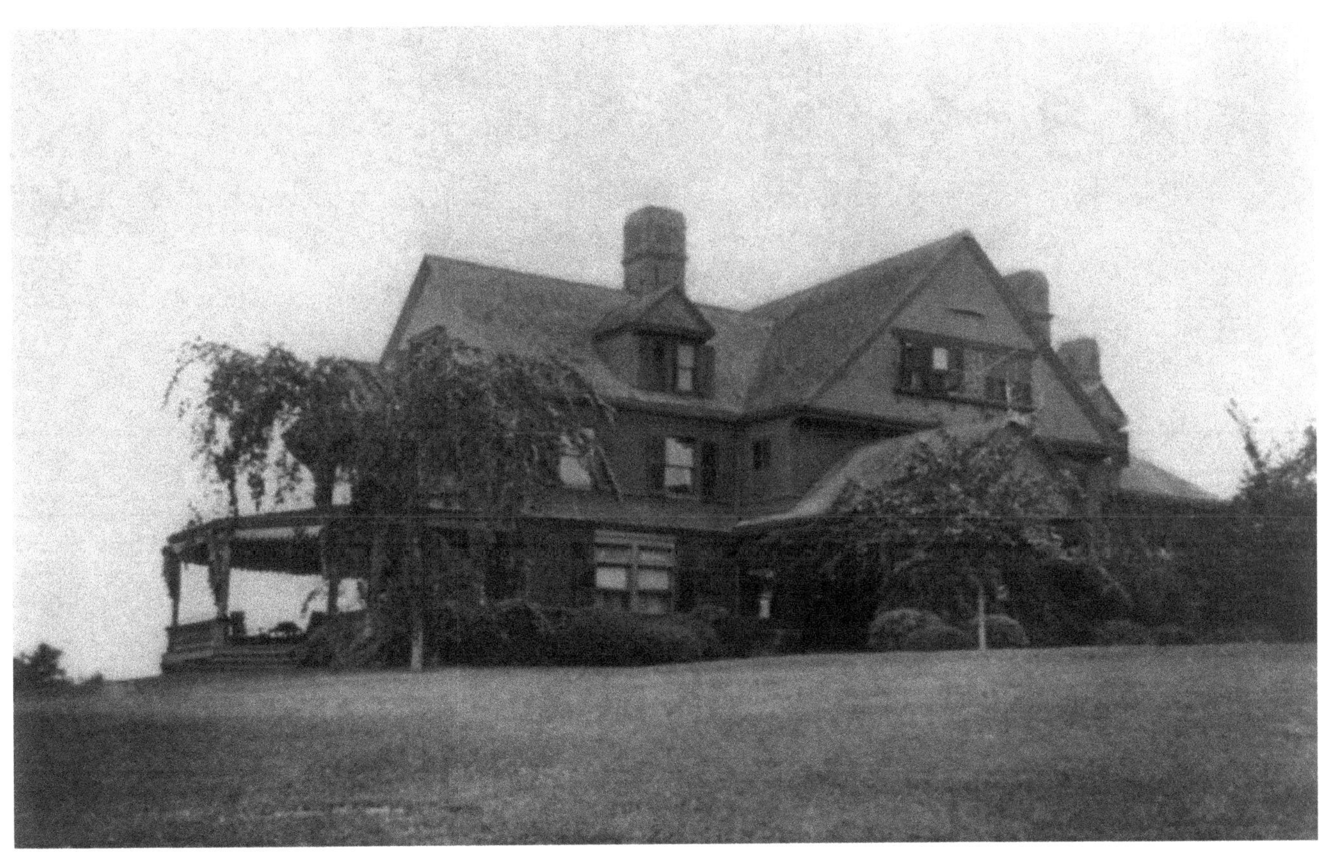

The house atop Cove Neck was originally going to be known as Leeholm, until Alice Hathaway Lee Roosevelt died. TR's eldest sister Anna oversaw the completion of the 23-room home, renamed Sagamore Hill after a local Native American chief. Theodore and Edith raised their children here, and while TR was president, Sagamore Hill was known as the "Summer White House."

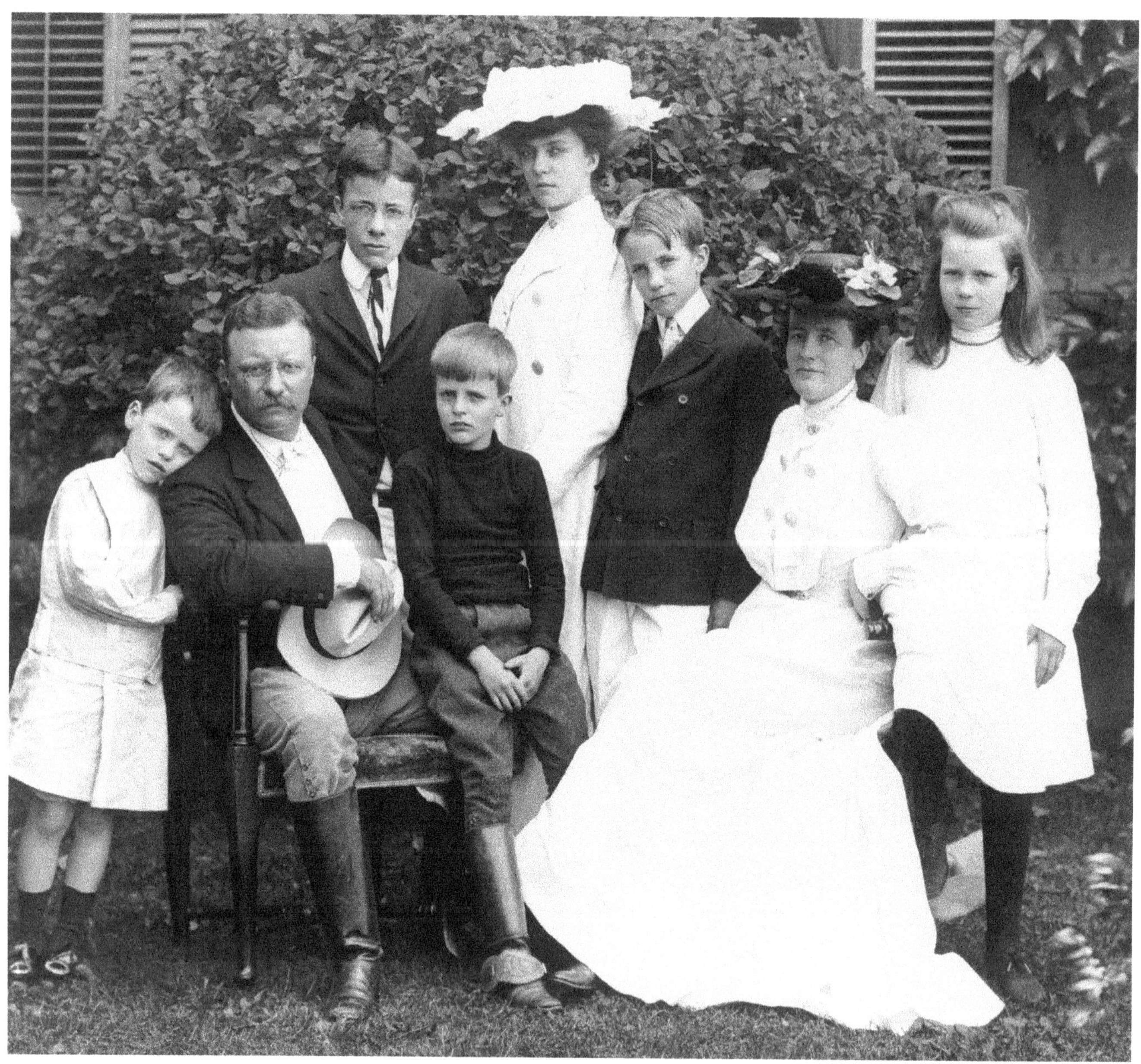

The Roosevelt family in 1903: Quentin, TR, Ted, Alice, Kermit, Edith, Ethel, and Archie on TR's lap. TR told his friend Western novelist Owen Wister in 1901 that his children "lead exactly the lives led by any other six children who live in a roomy house with a garden and go to school, and are on the whole pretty good, and are not always good at all."

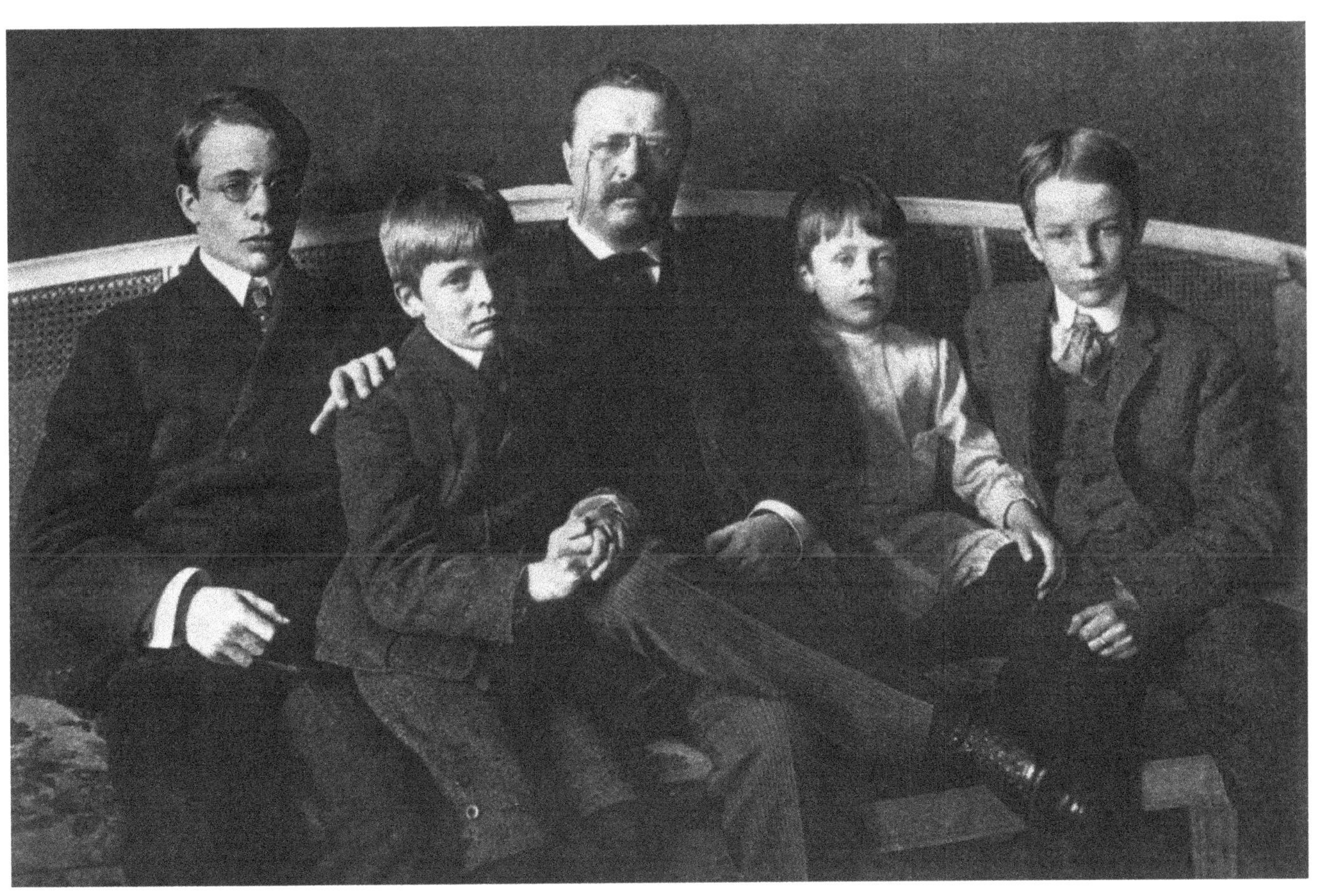

Roosevelt and his sons: Ted, Archie, TR, Quentin, and Kermit. The Roosevelt boys were the nucleus of what was called "the White House Gang." Friends and cousins swelled the ranks of this boisterous bunch who roller-skated through the White House, had snowball fights on the front lawn, staged mock attacks on federal buildings, and threw spitballs at Andrew Jackson's portrait. Darlings of the press, the White House Gang loved it best when the president joined in, as he frequently did.

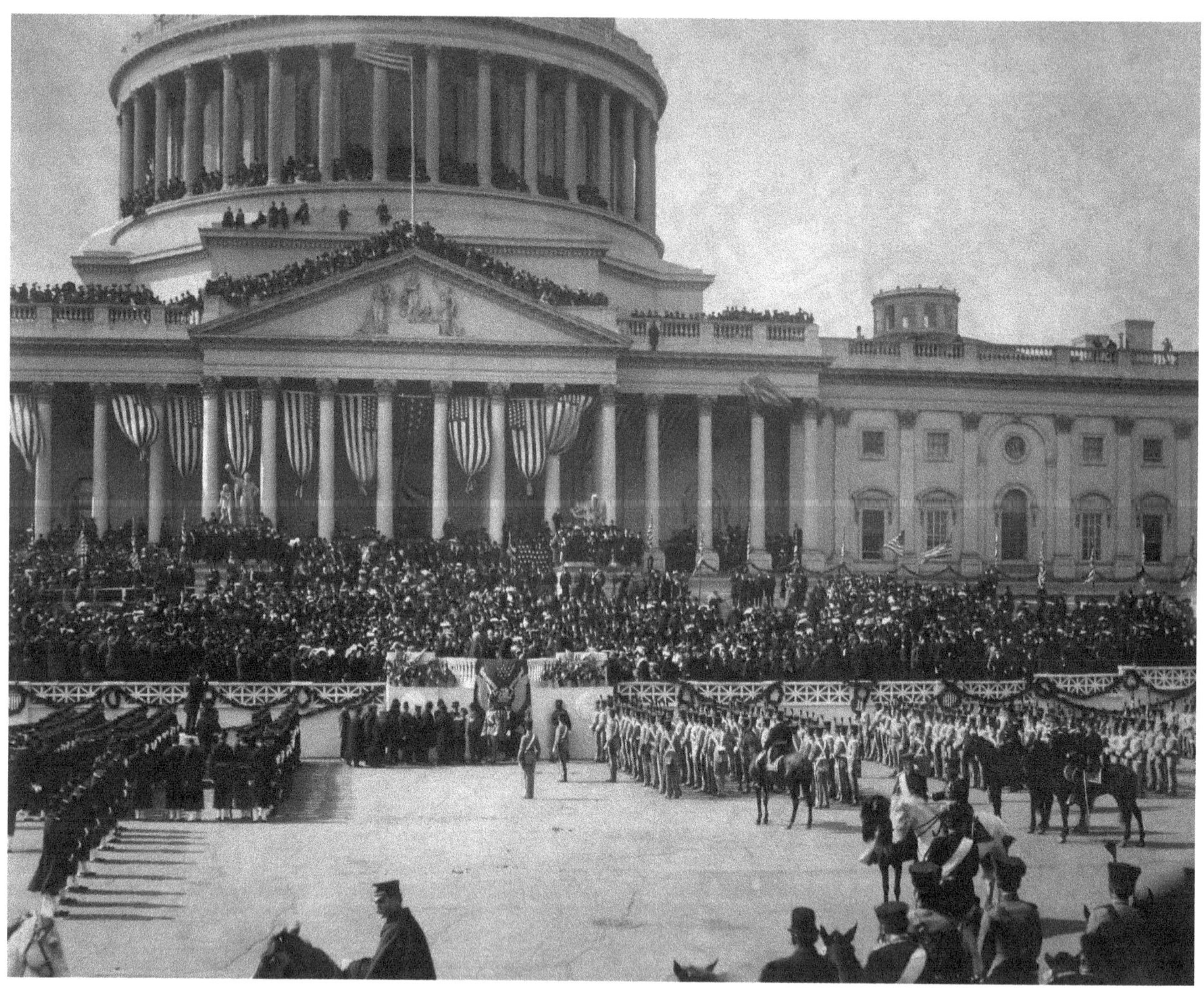

On March 4, 1905, Theodore Roosevelt took the inaugural oath for a second time. A believer in George Washington's model of two terms, Roosevelt told those gathered to congratulate him that he would not seek another four years. He hoped it would put him above politics, but instead it made recalcitrant lawmakers less inclined to work with him.

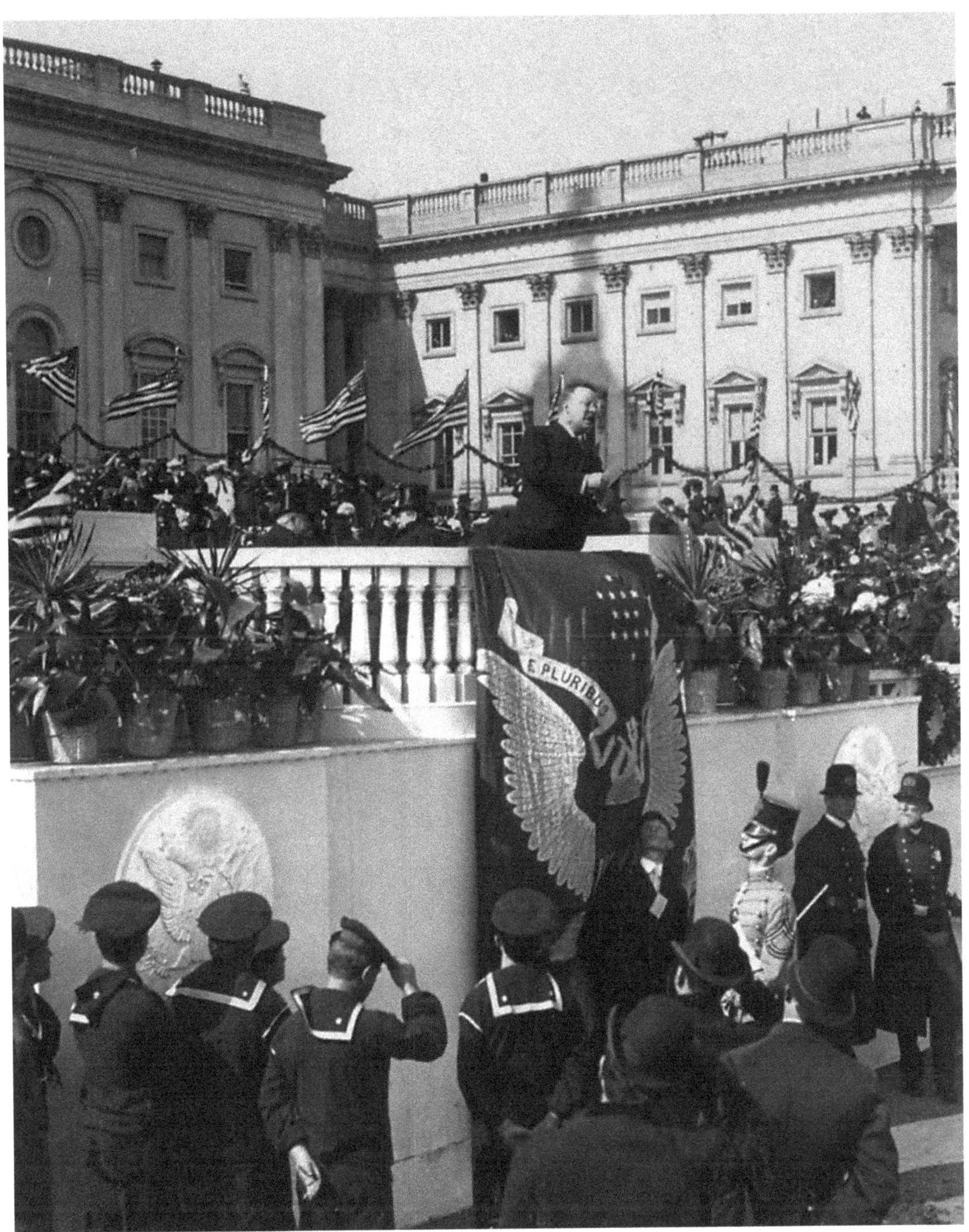

Roosevelt's inaugural address echoed the familiar strains of American exceptionalism. He called upon citizens to be faithful to the dreams of the Founders, and yet to be careful to leave a goodly portion to future generations. He reminded Americans that the difficult task of democracy called for "the qualities of practical intelligence, of courage, of hardihood, and endurance, and above all the power of devotion to a lofty ideal." For Roosevelt, that ideal was the American model of "free self-government."

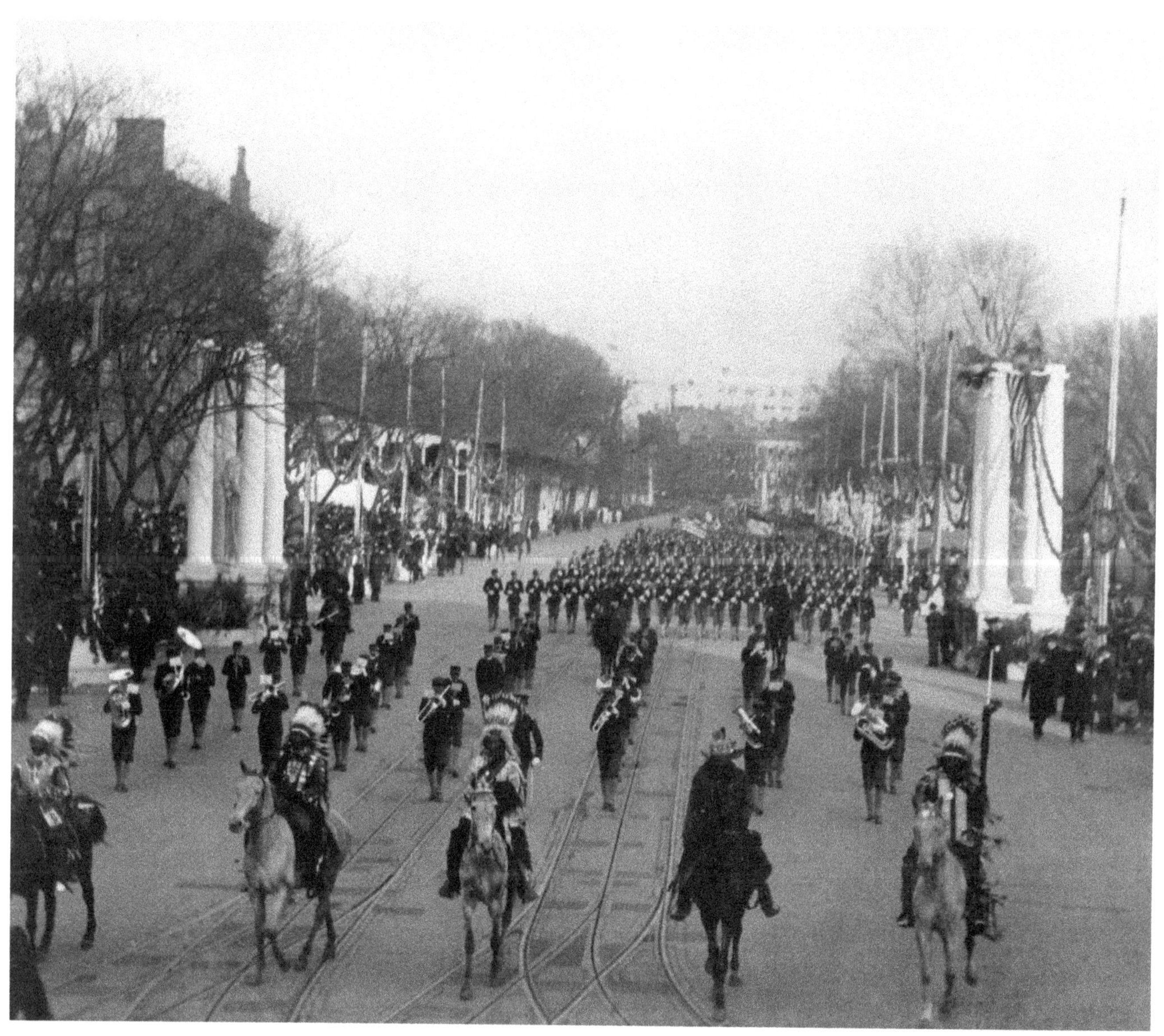

The famous Apache leader Geronimo passed before the presidential reviewing stand during the inaugural parade in 1905. Roosevelt, who had lived in the West and fought alongside Native Americans in 1898, assisted native peoples in ways that ranged from reforms for federal personnel who worked with Indians, to public demonstrations of admiration for Native American culture. As with African Americans, however, TR's record was mixed and he did not exert the farsighted leadership on their behalf that he might have.

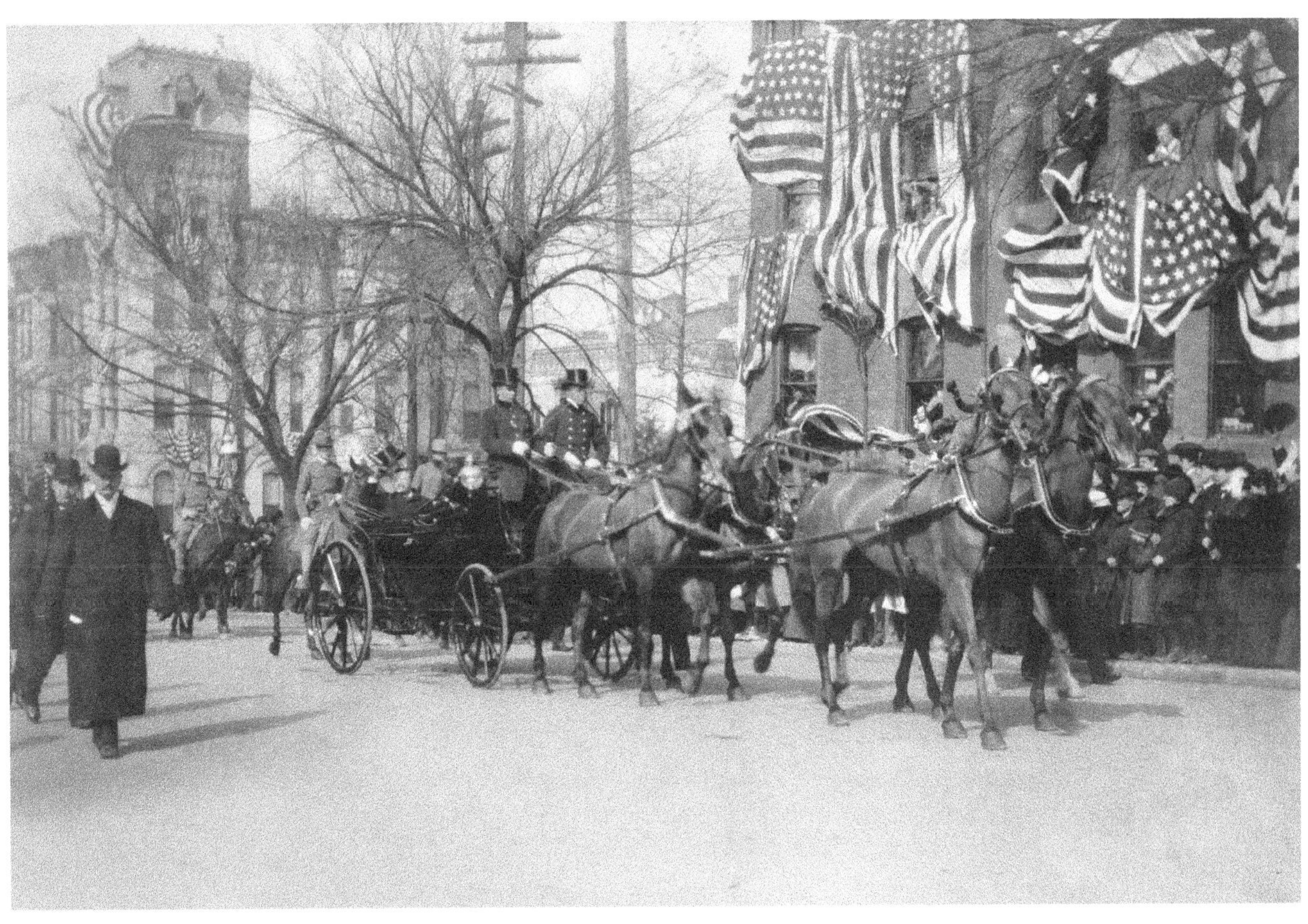

Roosevelt's popularity with the common American was extraordinarily high. Lauded across the nation for his efforts on behalf of working people, TR was elected by a handy majority. But inside Washington, he traversed a rockier path. Within the Republican Party a split was developing between conservative "stand patters" and progressive, reform-minded congressmen. This split would widen in TR's final four years and break wide open in his successor's.

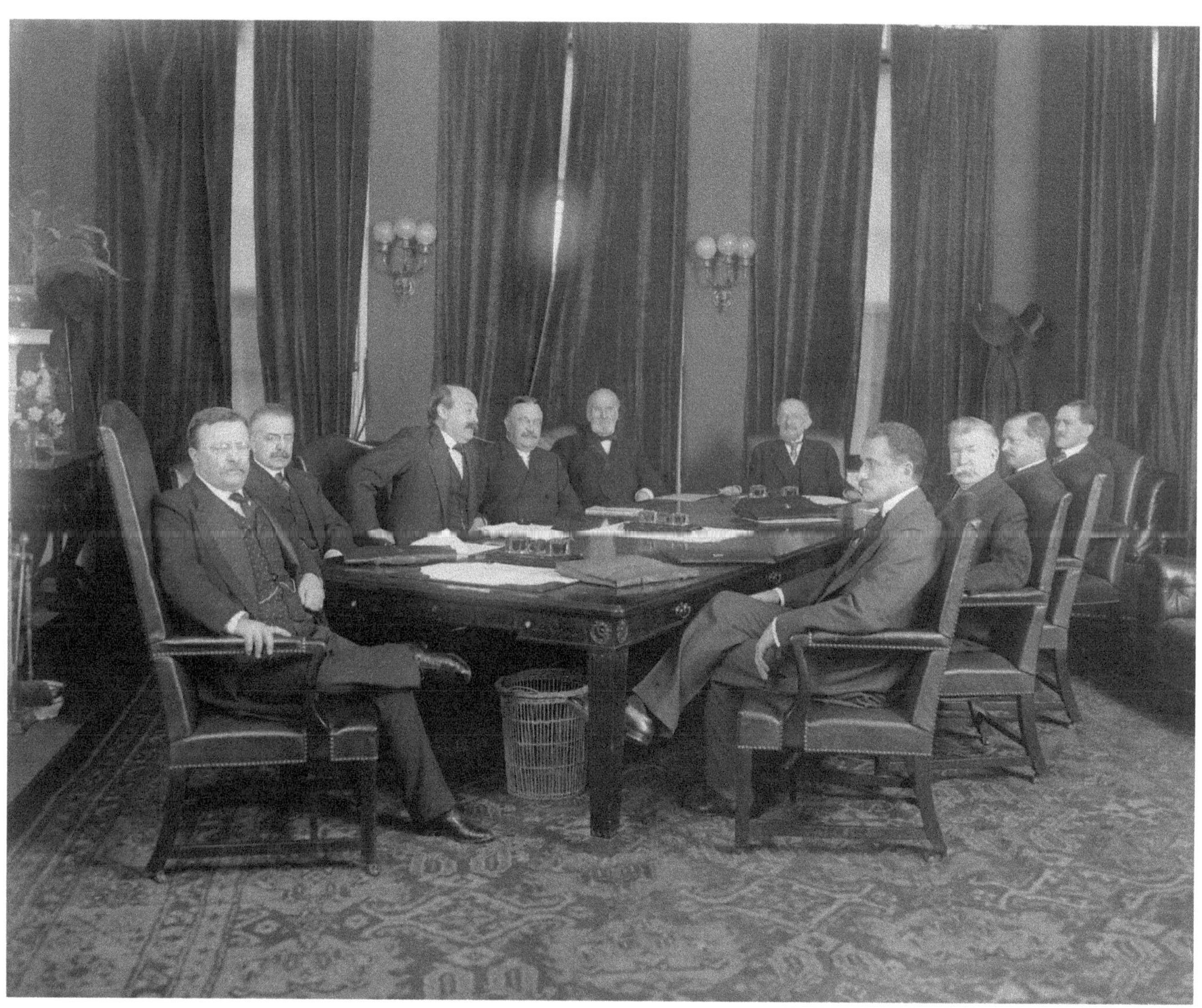

Roosevelt and his cabinet members, 1905. The first task after his election was the regulation of industry. Congress introduced most famously the Pure Food and Drug Act and the meat inspection rider, the latter spurred by Upton Sinclair's now-classic novel *The Jungle*. Although some industry giants, such as Heinz and Pabst, saw the benefit of the legislation in terms of increased public trust, most other businesses loathed what they saw as intrusive governmental interference in their affairs.

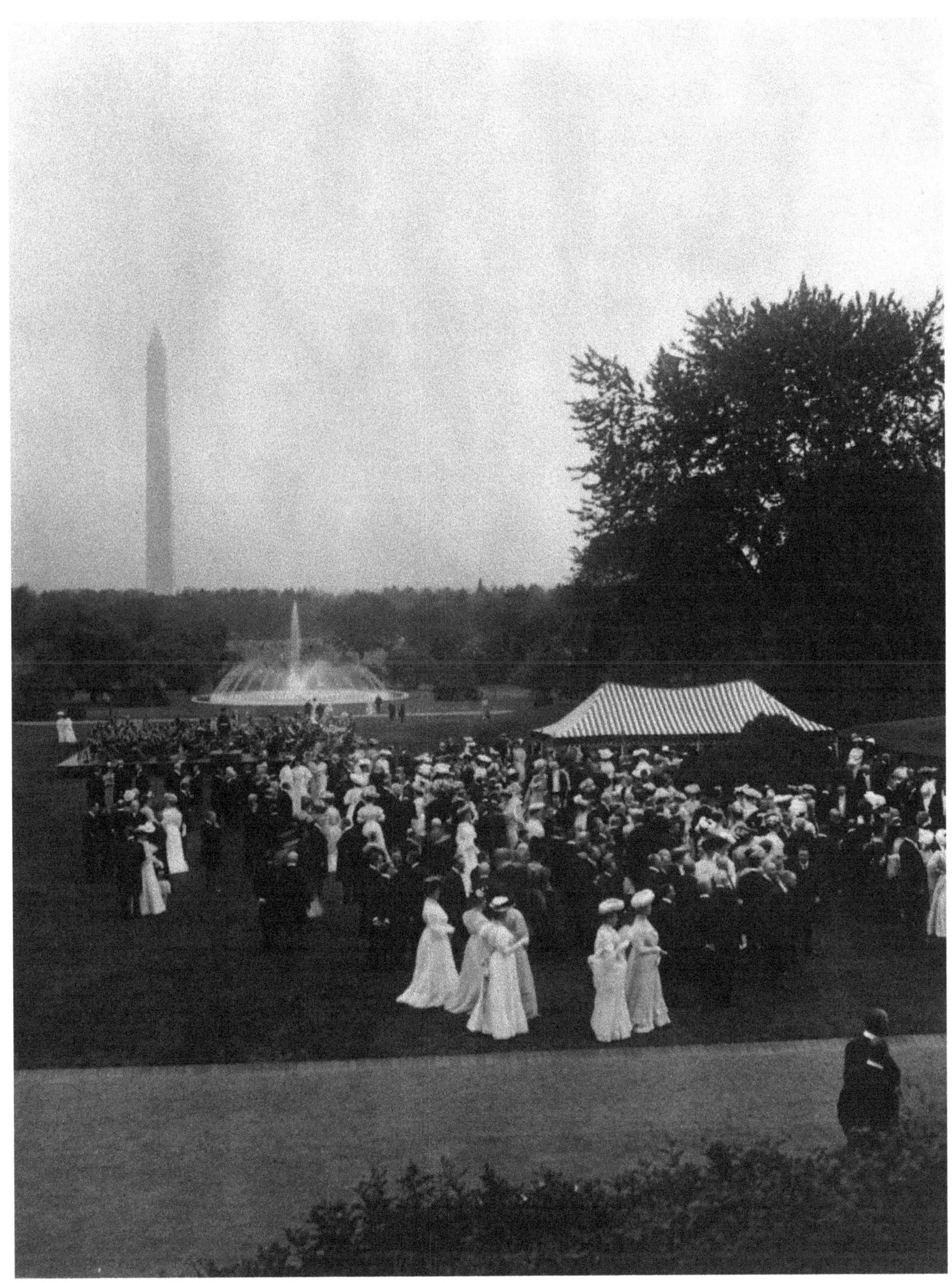

First Lady Edith Roosevelt was known as a calming influence on her ebullient husband. She pointedly left out of the White House invitation list any congressman with suspect morals, forcing TR to meet them at his sister's home. In addition to the White House renovation, Edith began the White House china collection and the First Ladies' portrait gallery. To manage official correspondence and seating arrangements, she hired the first social secretary, Isabelle Hagner. This garden party was just one of Edith Roosevelt's successful entertainments.

Theodore Roosevelt greets the former members of the First United States Volunteer Cavalry in 1905 at a Rough Rider reunion in San Antonio. TR looked after the men of his unit until the day he died, and after that, Edith and the children maintained the correspondence and assisted them whenever possible.

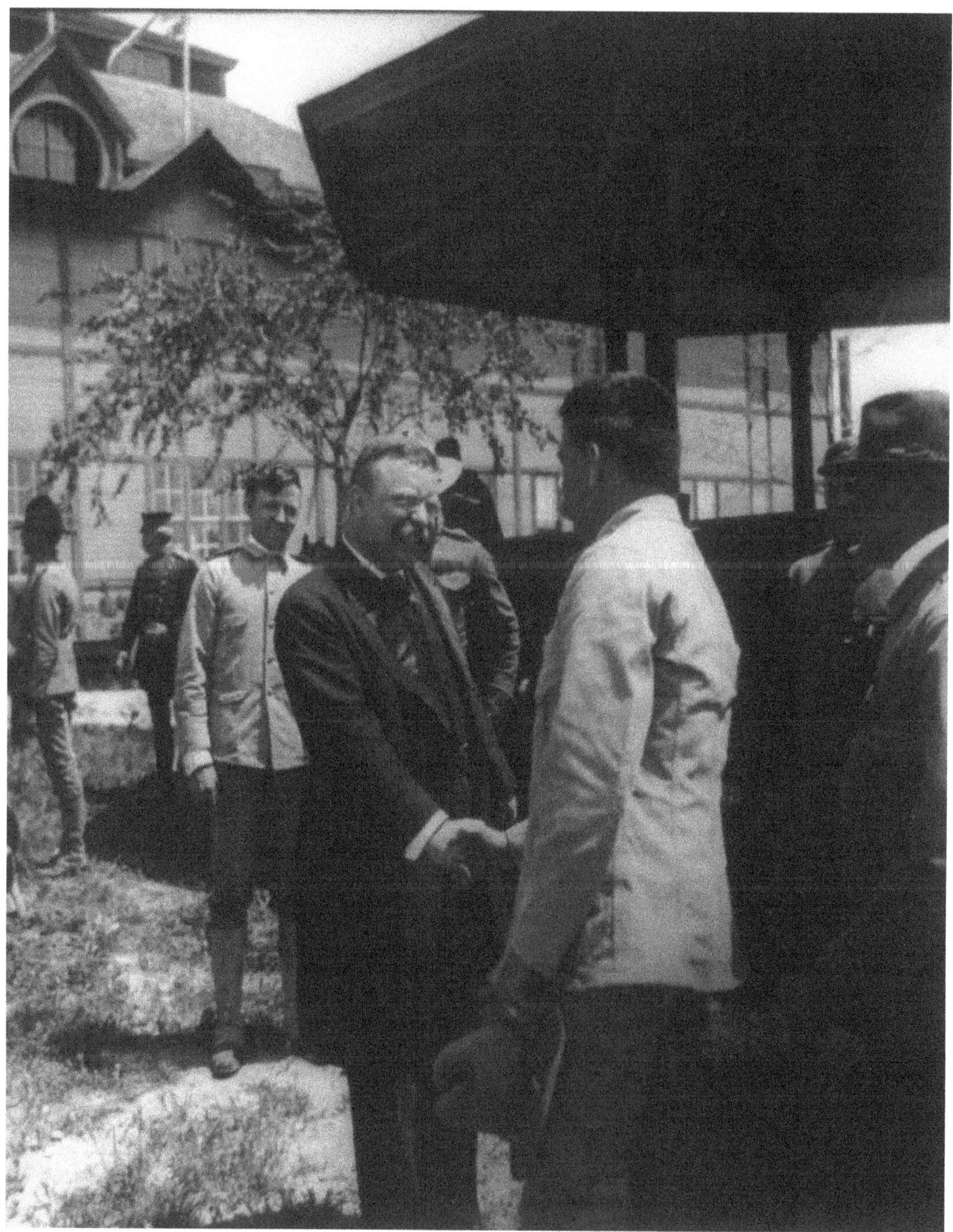

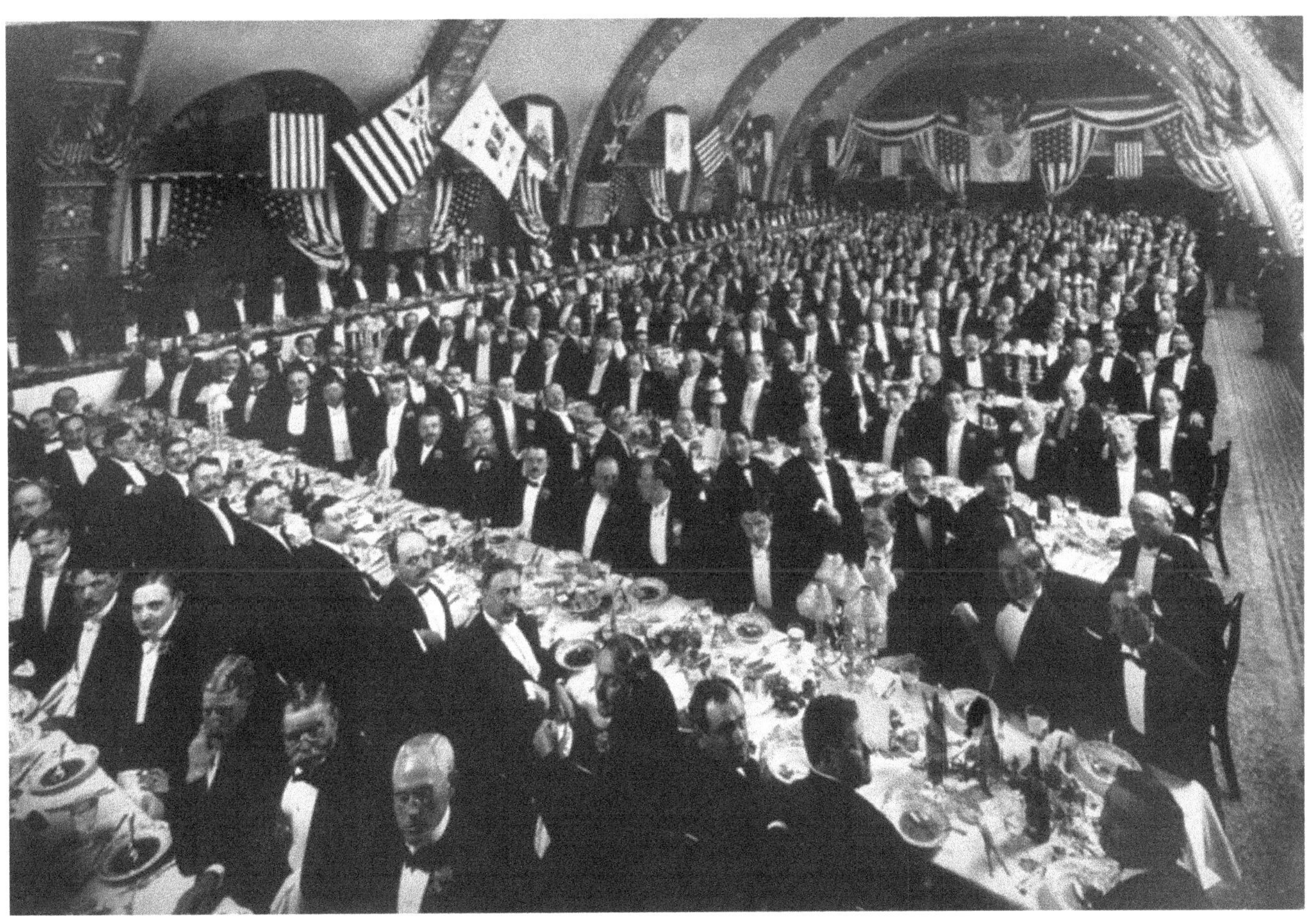

President Roosevelt speaking before the Iroquois Club in Chicago, 1905. The Iroquois Club was founded by Edward O. Brown and comprised young professional men from the Democratic Party. This was yet another venue for Roosevelt to explain the domestic reform agenda known as the Square Deal. TR's progressivism was beginning to make conservative Republican lawmakers even more suspicious of him.

When Roosevelt took office, America was 45 states strong. Here he is shown in 1905 urging the people of Durant to prepare themselves for the responsibilities of statehood. Oklahoma would become the nation's 46th state in 1907, but in the 1908 presidential election the Sooner State would go Democratic and vote for westerner William Jennings Bryan.

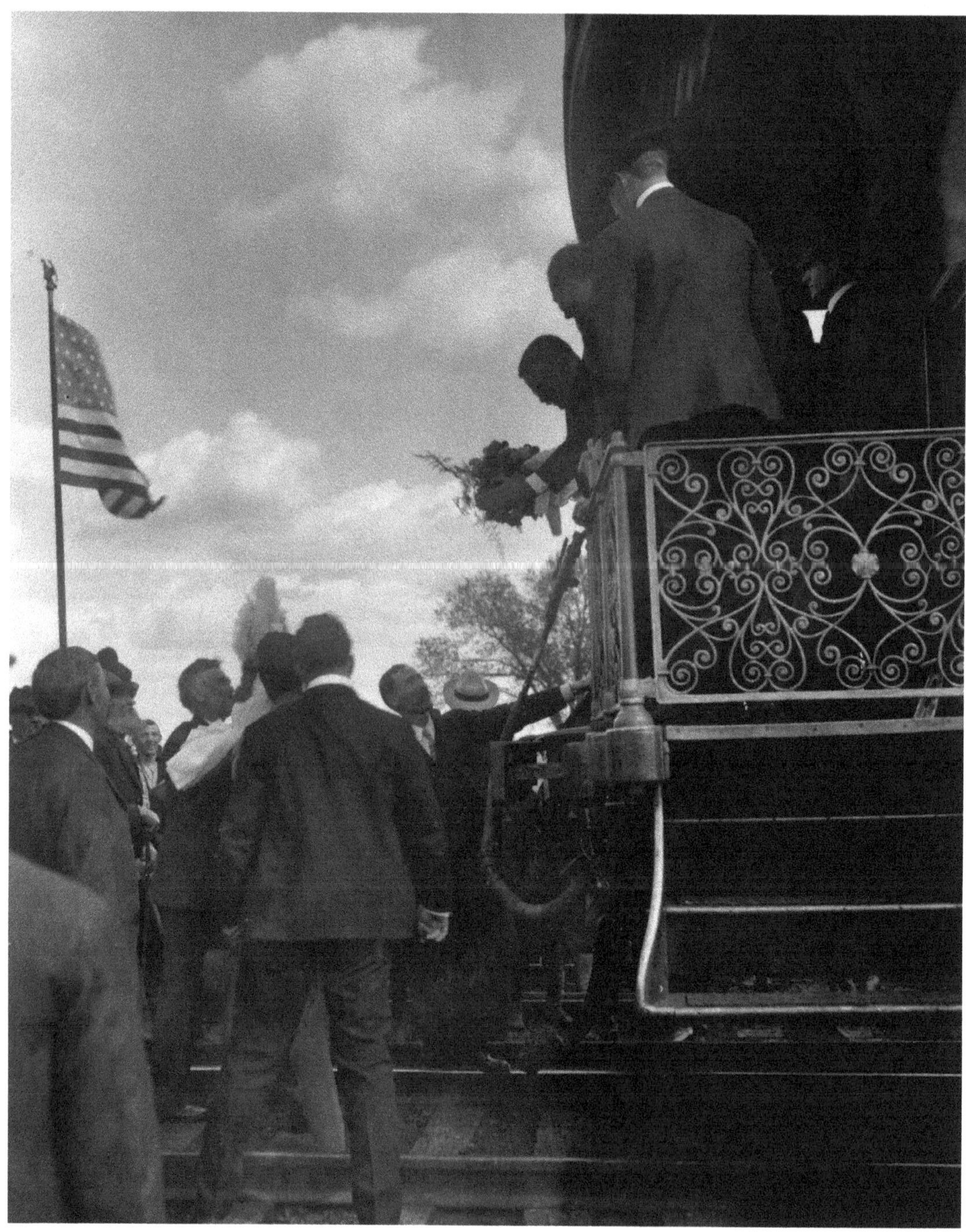

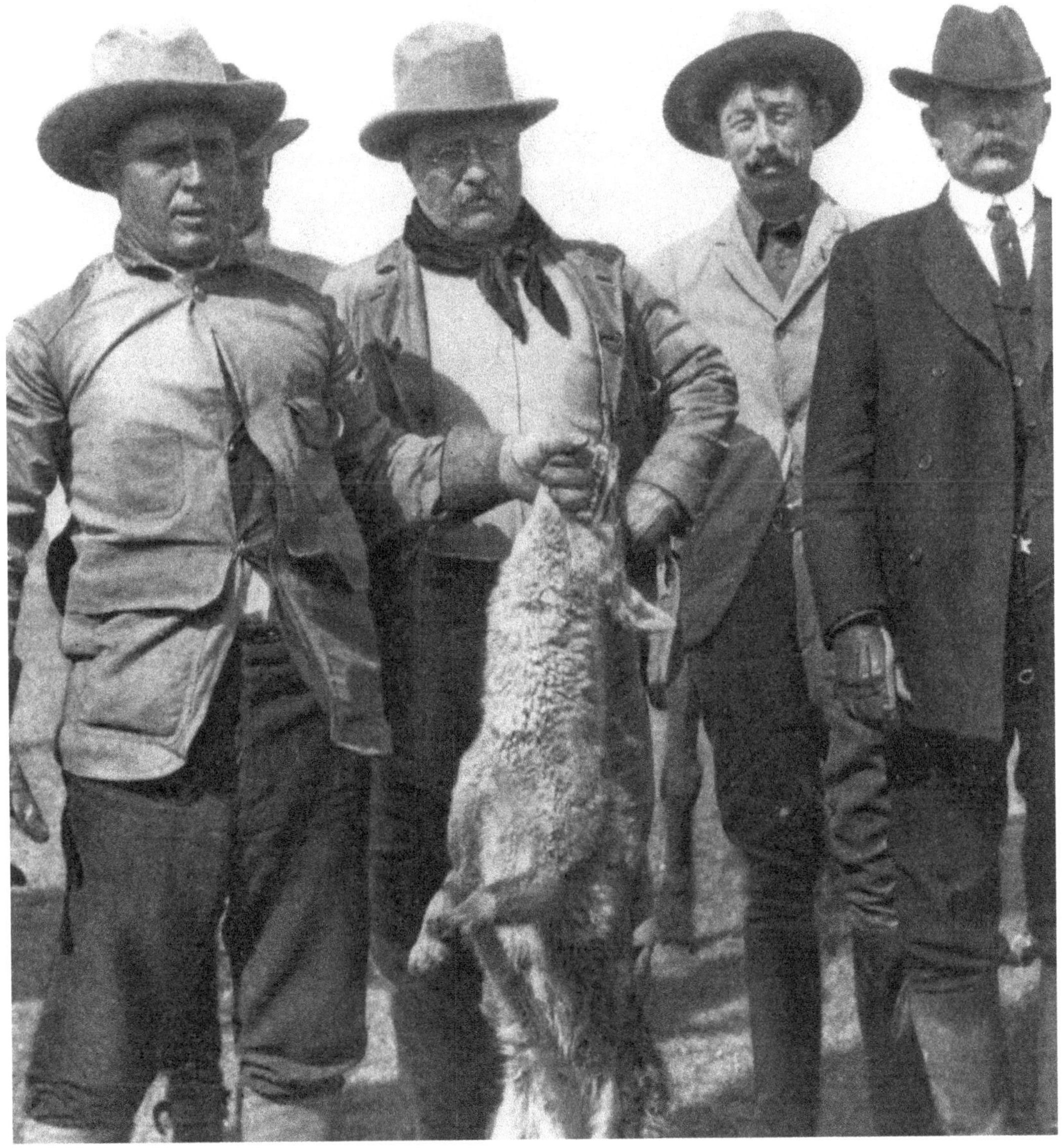

Another acquaintance, Jack Abernethy, hosted a coyote hunt for President Roosevelt. Abernethy is holding one of the seventeen coyotes TR crowed about to his son Ted in a letter of April 20, 1905. Roosevelt also shot a black bear on the Oklahoma trip. When Oklahoma became a state in 1907, President Roosevelt signed the proclamation. That year he also created the first federal game reserve there, the Wichita Mountain Wildlife Refuge.

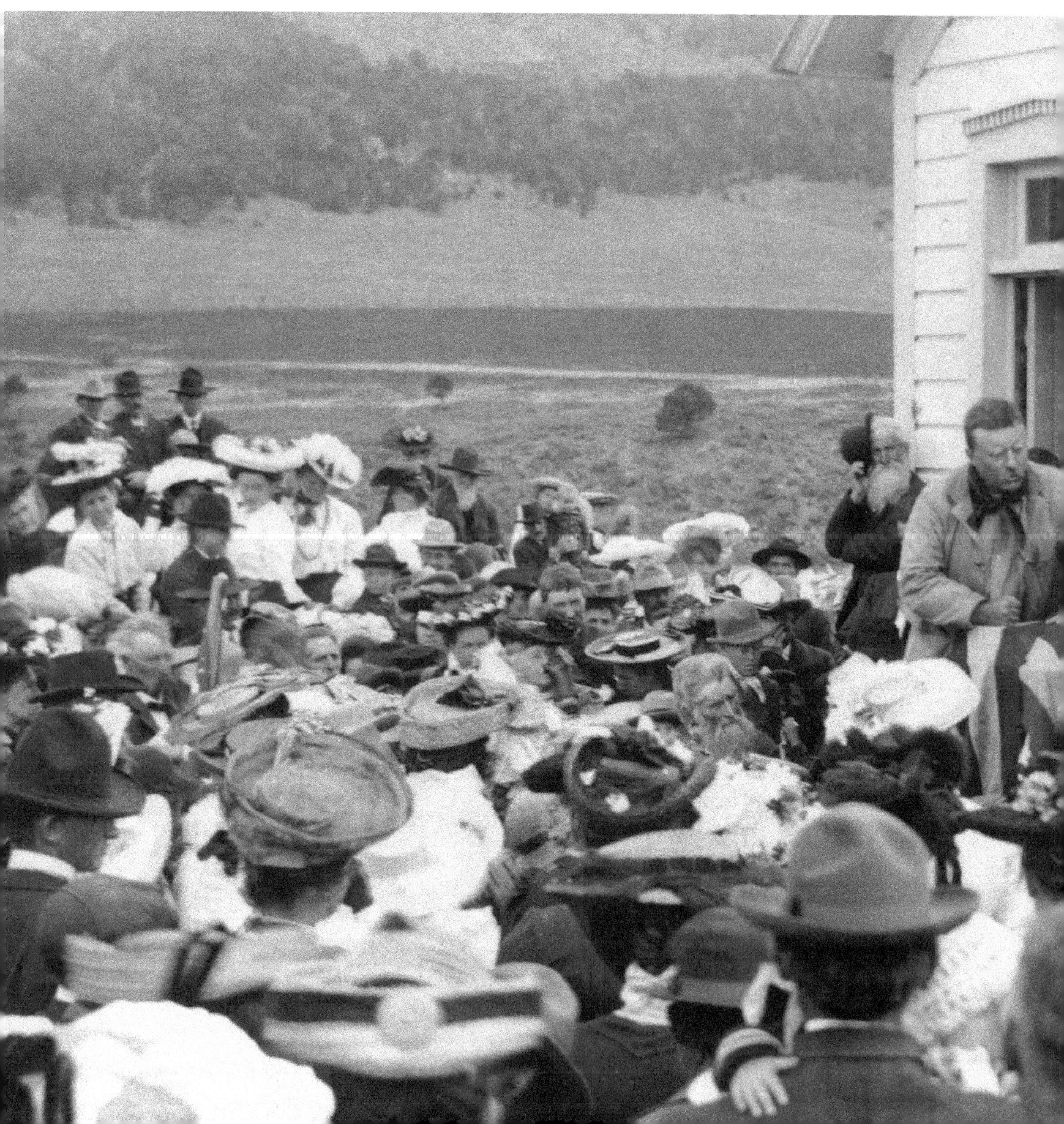

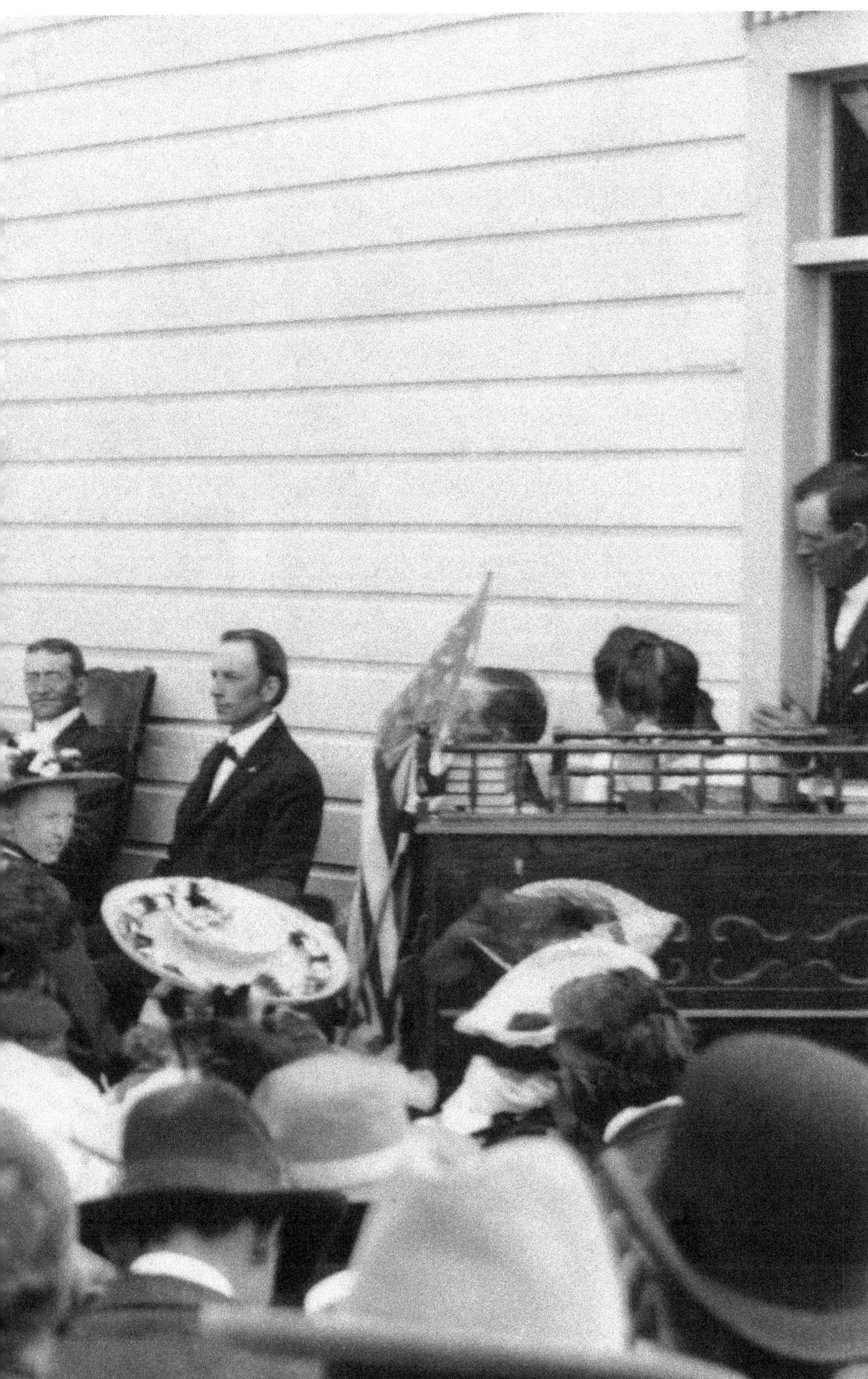

President Roosevelt speaking to a mixed crowd of men and women in Rifle, Colorado, in 1905. Western women gained suffrage before their eastern sisters, and in Colorado, women had been voting since 1893. While Roosevelt believed it was a woman's duty to produce children, he also believed in women's full legal equality. He embraced suffrage because so many of the female social reformers with whom he worked did. In 1912, TR would be the first major presidential candidate to back woman's suffrage.

Roosevelt spent twenty days hunting bear and bobcat in Colorado in the spring of 1905. Roosevelt saw that the numbers of big game animals had decreased since he had first hunted in the West. Consequently, in Colorado alone, he created seventeen national forests and established the Mesa Verde National Park.

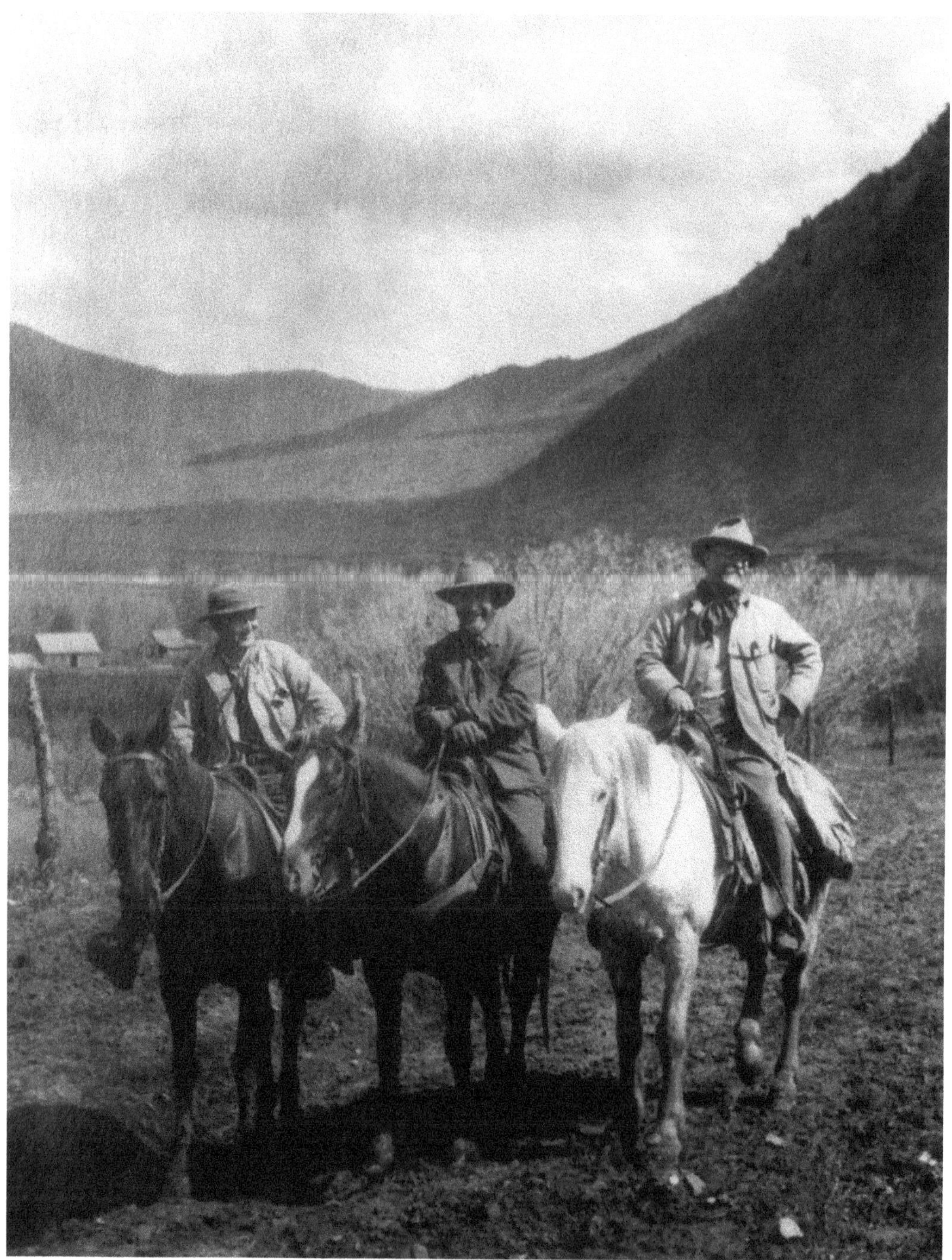

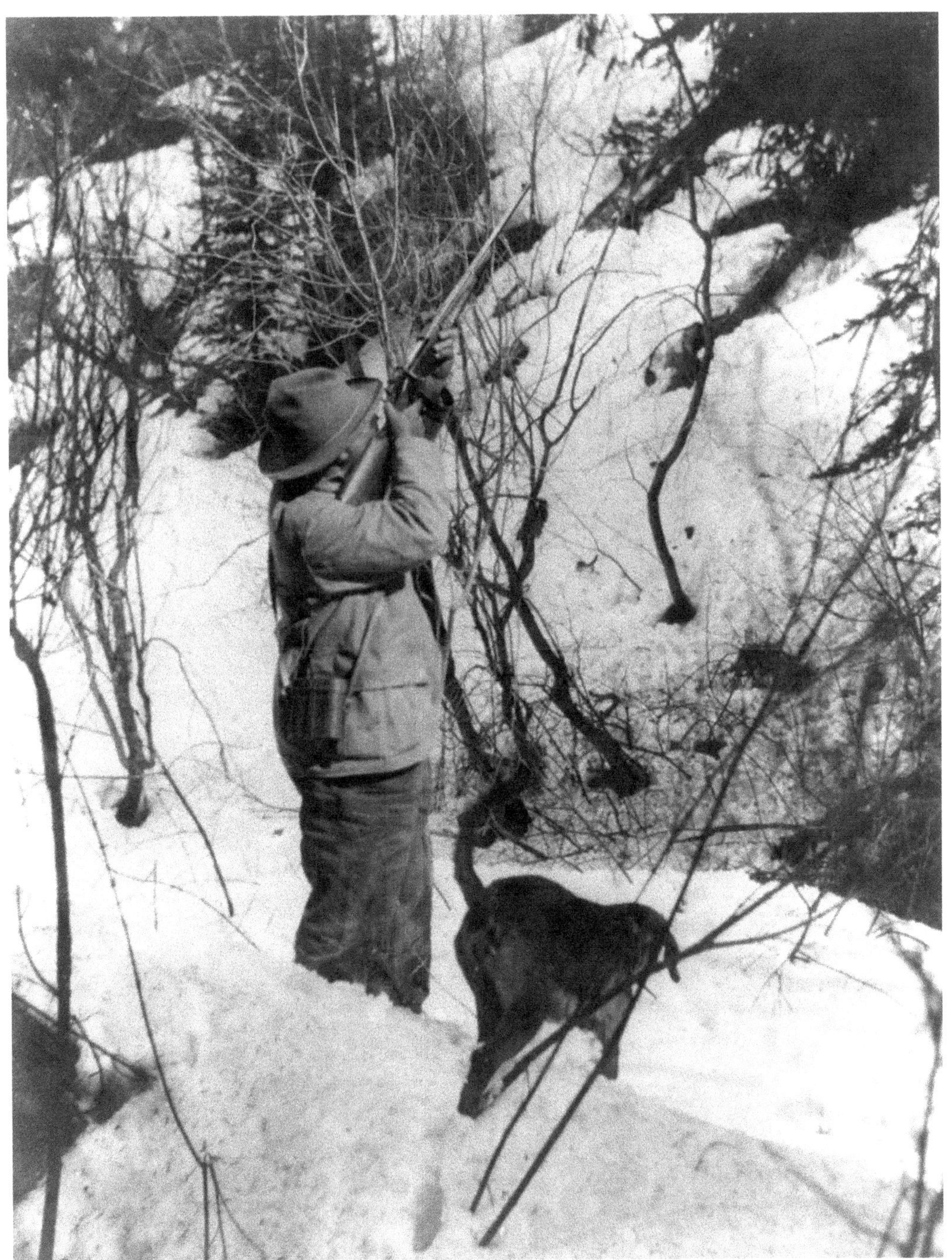

Roosevelt did enjoy bear hunting when the bear was able to put up a good fight. Before he became president, TR had established himself as an authority on the pleasures and responsibilities of hunting in books like *Hunting Trips of a Ranchman* (1885), *Ranch Life and the Hunting-Trail* (1888), and *The Wilderness Hunter* (1893). In his autobiography he recounts one "narrow escape" from a grizzly bear.

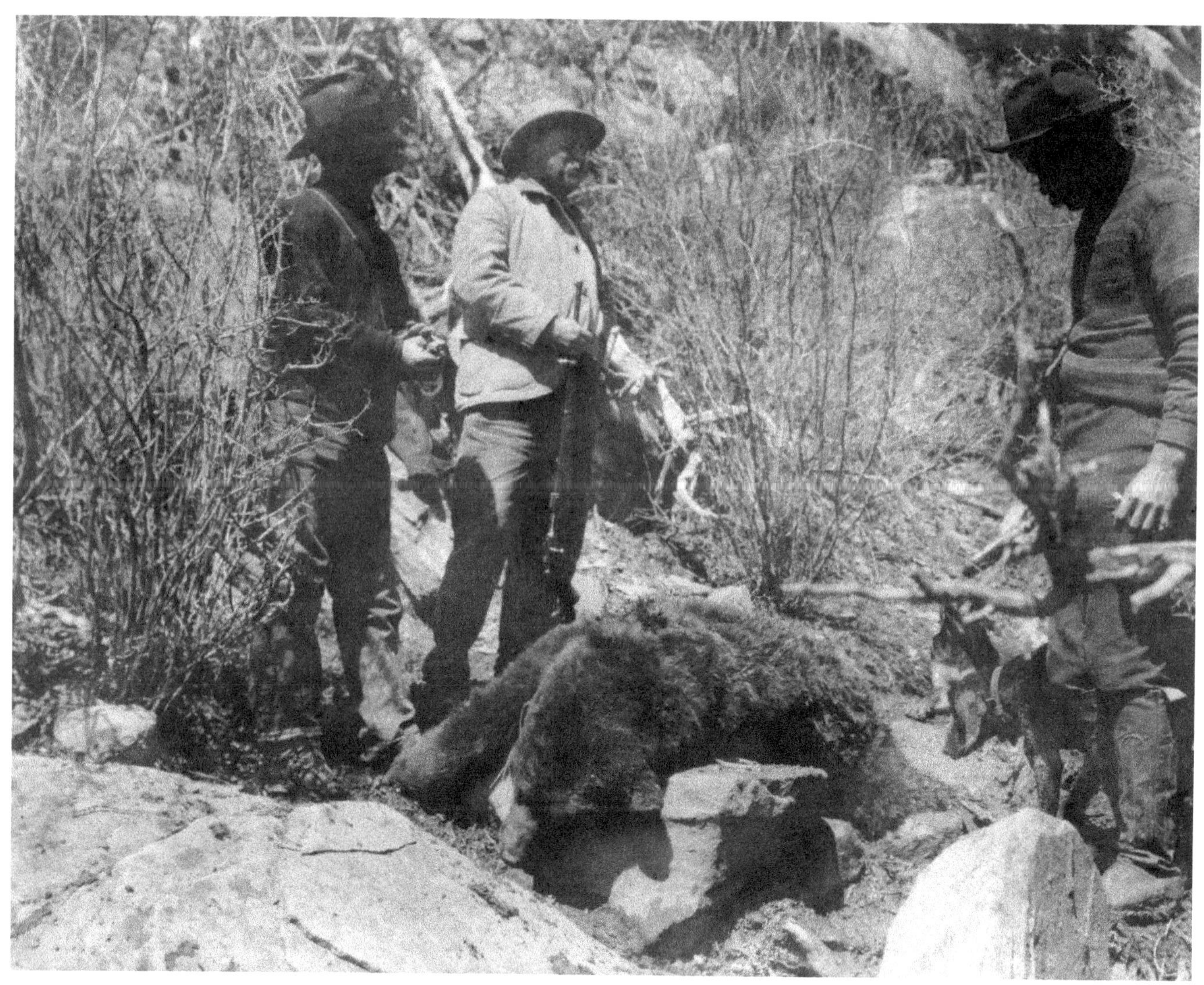

Roosevelt with his trophy, at West Divide Creek in Colorado, in April or May of 1905. TR considered cool-headedness the essential trait of the big game hunter, but admitted that it came only with practice.

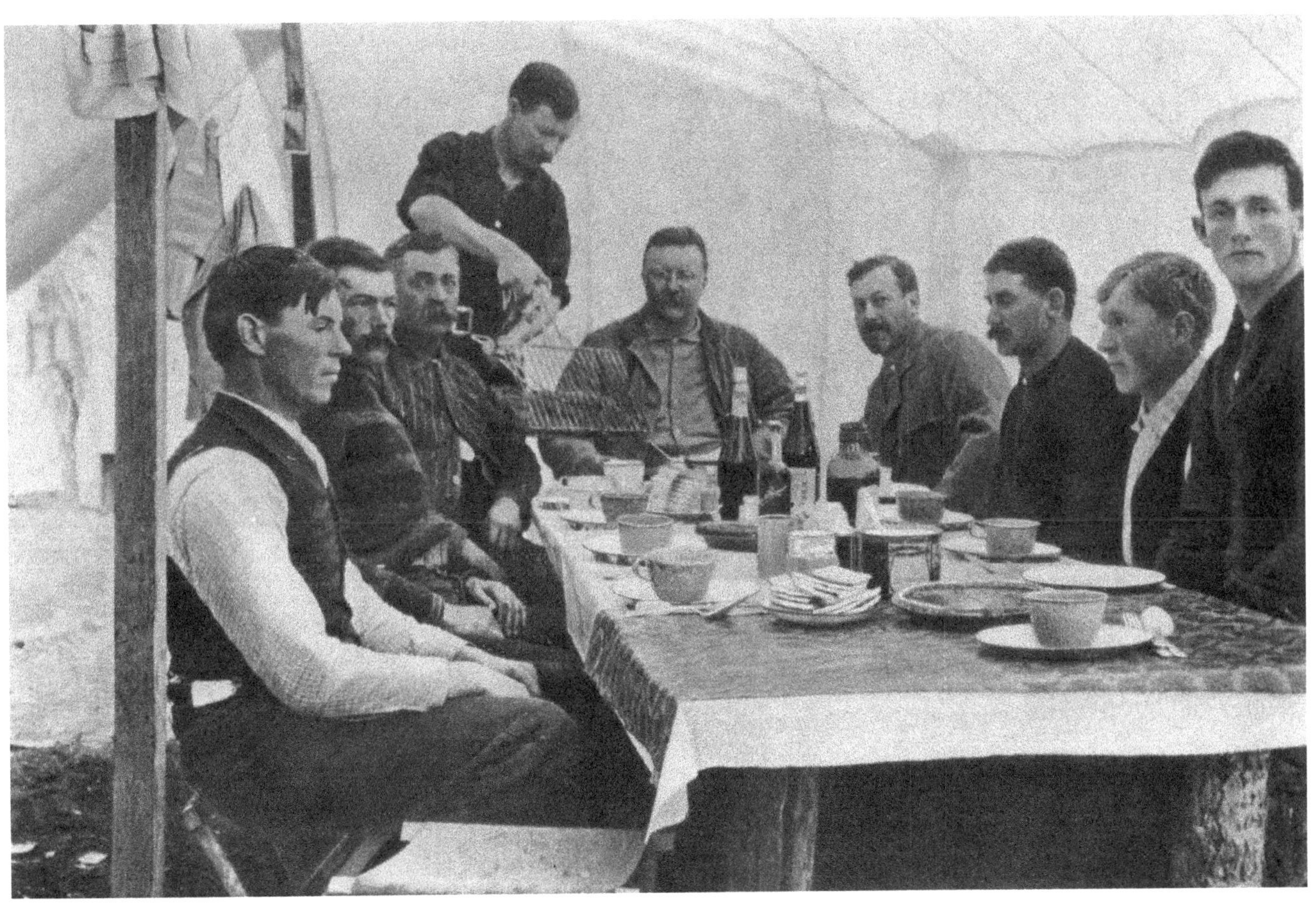

Seated at the head of the dining table, Roosevelt shares a victory supper with the men who accompanied him on the Colorado bear hunt.

Skip the terrier sits contentedly while TR reads during a break in the Colorado bear-hunting trip. In his autobiography, Roosevelt declared that "among those men whom I have known, the love of books and the love of outdoors, in their highest expressions, have usually gone hand in hand."

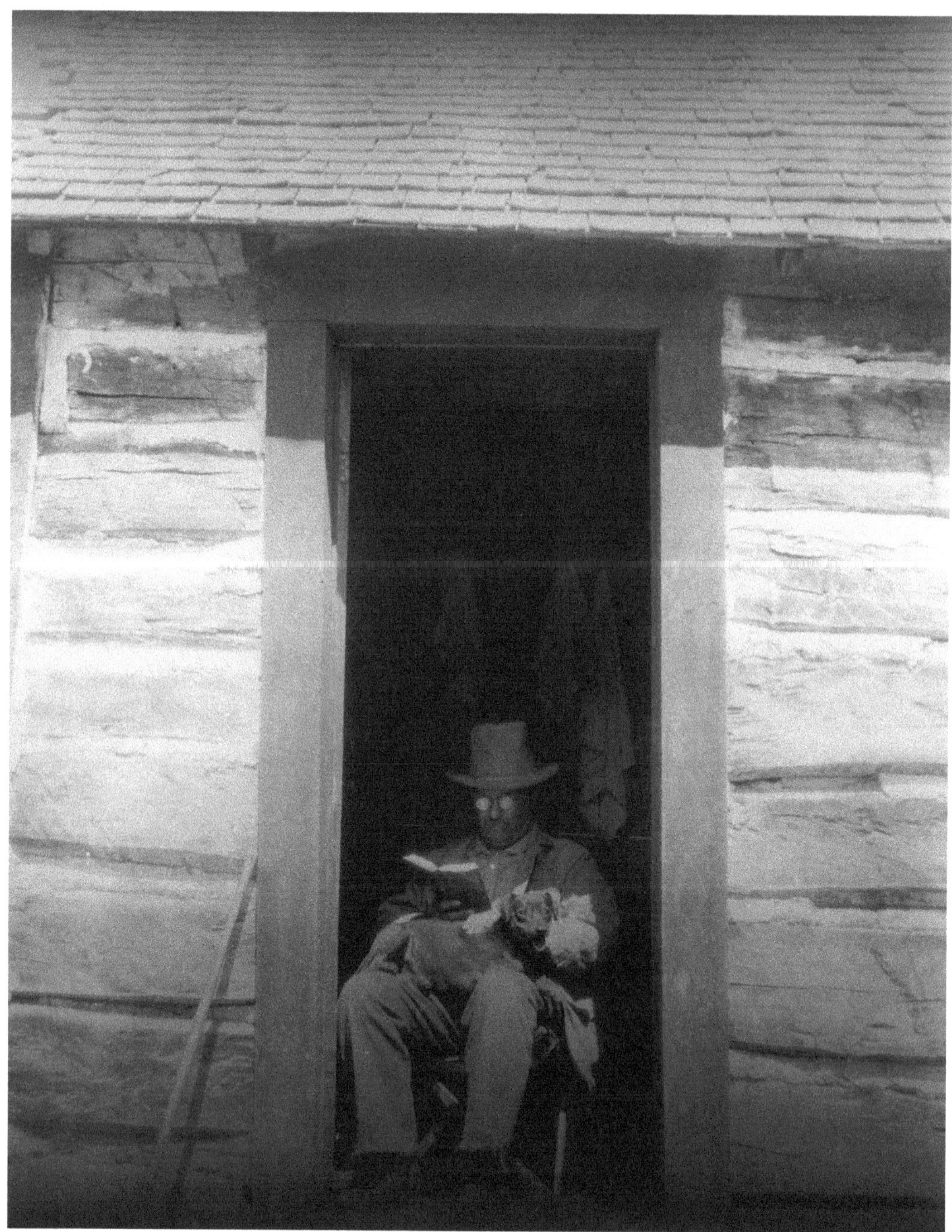

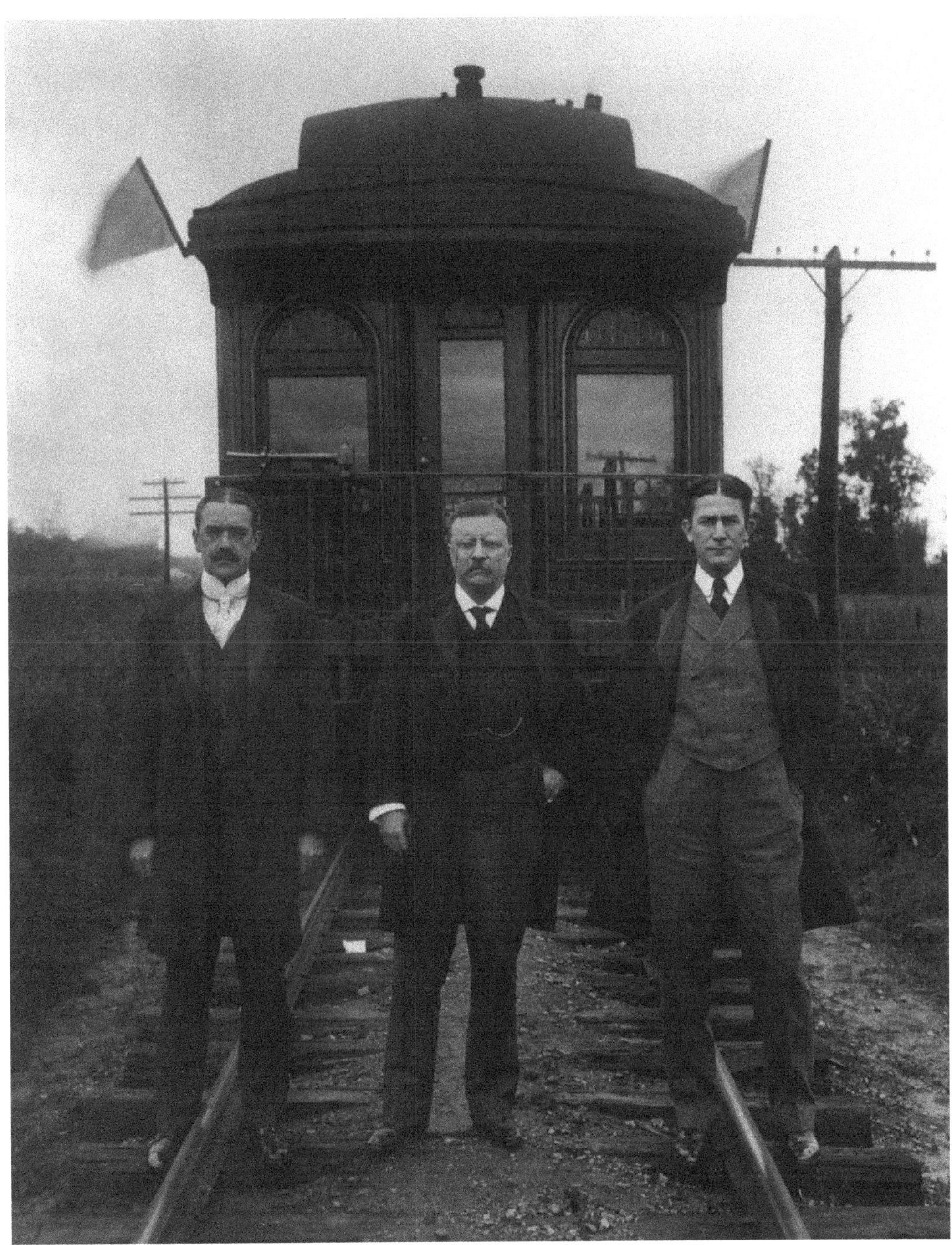

John Avery McIlhenny, Theodore Roosevelt, and John C. Greenway, on the railroad tracks near Little Rock, Arkansas, in October 1905. McIlhenny and Greenway had been Rough Riders in Cuba with Roosevelt and remained family friends. McIlhenny, a Democrat, was the scion of the famous Louisiana Tabasco sauce maker and a Louisiana state senator TR placed on the United States Civil Service Commission in 1906. Greenway was born in Alabama and worked in the mining industry in Arizona.

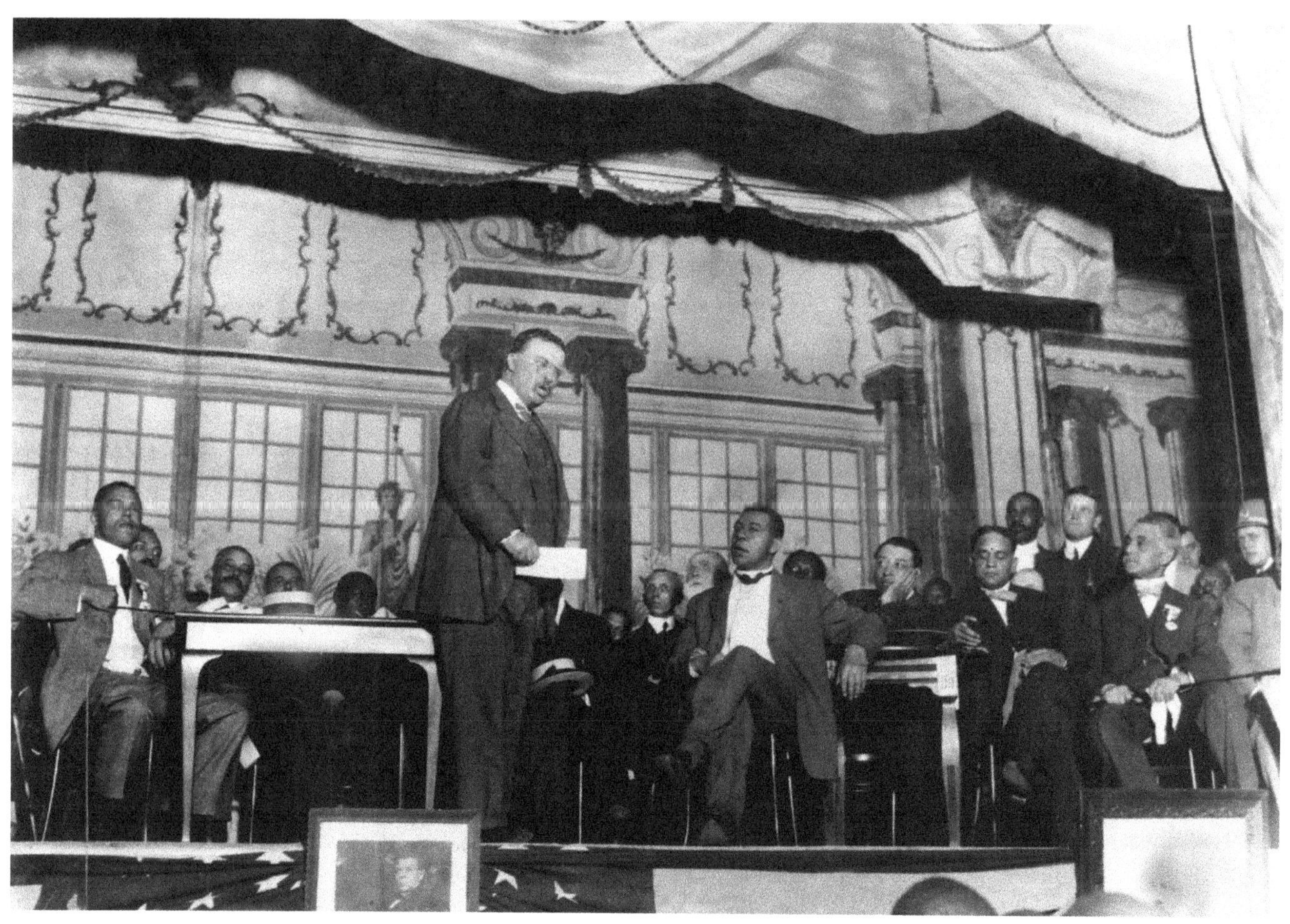

In October 1905, powerful author and educator Booker T. Washington invited Roosevelt to speak at Tuskegee Institute, the school for African Americans Washington founded in 1881. The two men consulted each other on appointments of interest to blacks and enjoyed a cordial relationship. Washington was furious when TR dishonorably discharged the African American soldiers at Brownsville without evidence of their guilt in 1906. By 1910, Roosevelt was serving on Tuskegee's Board of Directors at Washington's invitation.

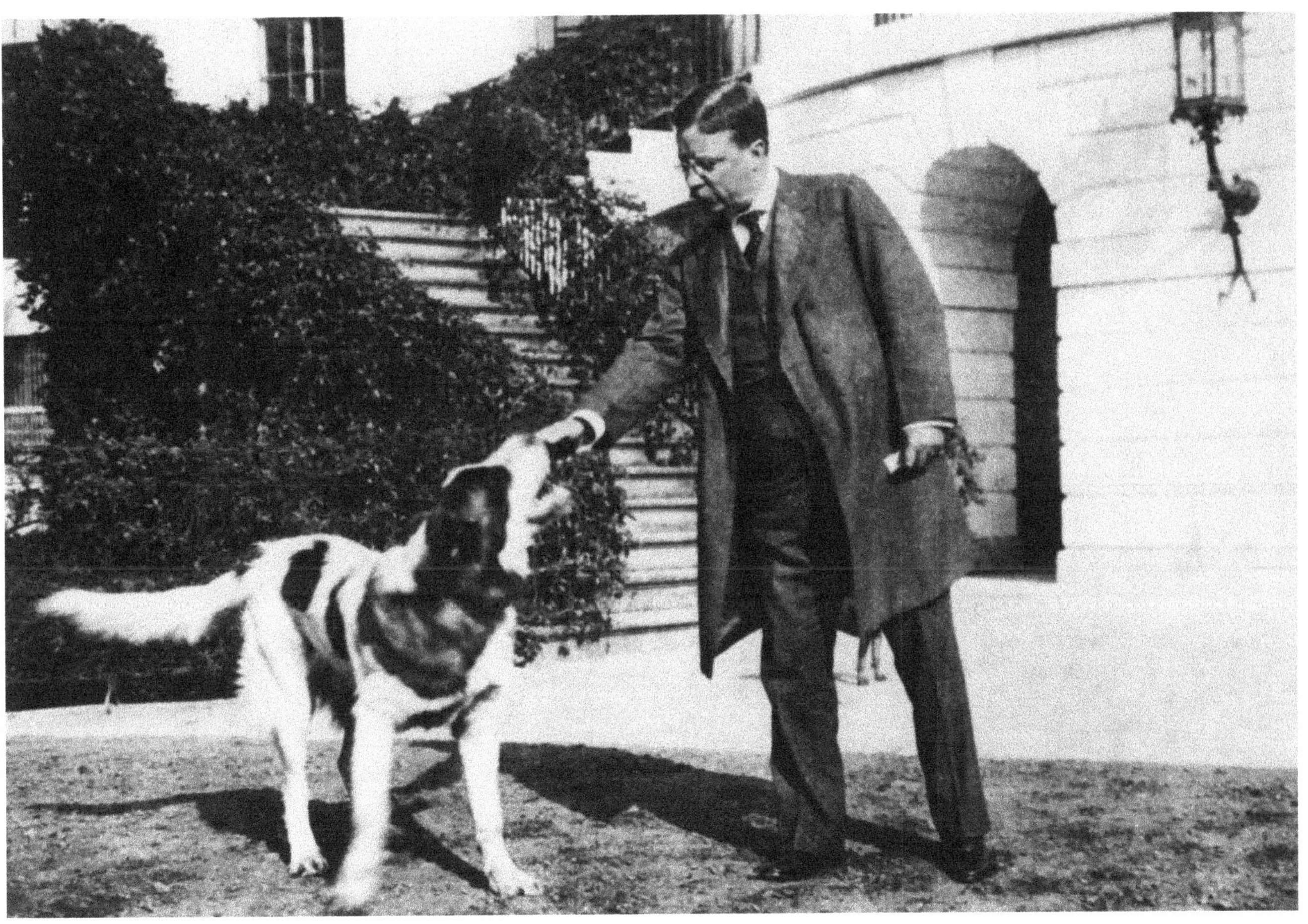

President Roosevelt outside the White House with his Saint Bernard, Rollo. The Roosevelt family members owned a disparate group of animals, among them Emily Spinach, Alice's green snake; Eli Yale, the macaw; Pony Grant and Algonquin, the ponies; Josiah, the badger; Bill, the lizard; Jonathan Edwards, the black bear; Jack, Gem, and Sailor Boy, the dogs; Jonathon the rat; a flying squirrel; two kangaroo rats; several guinea pigs; and Tom Quartz, the kitten.

In late 1905, when this photograph was taken, President Roosevelt was pursuing the progressive ideal of the efficient and honest government by reorganizing the Forest Service; struggling with more railroad regulation in the Hepburn Act; advocating for the Burke Act, which would make it easier for Native Americans to own their own land and grant them citizenship when they did; and fine-tuning the Isthmian Canal Commission so they could get the Panama Canal built more expeditiously.

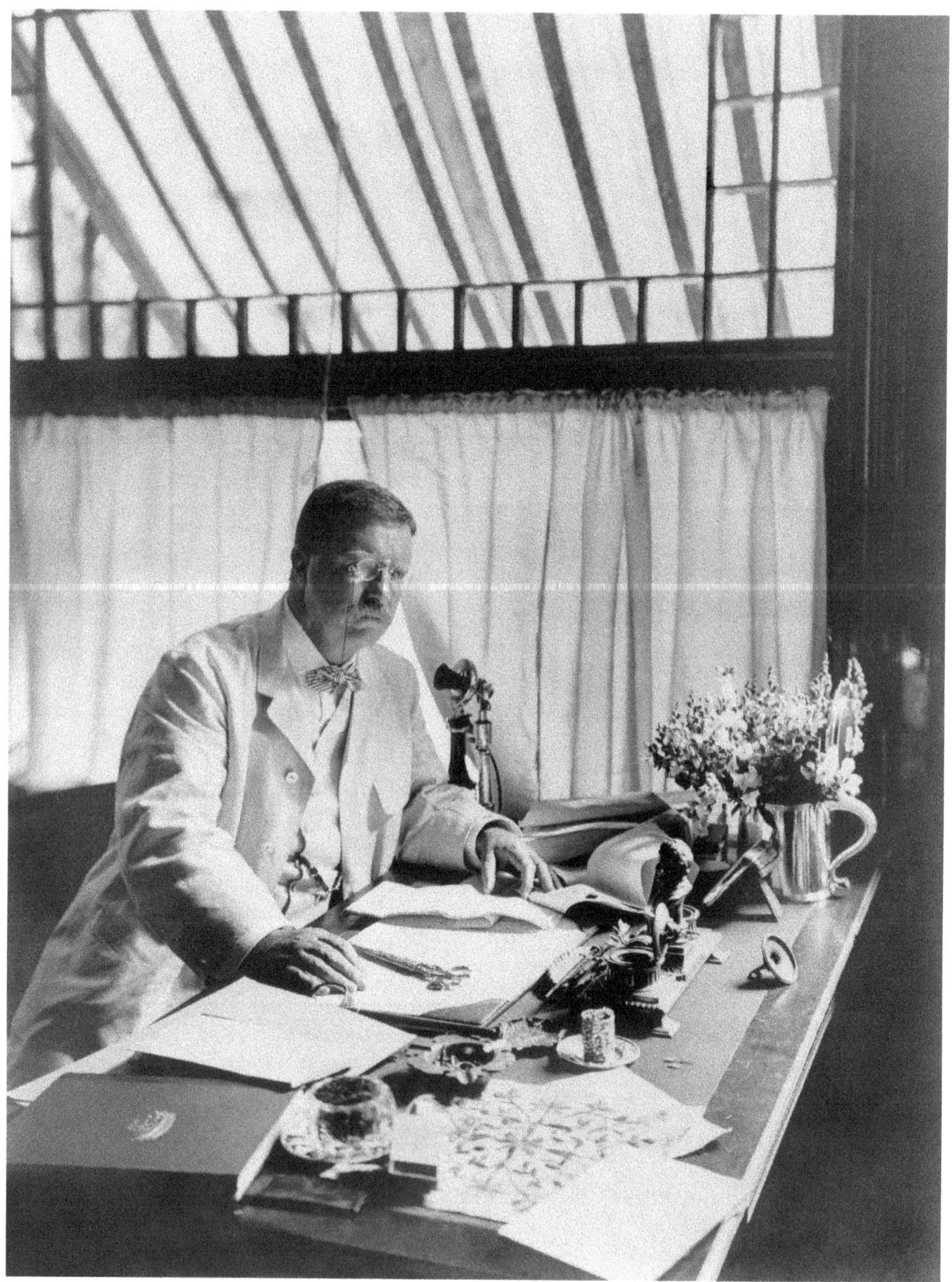

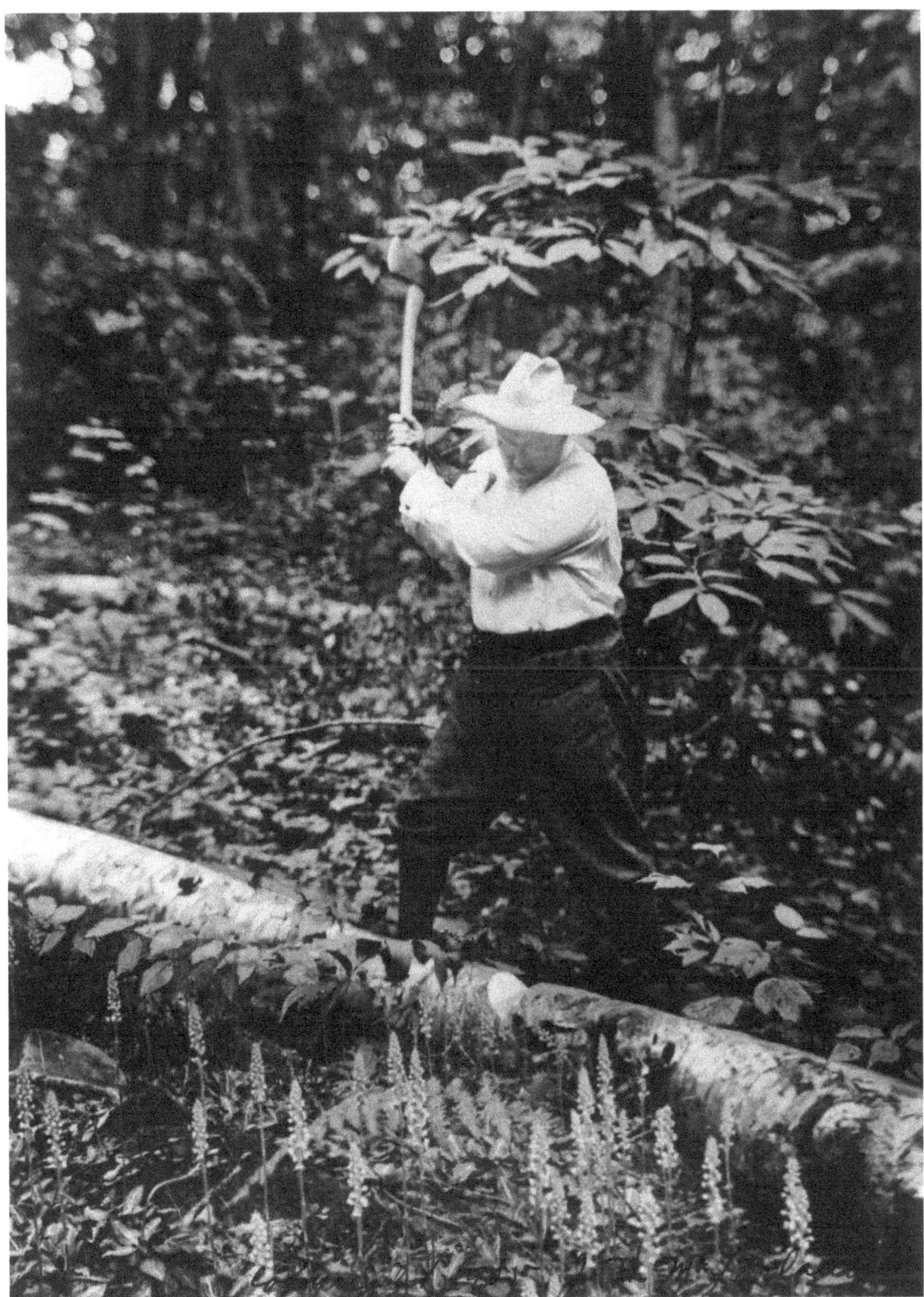

In his autobiography, Roosevelt professed his belief that "a man whose business is sedentary should get some kind of exercise if he wishes to keep himself in as good physical trim as his brethren who do manual labor." Chopping trees at Sagamore was one of Roosevelt's many physical pursuits, so natural to him that one of the first moving pictures ever made was of him chopping wood into logs.

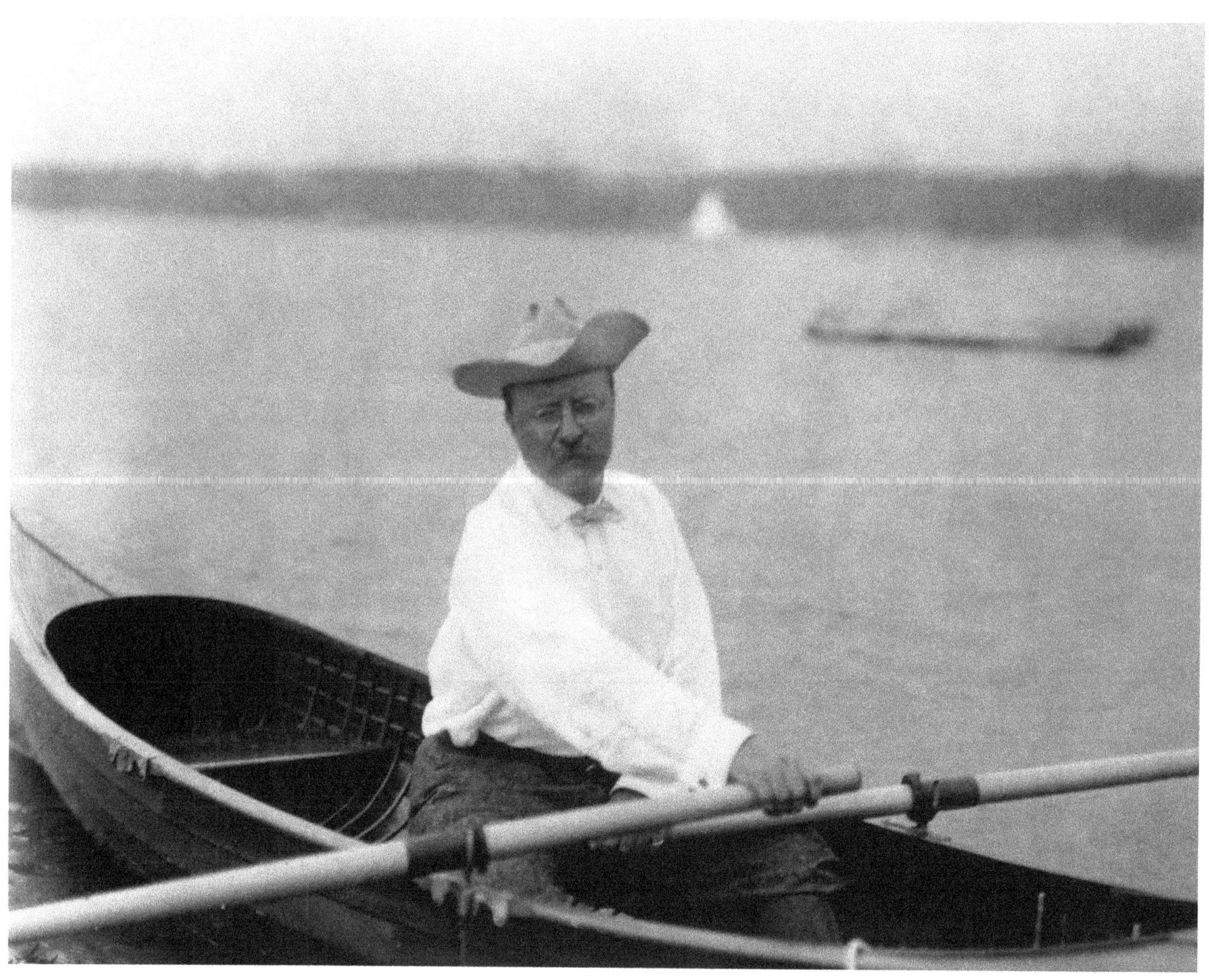

All his life Roosevelt preferred rowing to the less vigorous sailing, and all the Roosevelt cousins rowed happily through their summers at Oyster Bay.

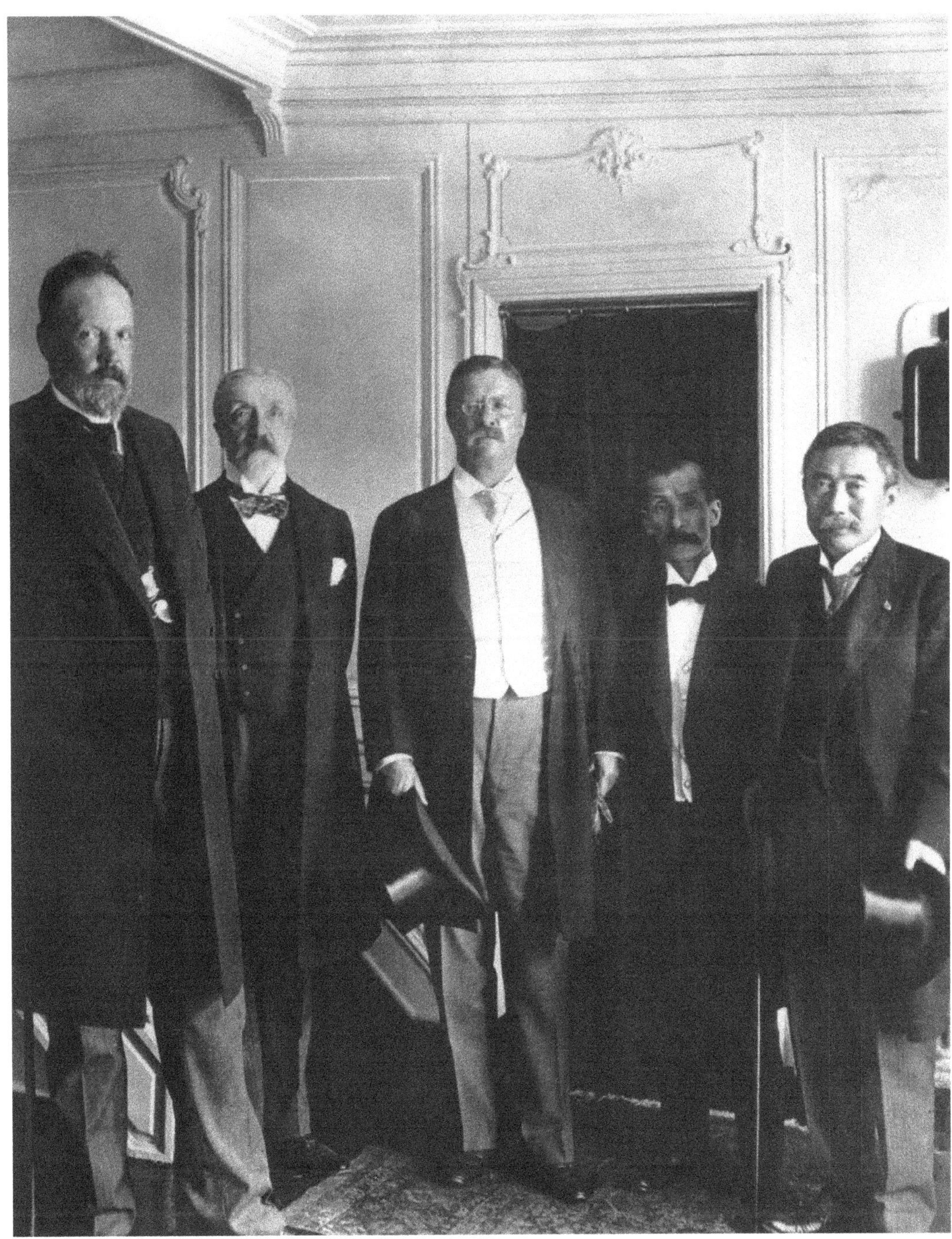

In February 1904, Japan attacked Russia and began the Russo-Japanese War. Although the U.S. remained neutral, the president wanted the result to be a balance of power in the Far East and so he became a mediator in the difficult peace process. For his help in the settlement of the Treaty of Portsmouth, Theodore Roosevelt won the Nobel Peace Prize in 1906. He was the first American to win the prestigious award.

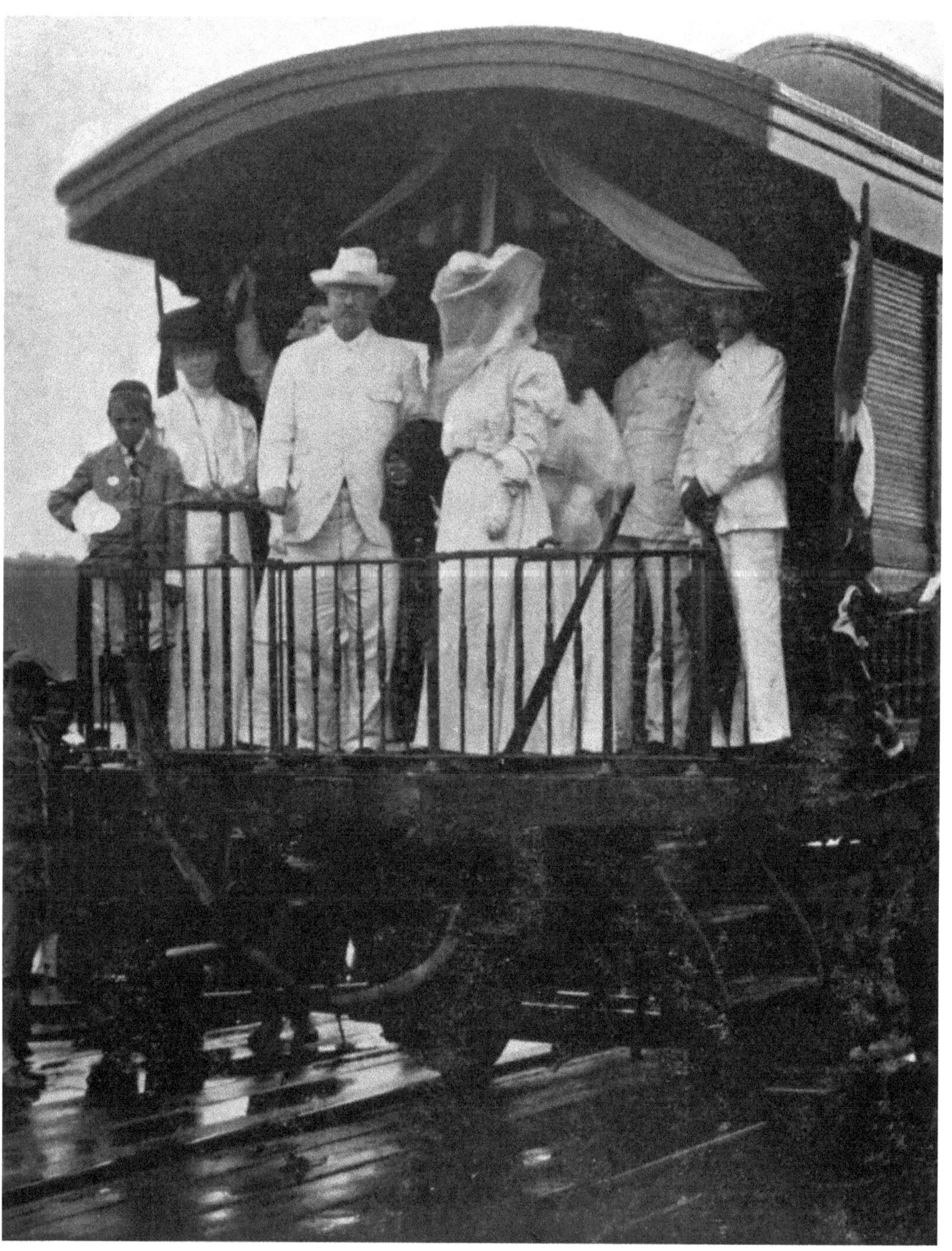

Roosevelt's 1906 trip to Puerto Rico and Panama made him the first president to leave the country while in office. His purpose in Panama was to inspect the progress of the Panama Canal building venture. This photograph is of Edith and Theodore Roosevelt and members of the presidential party at La Boca, the Pacific entrance of the canal.

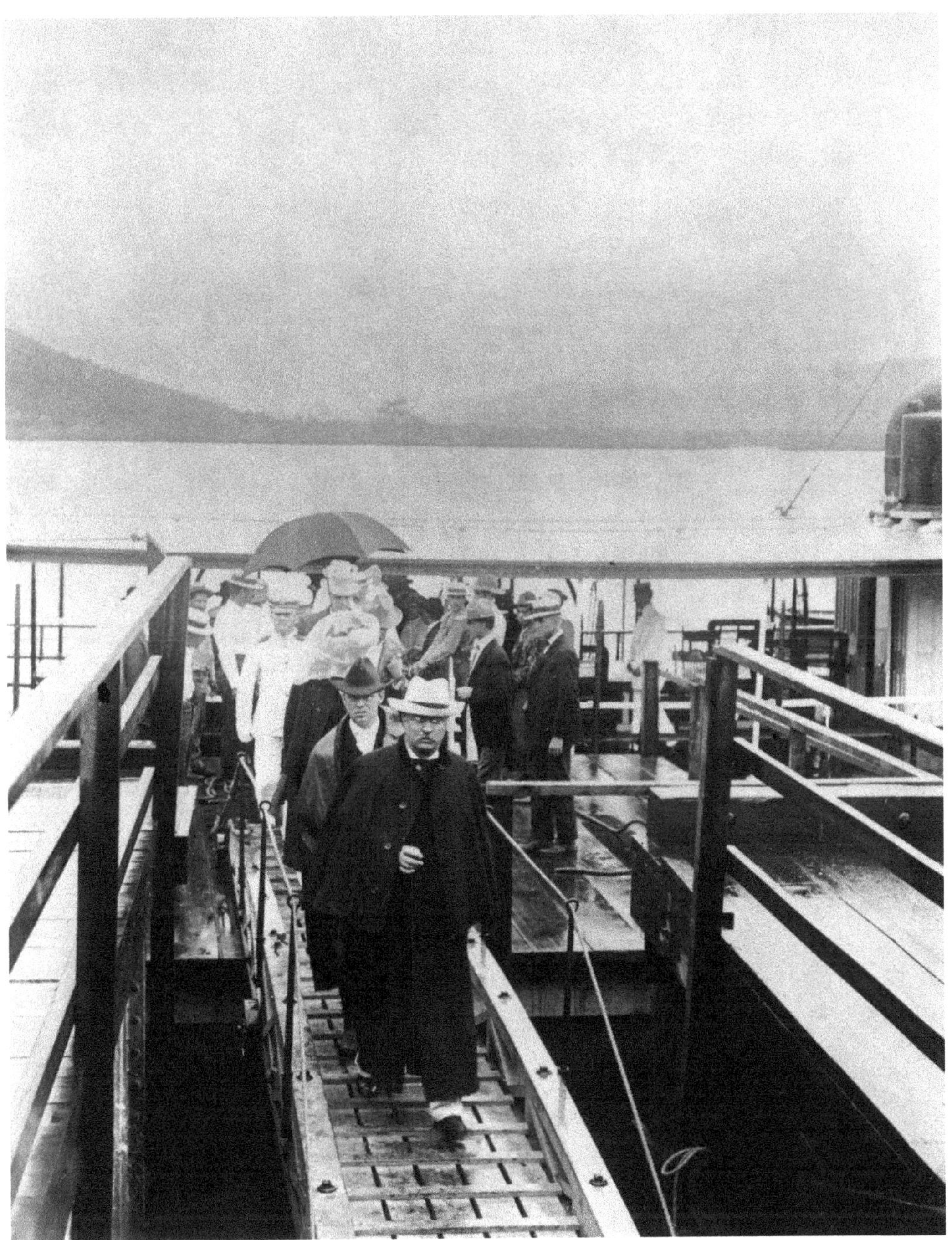

The Panama Canal was built to shorten the travel time for vessels crossing from the Atlantic to the Pacific. When Colombia rejected Roosevelt's deal, the administration turned to Panama, then a Colombian province. Roosevelt made the same offer to the Panamanians, who then declared their independence from Colombia, backed by the military presence of the U.S. Roosevelt is shown here walking up the gangplank at La Boca.

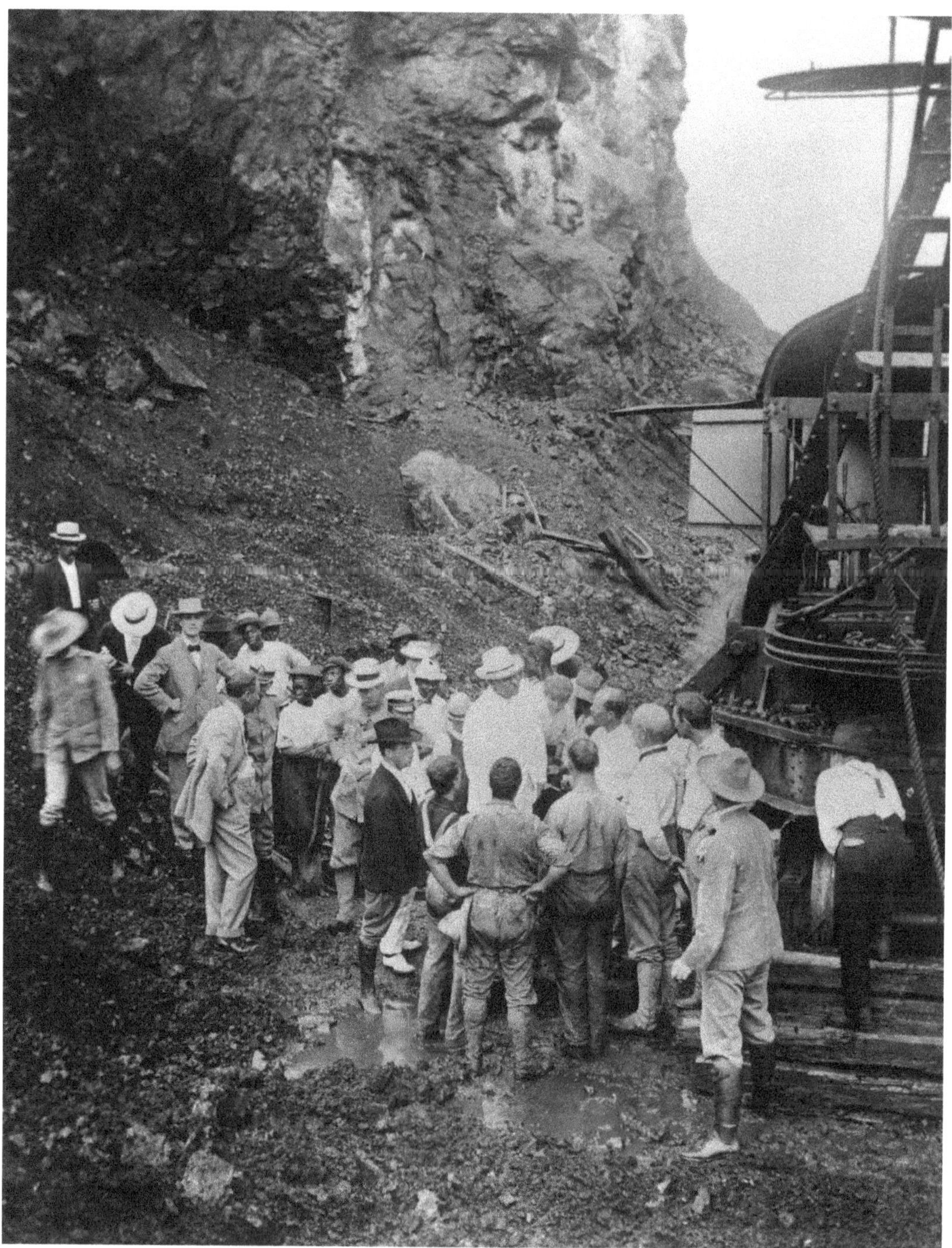

The presidential party at the Culebra Cut, the colossal engineering accomplishment that joins Lake Gatun on the Atlantic side to the Gulf of Panama on the Pacific side. The Culebra Cut was begun by French engineering teams in the 1880s and completed by Americans in 1913, after Roosevelt left office.

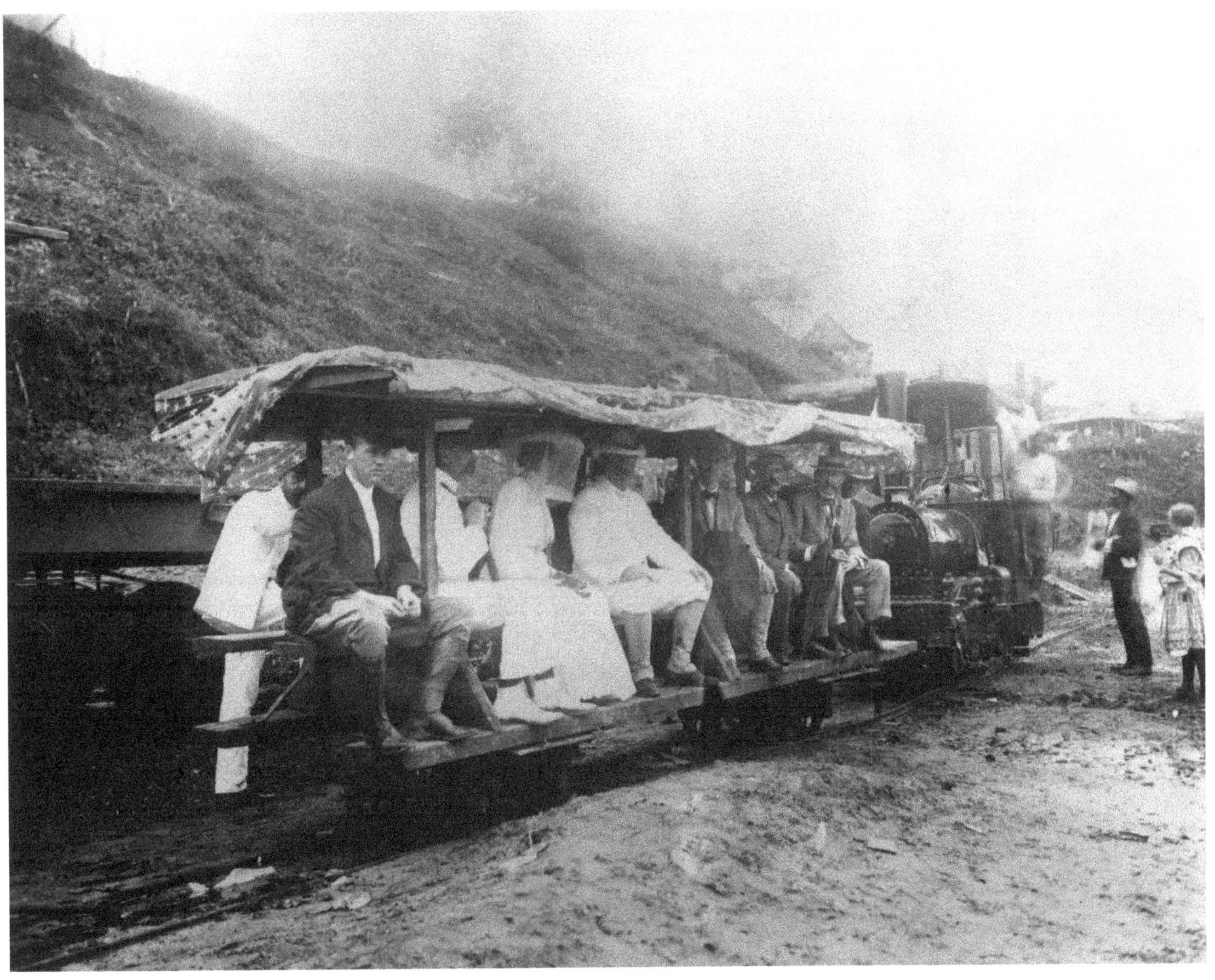

Edith and Theodore Roosevelt riding on the shuttle car at the Panama Canal site. The enormous building project transfixed Roosevelt, who took great pleasure in the work being done by men from the Antilles, Europe, and the U.S. TR also recognized the terrible human toll exacted by disease and accidents. In a letter to his son Kermit, Roosevelt called the canal building "an epic feat, and one of immense significance."

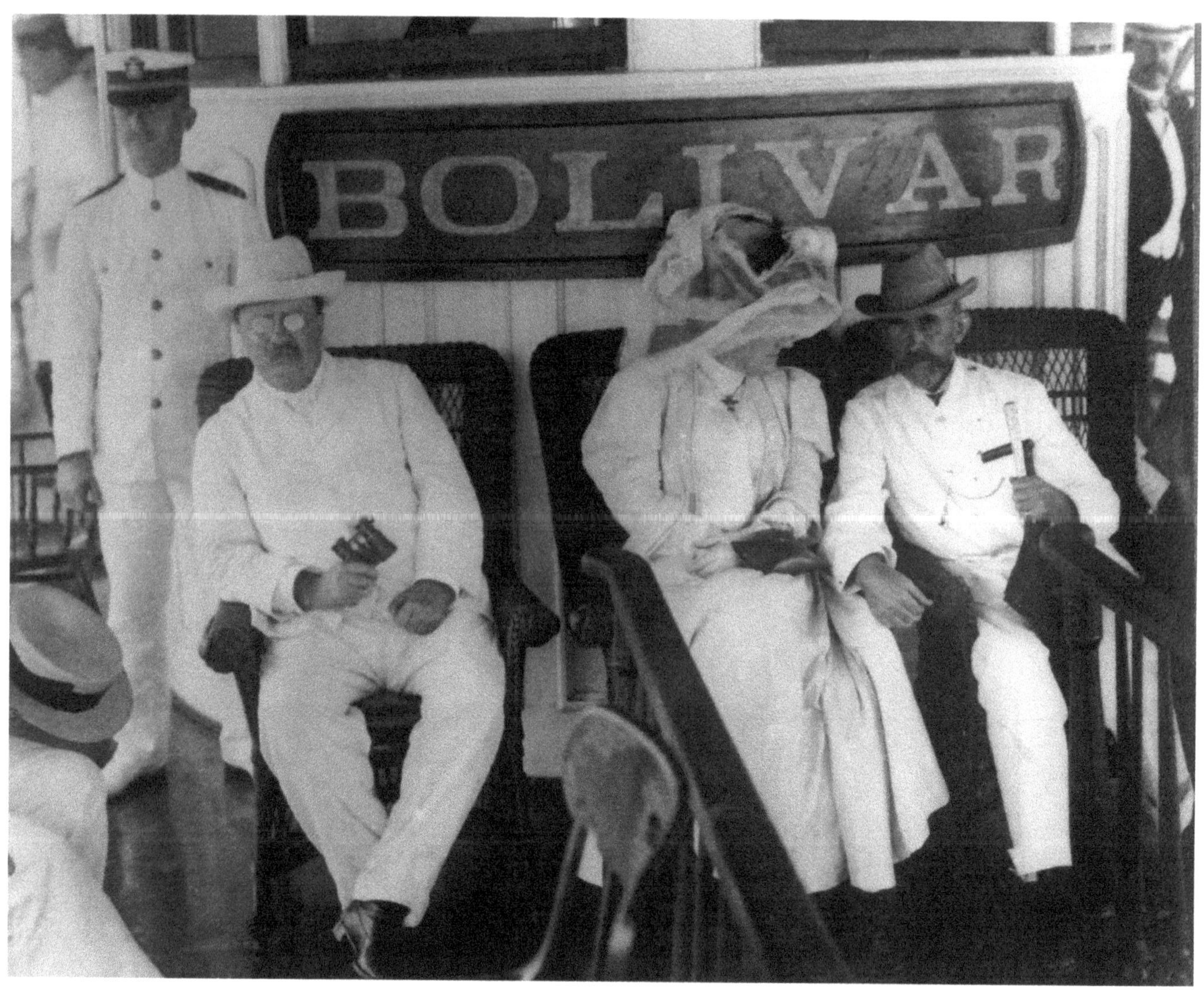

President Roosevelt and First Lady Edith Roosevelt aboard the *Bolivar* at the conclusion of their time in Panama. He returned home to congressional criticism of the work in the canal zone concerning the use of private contractors. Ultimately Roosevelt put the canal building into the hands of U.S. army major George W. Goethals, who completed the canal. The first ship passed through in 1914.

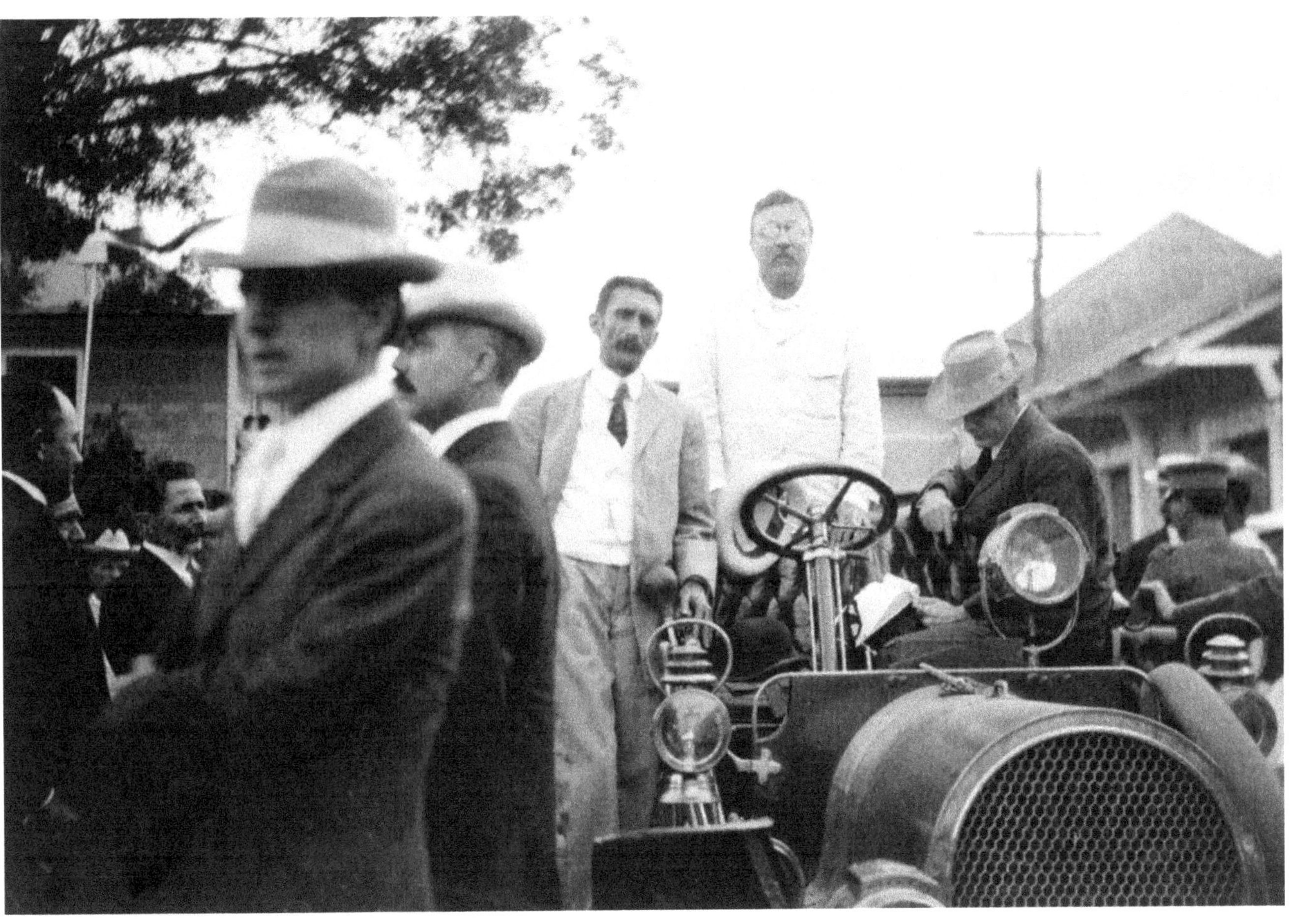

Roosevelt in Rio Piedras, Puerto Rico, 1906, which he visited after leaving Panama. The Roosevelts thought Puerto Rico surpassingly beautiful, but TR took a patriarchal view of its citizens, congratulating himself on the "good government" the U.S. was "giving them." TR did urge U.S. citizenship for Puerto Ricans, whose country had been an American territory since just after the Spanish-American War.

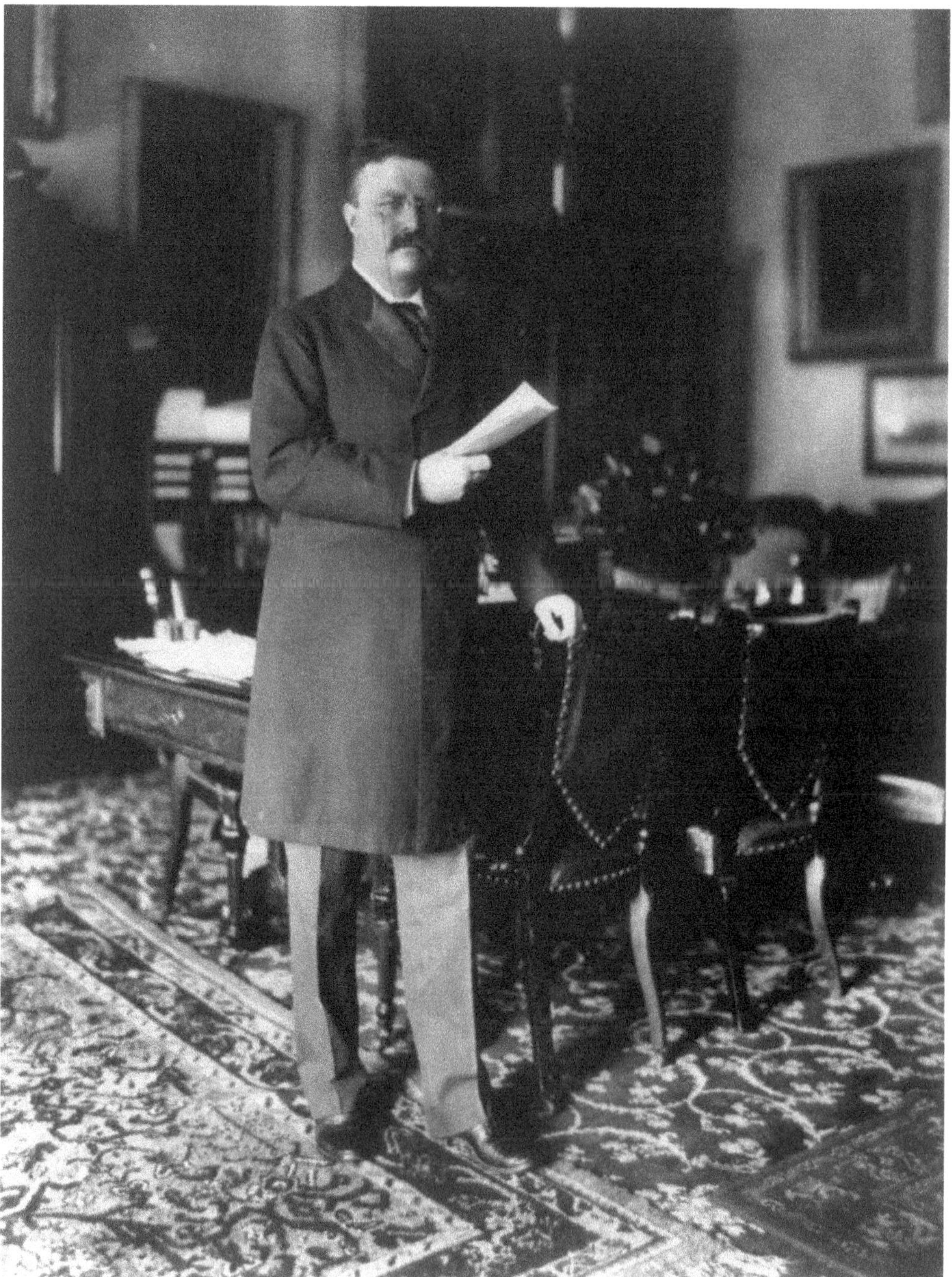

In 1907, as this official portrait photograph was taken, President Roosevelt could take credit for a significant record on environmental conservation, several important trust-busting cases, the successful settlement of the anthracite coal strike, the establishment of the Department of Commerce and Labor, the Panama Canal Treaty, legislation to curb unfair railroad practices, the Portsmouth Treaty, mediation of the Algeciras Conference, the Roosevelt Corollary, and critical consumer protection legislation.

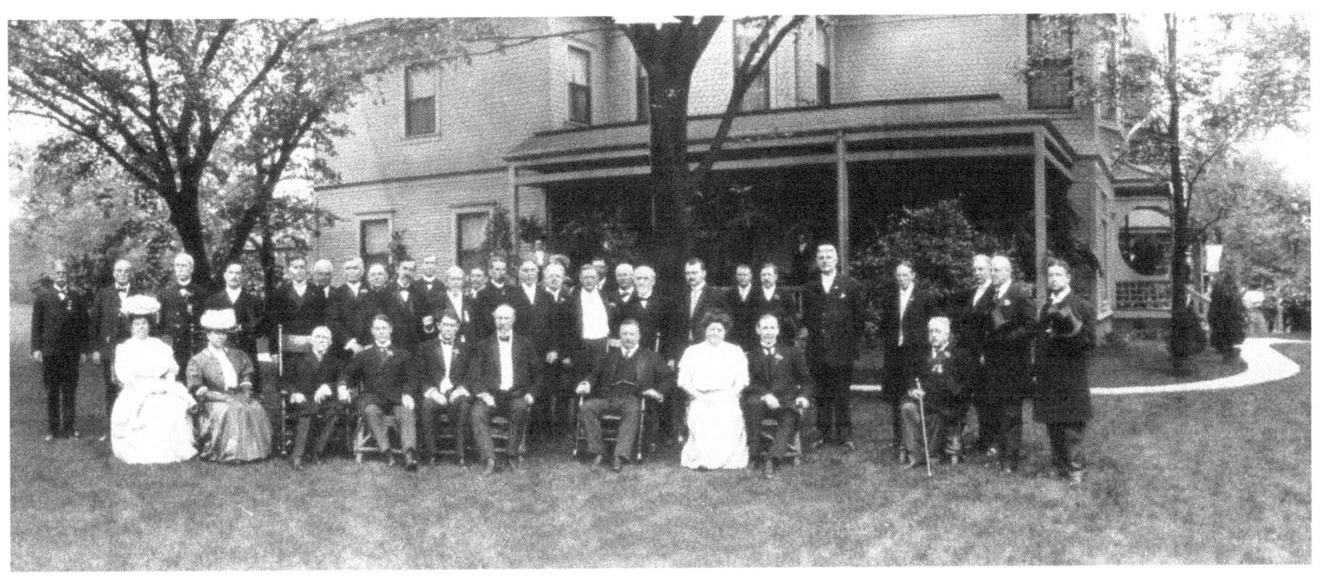

Vice-president Charles W. Fairbanks hosted President Roosevelt on May 30, 1907, at his home in Indianapolis. Fairbanks, a good friend of McKinley, had been a popular and ambitious senator before his election to the vice-presidency, which was brought about by the conservative wing of the G.O.P. "The Indiana Icicle," as he was called for his detached deportment, had few tasks given him by President Roosevelt, whose own political leanings were to the left of his second-in-command.

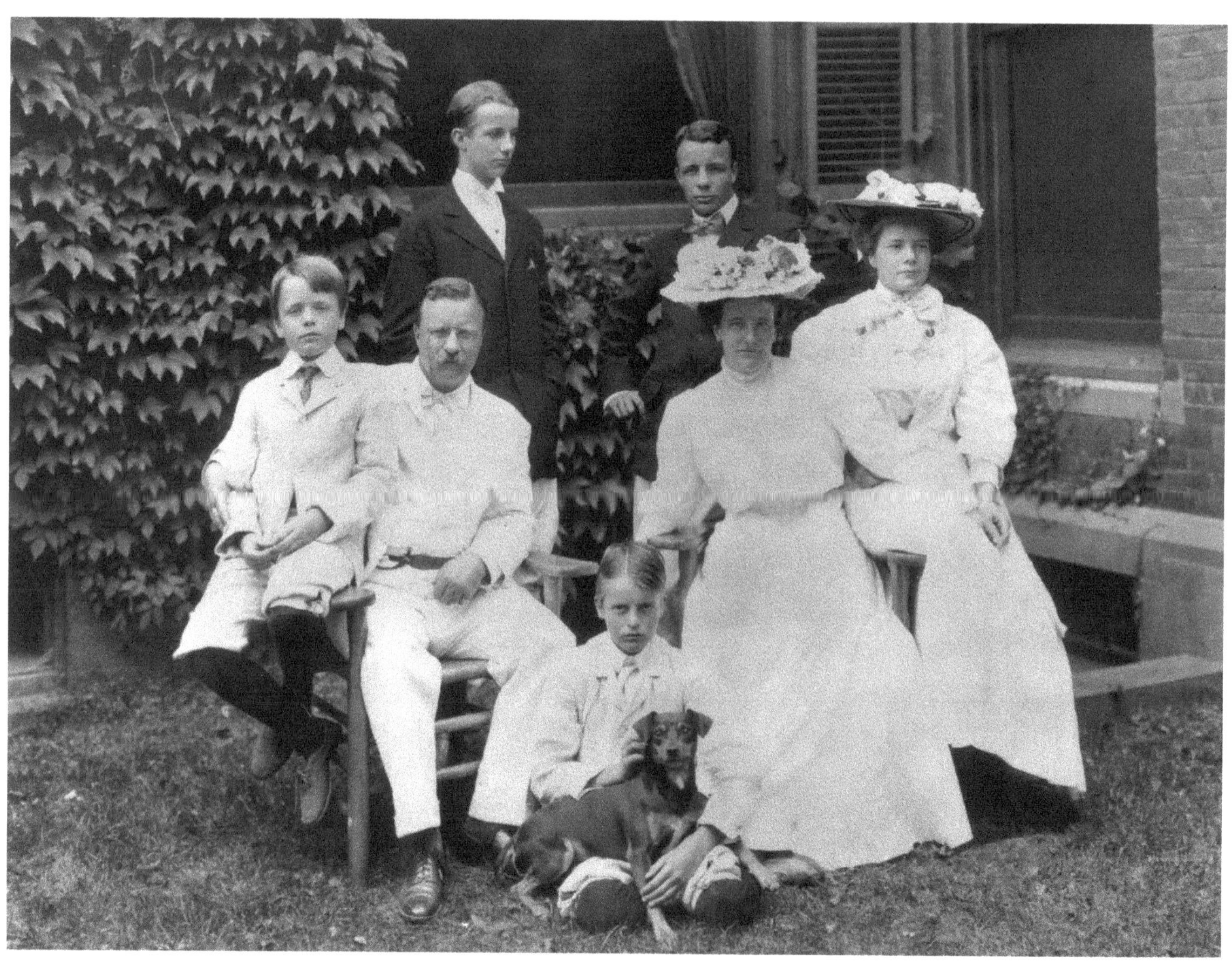

The most brilliant entertainment in the Roosevelt White House was Alice Roosevelt's February 1906 wedding to Ohio Representative Nicholas Longworth. This photo shows the Roosevelt family absent the celebrated "Princess Alice." Quentin, TR, Kermit, Archie, Ted, Edith, and Ethel are grouped here at Sagamore Hill. The dog is probably Skip.

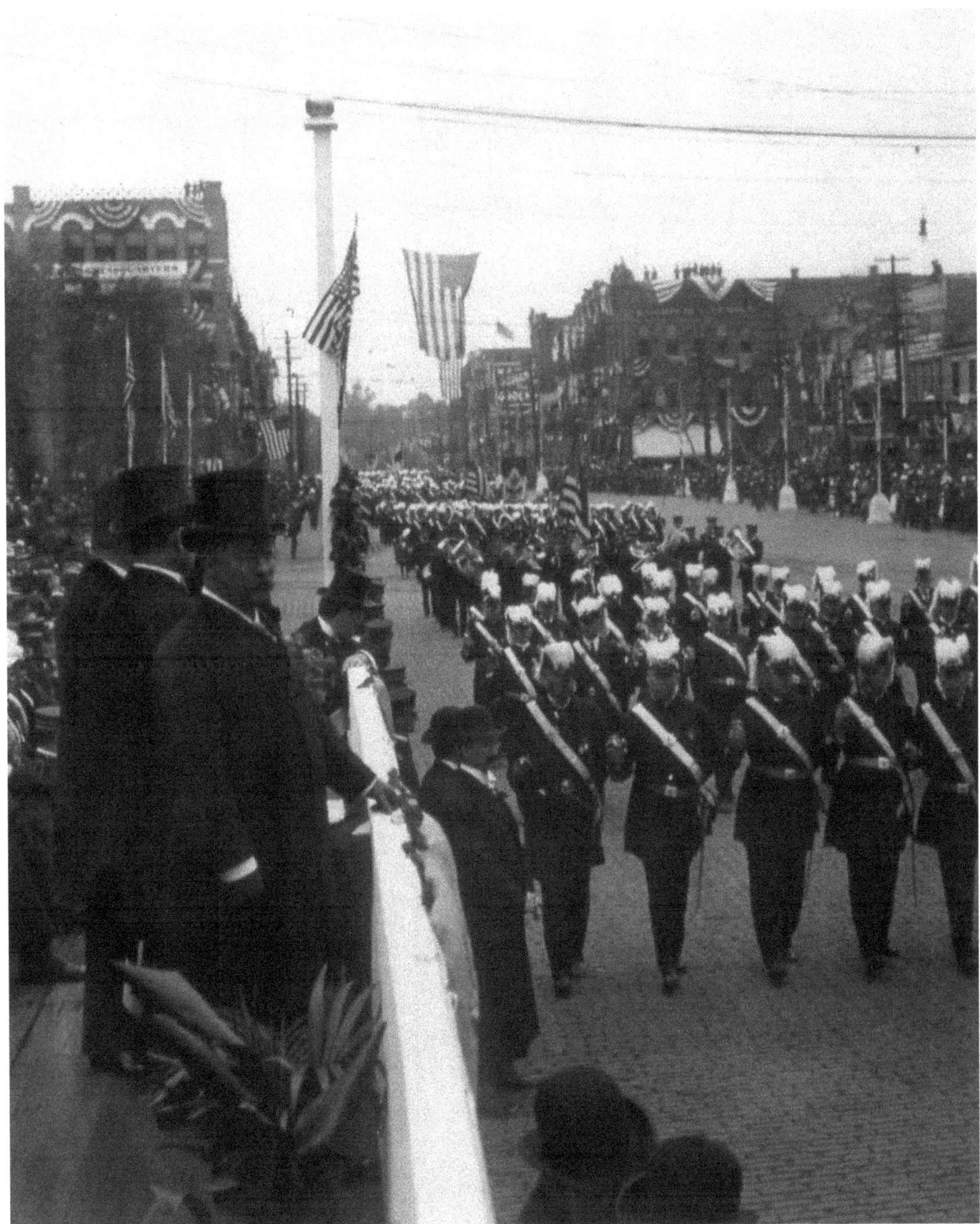

The parade in Canton, Ohio, was in memory of former president William McKinley, who had been assassinated six years earlier. Roosevelt is on the reviewing stand for the somber occasion.

President Roosevelt in a group photograph taken aboard the U.S.S. *Mississippi* on its way down the Mississippi River. A steam train had carried him across the Midwest where he boarded the steamboat at Keokuk, Iowa. From both conveyances he made a number of speeches as he passed through small towns. Sailing beside him were seventeen governors and delegations from the river towns, all in their own boats. In Louisiana, Roosevelt went on another hunting trip.

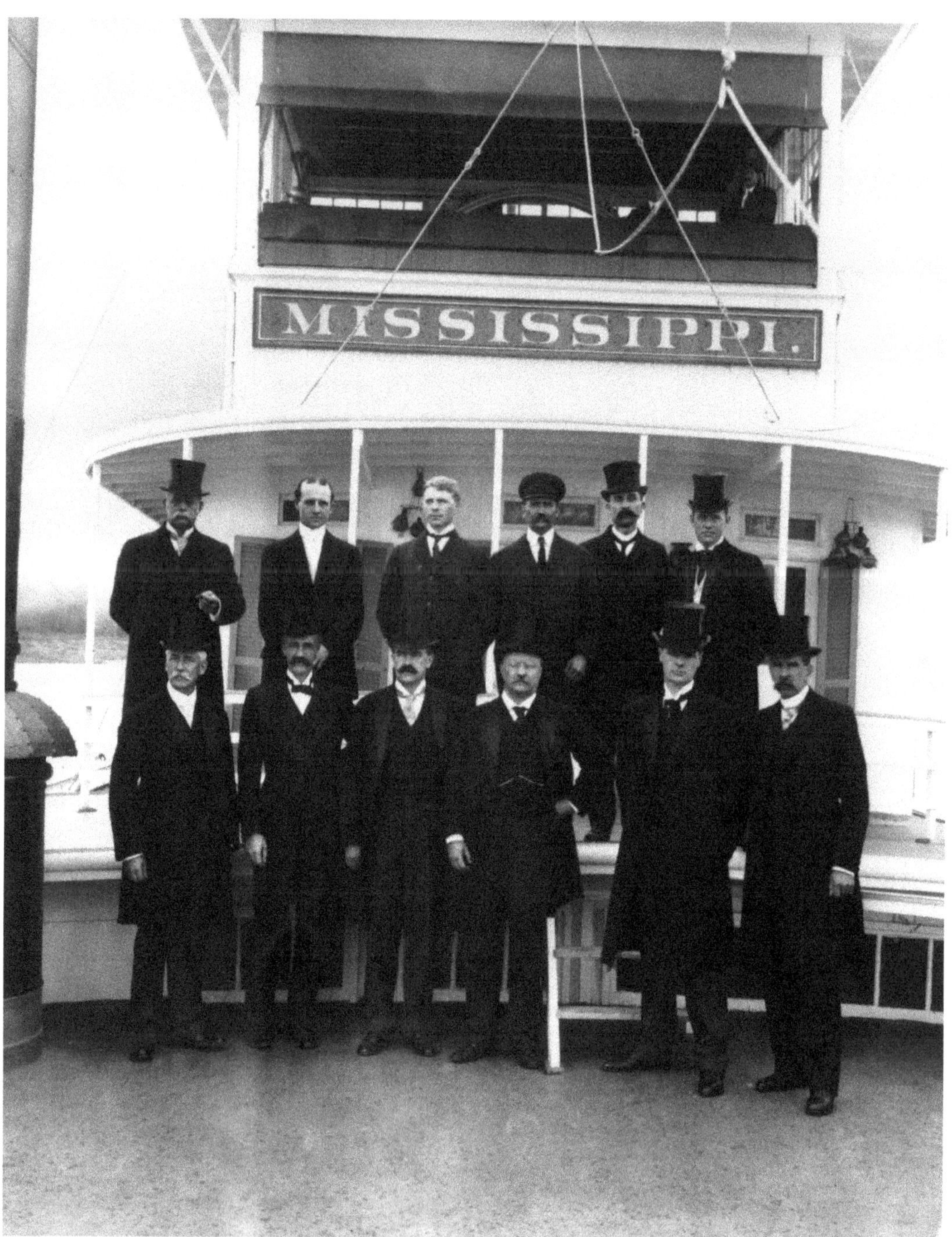

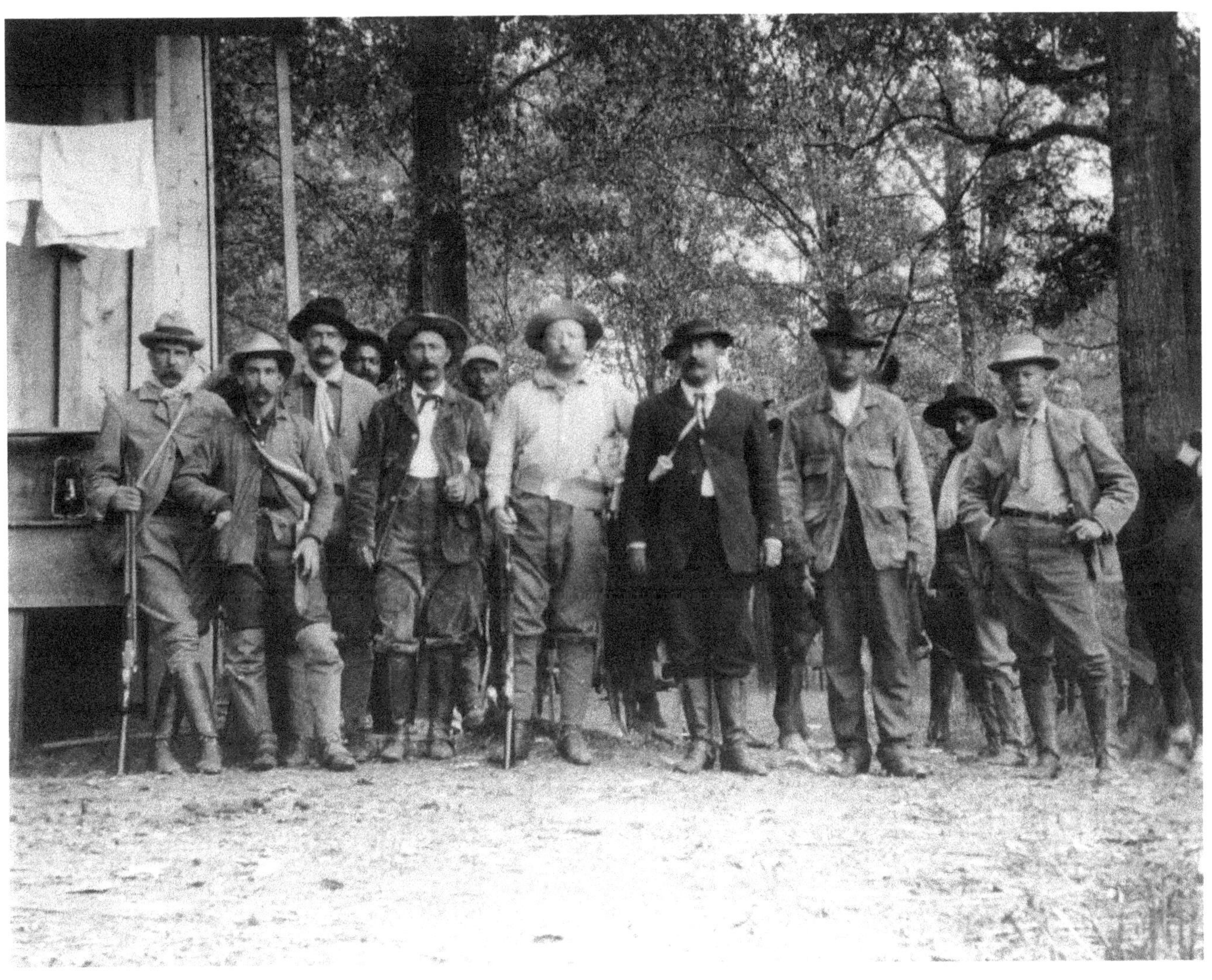

In Tenesas Bayou, Louisiana, President Roosevelt shot a bear and four deer, as he reported to John Burroughs on October 13, 1907. He included a list of the wildlife he had seen: wolves, black fox squirrels, red-bellied woodpeckers, ivory-billed woodpeckers. The cypress, red gum, and white oak trees he thought "magnificent."

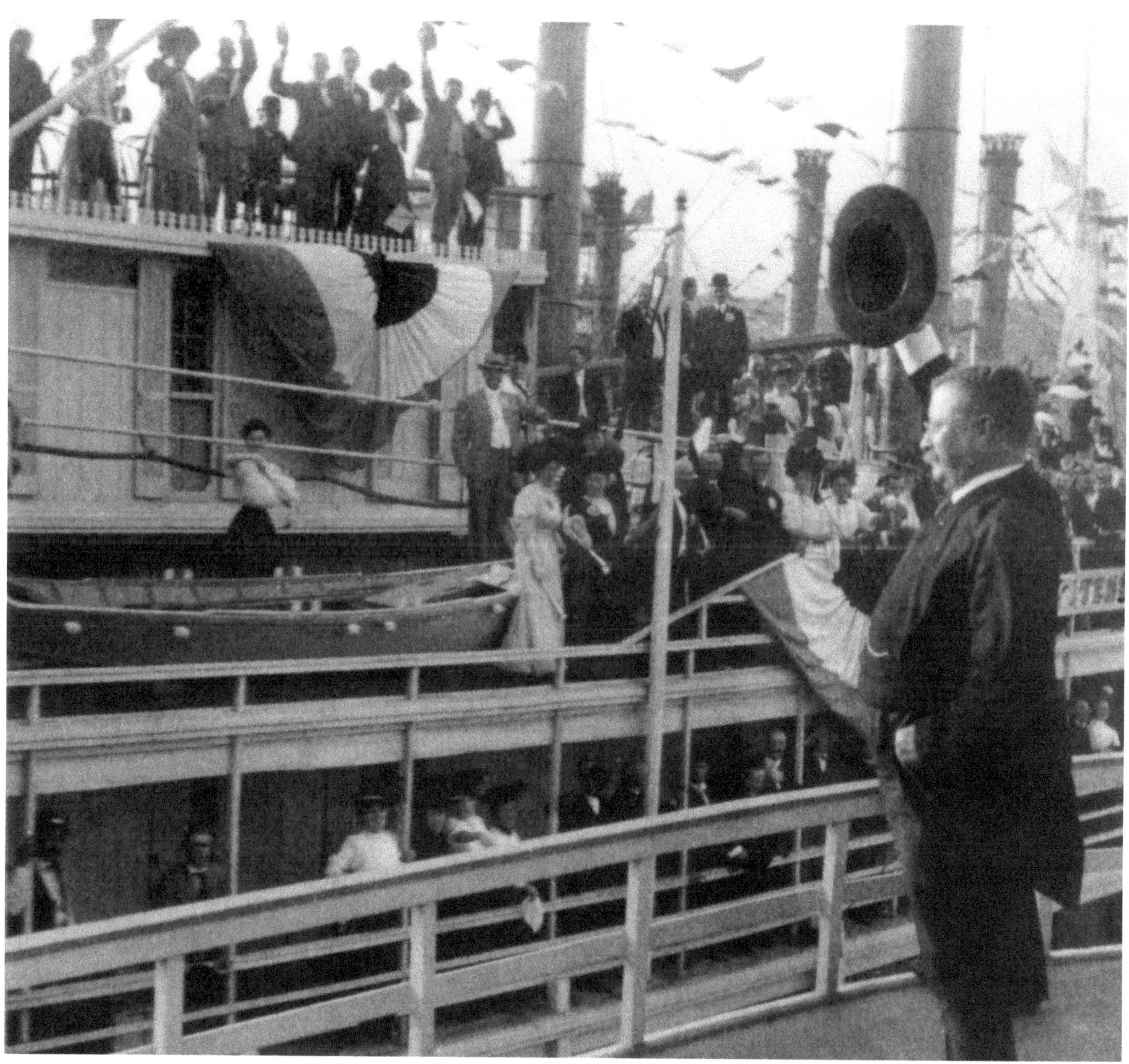

Roosevelt is shown here leaving St. Louis, Missouri, waving to another ship in the presidential steamboat parade and its enthusiastic fans. When TR wasn't waving to crowds or speechmaking, he held meetings with local politicians, dictated letters, and read. He was just then in the middle of *Puck of Pook's Hill,* by his friend Rudyard Kipling.

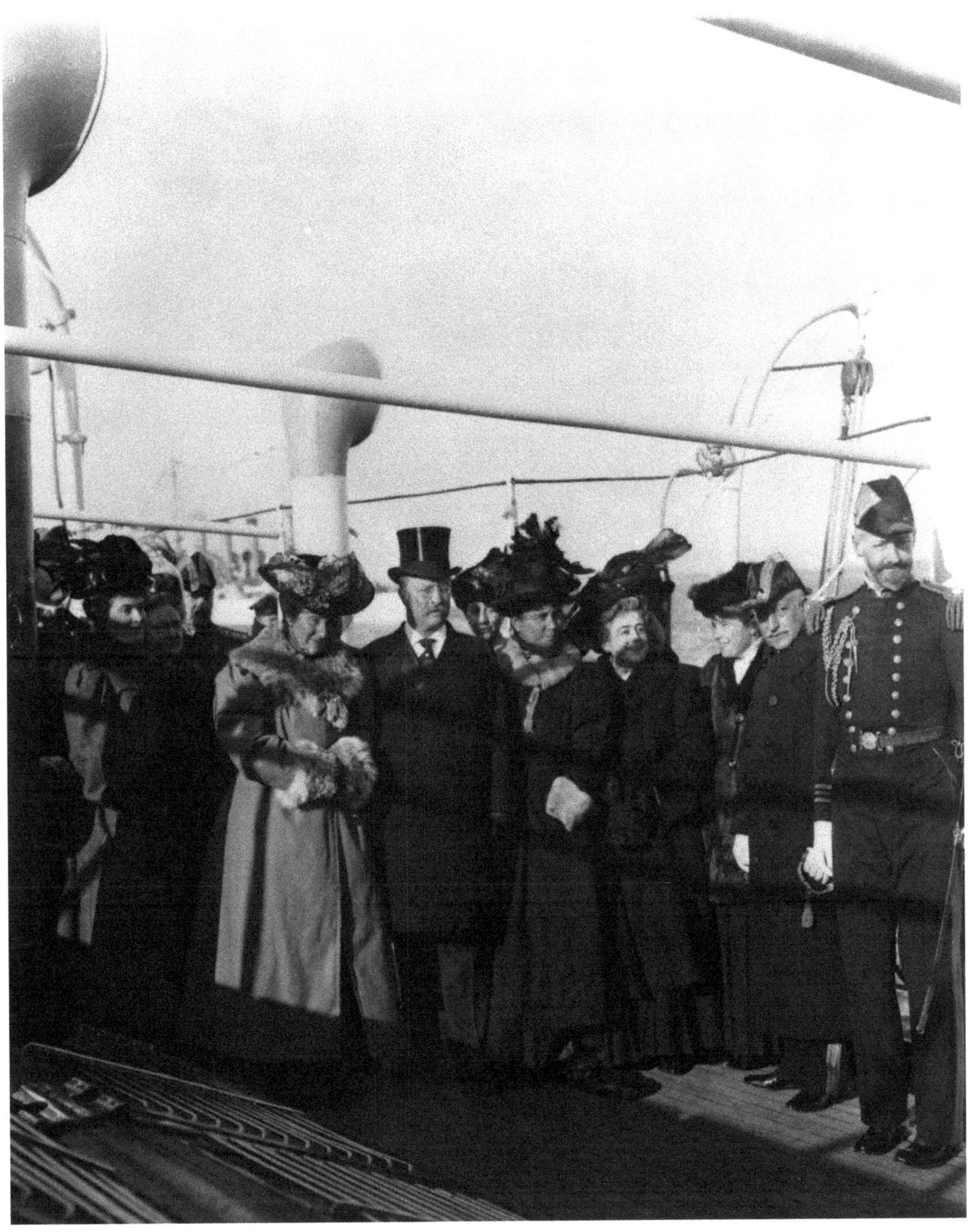

President Roosevelt stands proudly on the deck of the *Mayflower* on December 16, 1907, with Edith and Ethel beside him. The occasion was the launch of the Great White Fleet on its voyage around the world, the victorious embodiment of TR's consistent urging for naval preparedness. As the progressive-conservative split widened within the G.O.P., Roosevelt faced obstinate senators who wanted to punish him by denying the funding for the ships. Roosevelt prevailed with the aid of loyal, progressive senators working on his behalf.

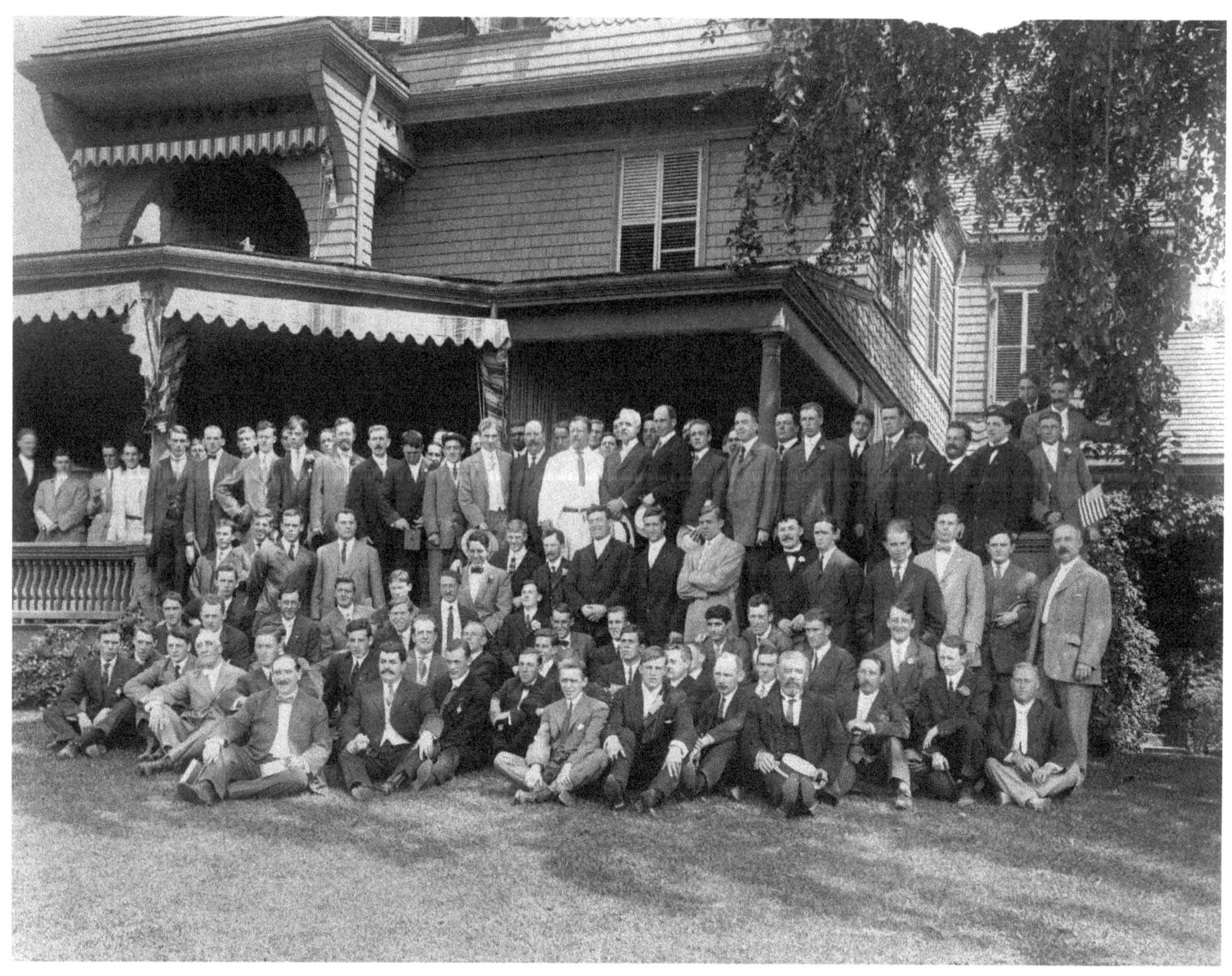

Theodore Roosevelt stands in the center of the 1908 U.S. Olympic team. The Olympics were held in London. At the games, competing in track and field, John Baxter Taylor became the first African American athlete to win an Olympic gold medal.

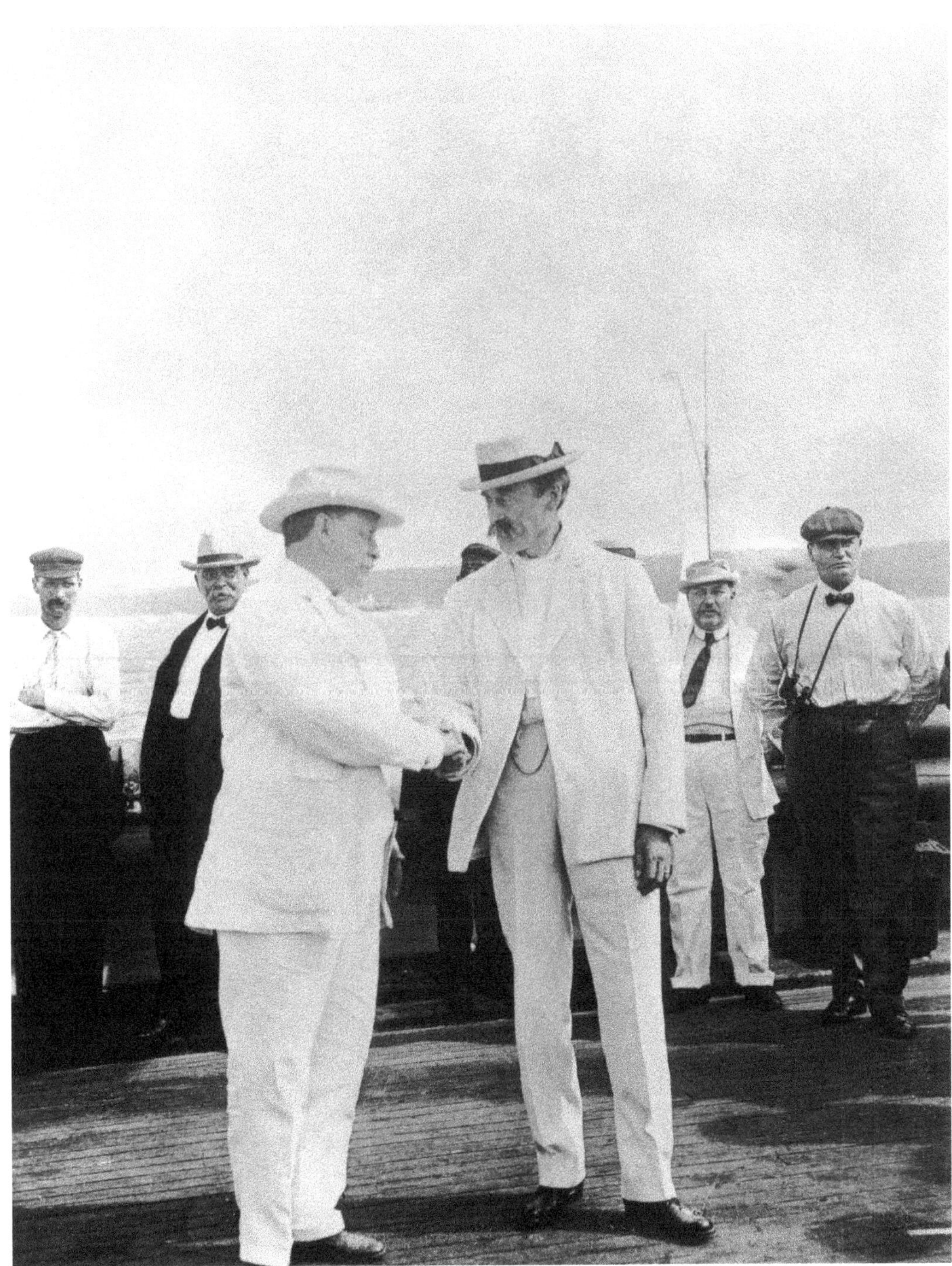

On July 7, 1908, President Roosevelt bids Commander Robert Peary good luck as he leaves for another Arctic expedition aboard his ship, the *Roosevelt.* Naval officer, civil engineer, explorer, and amateur anthropologist, Peary was famous around the globe for his journeys to the top of the world. In 1909 he and African American explorer Matt Henson believed they had won the race, declaring, "We have planted the Stars and Stripes at the North Pole."

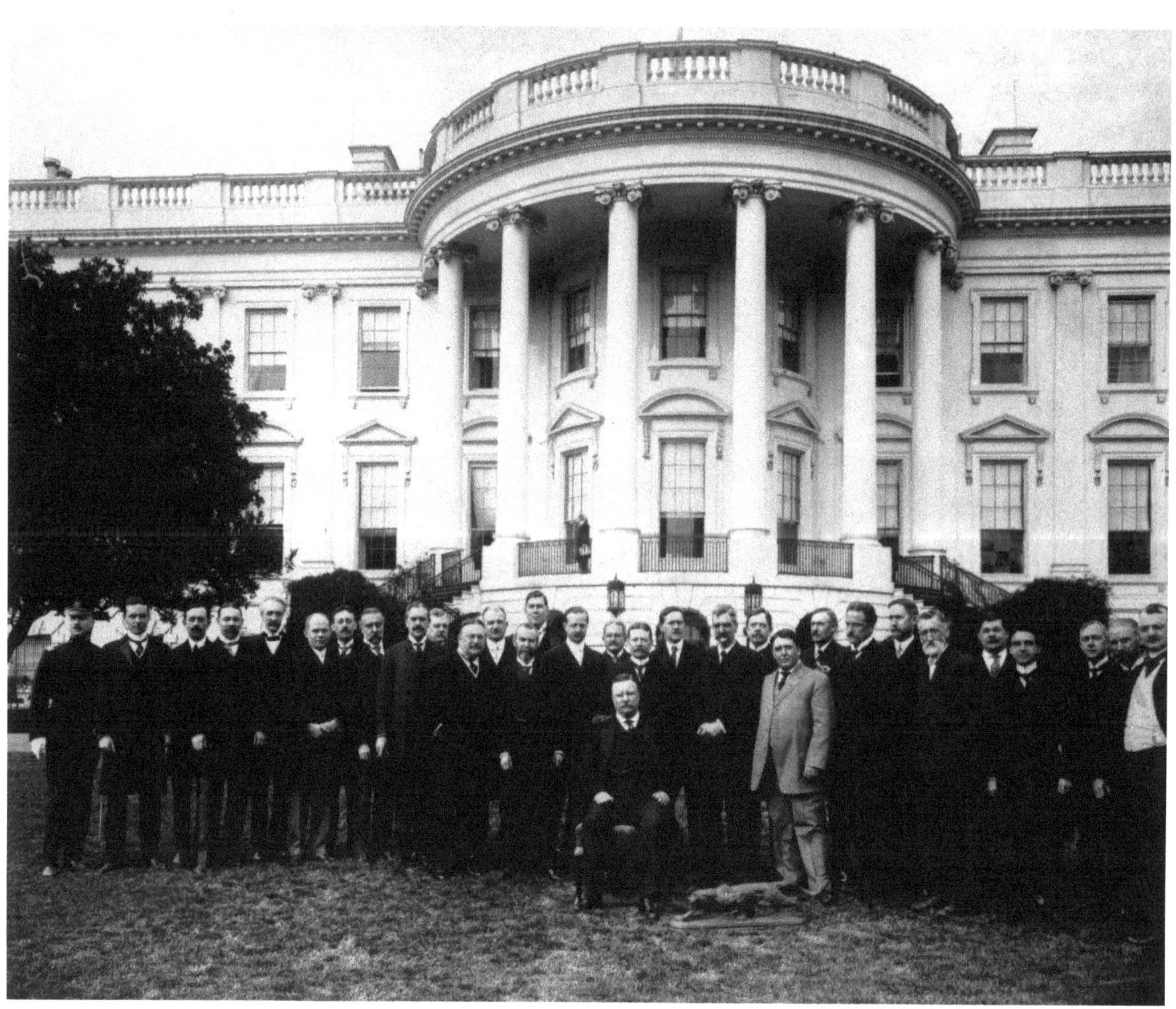

Theodore Roosevelt had a group of advisors called the Tennis Cabinet. Consisting of men with whom he could play tennis and discuss national and foreign affairs, this unofficial but influential cadre was one way TR maintained his channels of communication and good spirits among his intimates. This was a farewell photograph taken on the eve of Roosevelt's departure from the White House.

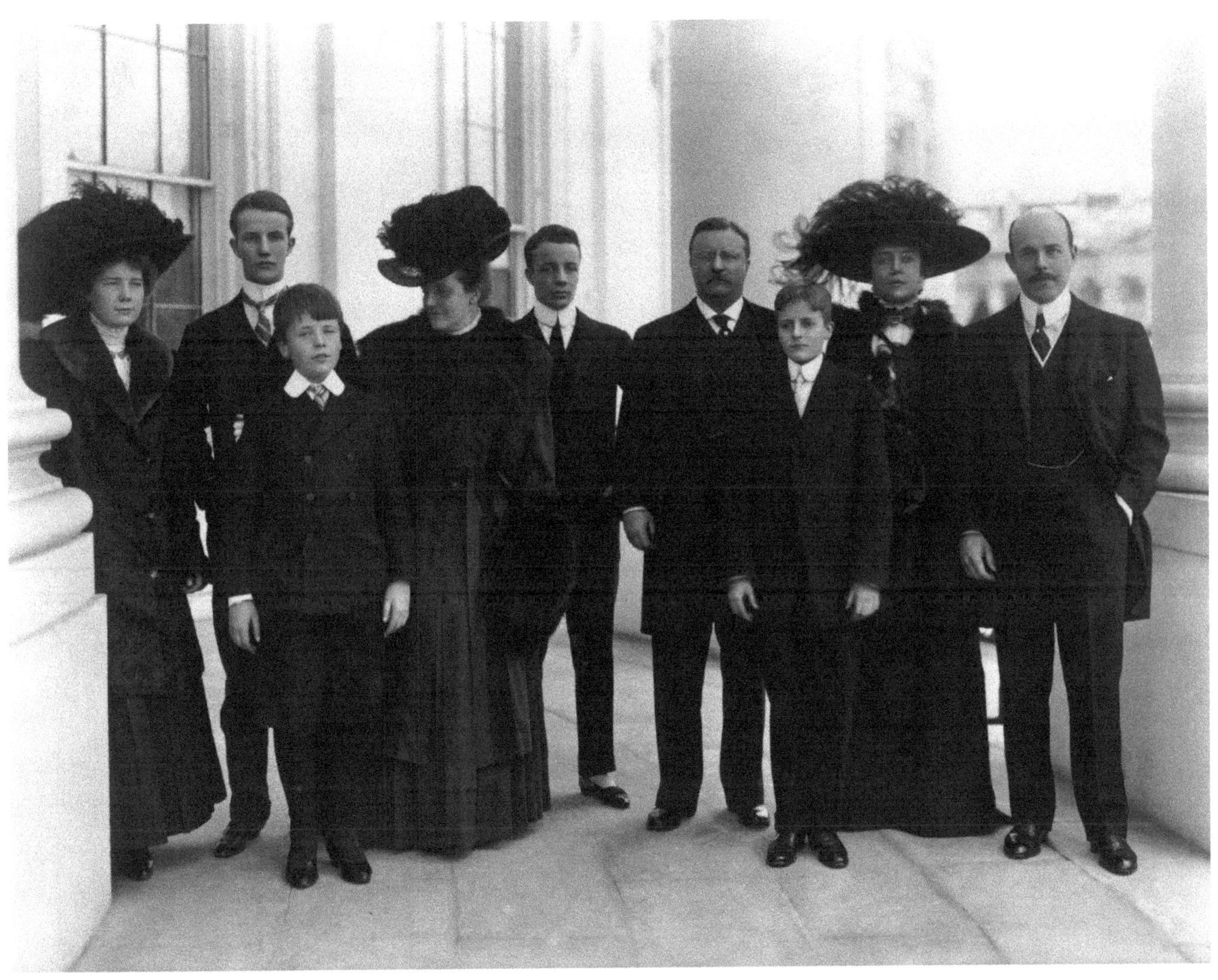

The Roosevelt family leaving the White House. Alice Roosevelt Longworth thought they looked as though they had been "expelled from the Garden of Eden." They all—with the possible exception of privacy-loving Edith—felt that way, too. Ethel, Kermit, Quentin, Edith, Ted, TR, Archie, Alice, and Nick Longworth.

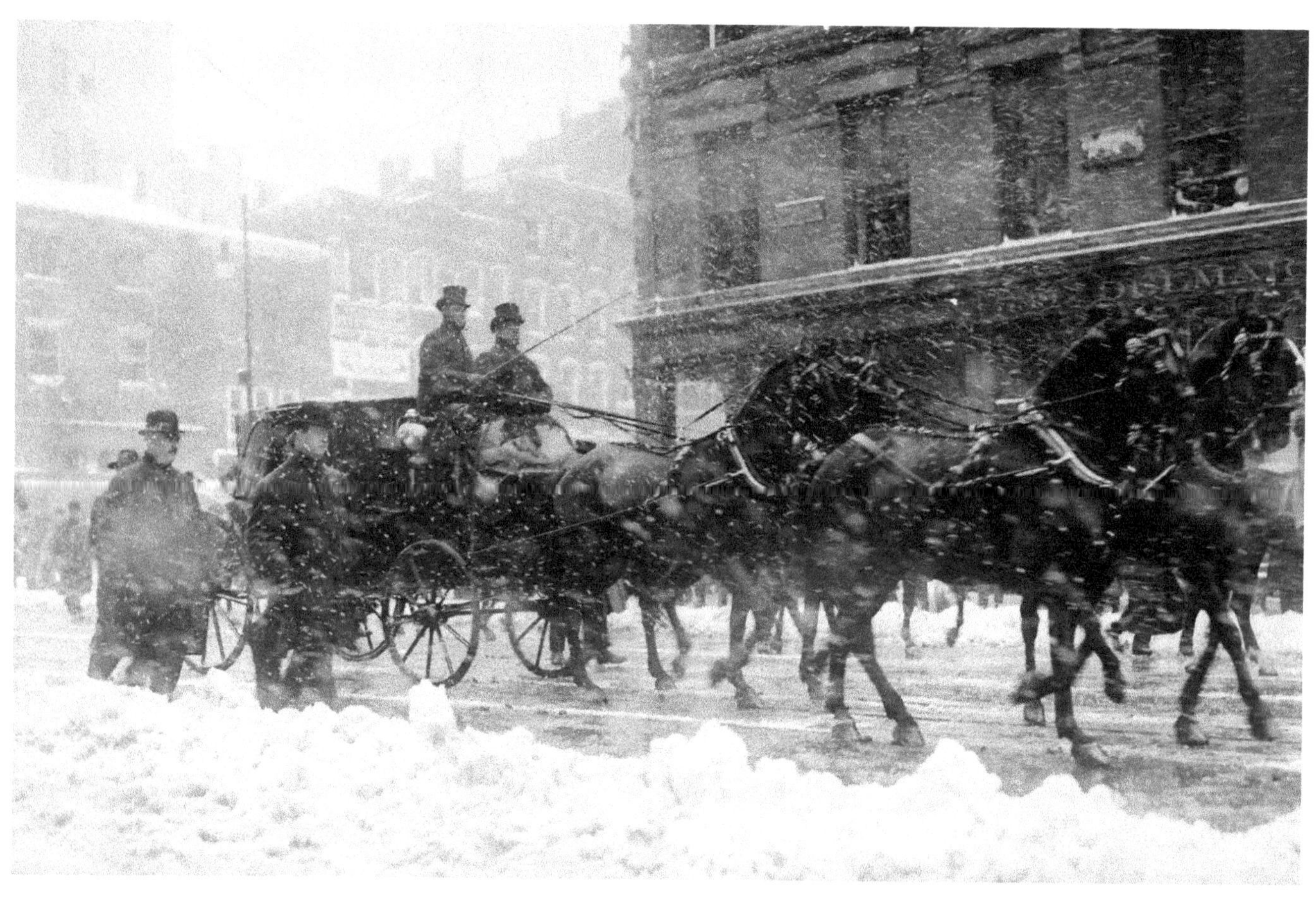

On a cold, snowy Inauguration Day, March 4, 1909, Roosevelt rode to the capitol with president-elect William Howard Taft. Roosevelt had desperately wanted to stand for reelection in 1908 but felt he had to honor the promise he had made about two terms. He was so popular, however, that he could choose his successor, Taft. Roosevelt convinced himself that he and Taft thought alike, although in important ways Taft's conservative tendencies would appear only after he took the oath of office. Taft and Roosevelt had been close, but the friendship would quickly unravel.

The Post-Presidential Years (1909–1919)

As President Roosevelt's hand-picked successor William Howard Taft took the oath of office on March 4, 1909, fifty-year-old TR became the youngest former president. Combining his love of big game hunting, his scientific avocation, and his desire to let the newspapers focus on Taft, Roosevelt embarked on a lengthy African safari and a statesman's tour of Europe. Eschewing political news while away, Roosevelt returned to find the Republicans bitterly factionalized between progressives and conservatives.

TR listened to pleas that he run for the presidency again. Ignoring Taft's control of G.O.P. funds, Roosevelt threw his hat into the ring. As founder of the Progressive Party, he survived an assassin's bullet but could not overcome his late start in the race. The 1912 presidential election changed the timbre of both parties, and the G.O.P. split handed the White House to Democrat Woodrow Wilson.

After penning his autobiography, TR took his "last chance to be a boy" and embarked upon a dangerous scientific exploration of an uncharted Brazilian river. He nearly lost his life.

In 1916 Roosevelt declined the Progressive Party nomination for president and turned all his efforts toward American preparations for the European war that had begun in 1914. President Wilson denied Roosevelt a final opportunity for military combat, but TR sent all four of his sons to battle instead. Only three came back.

Six months after Quentin was shot down in France, a coronary embolism killed Theodore Roosevelt, who died peacefully in his sleep on January 6, 1919.

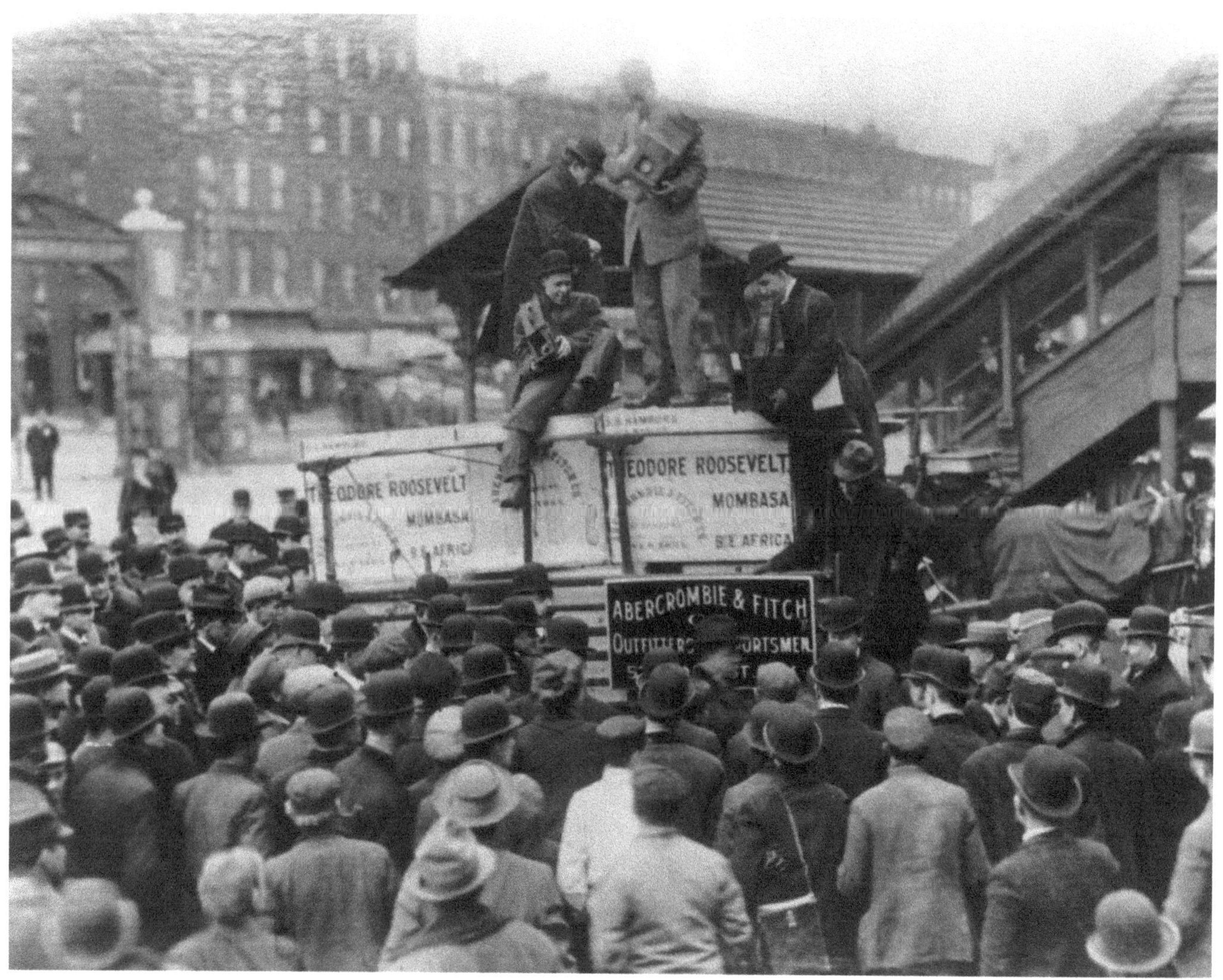

To allow President Taft to work out his own destiny, Colonel Roosevelt (as he wanted to be called, post-presidency) left on a fifteen-month hunting trip in Africa. The $75,000 (in 1909 dollars) cost of the trip came from his own savings, benefactors like Andrew Carnegie, and the $50,000 Scribner's Magazine paid him to write about his adventures. Crowds of admirers watched as his baggage was loaded onto the ship.

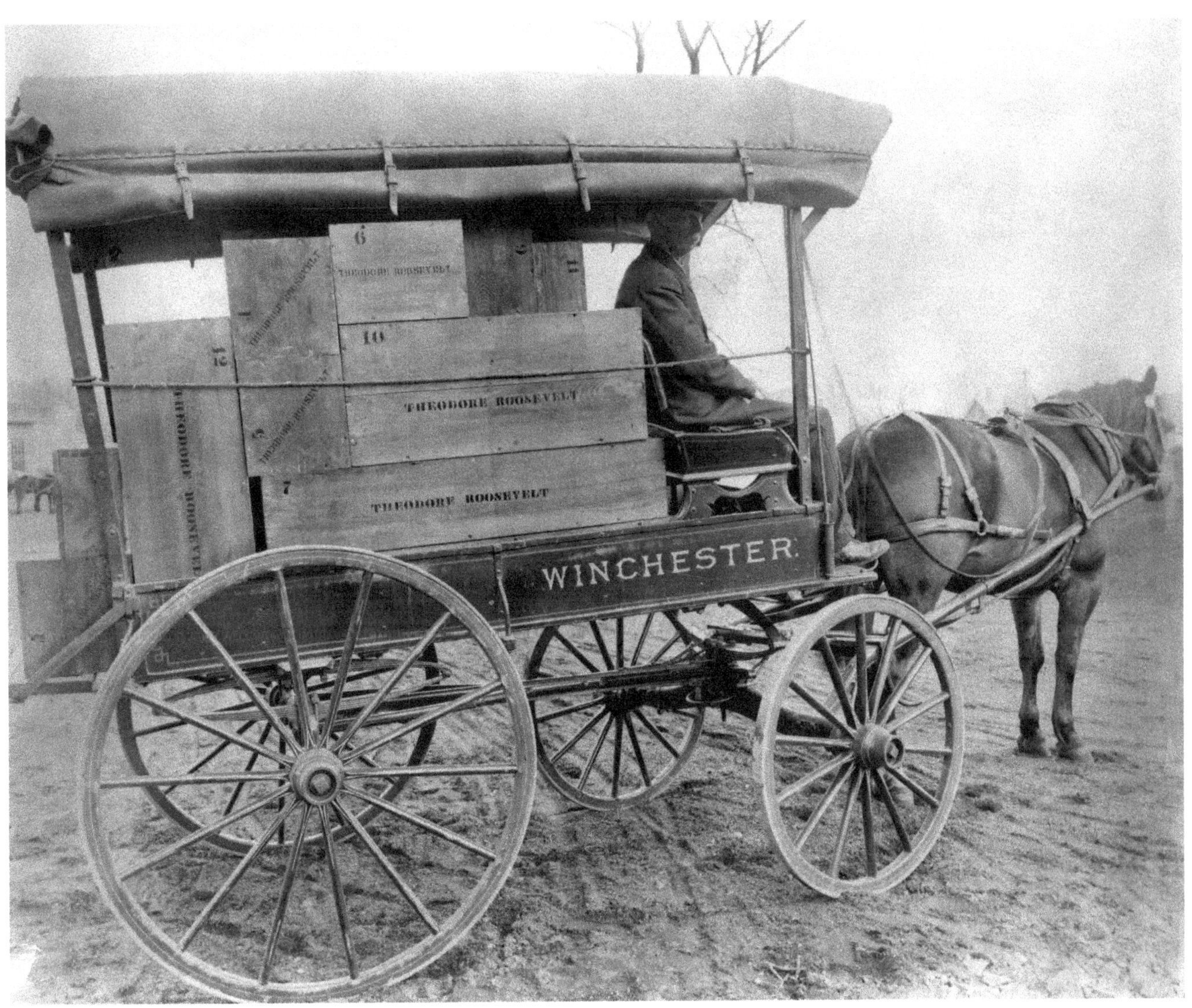

Winchester rifles were only a few of the kinds of weapons TR carried to bring down lions, elephants, and other African game. With him also went nine extra pairs of glasses and sixty pounds of the famous "pigskin" library of classics—a gift from his sister Corinne Roosevelt Robinson—to be read along the trail. Most important of all, his son Kermit—an accomplished hunter—accompanied Roosevelt.

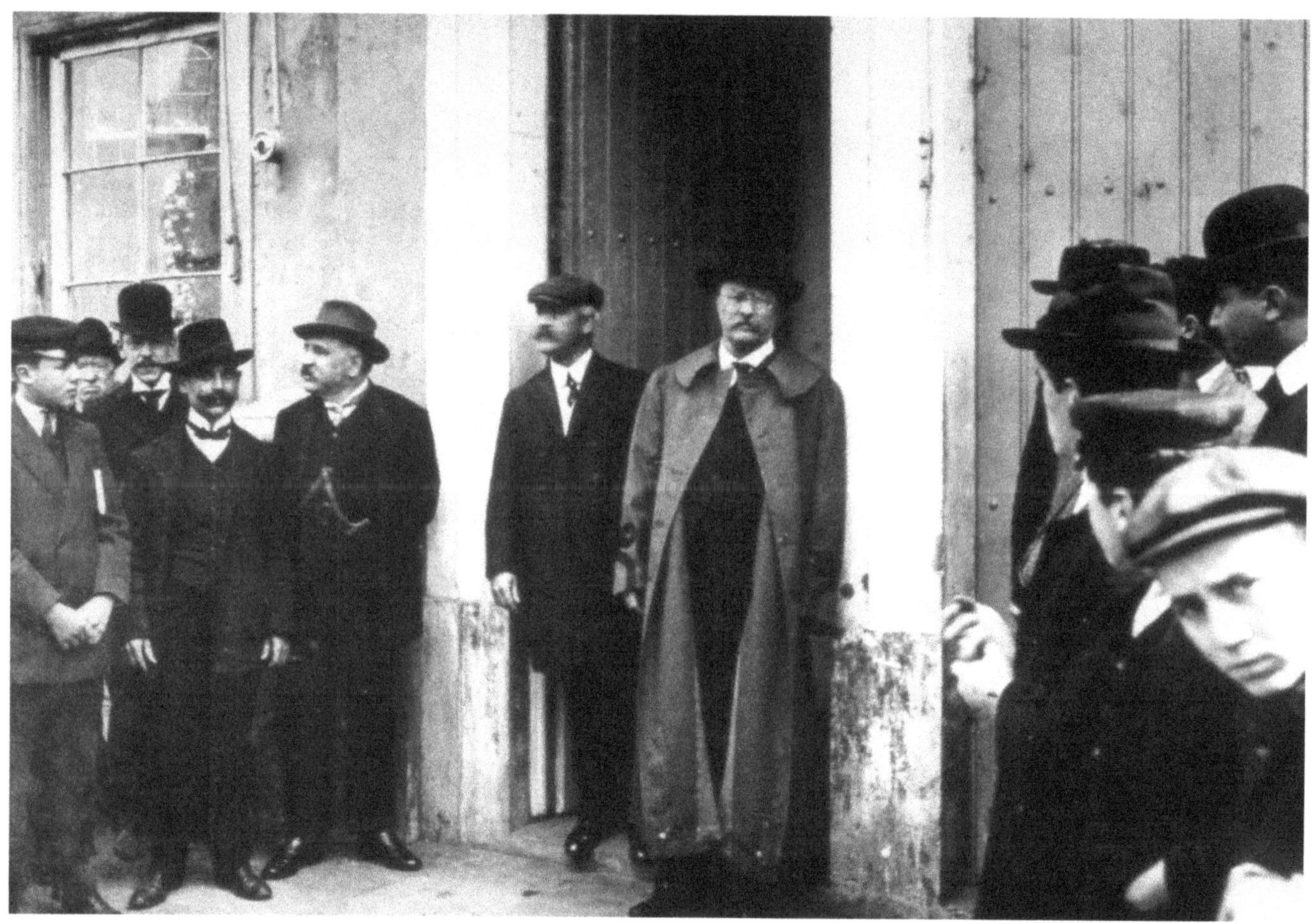

On the way to Africa, Roosevelt stopped in at the Azores to meet with the American consul there. Although well-wishers had crowded New York harbor and thronged the streets to see him off, and there were devotees in places like the Azores, the conservative wing of the G.O.P. and many business leaders were glad to see TR go far away on safari. At the news, Wall Street financier J. P. Morgan reportedly lifted his glass to intone, "America expects every lion to do its duty."

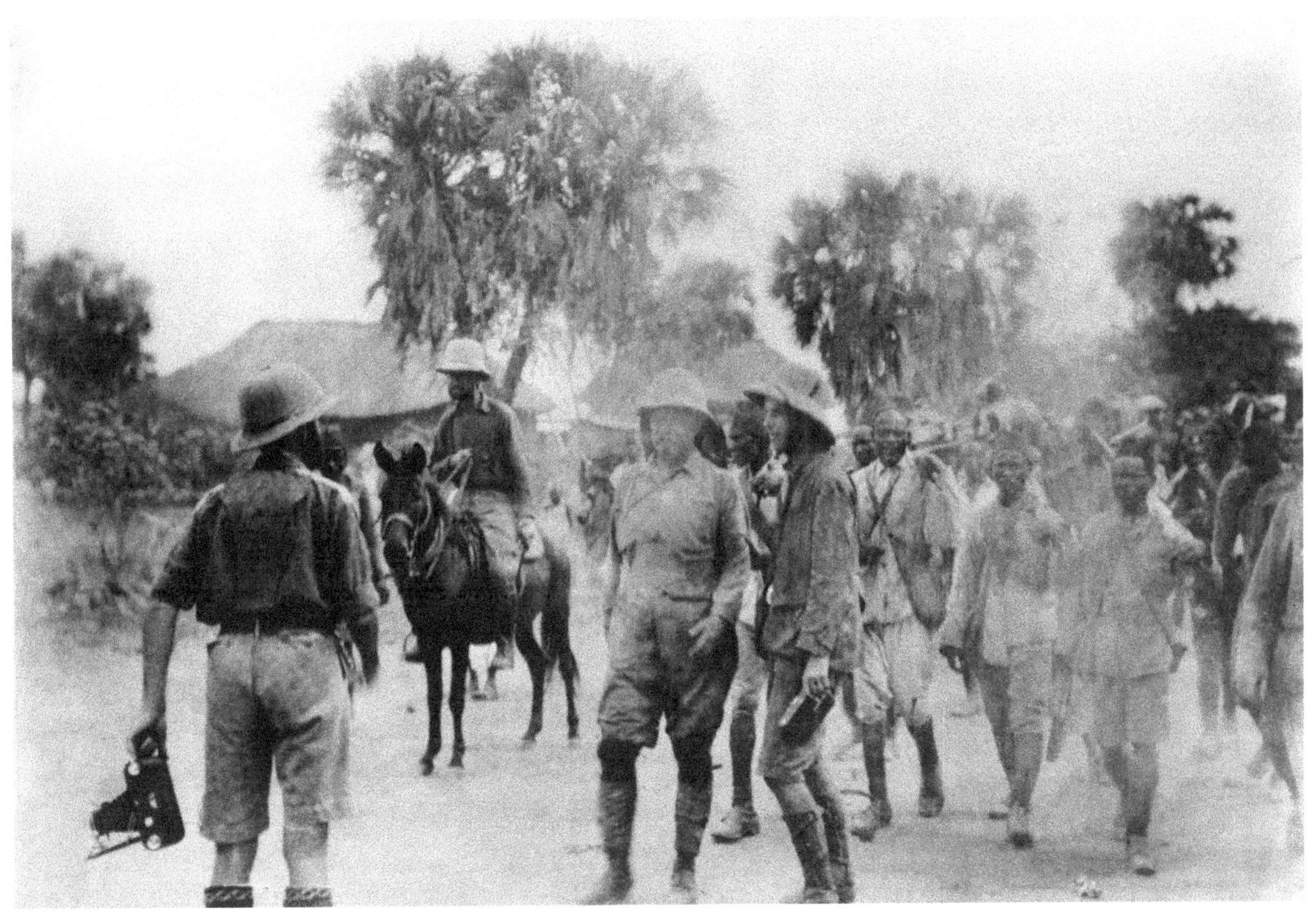

In his first article for Scribner's, TR wrote in detail about the journey from Mombasa where his safari actually began on April 24, 1909. Roosevelt rode on the cowcatcher of the train most of the way. They stayed with friends en route and shot a lion, a giraffe, and a rhinoceros. Kermit, that "very dearest traveling companion," and TR are captured in an informal photograph with others in their group.

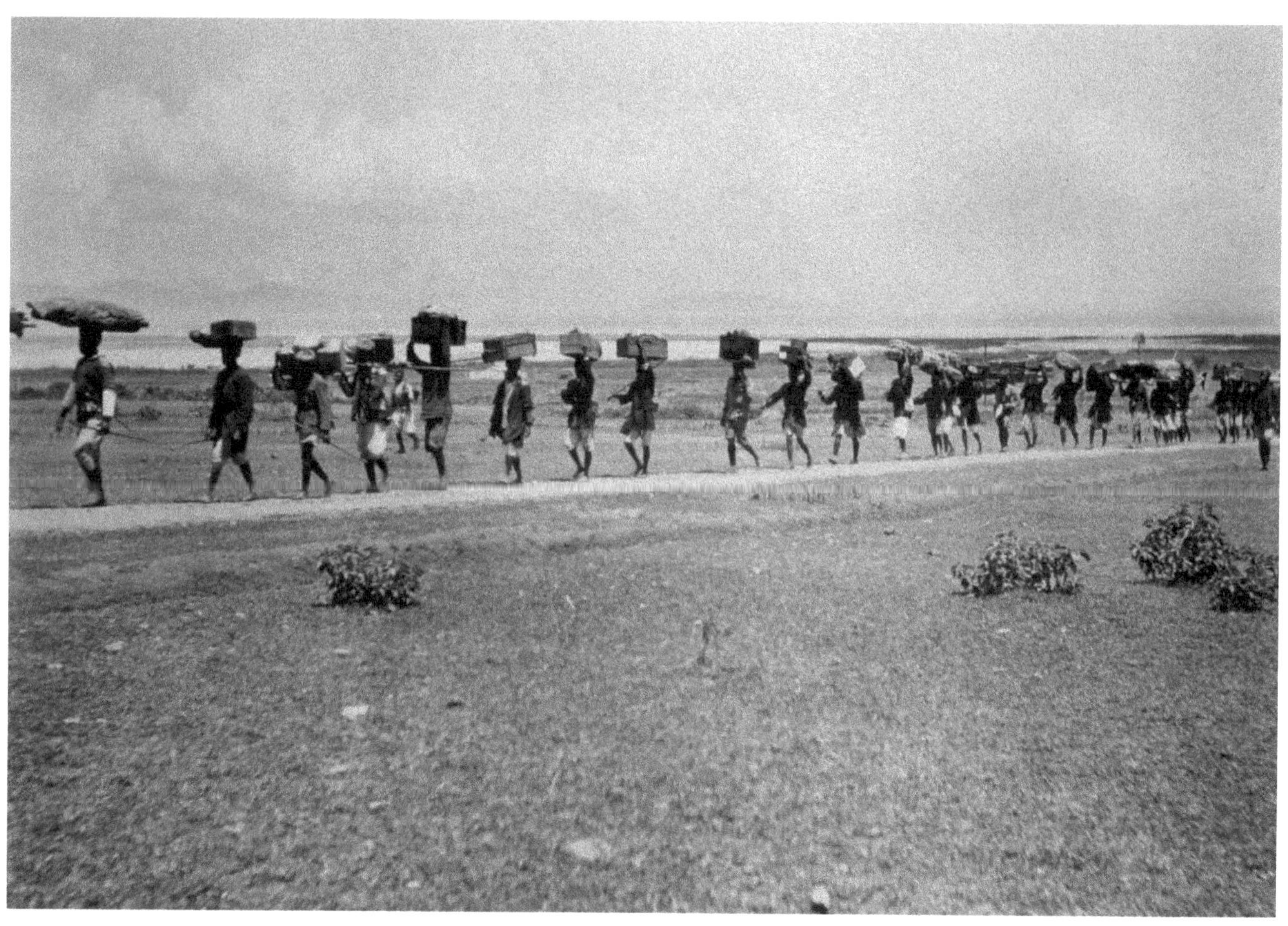

This photograph shows the long line of African bearers in Roosevelt's party. Two hundred and sixty Africans accompanied TR, and all but sixty of them carried scientific equipment. The three naturalists conducted the largest scientific expedition ever to cross eastern Africa, especially focused on small mammals, birds, and vegetation, on behalf of the Smithsonian Institution. Roosevelt co-authored the scientific record of the trip in *Life Histories of African Game Animals.*

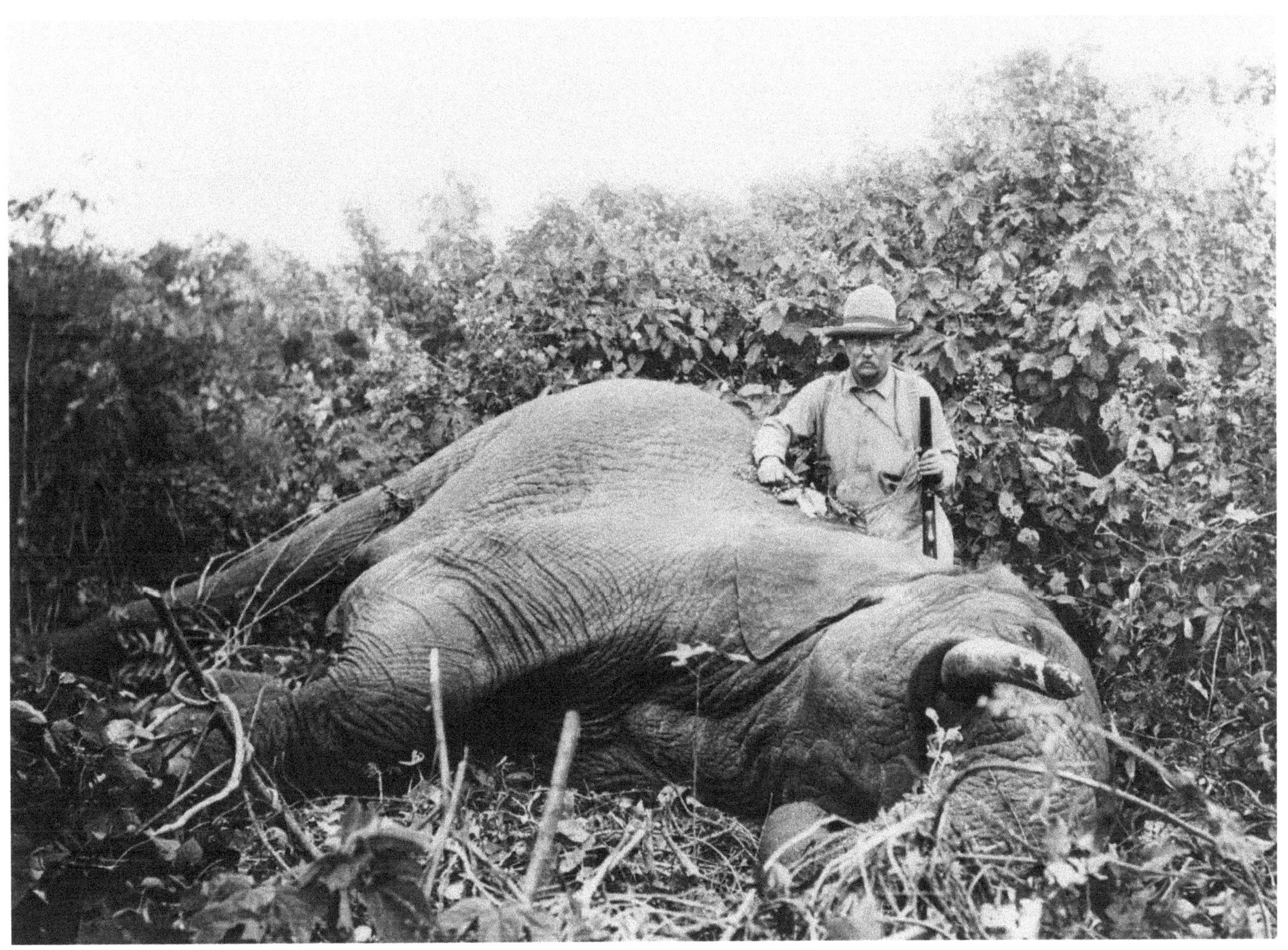

The few letters TR wrote home were full of the tally of their hunt: six lions, two bull giraffes, one hippo, a leopard, a hyena, a zebra, a waterhog, two rhinoceros, an eland, "various antelopes, etc." They killed for meat or for science, but Roosevelt particularly relished the physical danger when an animal fought back.

Photographs with their trophies were *de rigueur.* Some of the pictures accompanied TR's articles and some went to his book *African Game Trails,* where he wrote most dramatically about killing his first lion. The American public stayed well apprised of the colonel's adventures—partly because, as he had done in Cuba, TR allowed journalists to follow him for the inside story.

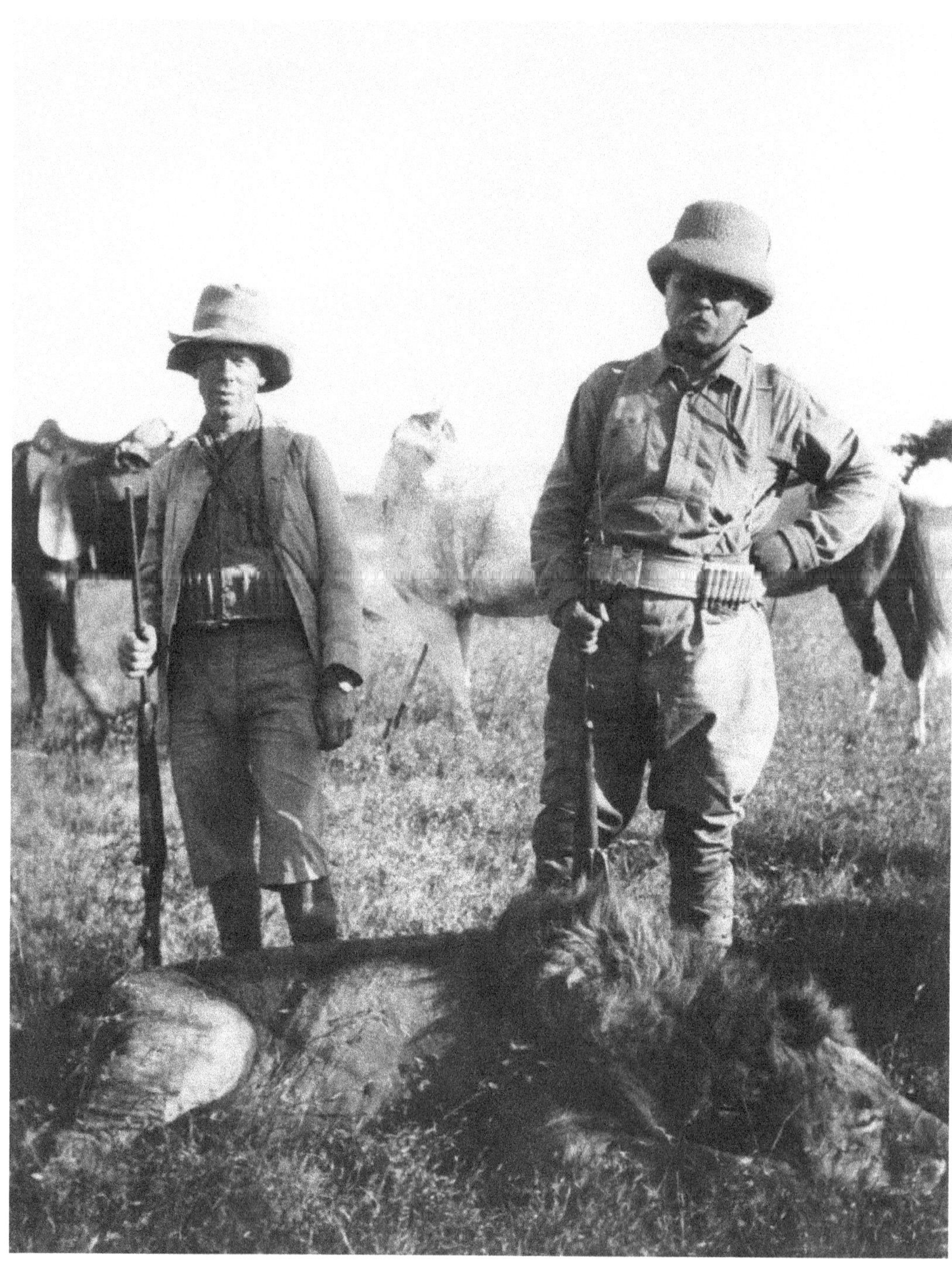

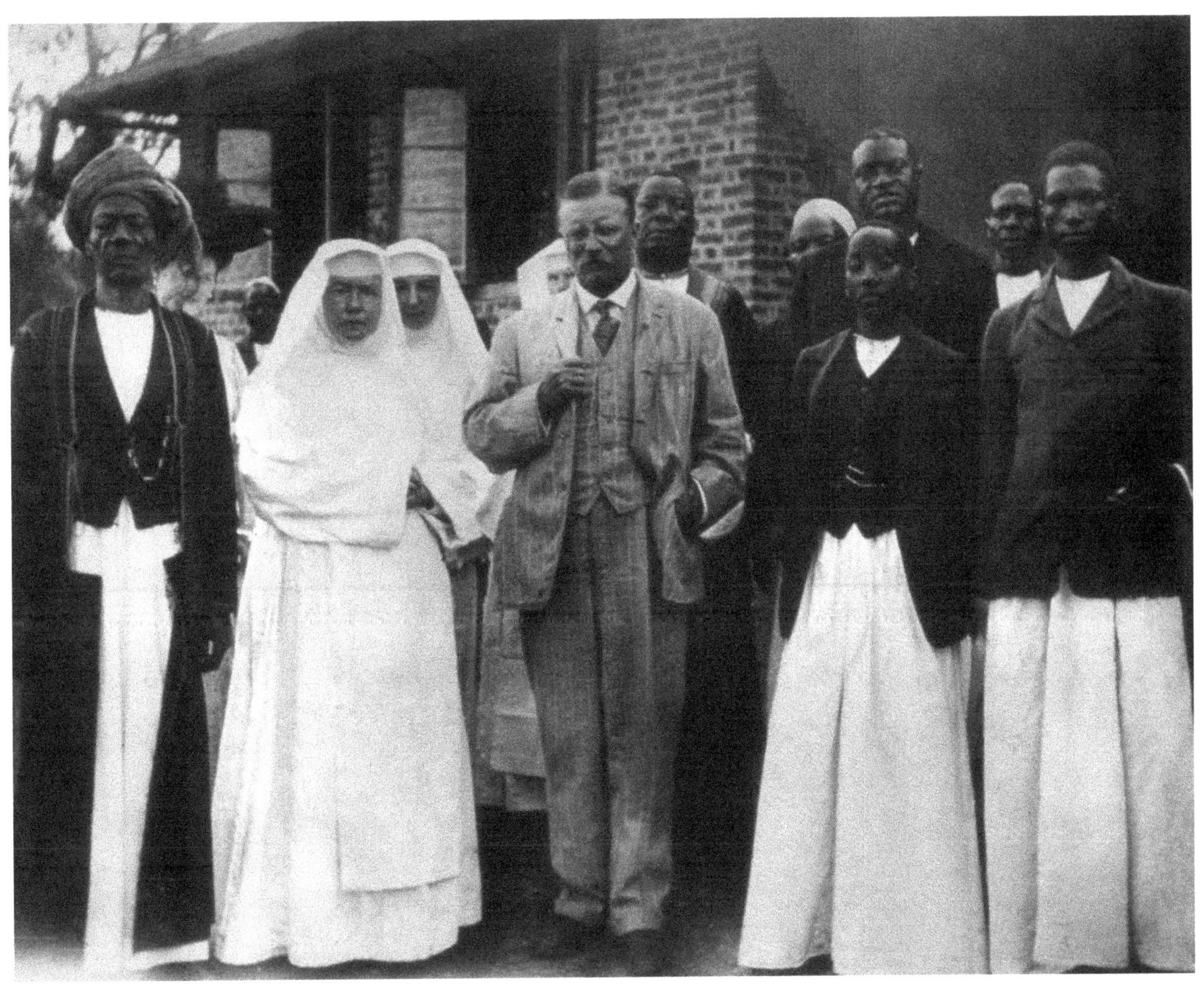

At the conclusion of the safari, Colonel Roosevelt posed with a group of religious at St. Mary's Convent near Kampala, in British East India, just before Christmas 1909. Roosevelt was raised in the Dutch Reformed Church and attended Christ Episcopal Church with his family in Oyster Bay because there was no Dutch Reformed church there. In Albany and Washington, TR worshiped at German Reformed churches—the precursor of today's United Church of Christ.

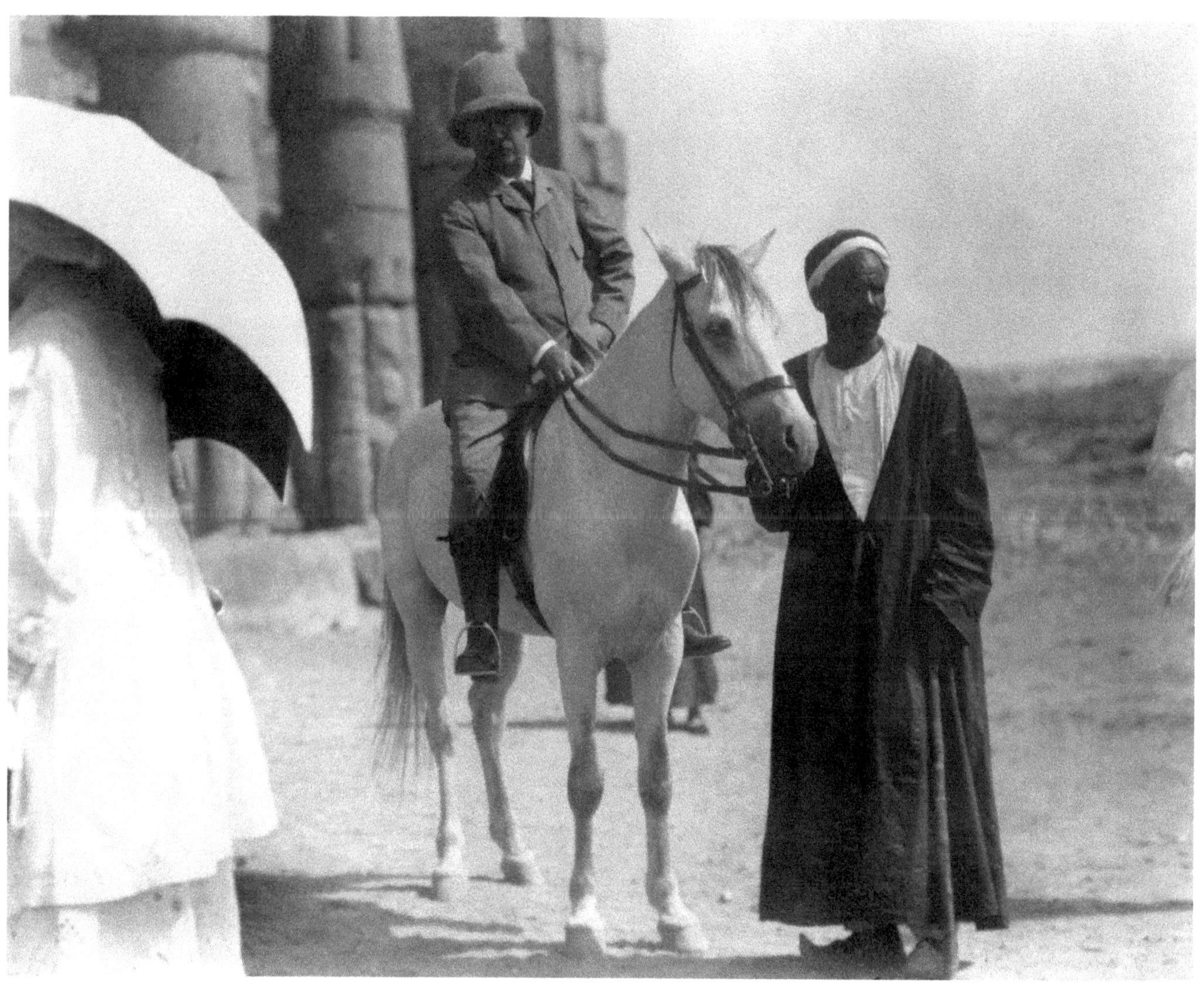

The safari was a rousing success both personally and scientifically. Five museums gained from the expedition, and the Smithsonian alone received more than 500 large mammals, more than 3,500 small mammals, and nearly 3,000 birds. By the end of February, the Roosevelts had reached Egypt, where TR had not been since he was a boy. Edith and Ethel joined them there for some sightseeing in Luxor, where this photograph was taken.

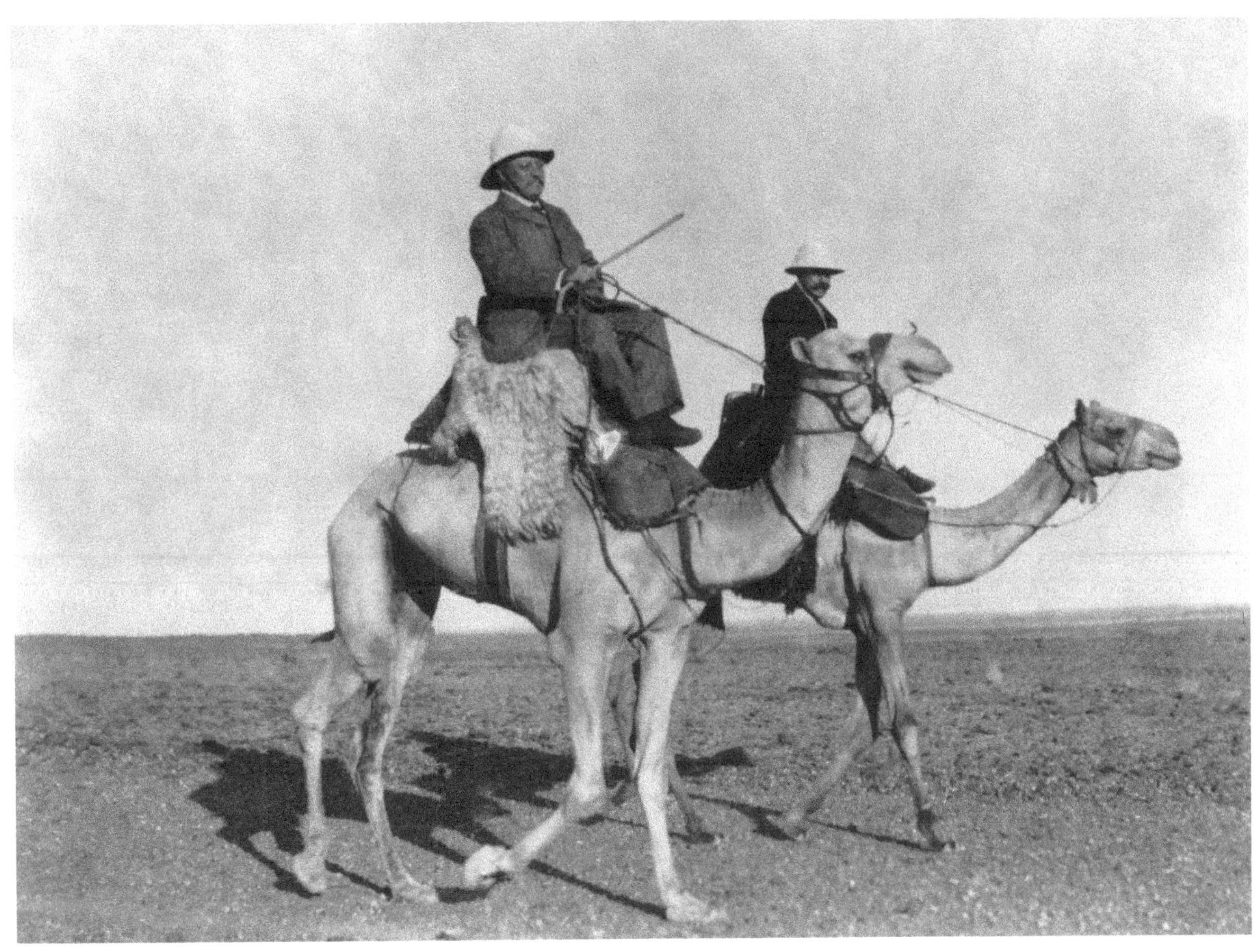

Roosevelt astride a camel in Kerrei, the site of the 1898 Battle of Omdurman where Sir Horatio Kitchener defeated the Sudanese in the attempt to control the Sudan. Roosevelt's colleague on the camel ride is the Austrian baron Rudolph Slatin, who had spent three decades in Northern Africa as a soldier, adventurer, and civil servant.

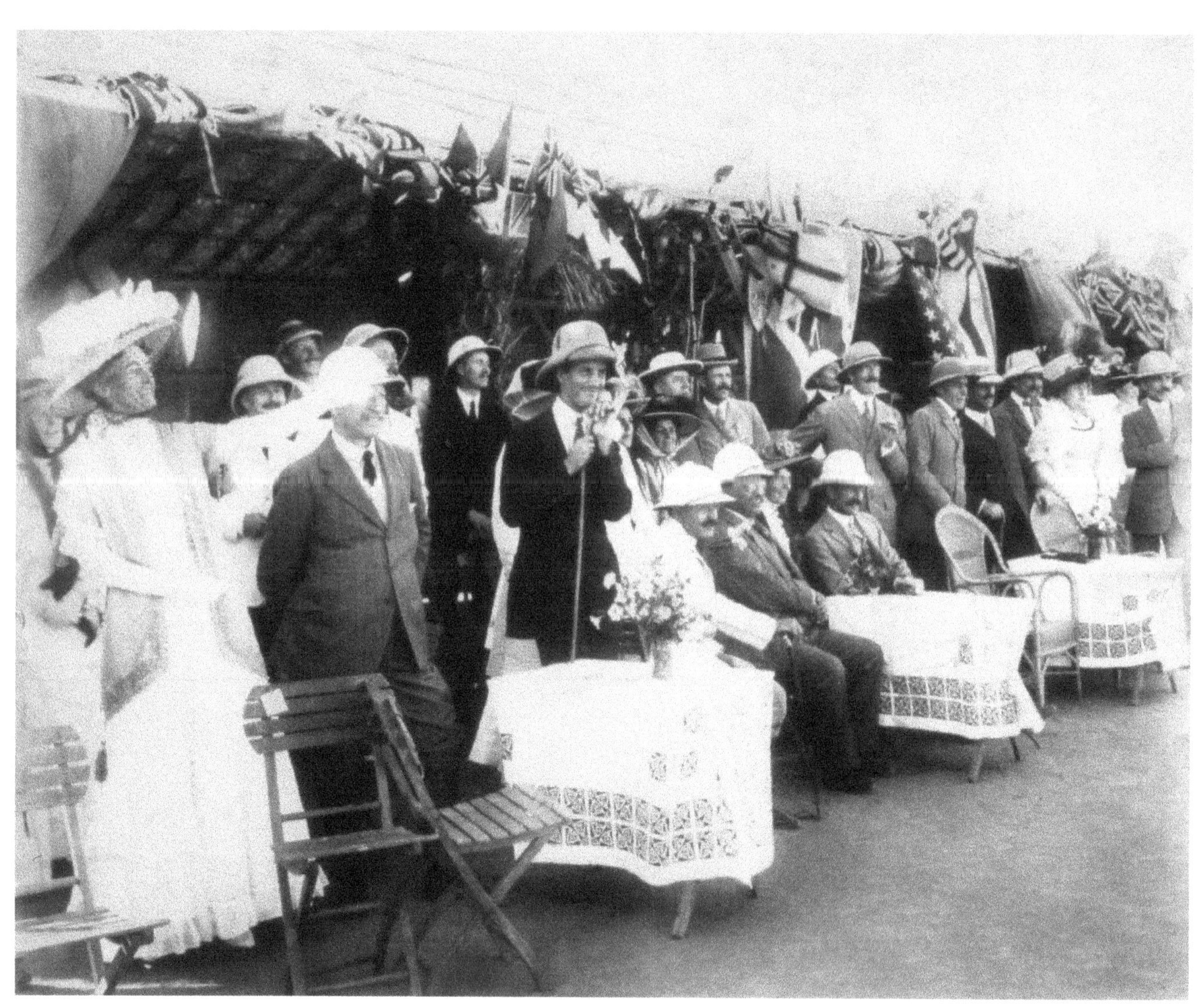

Roosevelt watching a horse show in Khartoum on March 16, 1910.

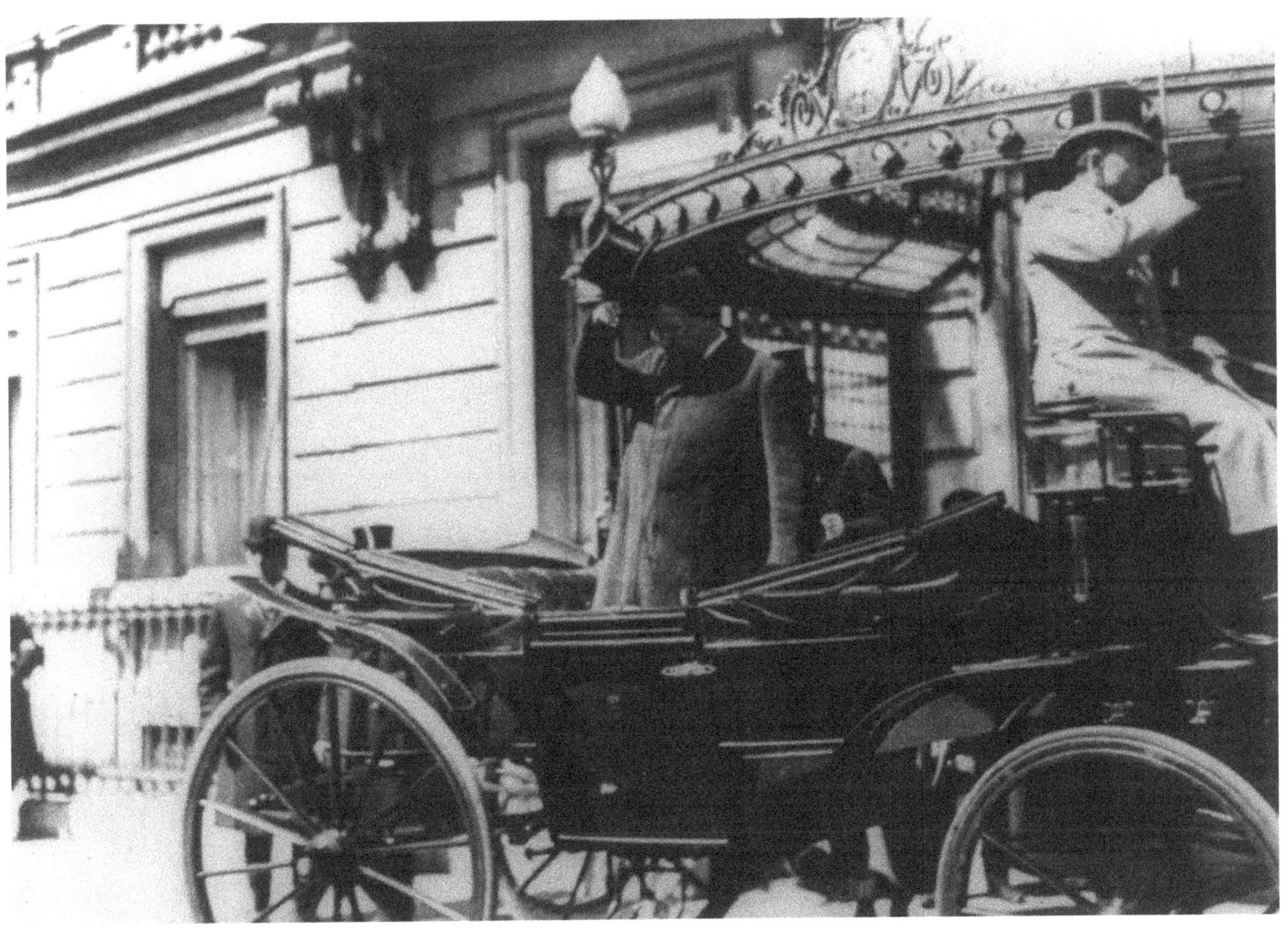

Leaving Egypt, Edith and Theodore went to Europe. His fame as a statesman and a scientific explorer preceded him. Every day passed, he wrote a friend, in "a perfect whirl." In this photograph, the former president is saluting the crowd gathered to see him in front of the Des Indias Hotel at the Hague, the site of two world conferences on peace. Elsewhere in Europe, TR cautioned nations against "unhealthy militarism" and urged reliance on diplomacy first, through a league of peace.

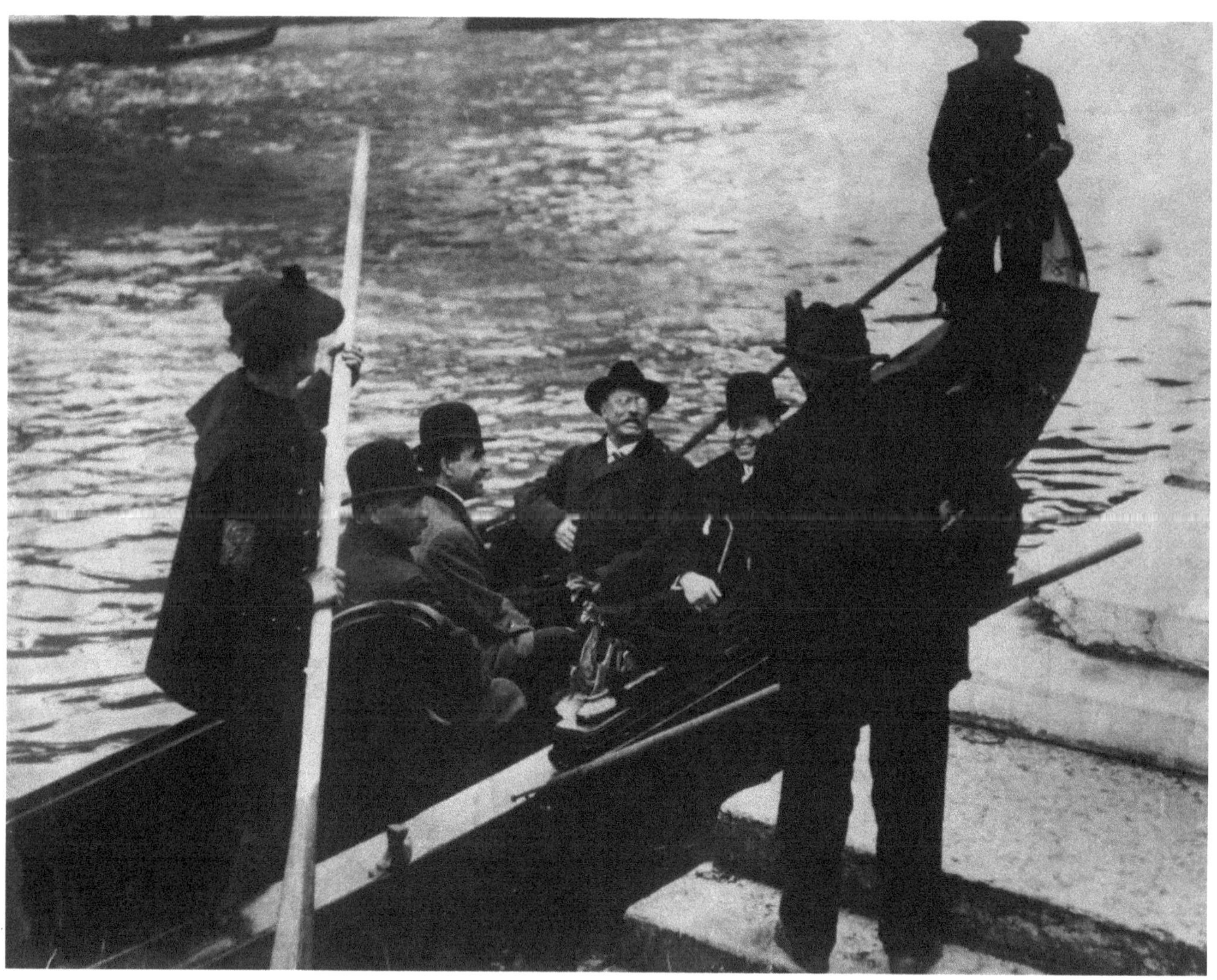

Edith and Theodore went to Europe where he was always the center of adoring crowds. He had promised Edith time alone together to get reacquainted, but that was difficult—he was bombarded with requests for speeches and appearances. The couple did get away to Italy for a second honeymoon. This photograph demonstrates that business interfered even in Venice—Edith is not in the gondola with TR on the Grand Canal.

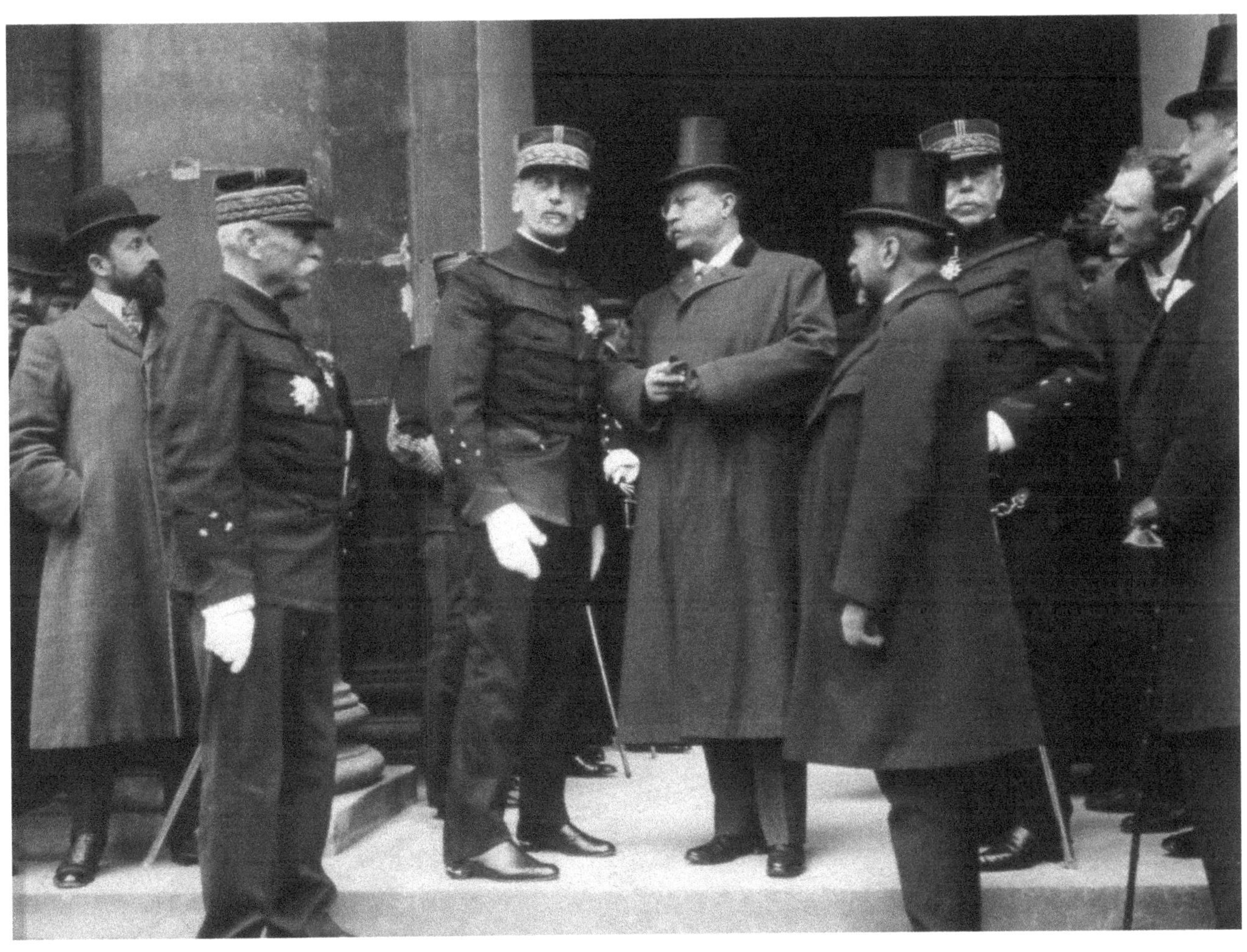

Roosevelt gave several prestigious talks in Europe, among them "International Peace," the acceptance speech for his Nobel Prize in Norway, and an address entitled "Citizenship in a Republic" at the Sorbonne, in Paris. The latter was a marker of how far to the left Roosevelt had moved in his political thinking, as in it he spoke approvingly of nationalizing utilities and railways. Roosevelt, in this April 1910 photograph, stands in front of Les Invalides, where Napoleon is buried.

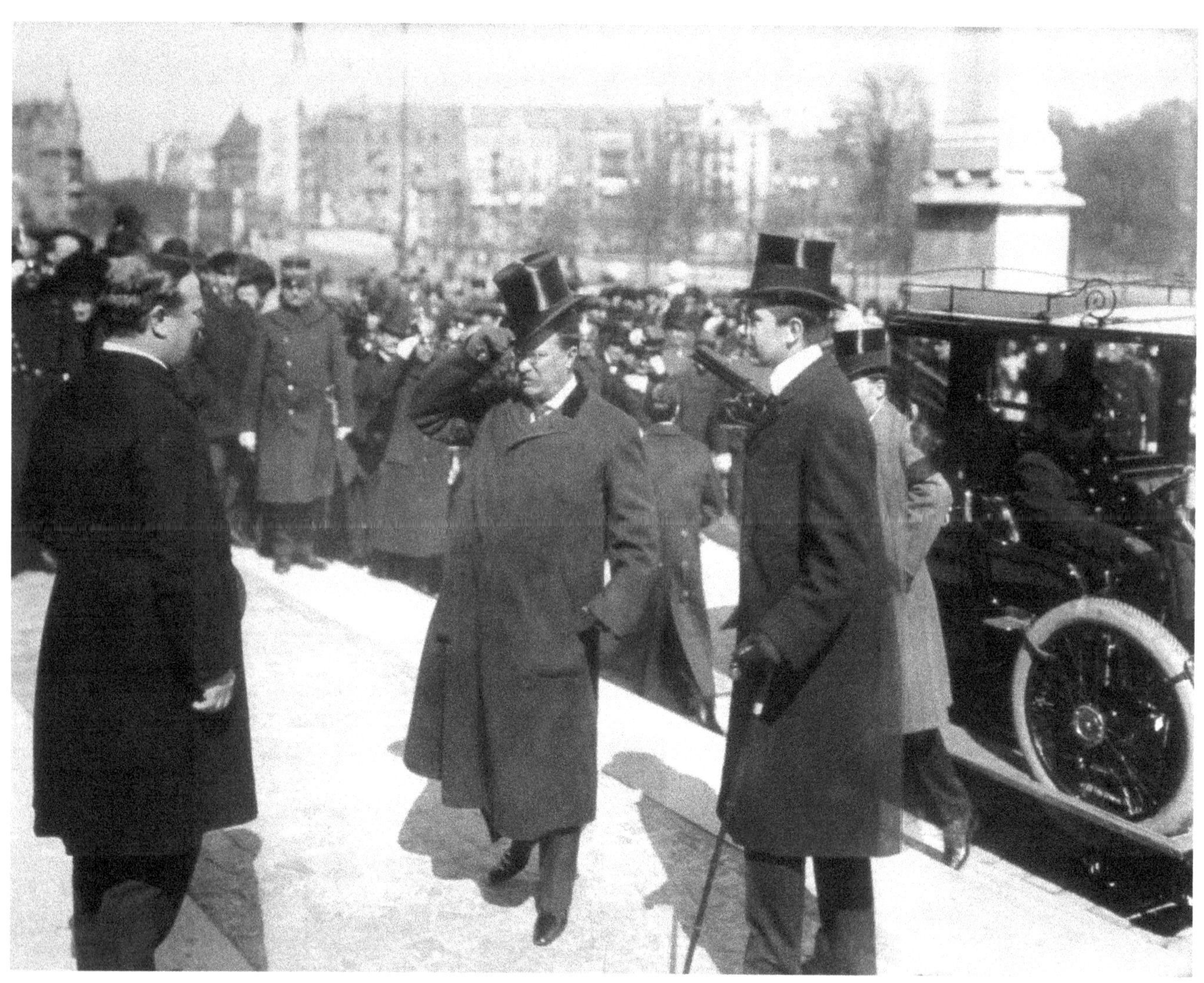

From Christiana, Norway, Roosevelt wrote to his friend Henry Cabot Lodge, "The various sovereigns have vied with one another in entertaining us," but he found the "popular reception" to have been "even more remarkable. I drive through dense throngs of people cheering and calling, exactly as if I were President." In this photograph, Roosevelt tips his hat in Stockholm, Sweden, in May 1910.

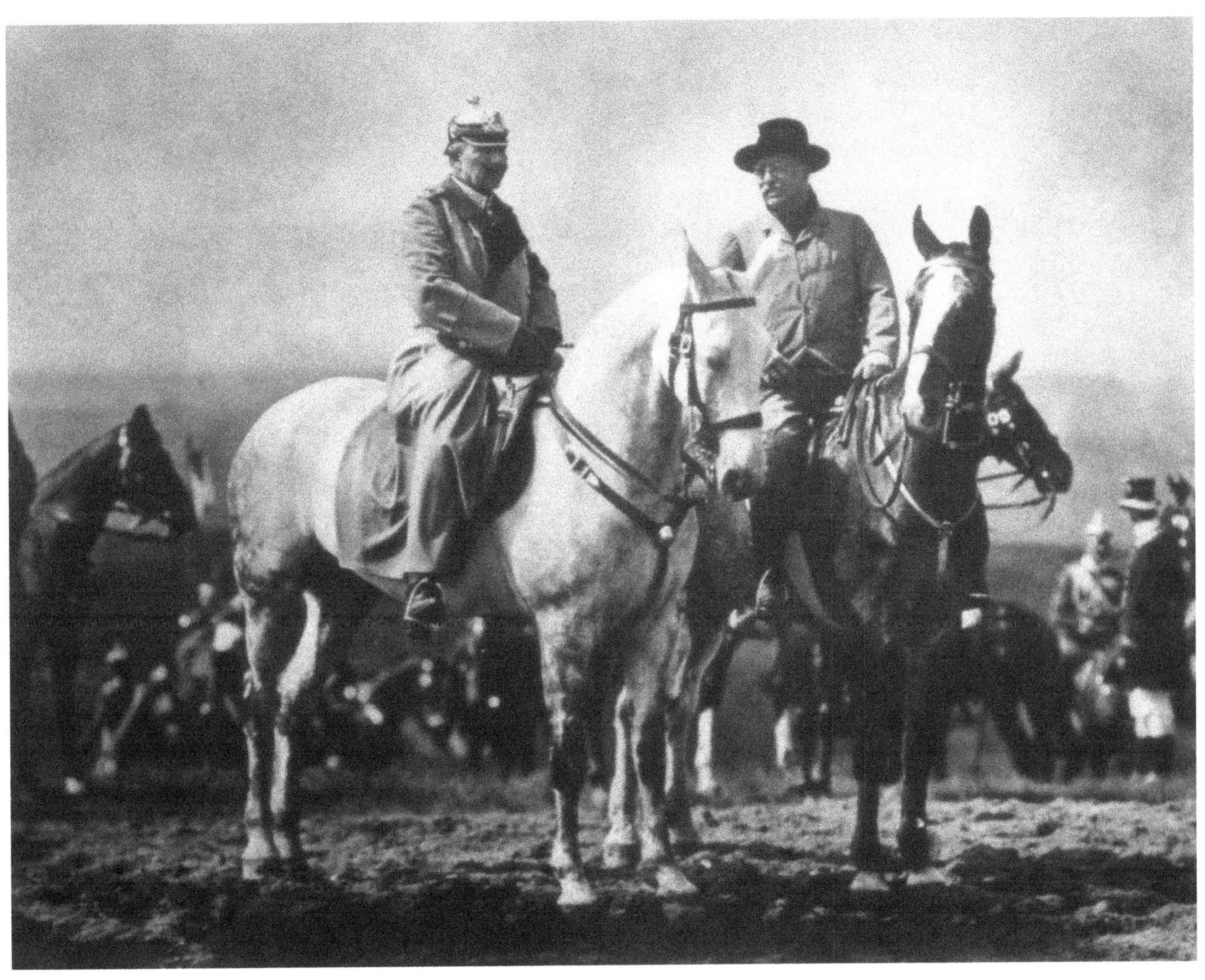

Roosevelt accepted an invitation from Kaiser Wilhelm to Berlin, which included a trip to Doberitz to view the German army's field maneuvers. Roosevelt was impressed but troubled by the evidence of growing militarism he saw across the continent. In his Berlin address, "The World Movement," TR lauded both the soldier and the philosopher but stressed overall how interdependent was the world and thus how interconnected every country's fate.

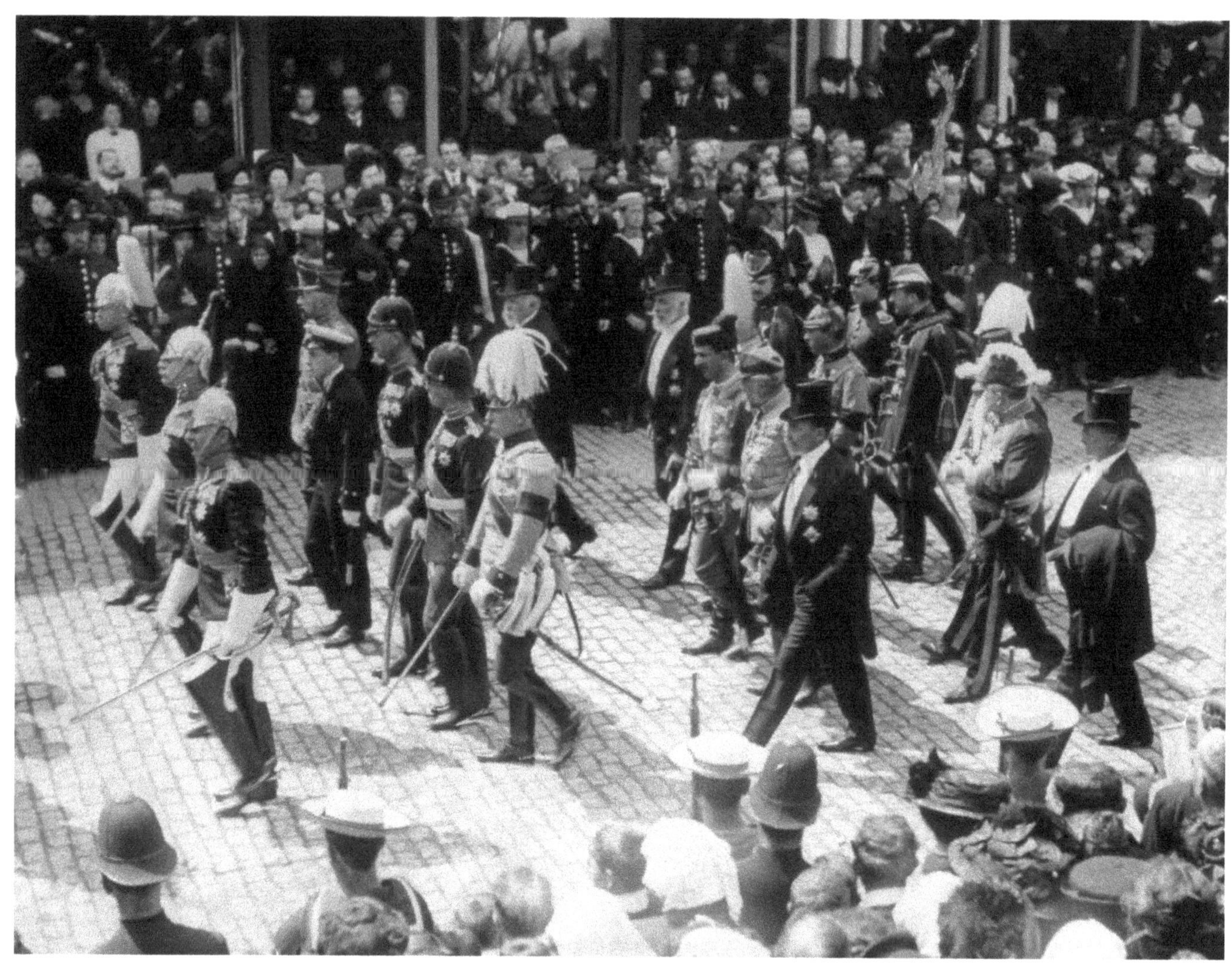

President Taft wired Roosevelt to ask him to represent the United States at the funeral of England's King Edward VII. Special Ambassador Roosevelt is shown here walking in the funeral procession along with dignitaries from other nations.

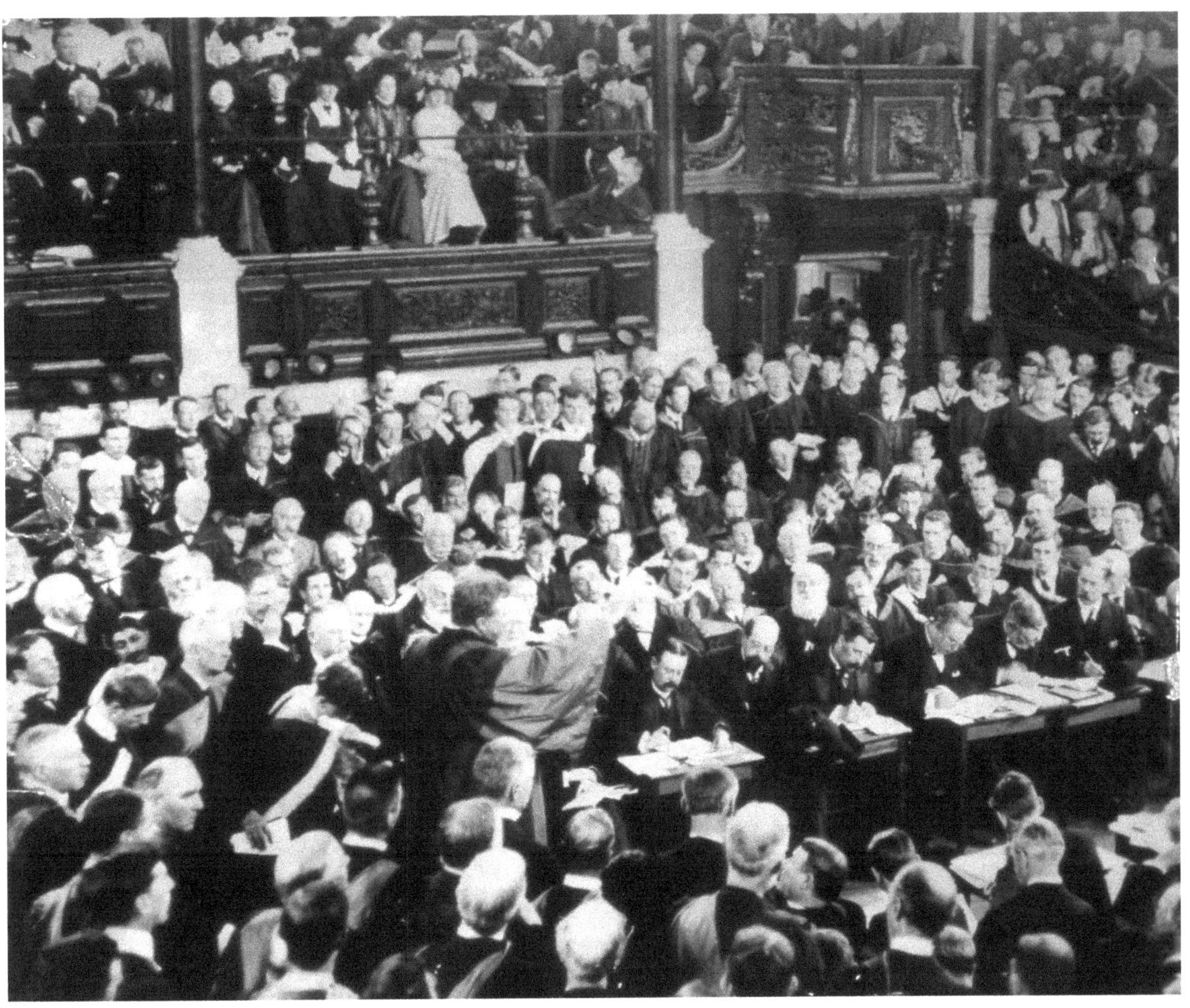

In Oxford, Roosevelt delivered the Romanes Lecture at the Sheldonian Theatre. His topic was "Biological Analogies in History." His conclusion called for the application of moral law internationally and exhorted his listeners that "we should tolerate lawlessness and wickedness neither by the weak nor by the strong."

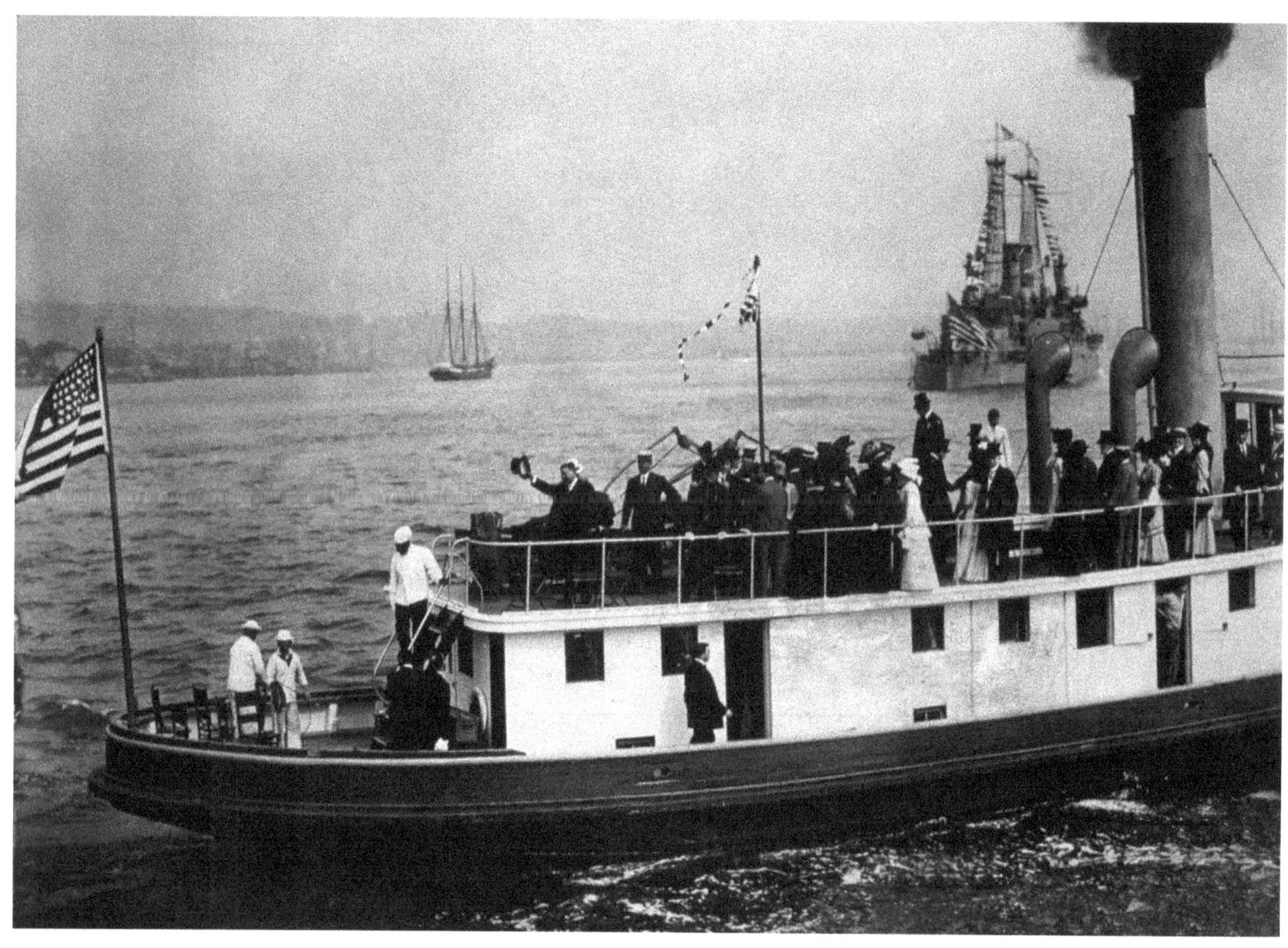

On June 18, 1910, the Roosevelts docked in New York. One hundred thousand people clogged the streets and the harbor to welcome them. The Colonel was overwhelmed. He had written to a friend on May 5: "Ugh! I do dread getting back to America, and having to plunge into the cauldron of politics," but in a speech on his homecoming Roosevelt rhapsodized about being "back in my own country . . . eager to do my part."

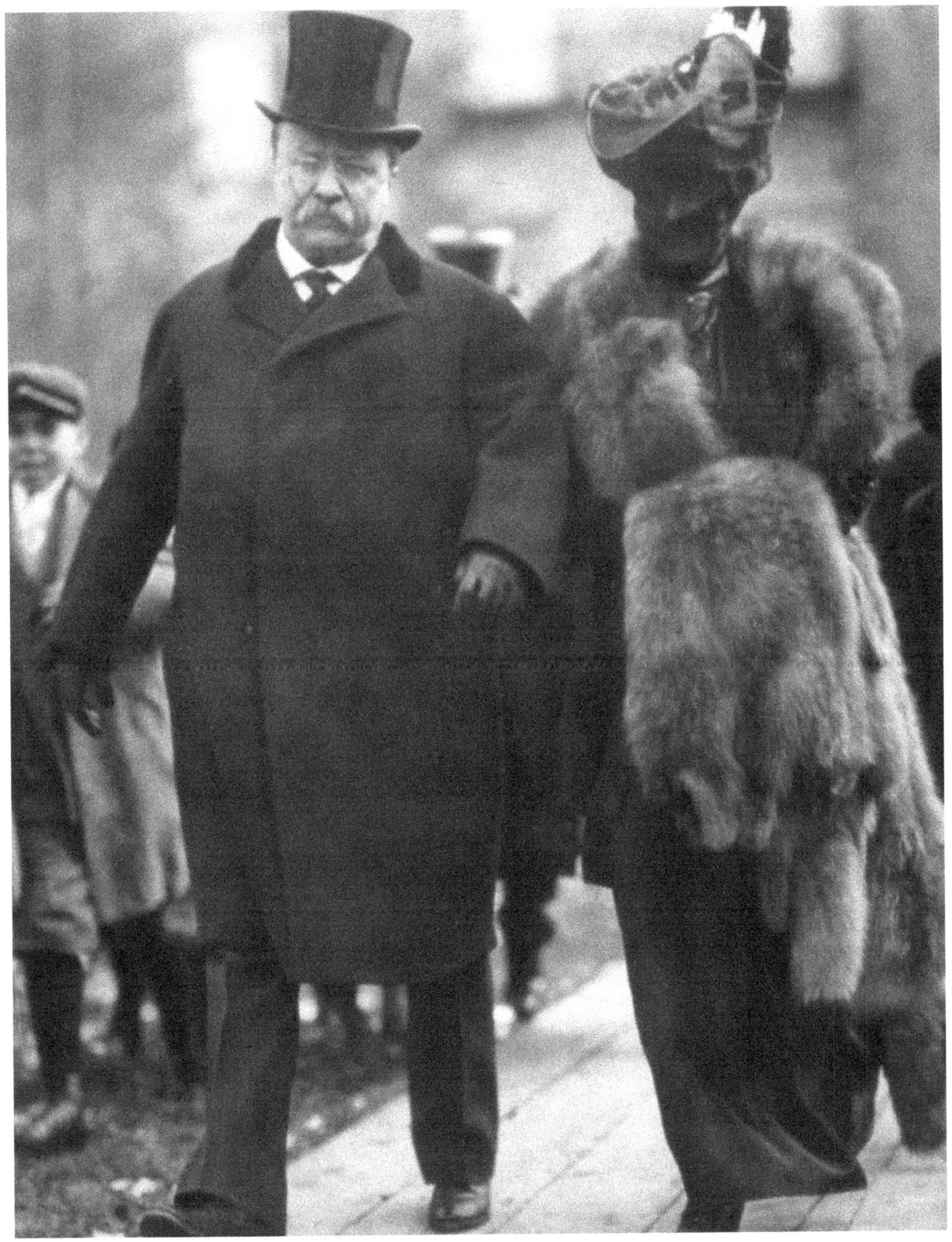

Edith and Theodore Roosevelt in 1910. The couple's devotion to each other had not ceased in the nearly quarter-century they had been married. Edith was especially happy to be away from the crowds in Europe and to have TR home again in Oyster Bay. In 1905, Edith had purchased a rustic cabin named Pine Knot, in Virginia, as an escape from Washington duties. The couple also planned to spend more time there after the presidency.

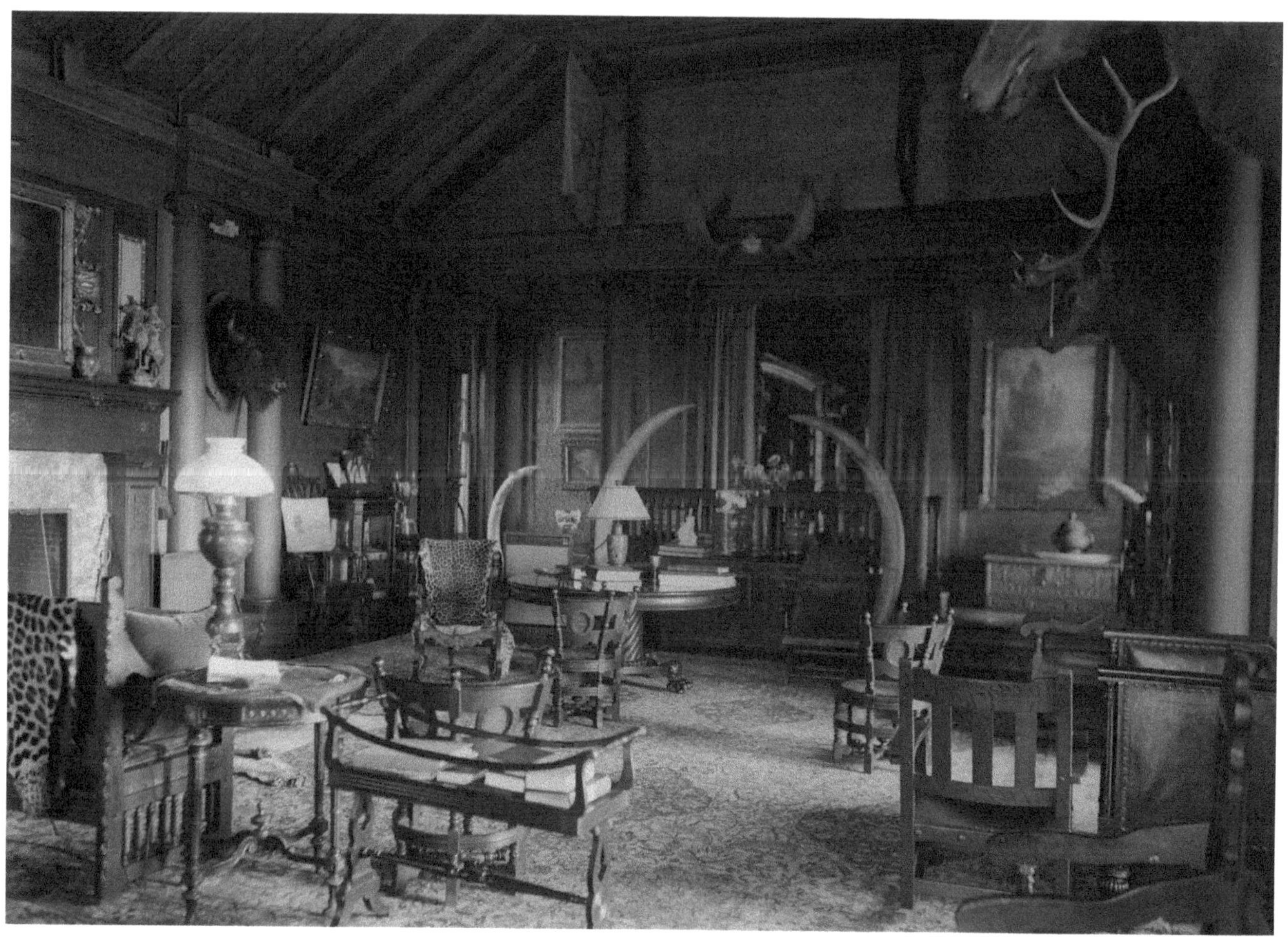

Roosevelt was overjoyed to return to Sagamore Hill. His Trophy Room was redecorated with the skins of animals bagged in Africa. Soon, however, there were more politicians than animal heads at Sagamore. Roosevelt learned that Taft had widened the split in the Republican Party, and further, that unhappy congressmen loyal to him were talking by then of a Progressive movement.

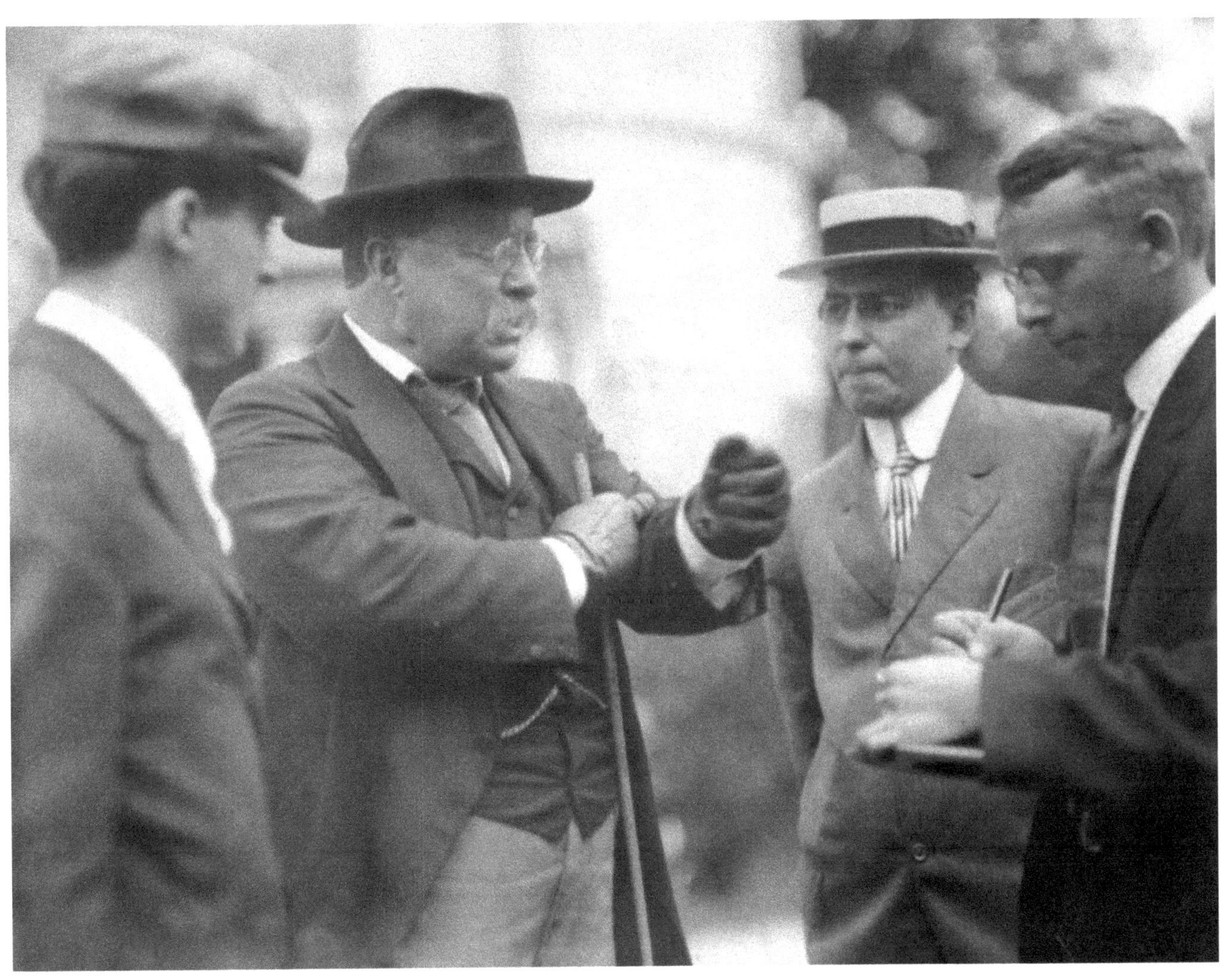

"Doing his part" began with a western tour to lend support to Republican candidates in the 1910 campaign. He left from his sister Corinne Roosevelt Robinson's home in Herkimer, New York. Roosevelt's goal was to heal the rift, but he found it impossible. His heart was with the progressives.

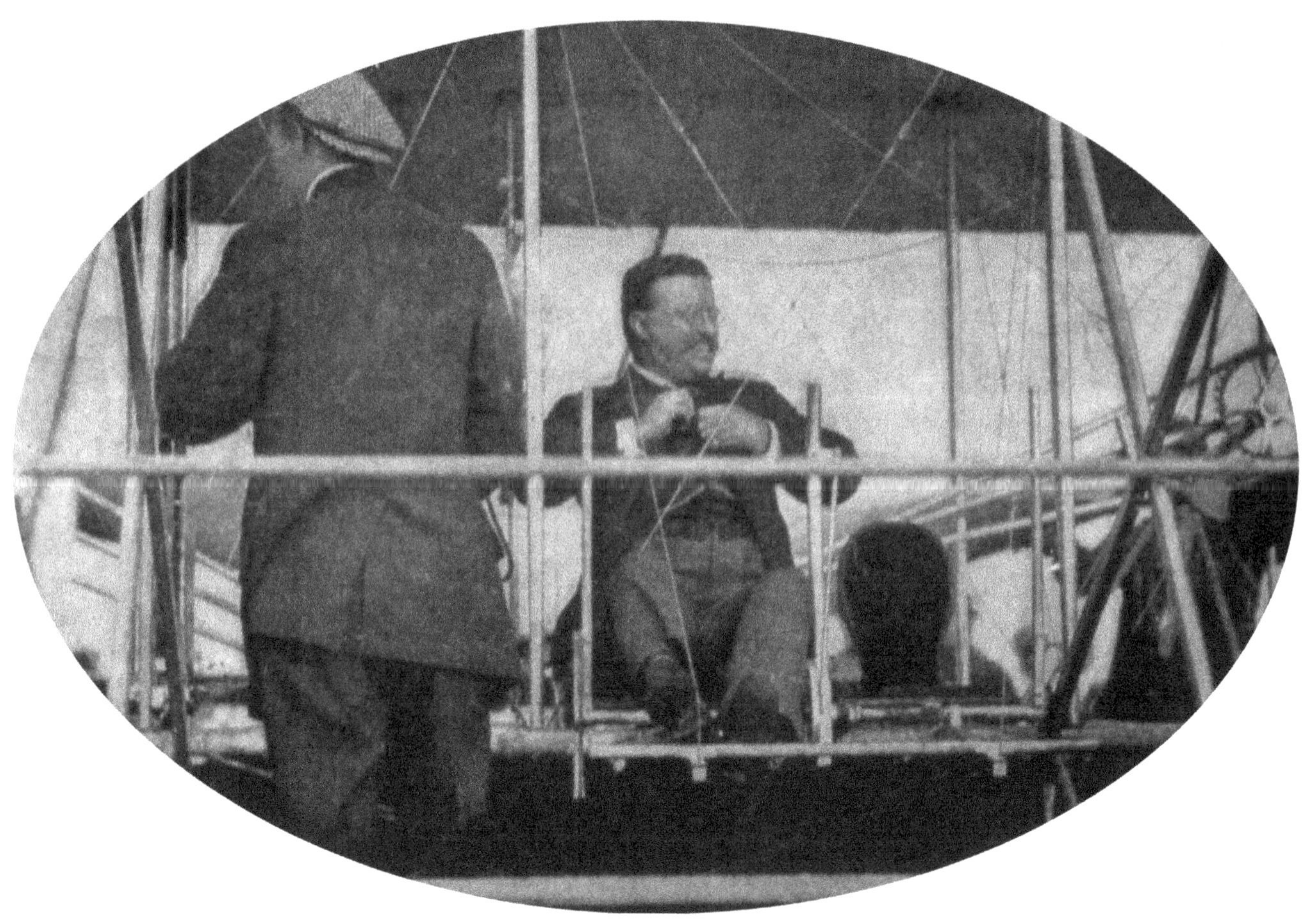

Theodore Roosevelt was the first president ever to fly in an airplane. On October 11, 1910, pilot Arch Hoxsey took TR up fifty feet in the air for a four-minute flight over the St. Louis airfield. The event—along with the former president's bravery—was filmed using the new motion picture camera. The whole Roosevelt family had been interested in flight since hearing aviation pioneer Samuel P. Langley discuss his experiments in the 1890s.

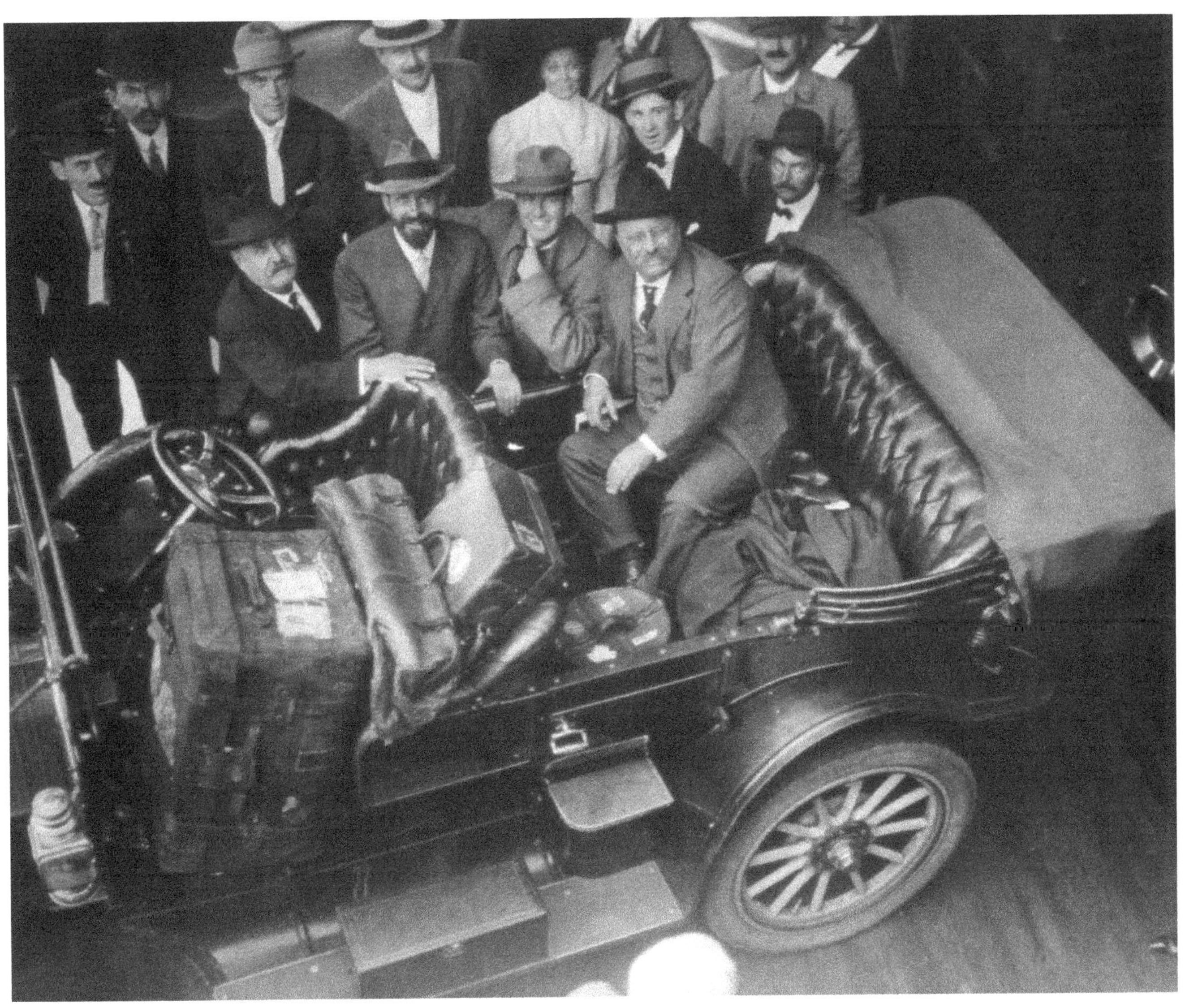

Here he is looking up from the backseat of an automobile in North River Ferry, New York, on September 11 at the end of the trip. Americans mused about the Colonel's speech of August 31 in Osawatamie, Kansas. "The New Nationalism" laid out TR's commitment to a panoply of progressive ideals like driving "special interests out of politics" and ascertaining that "property shall be the servant and not the master of the commonwealth."

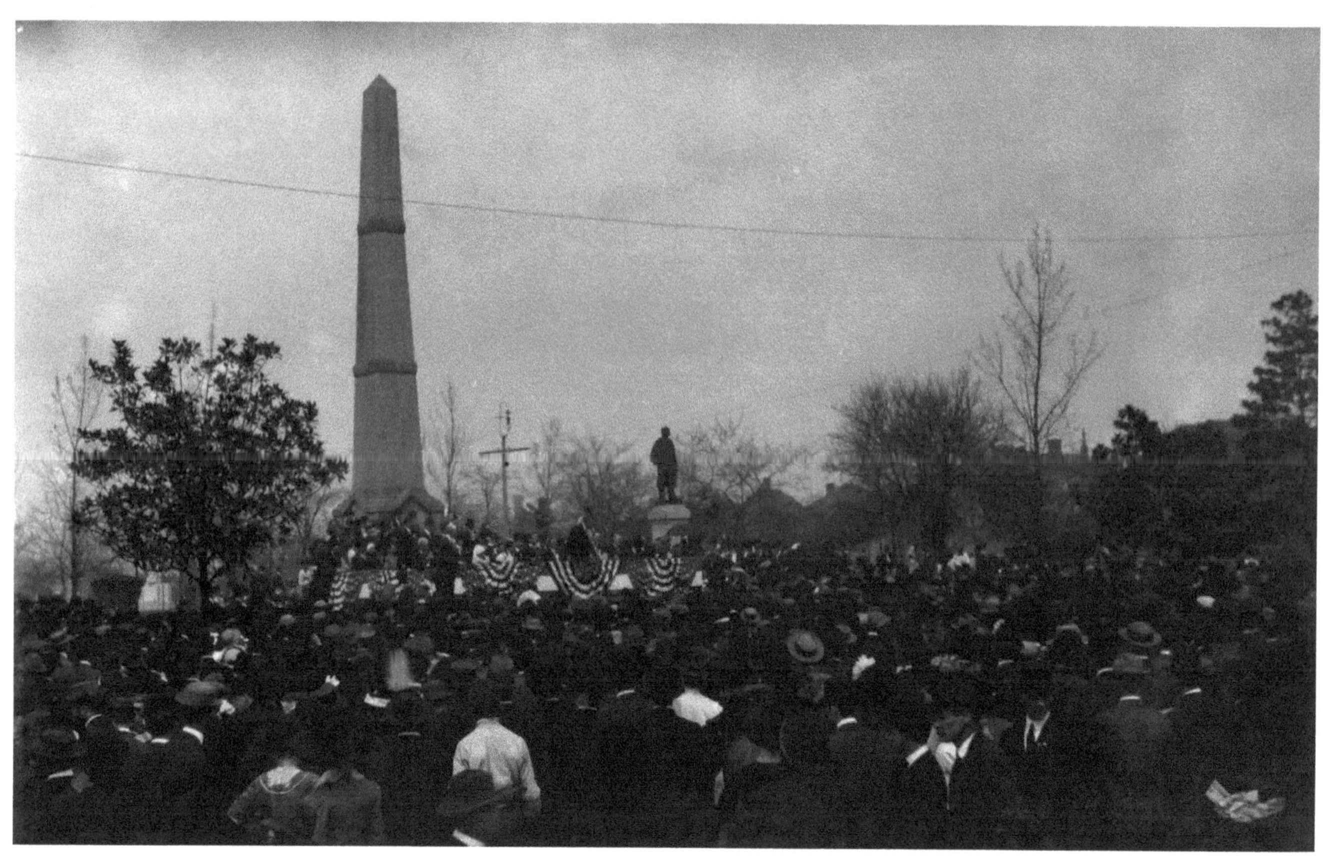

The National Child Labor Committee worked on a progressive goal: stricter laws against the exploitation of children in industrial jobs. Roosevelt gave an address before the NCLC in Birmingham, Alabama, in March 1911. Well-known labor advocates and social reformers like Jane Addams, Florence Kelley, and Lillian Wald worked with the NCLC, helping shape TR's views on women's suffrage as well as child labor.

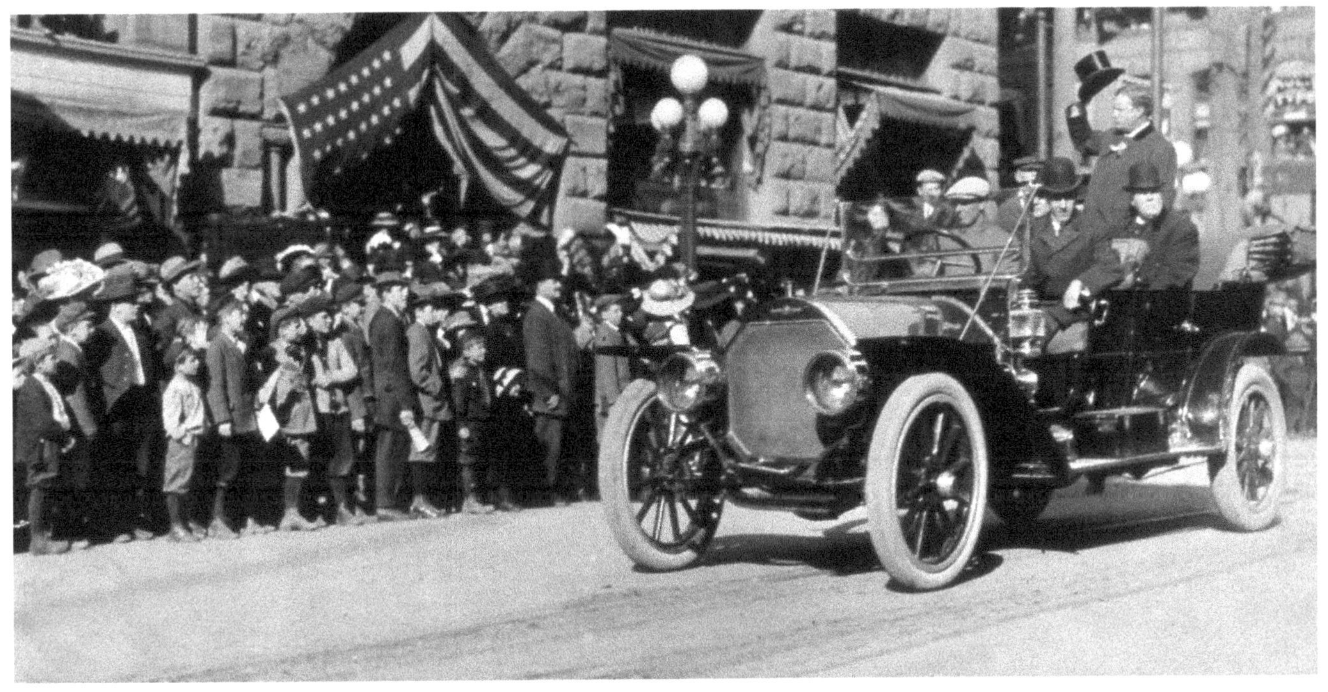

Roosevelt greeting crowds in Spokane, Washington, in early April 1911. Roosevelt had traveled to the West coast in mid March, but not before penning a letter to President Taft about the unrest in Mexico. Should the U.S. enter a war against Mexico—the sort where Japan might back Mexico—then, TR requested, he would like permission to raise a voluntary cavalry division of 12,000 men as he had done in Cuba. He had already chosen his officers, down to the majors and captains. Such a war never came about, but Taft might have had a difficult time turning down the very popular Colonel.

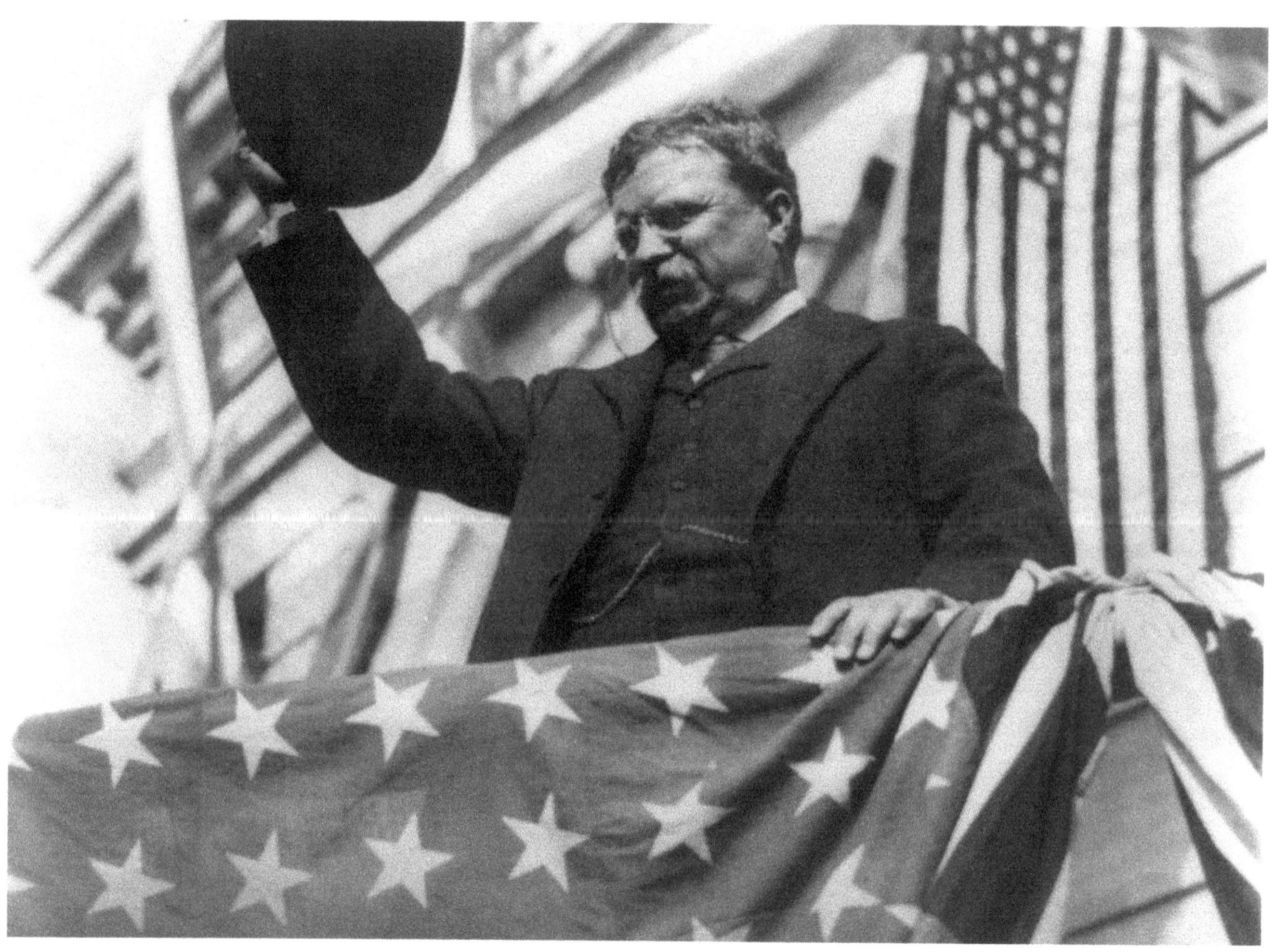

In January 1912, Roosevelt announced his intention to run for the Republican Party nomination against the incumbent, Taft. This momentous decision came because TR felt Taft ignored the progressive reform agenda. The crowds of people who came to see TR also persuaded him that Americans wanted him to run. At the G.O.P. convention he charged that the nomination was unfairly stolen from him, and so he launched a third party, called the Progressive Party (and nicknamed the Bull Moose Party) to challenge both the Republicans and the Democrats. "We stand at Armageddon," Roosevelt thundered, "and we battle for the Lord!"

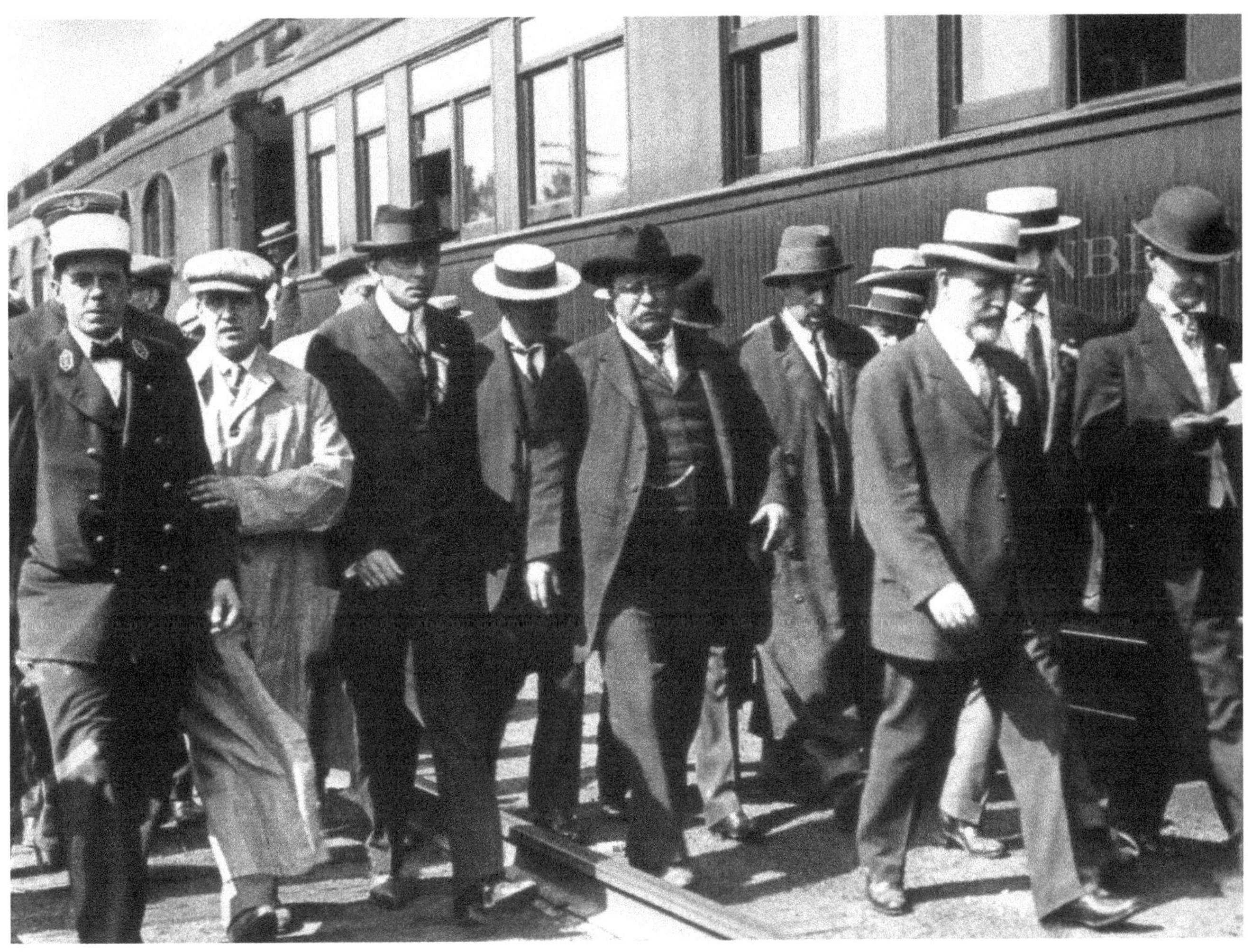

The Progressive Party platform avowed, "It is time to set the public welfare in the first place." It called for direct primaries, direct election of senators, initiative, referendum, and recall, an expedited process to amend the Constitution, equal suffrage for women, prohibition of child labor, a minimum wage for women workers, a six-day workweek, an eight-hour workday, and workers' safety laws, some form of retirement, campaign reform, an end to injunctions during labor strikes, a climate favorable to trade unions, an inheritance tax, and conservation of natural resources, among other things.

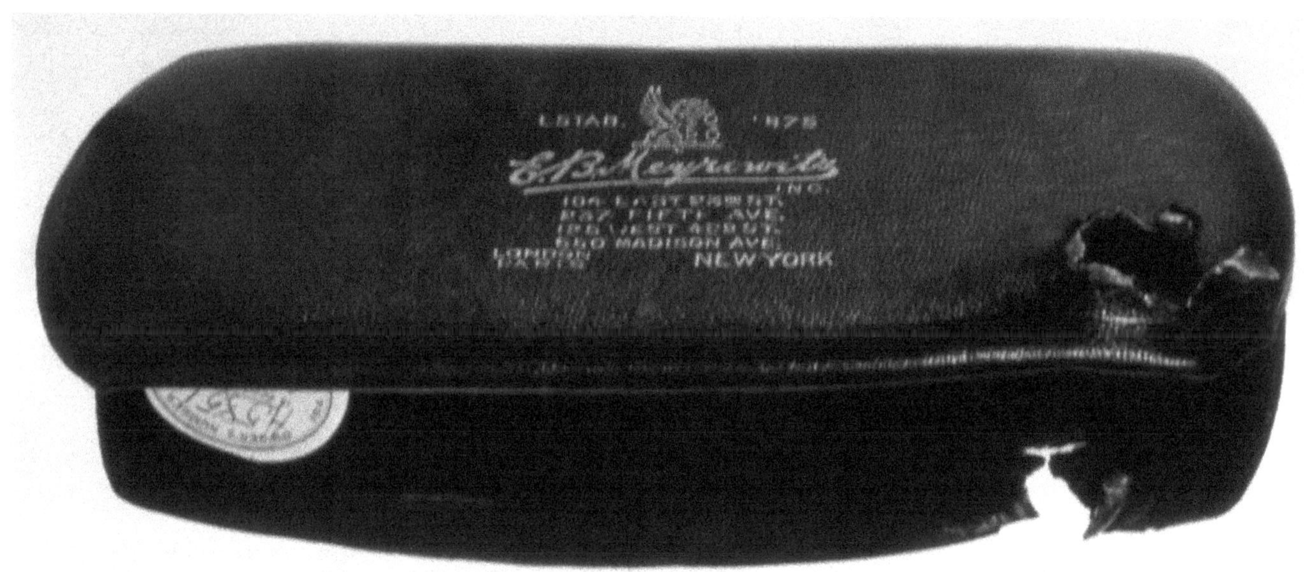

While campaigning in Milwaukee, Wisconsin, on October 14, 1912, Theodore Roosevelt was shot by John F. Schrank. The assassin's bullet hit TR in the chest as he was entering the hall to speak. Luckily for Roosevelt, the bullet passed first through his heavy overcoat, then through his folded-up speech, and finally through his steel eyeglasses case. The combination slowed the bullet, which missed his lung and lodged in a rib. Roosevelt insisted on giving his speech, which he did, before being hospitalized.

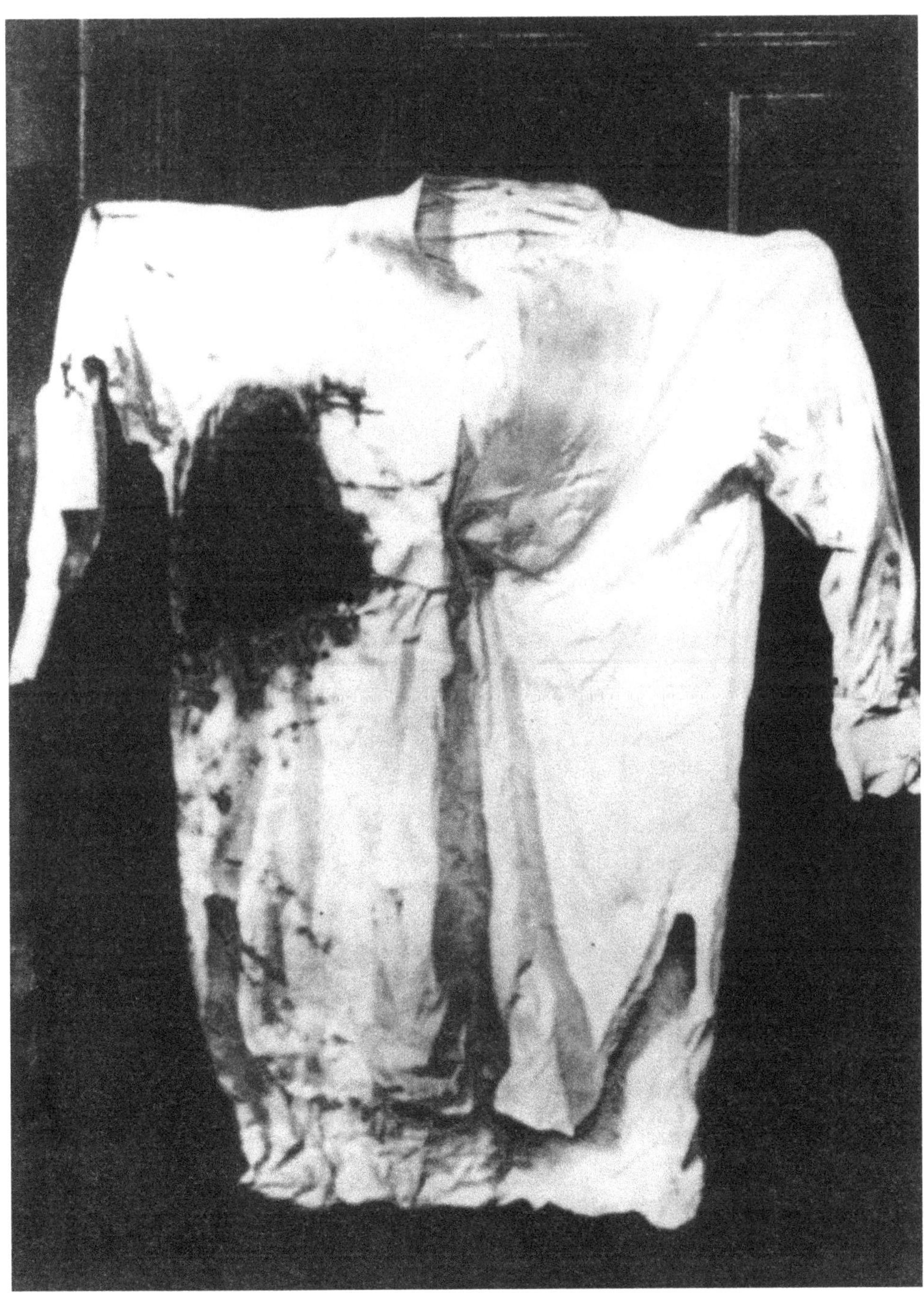

The shirt Roosevelt was wearing during the assassination attempt.

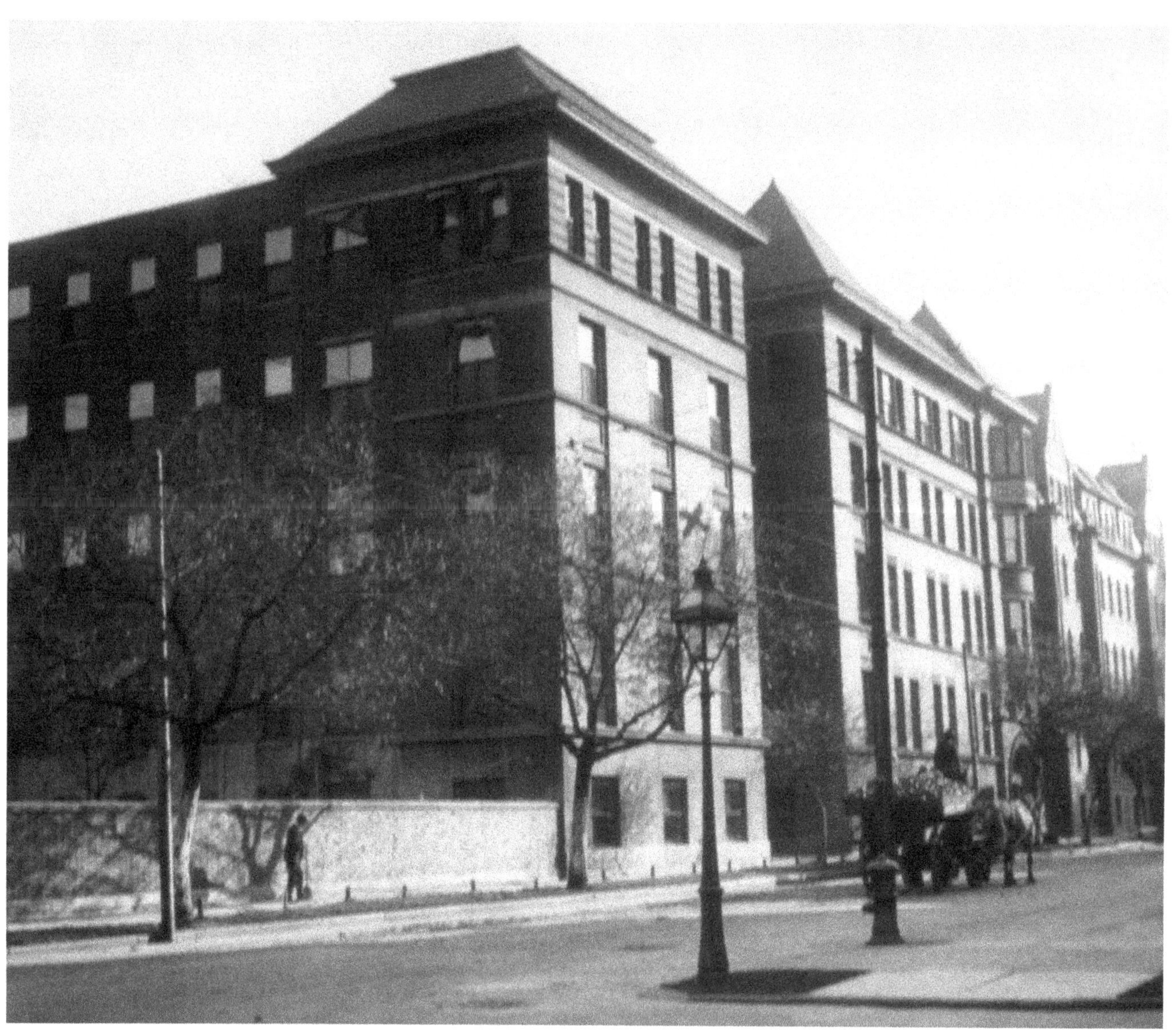

Roosevelt was moved to Mercy Hospital in Chicago, where his family joined him. In deference to their colleague, all campaigning stopped while Roosevelt was recuperating. The *x* on this photograph indicates Theodore Roosevelt's hospital room.

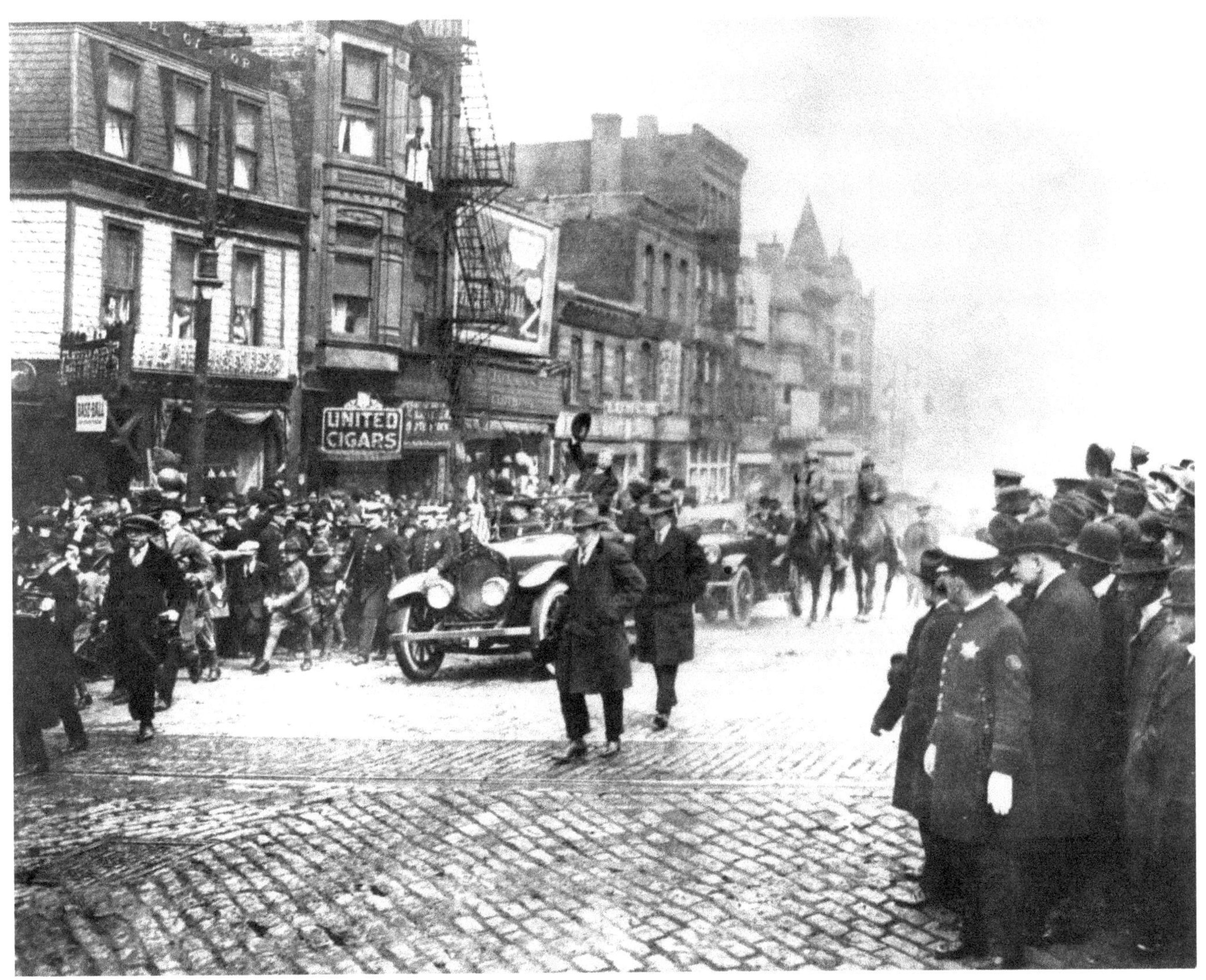

Roosevelt back on the campaign trail. His enemies were the same in 1912 as they had been in 1904. As he put it on May 27, 1903, "The big New York and Chicago capitalists—and both the criminal rich and the fool rich—will do all they can to beat me." Taft's control of the G.O.P. machinery also hampered his fight.

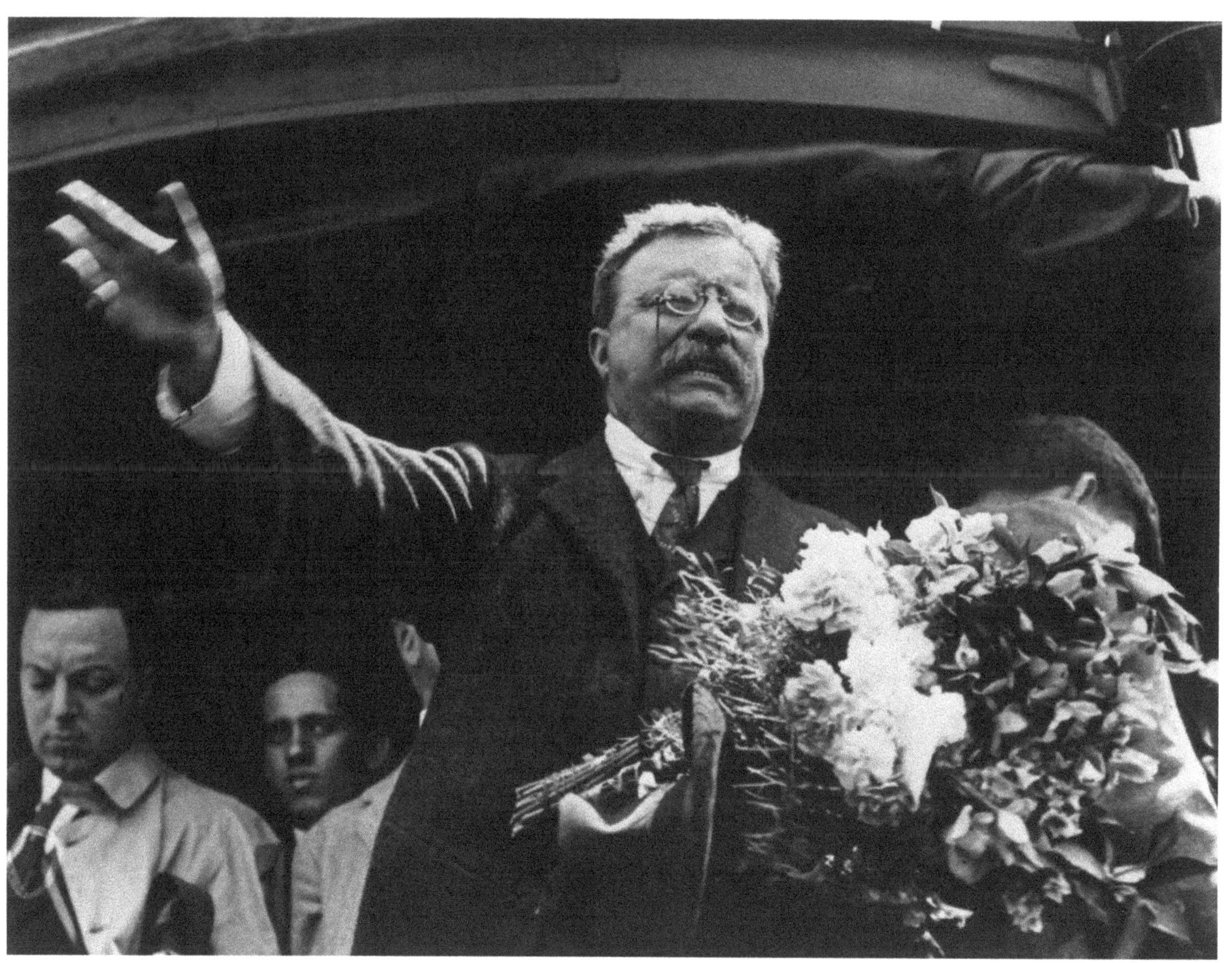

Roosevelt holding a bouquet of flowers. Although his popularity remained undimmed among Americans, Roosevelt lost the 1912 election. Progressive Democrat Woodrow Wilson was the country's choice. TR's electoral college tally of 88 trounced Taft's 8.

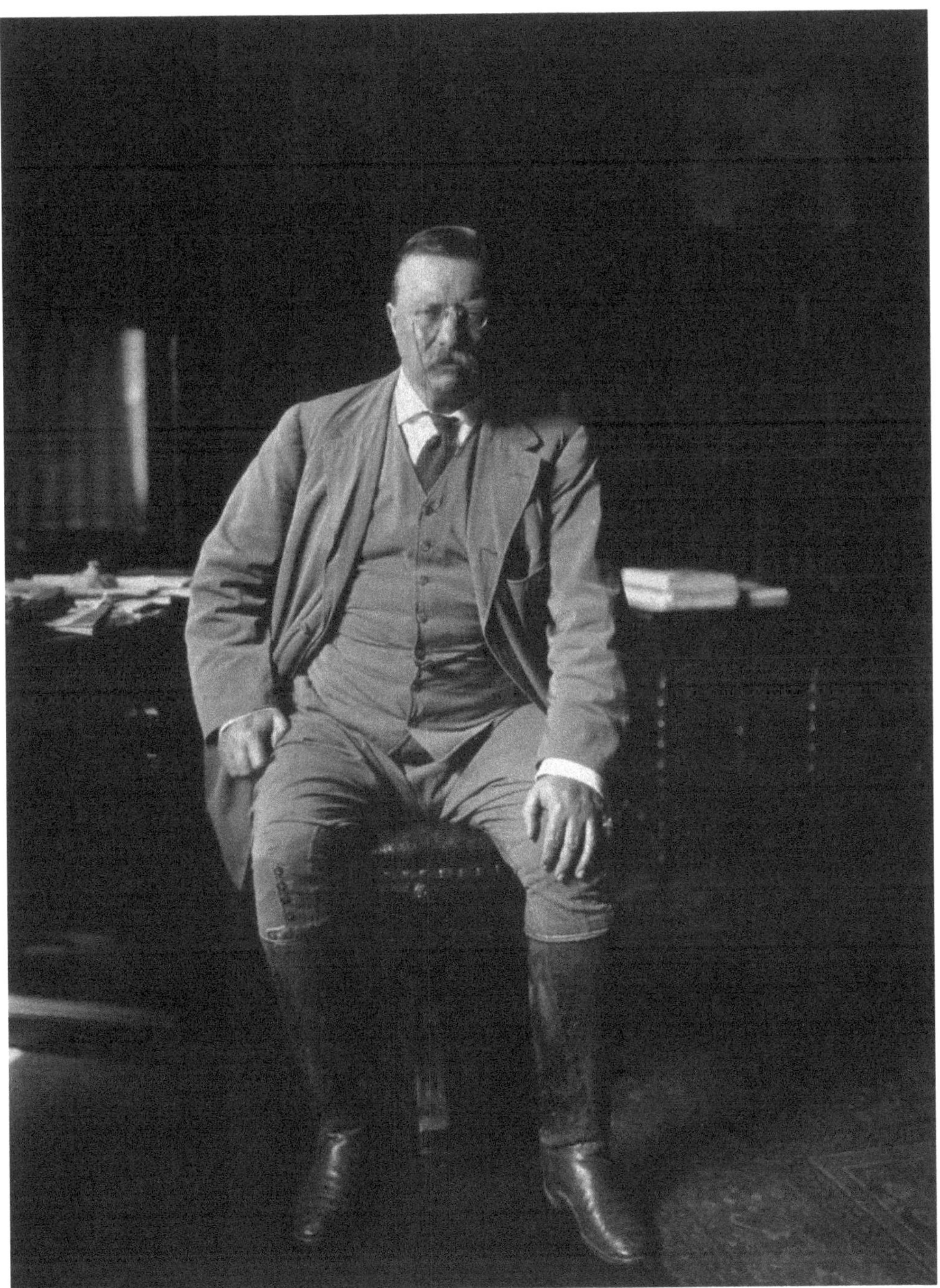

Theodore Roosevelt in the library at Sagamore Hill. After the loss in 1912, Roosevelt wrote his autobiography and served as president of the American Historical Association. With the publication of *History as Literature, and Other Essays,* he was nearing his twentieth book.

Leonard Wood had been Roosevelt's superior at the onset of the Spanish-American War. He subsequently became the military governor of Cuba, then fought in the Philippine-American War and was promoted to major general in 1903. In 1910, Wood served as Army Chief of Staff, implementing several innovations. During World War I, he trained infantry divisions. He stands next to his old friend TR.

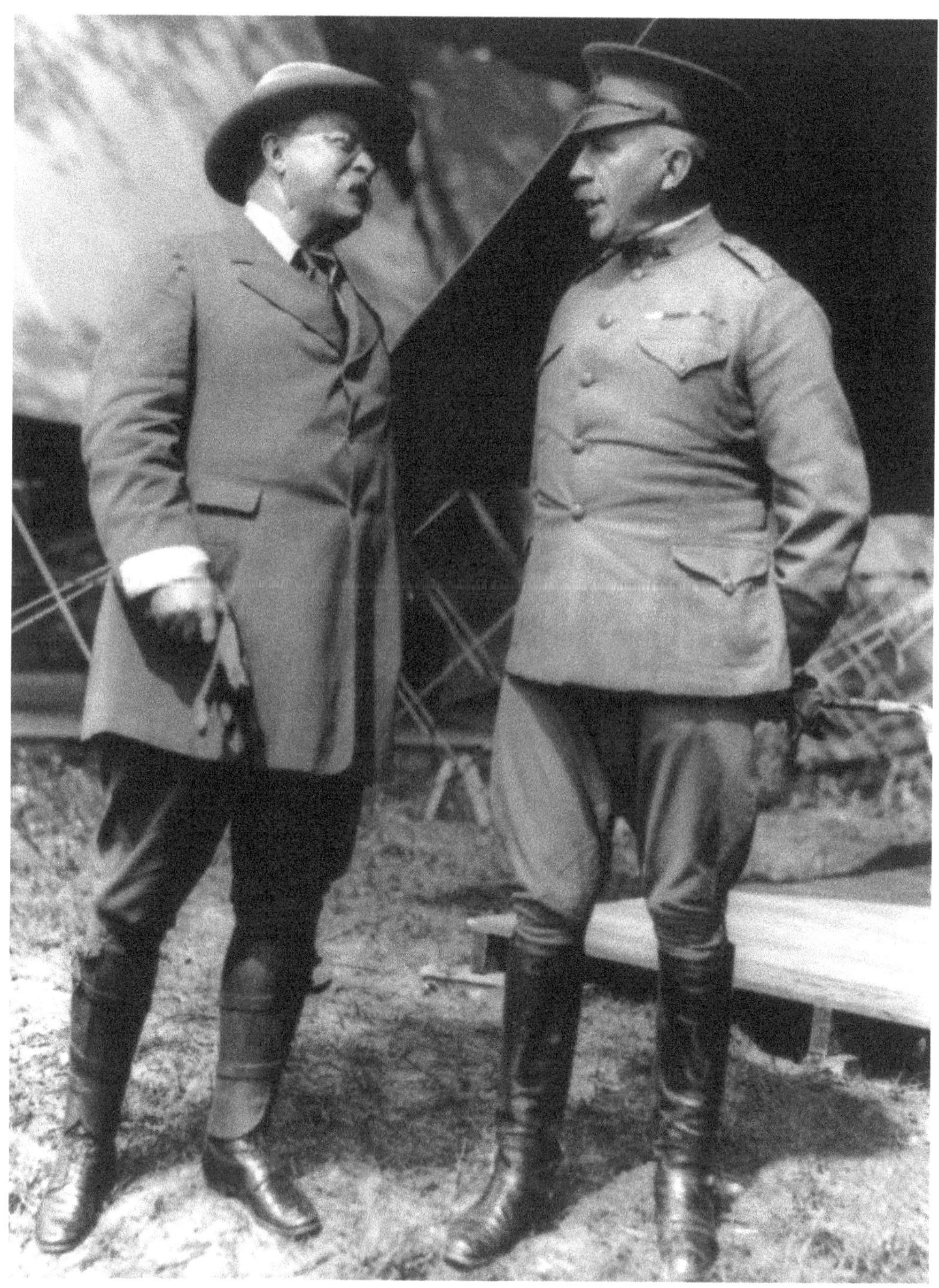

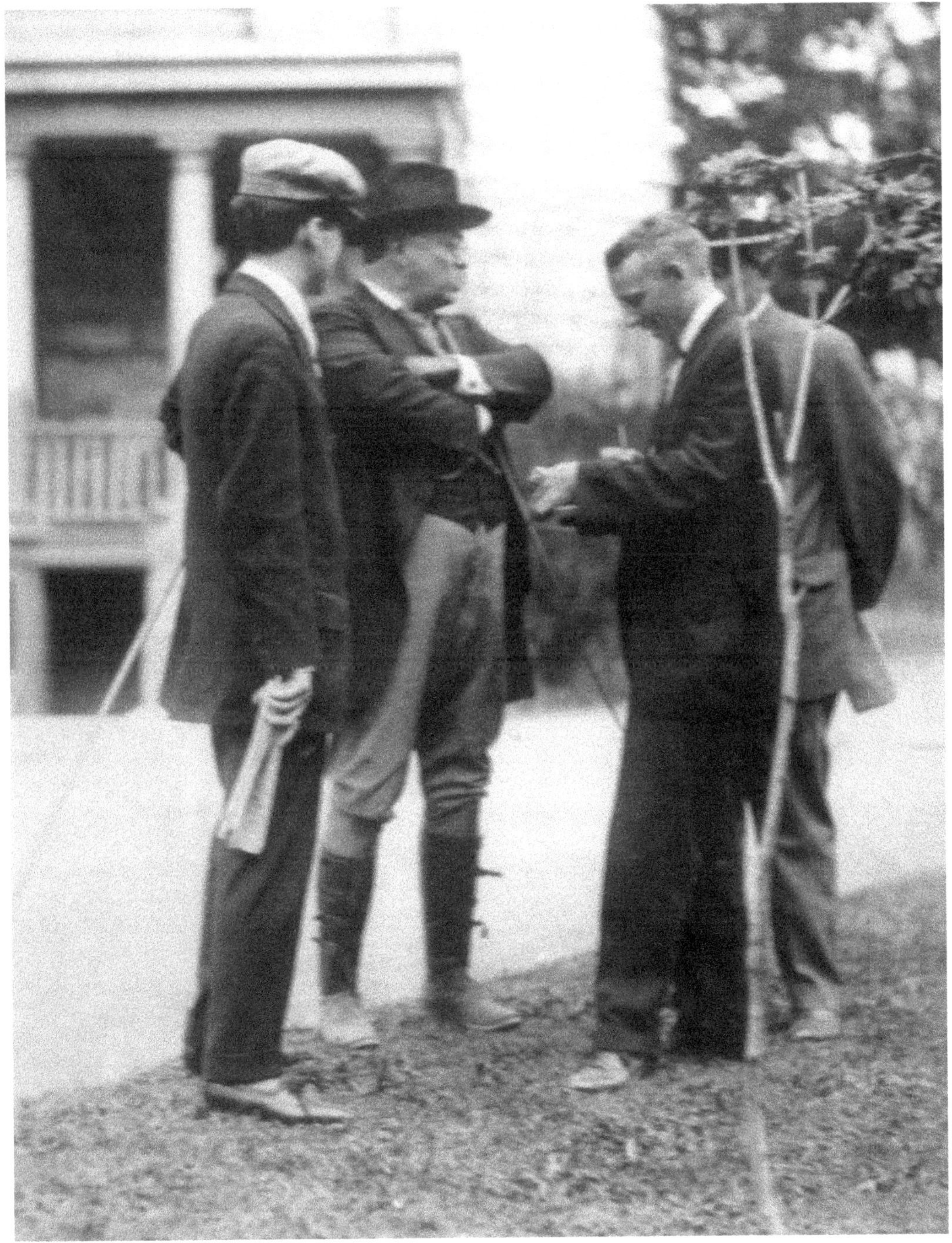

Theodore Roosevelt in 1914, pausing at his sister's home in the middle of a speaking tour. As head of the Progressive Party, a man of letters and of science, TR was frequently asked to deliver lectures to audiences of every sort.

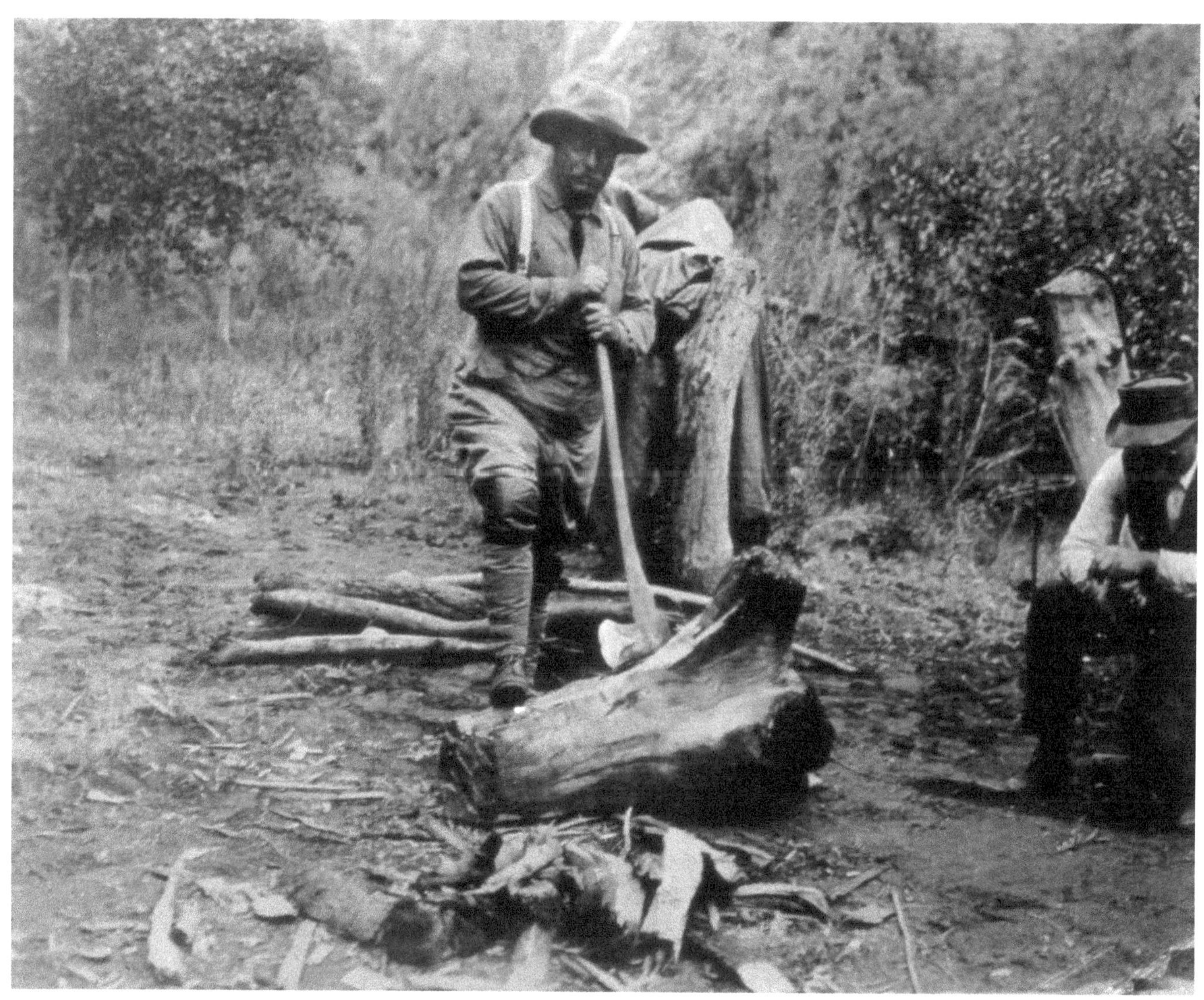

Roosevelt stands on the North Rim of the Grand Canyon in a characteristic pose, chopping wood, in July 1913.

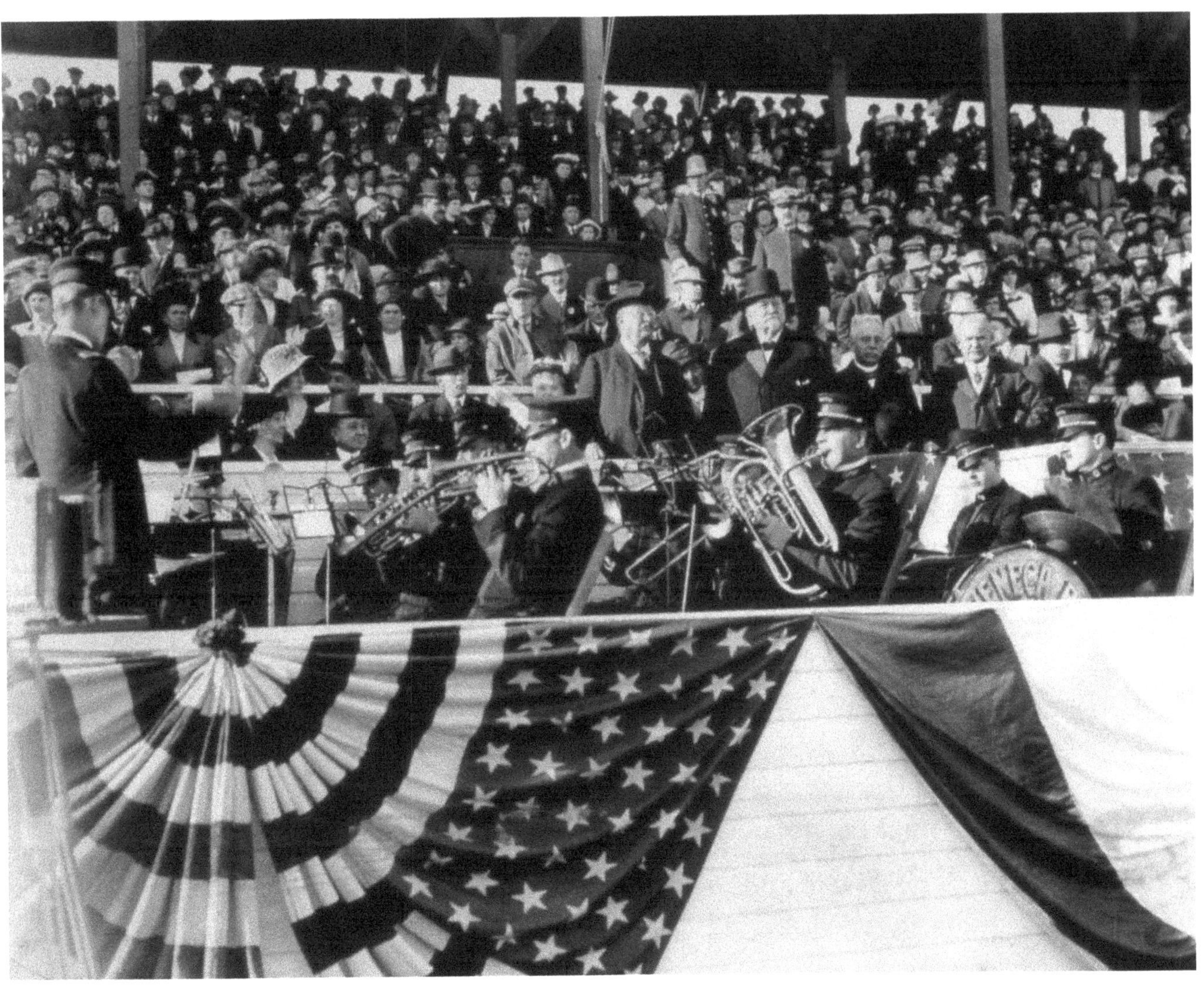

This photograph was taken not long after TR returned from five weeks in New Mexico and Arizona, and one month before Roosevelt prepared to leave on an exploration of an uncharted river in South America. Roosevelt is giving an address at the Rochester Exposition in New York.

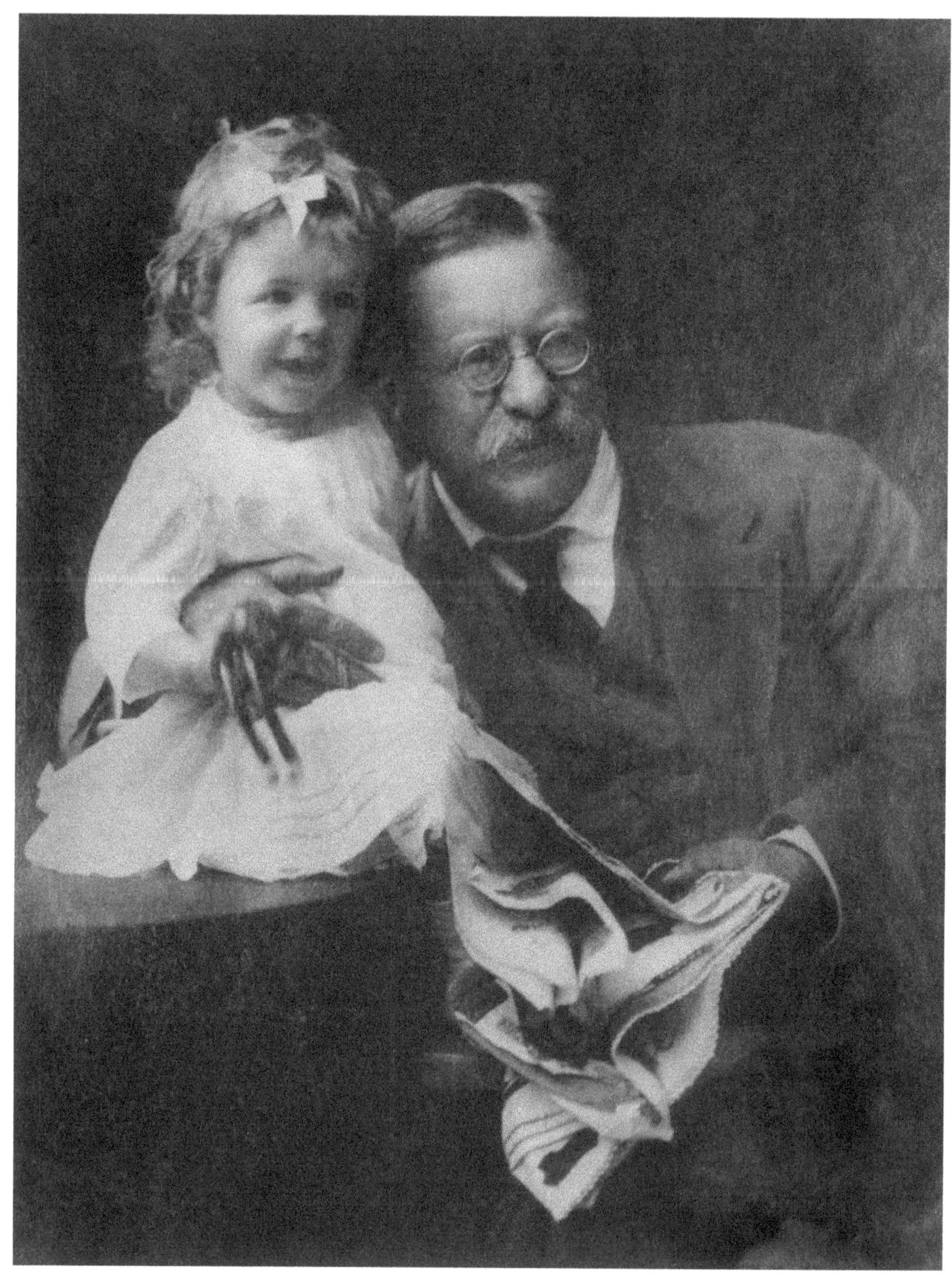

Roosevelt with his first grandchild, Ted and Eleanor's daughter Grace Green Roosevelt, born in the fall of 1913. Because Edith was suffering from a riding accident, the new grandparents did not immediately see Gracie, who was born in California.

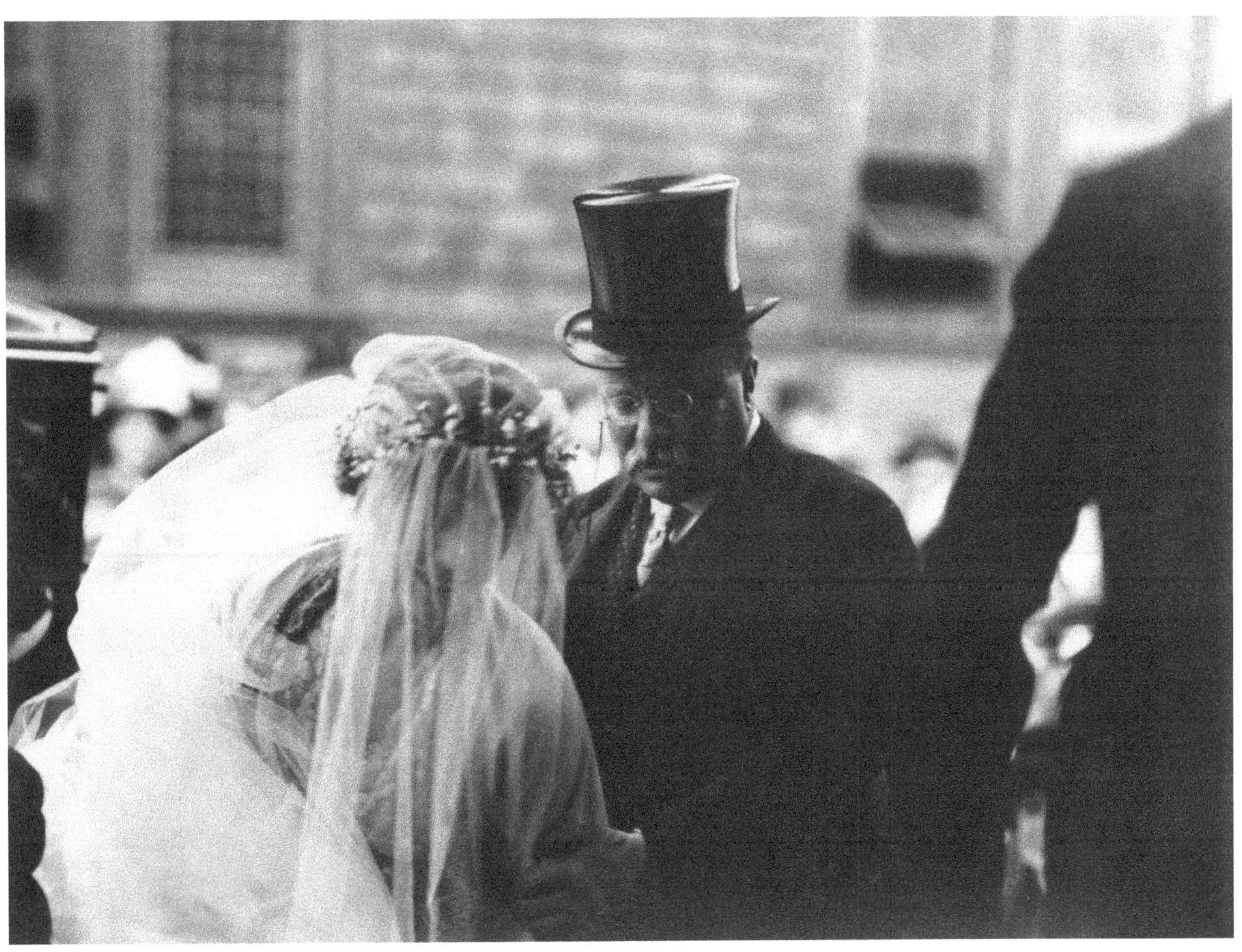

On April 4, 1913, Ethel Roosevelt wed Richard Derby at Christ Episcopal Church in Oyster Bay. TR heartily approved of his physician son-in-law, and in this photograph is ready to give the bride away. Of his two daughters, Ethel was the dutiful homebody. Like her mother, she preferred privacy. Ethel served as the glue that held the siblings together.

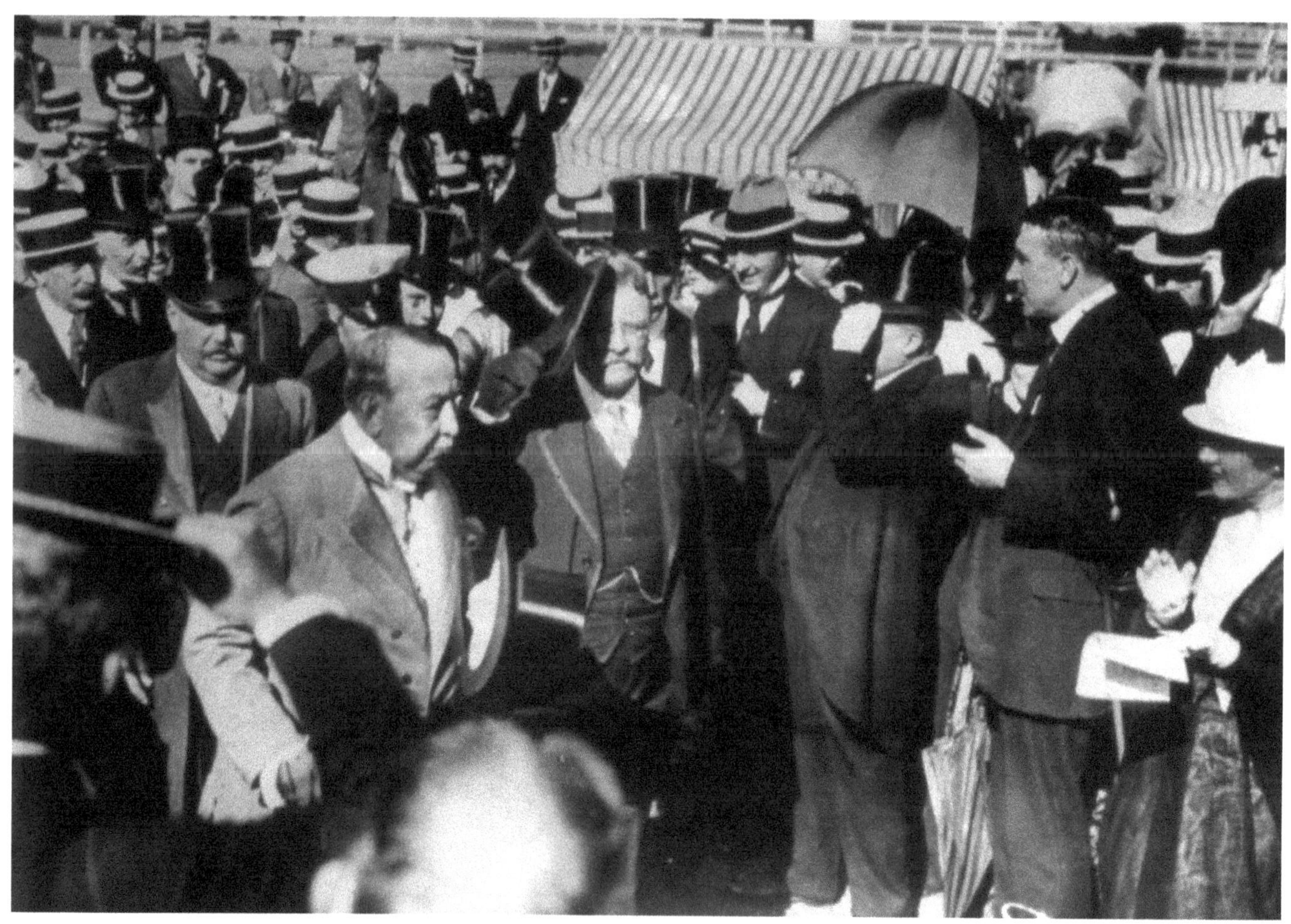

Surrounded by a crowd in Buenos Aires—one of several cities on his lecture circuit—Roosevelt reinterpreted the Monroe Doctrine. He then left for the South American wilderness on a new expedition, which he called his "last chance to be boy."

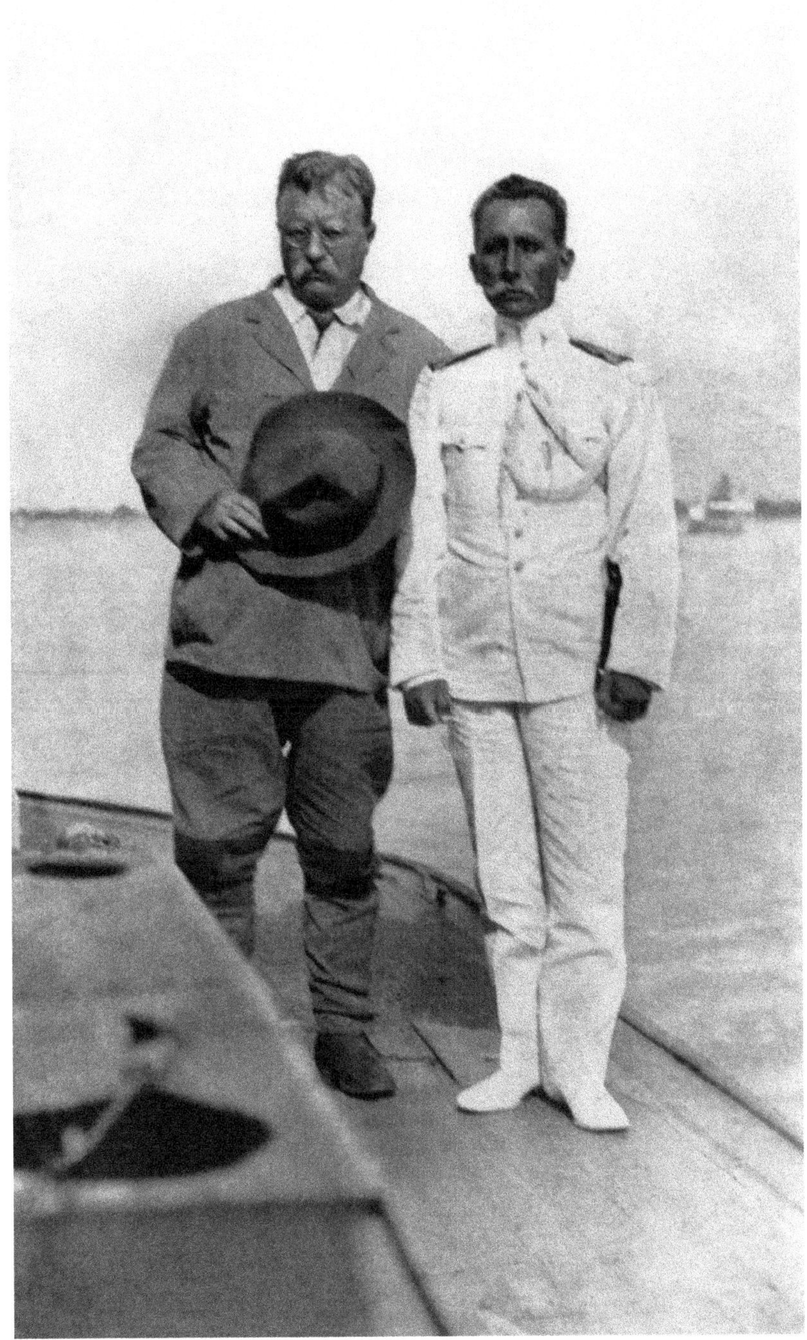

Colonel Candido Mariano da Silva Rondon was Roosevelt's fellow explorer. Their plan was to map an uncharted Brazilian river that Rondon had noticed on an earlier surveying mission. He referred to the river as the River of Doubt.

The exploration of the River of Doubt was financed similarly to the African safari—the American Museum of Natural History would provide funding and a cadre of naturalists to assist Roosevelt in the acquisition of a variety of plants and animals, and Scribner's Magazine promised remuneration for TR's articles about their trip.

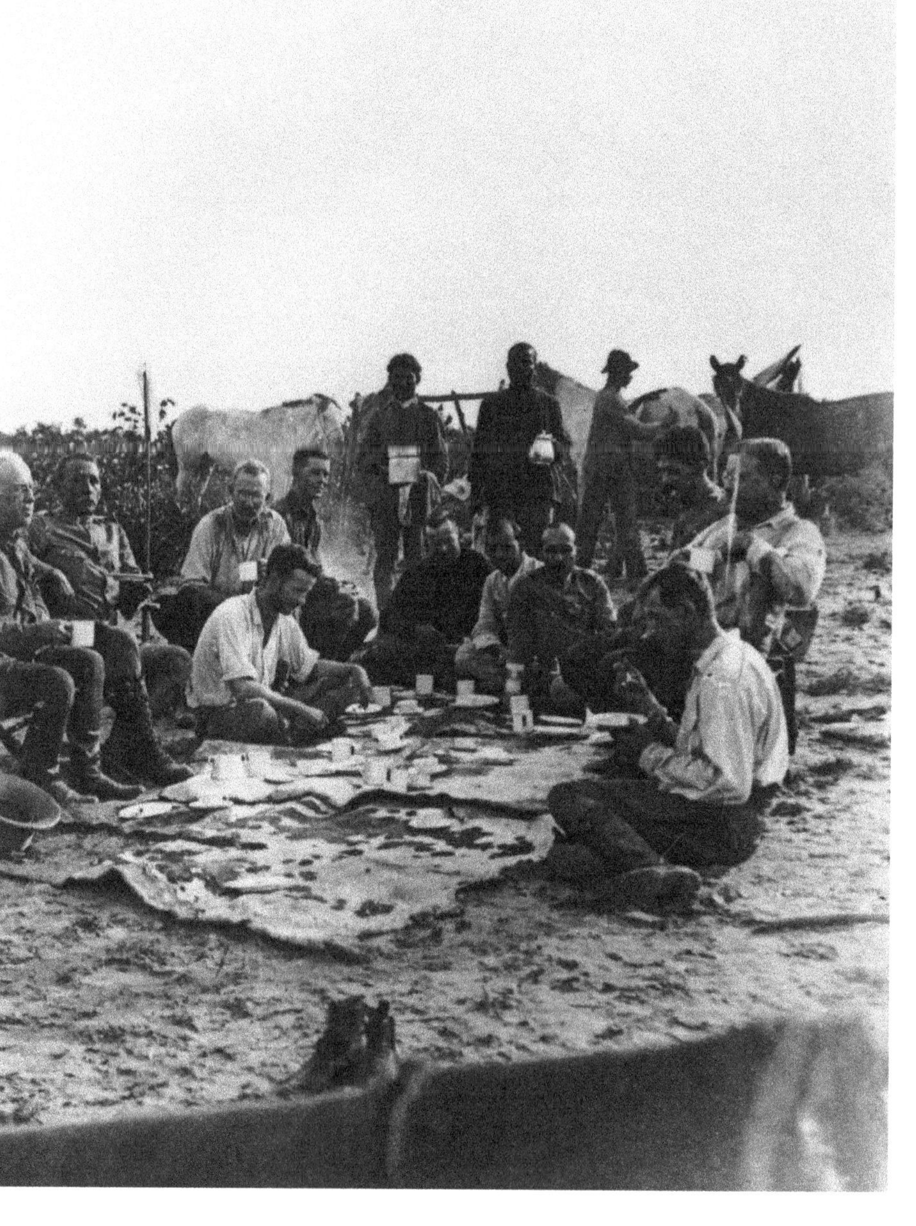

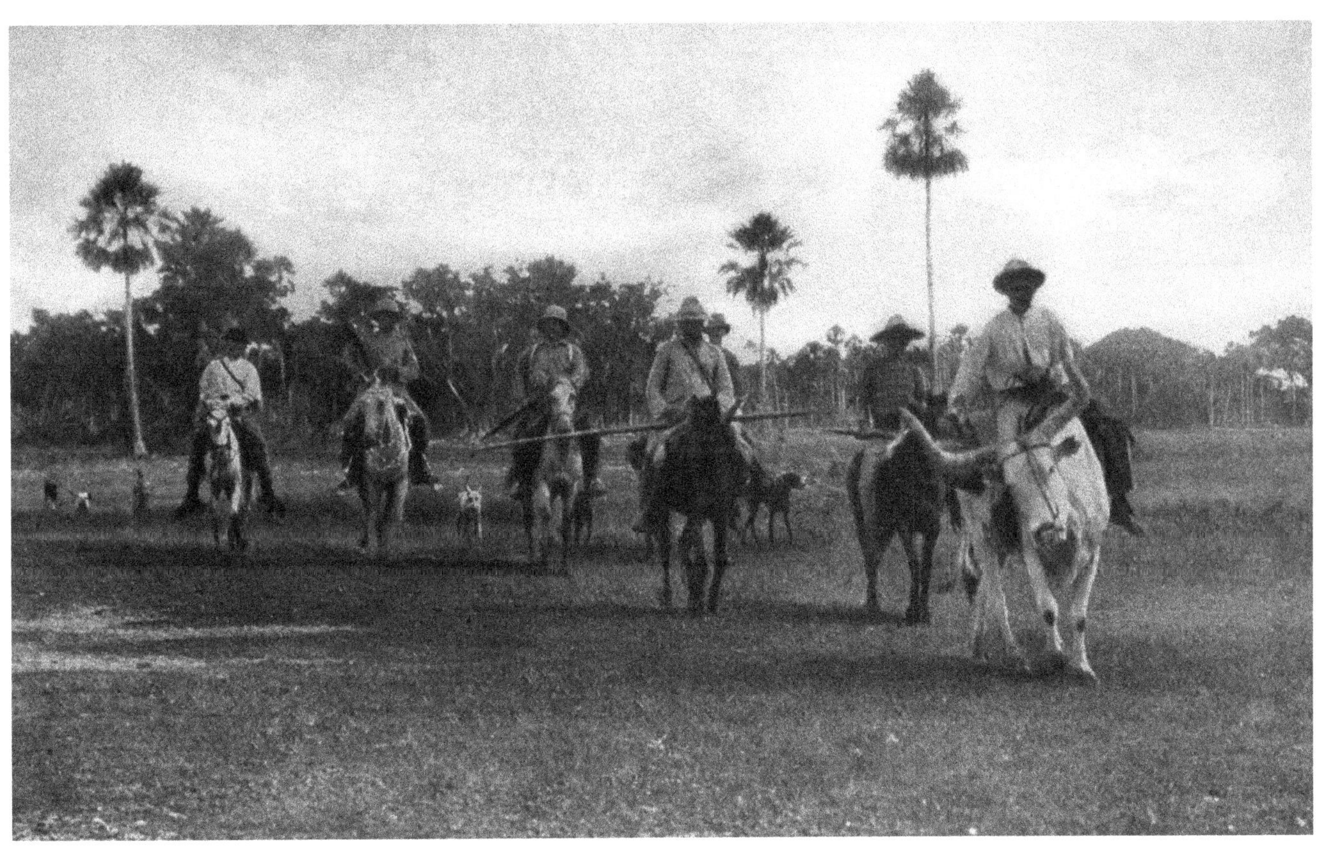

Roosevelt and some of his party at a ranch near Rio Taquary in Brazil. Edith Roosevelt asked Kermit to accompany his father on this trip as well, thinking that the 56-year-old might need his son's assistance. In *The Long Trail,* Kermit told of the difficulties they encountered, like losing six of their ten canoes with the supplies and food they carried, how the river had very few fish, and how they existed on half-rations.

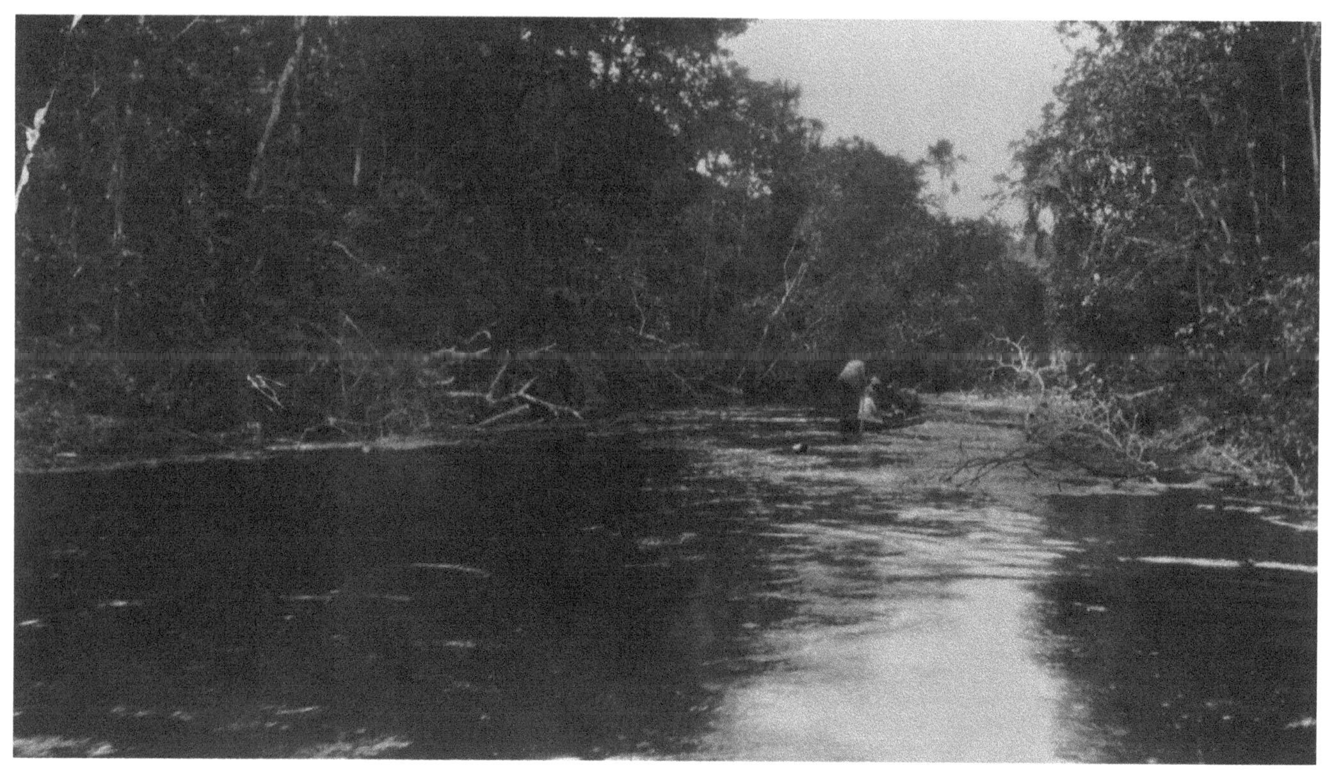

Starting down the River of Doubt, February 27, 1914.

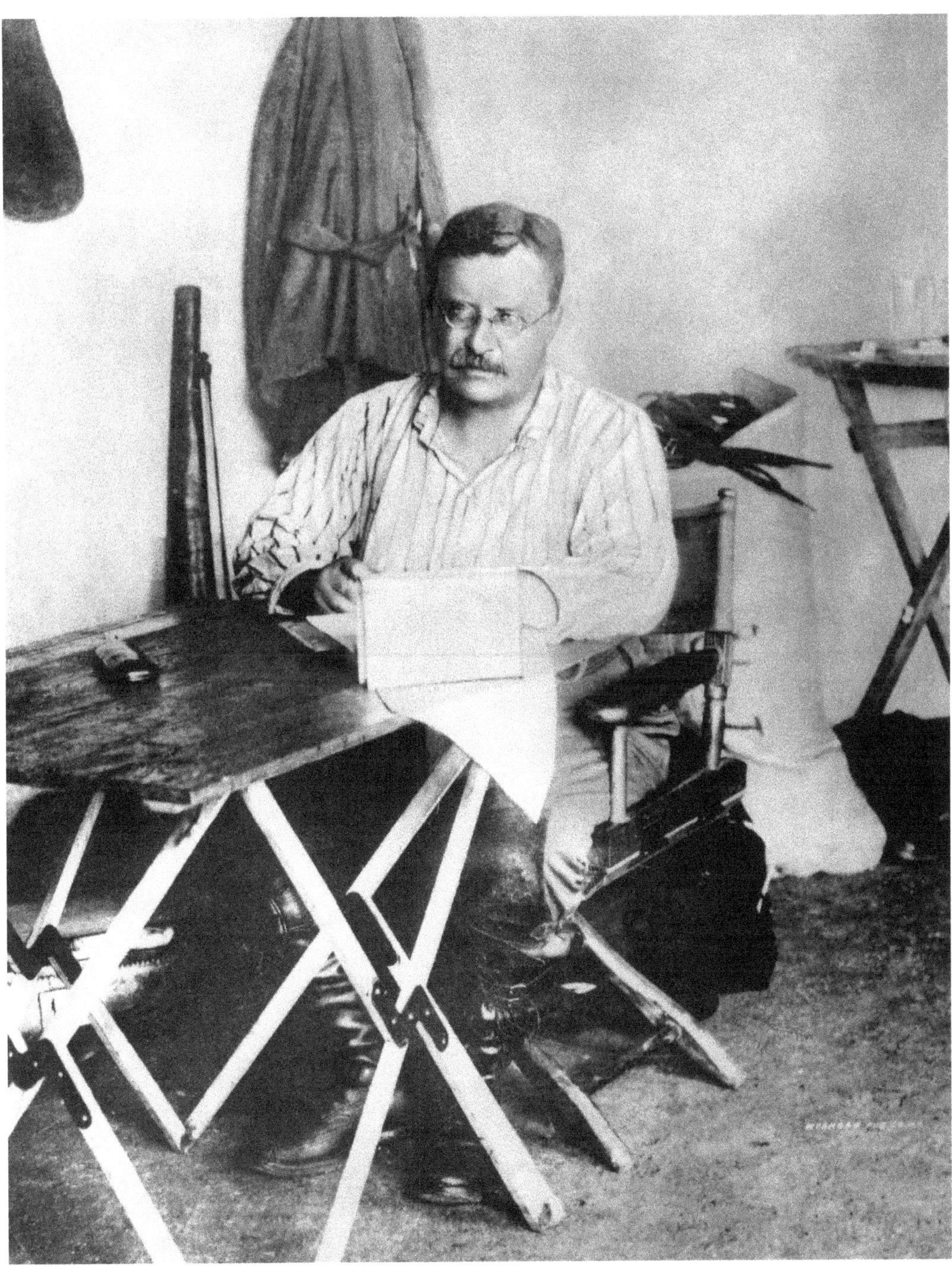

Kermit and Rondon did the surveying. The former was the sighting scout, whose job was to push ahead in the tortuous river seeking clear spaces to plant the sighting pole for the measurements that Rondon took. When they set up camp, TR wrote letters home, made notes about the flora and fauna, and worked on his Scribner's articles.

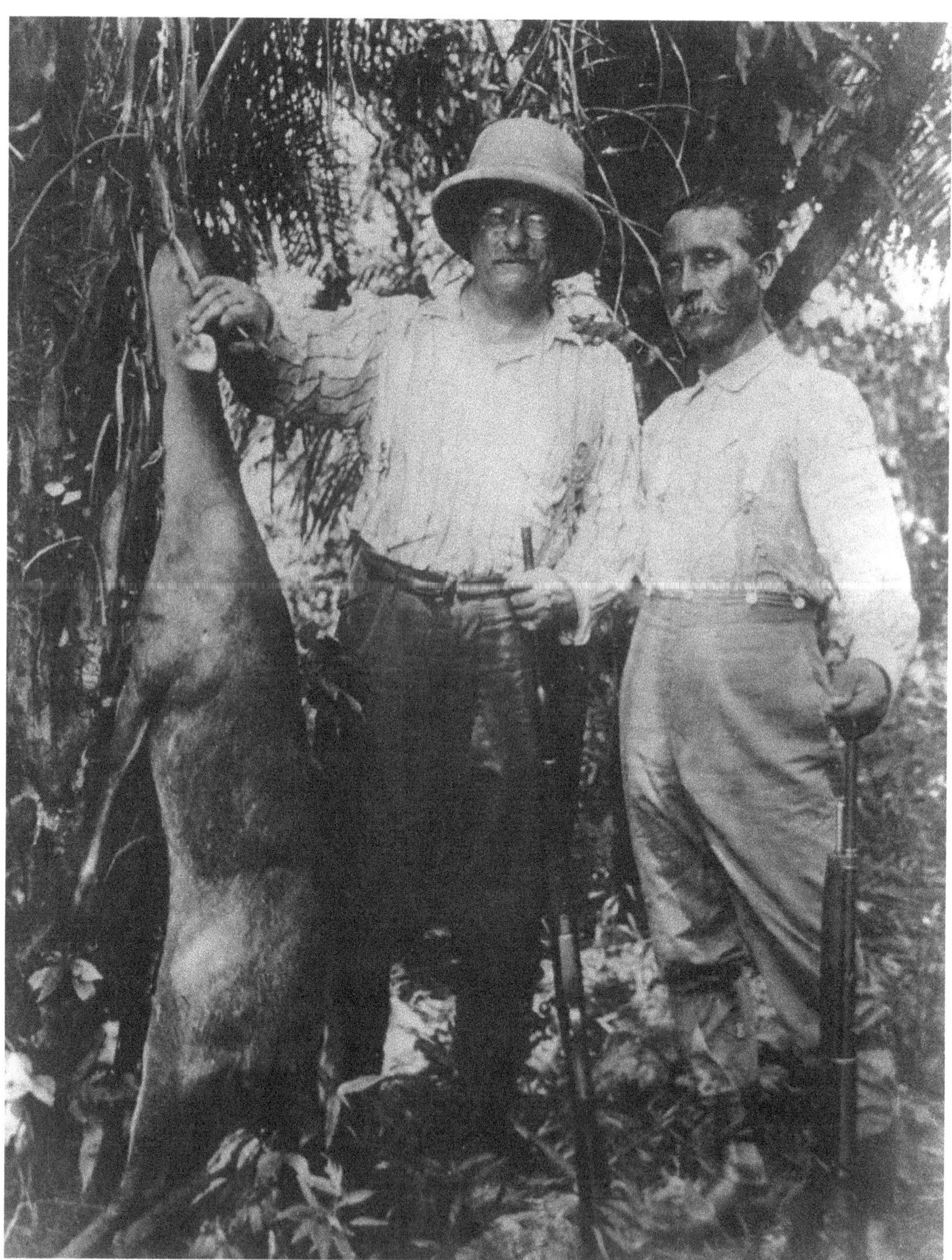

Roosevelt and Rondon pose with the bush deer they shot near Porto Campo.

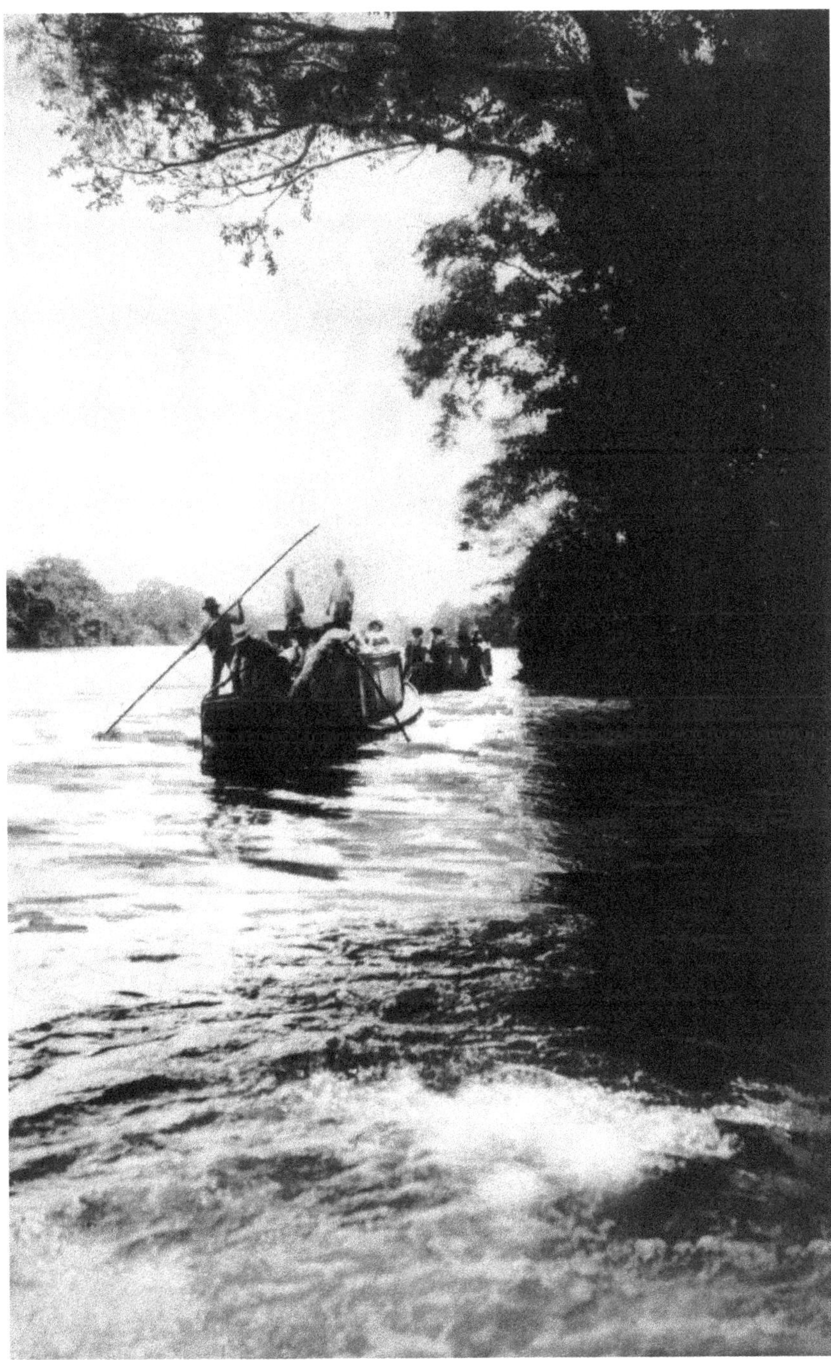

The boats being poled up the river. The explorers fought heat, debris from hammering rainstorms, mosquitoes, sand flies, wasps, rapids that forced them out of the river, and malnutrition.

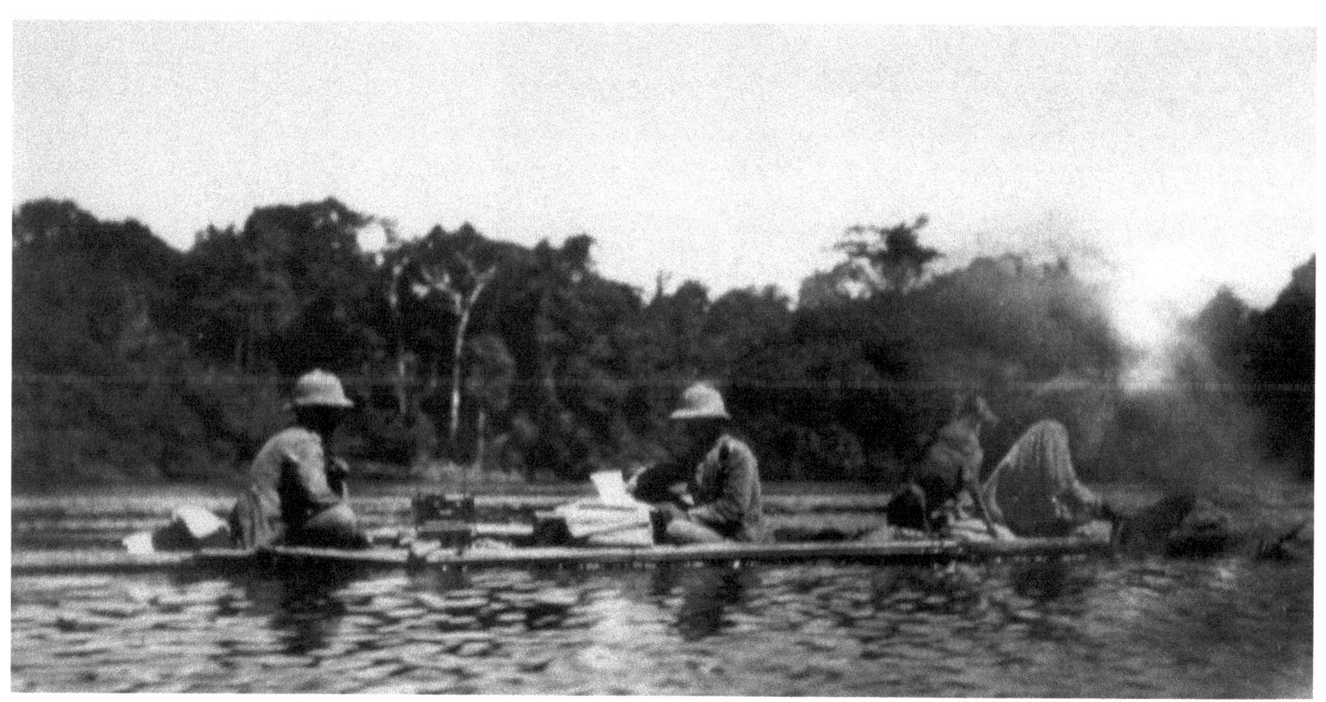

The worst time for TR on the River of Doubt came after he hurt the same leg in the same place that he had injured it in the 1902 electric trolley collision. As Kermit put it, "Then he came down with fever, and in his weakened condition was attacked with a veritable plague of deep abscesses." At one point, TR was out of his mind with the fever and recited poetry over and over, especially Samuel Taylor Coleridge's "Kubla Khan." He told Kermit to leave him behind. Kermit refused.

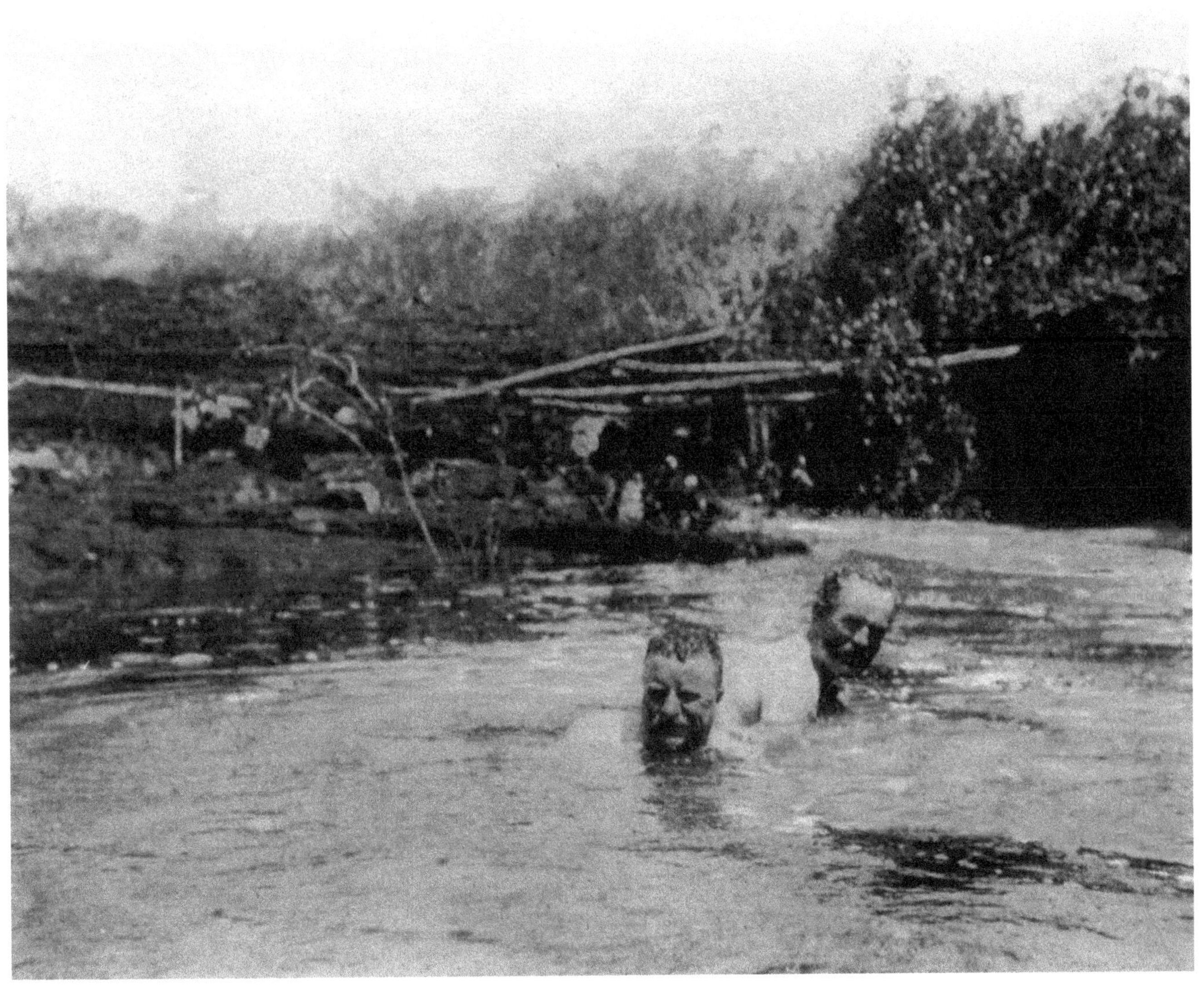

Gradually the physician drained the abscesses enough that TR could go on. But he contracted malaria and was never physically the same after the three-month ordeal in the Brazilian jungles. This photograph, taken by Kermit, shows Theodore swimming, despite the piranhas.

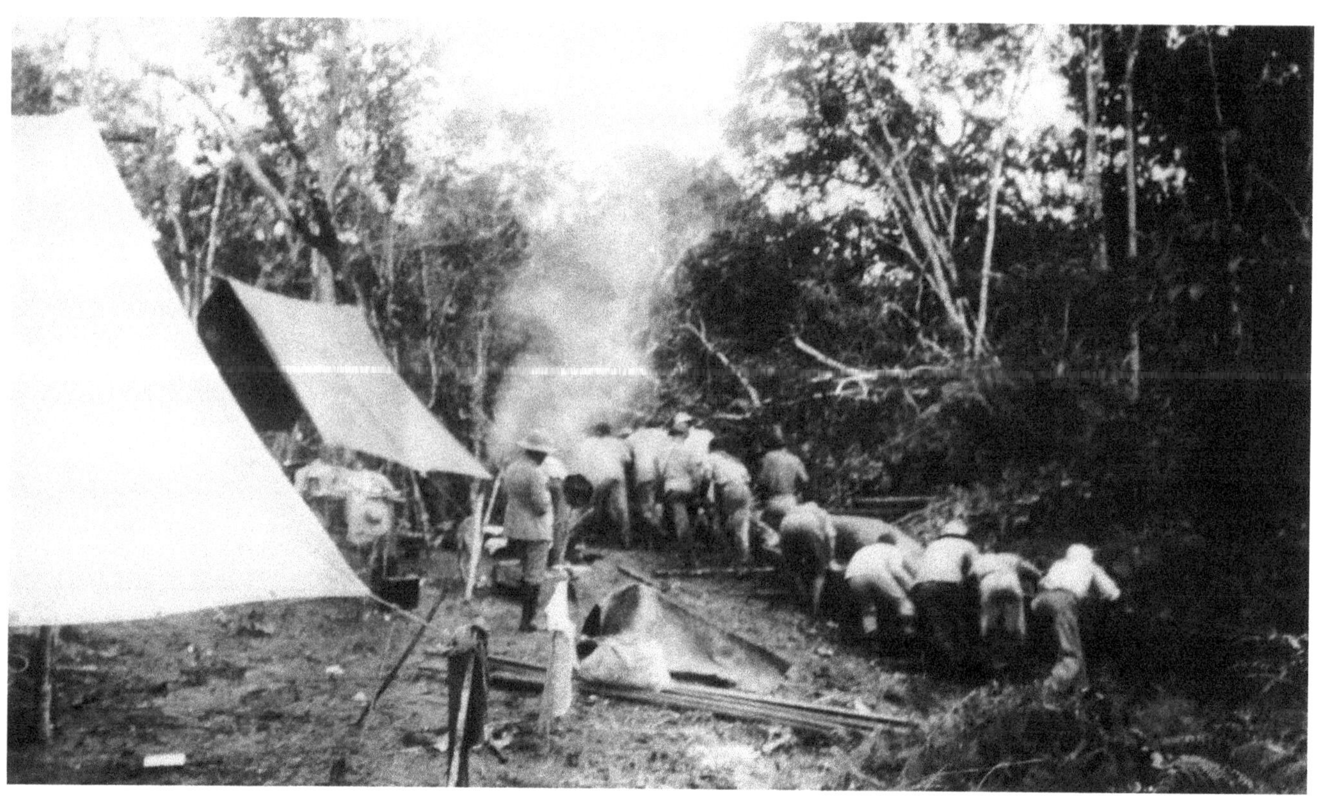

Portage was tedious and back breaking, but the rapids were so fierce they had no choice.

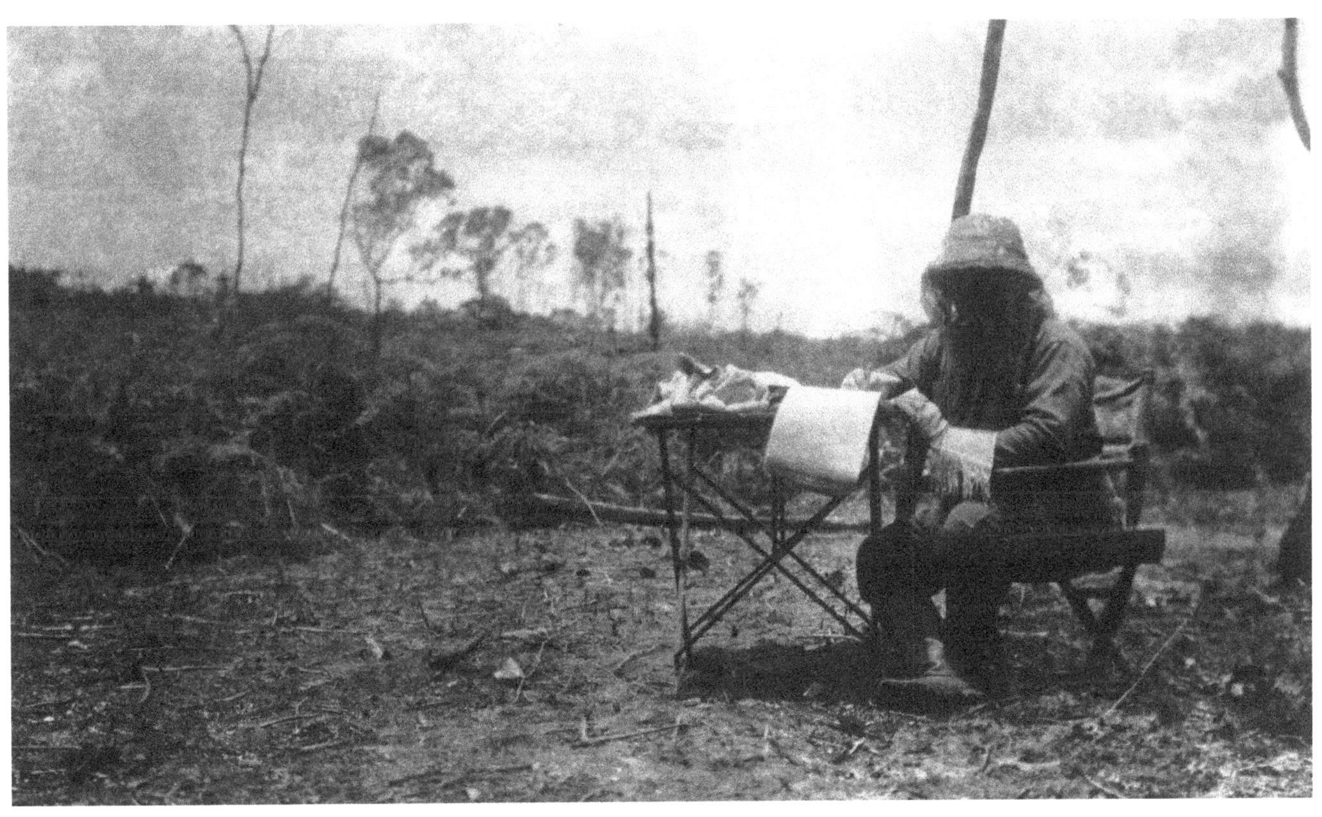

Roosevelt had much to write about, under his mosquito netting. They lost three men and endured physical suffering, but they increased the amount of information available about the Brazilian interior, and successfully charted the River of Doubt. In his honor, Colonel Rondon renamed it the Rio Roosevelt.

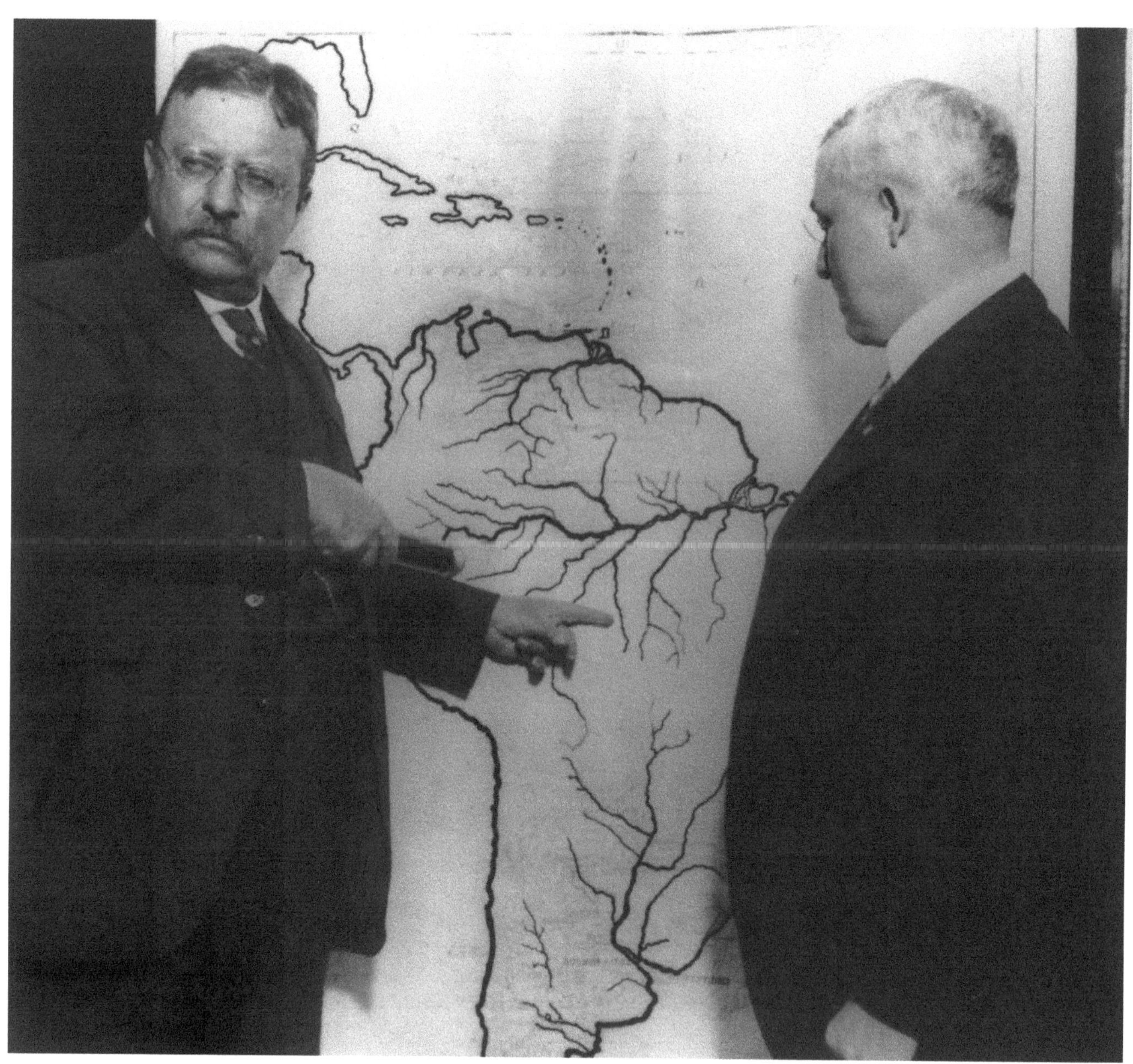

When at last the Roosevelts returned to the United States, TR made it his duty to share their discoveries. He published *Through the Brazilian Wilderness,* and gave talks, such as this one in Chicago with University of Chicago geography professor, Paul Goode, on October 18, 1914.

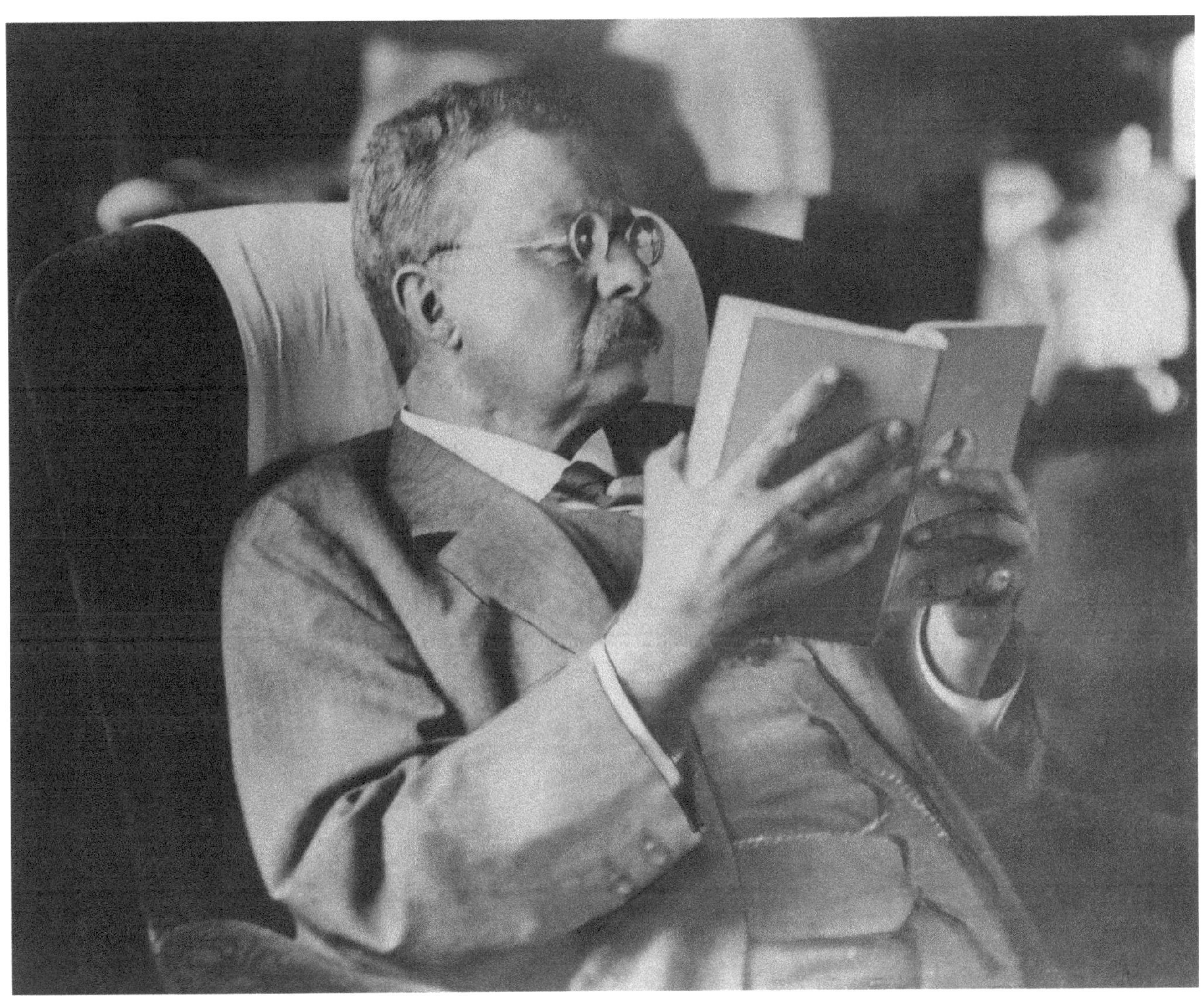

"Now and then I am asked as to 'what books a statesman should read,' and my answer is, poetry and novels—including short stories under the head of novels. I don't mean that he should read only novels and modern poetry. If he cannot also enjoy the Hebrew prophets and the Greek dramatists, he should be sorry. He ought to read interesting books on history and government, and books of science and philosophy; and really good books on these subjects are as enthralling as any fiction ever written in prose or verse." TR, from his autobiography.

Arthur Hamilton Lee and his wife, Ruth, were close friends of the Roosevelt family. Lee and TR are shown here leaving the Natural History Museum in London in 1914. Lee was a Conservative member of the House of Commons and the two families shared a love of art, politics, literature, and nature.

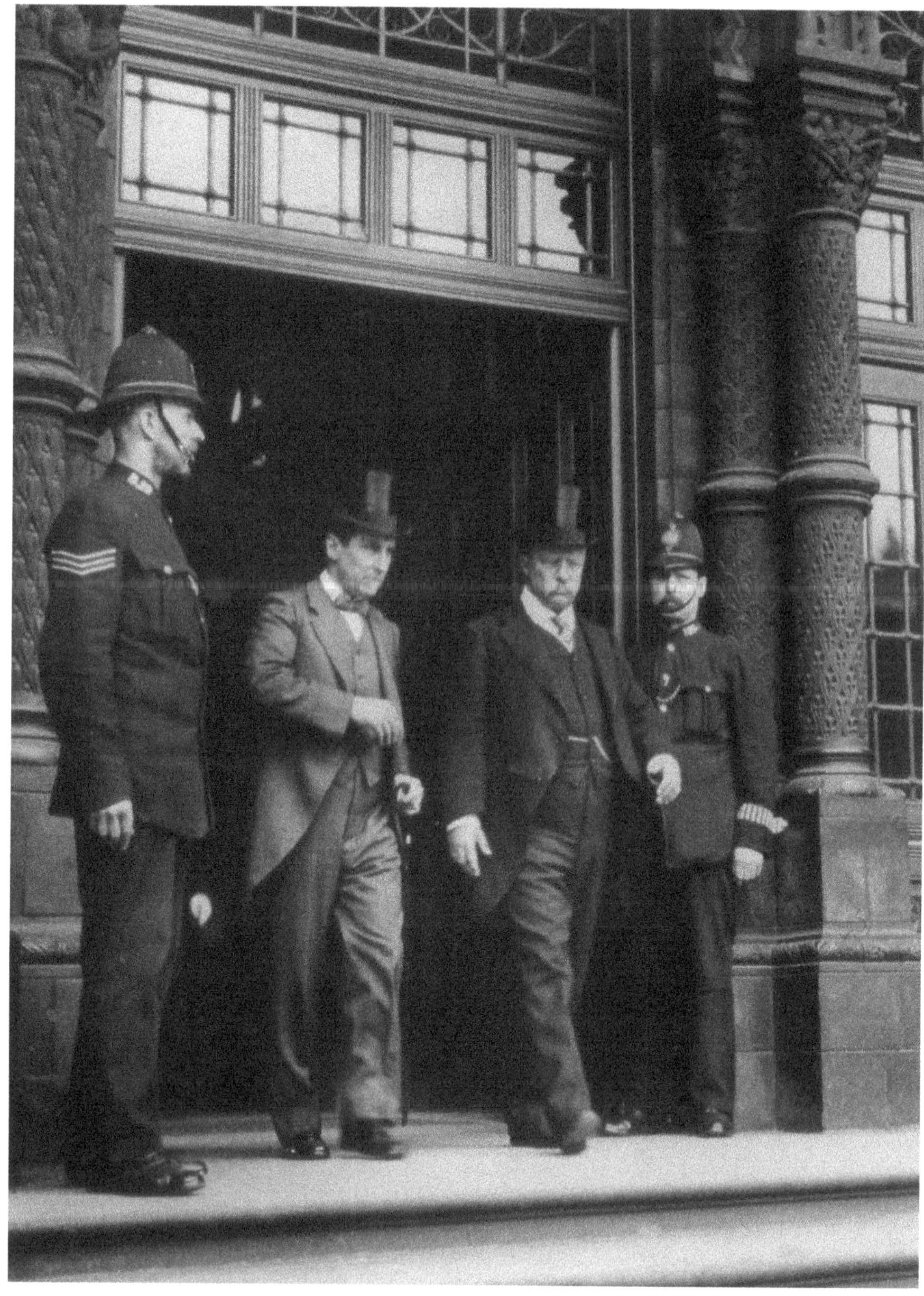

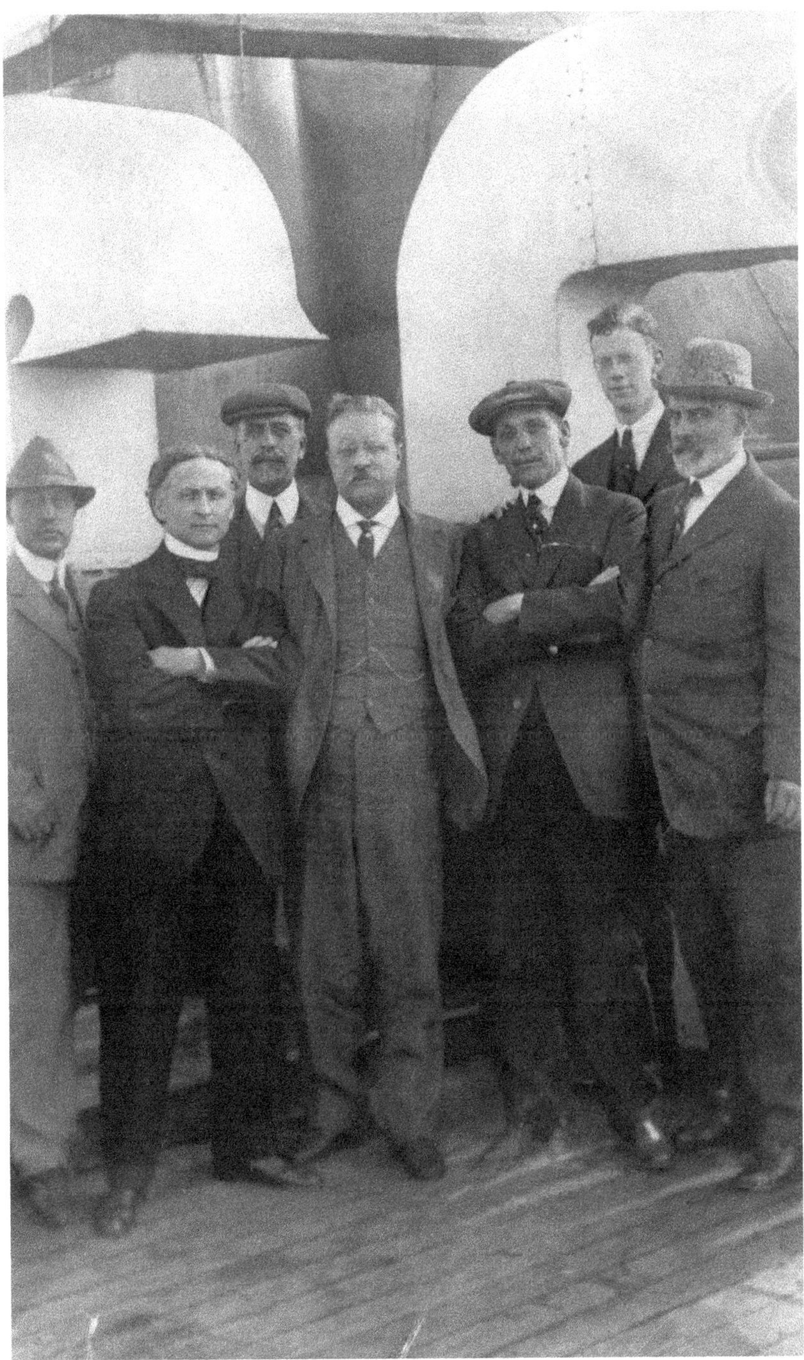

Harry Houdini was the famous escape artist and magician of the era. Roosevelt poses on Houdini's left aboard the Hamburg American Liner *Imperator,* June 23, 1914.

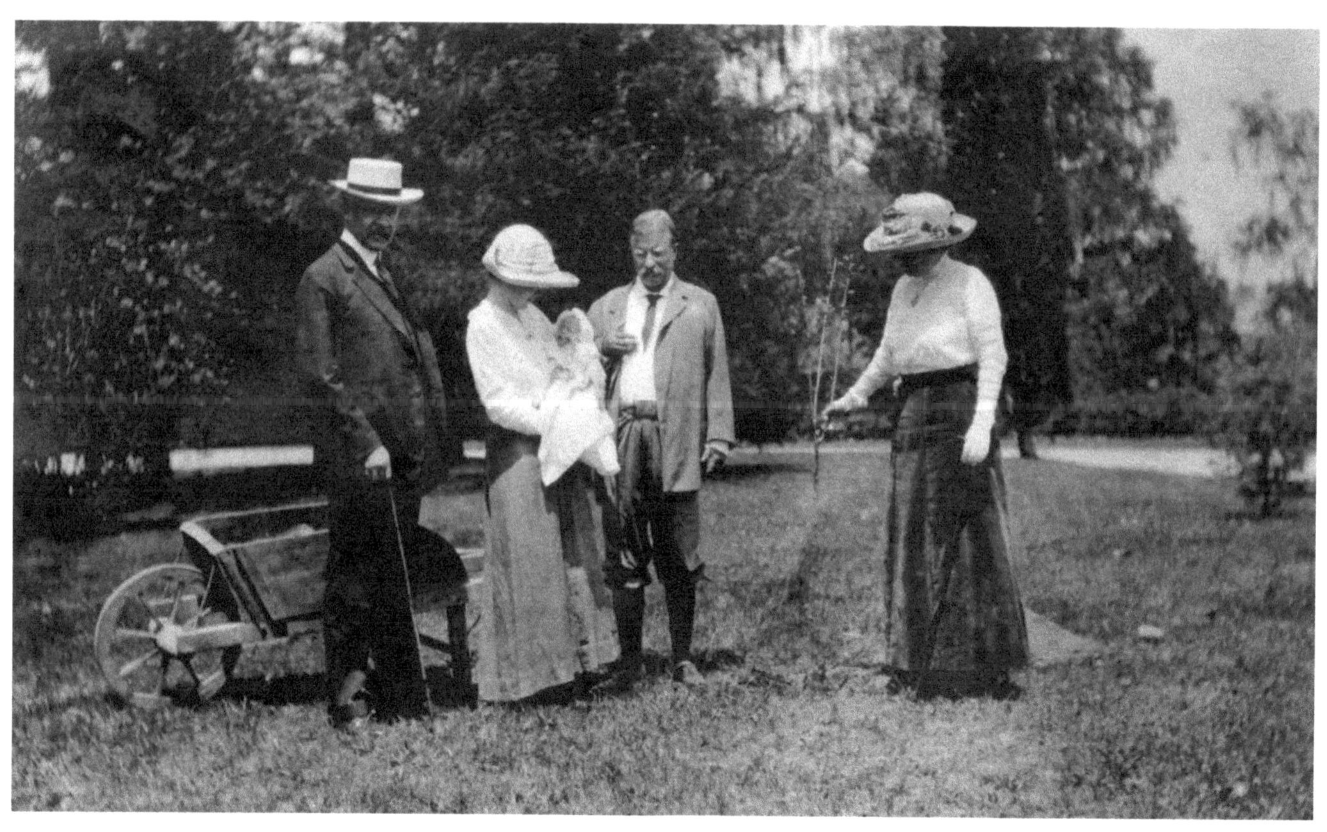

Edith and Theodore plant a cherry tree at Sagamore Hill in honor of their new grandson, Richard Derby, Jr., "a fine little fellow," TR wrote to his friend Arthur Lee on May 20, 1914. The child was the son of Ethel and Richard Derby, who are looking on.

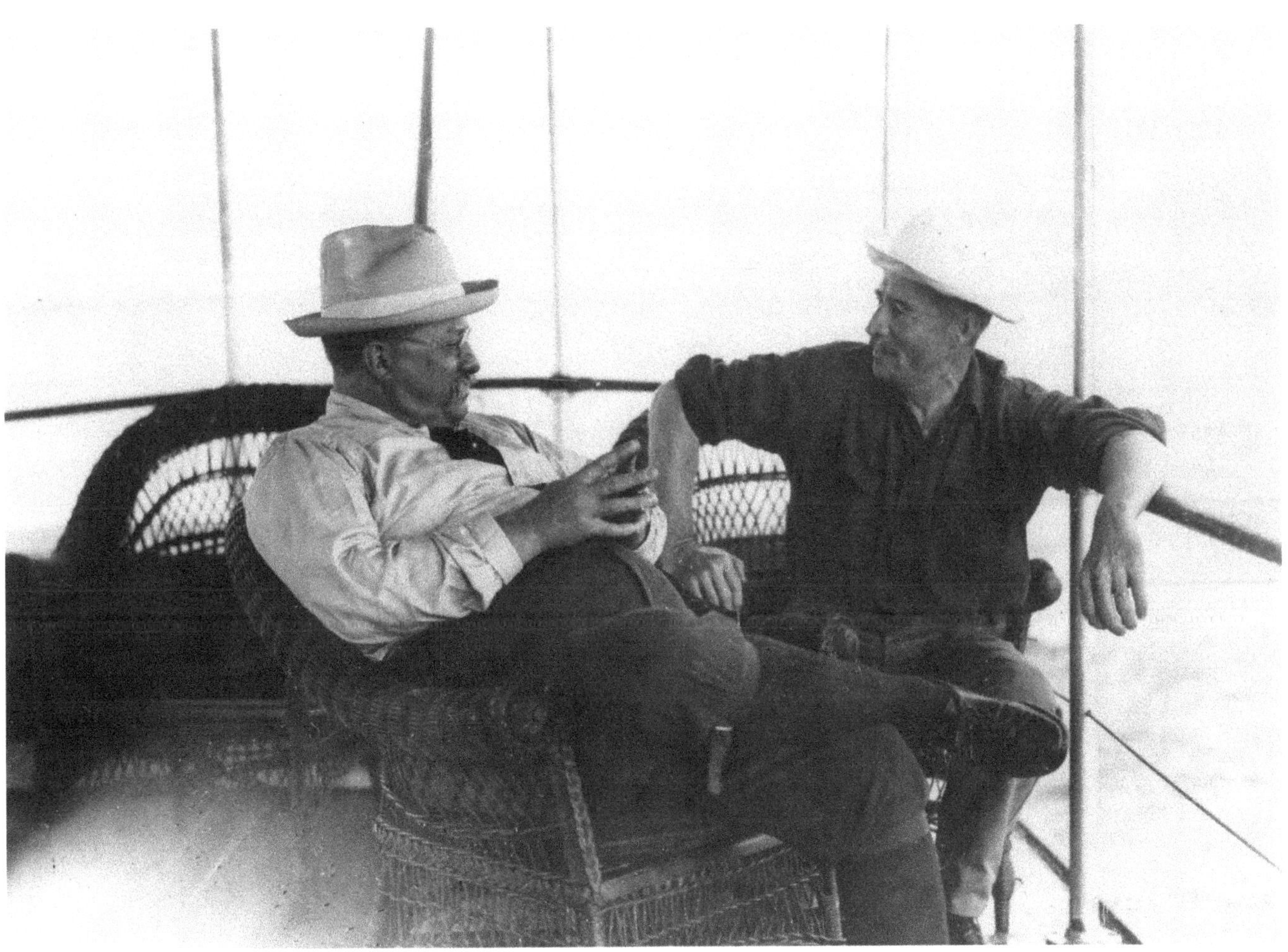

Roosevelt's first two publications, *The Summer Birds of the Adirondacks* and *Notes on Some of the Birds of Oyster Bay*, were written when he was college age. Roosevelt was an ornithologist who studied bird behavior, knew birds by their calls, wrote about their habits, and created 51 bird refuges as president. In this photo, he and Mississippi governor John M. Parker relax on board the *Daisy* in between visits to bird sanctuaries at the mouth of the Mississippi River in June 1915.

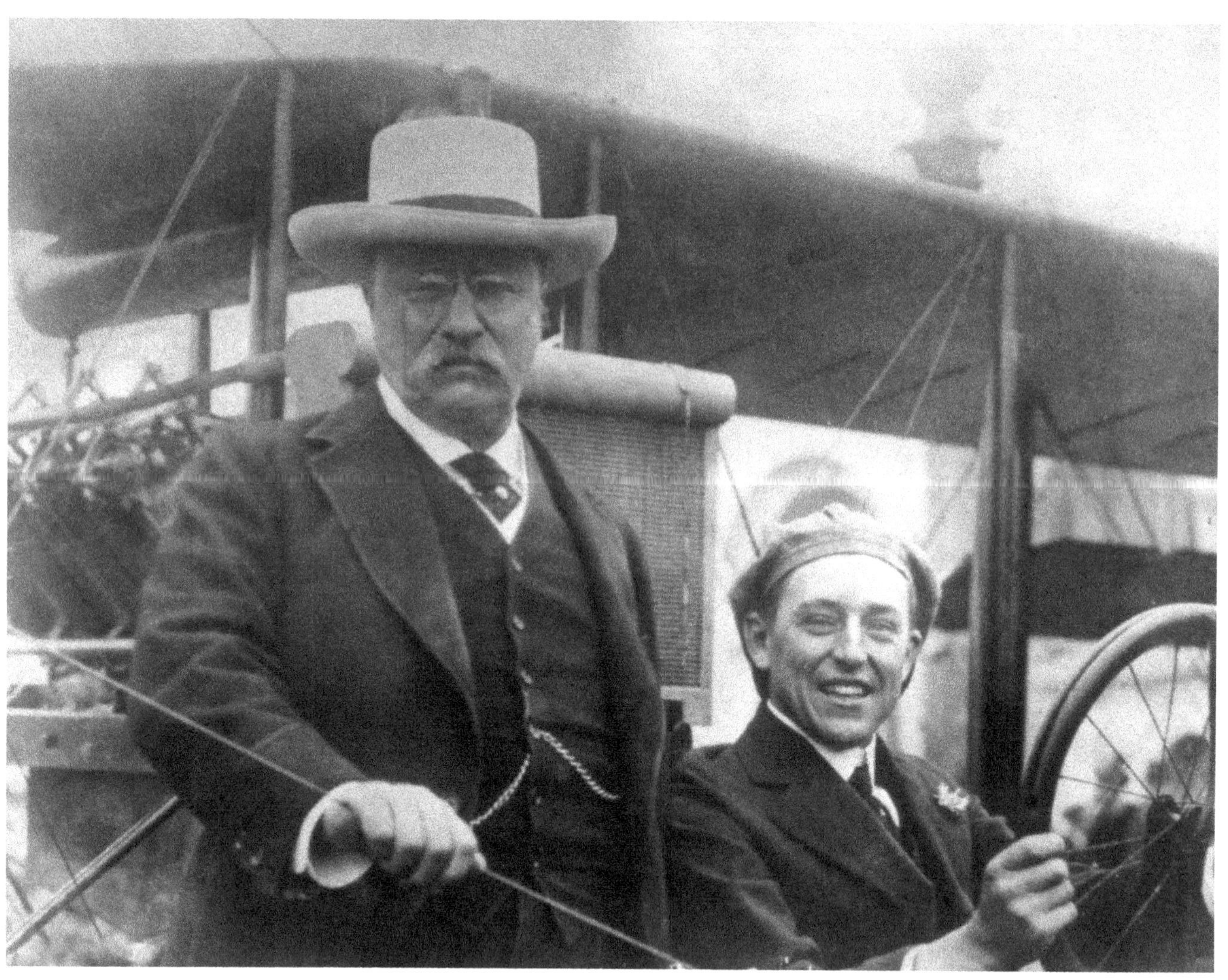

A film was made of Theodore Roosevelt speaking on "Roosevelt Day" at the San Francisco Panama-Pacific Exposition in July 1915. This photograph shows him with famous barn-storming, daredevil aviator Arthur Roy "Art" Smith.

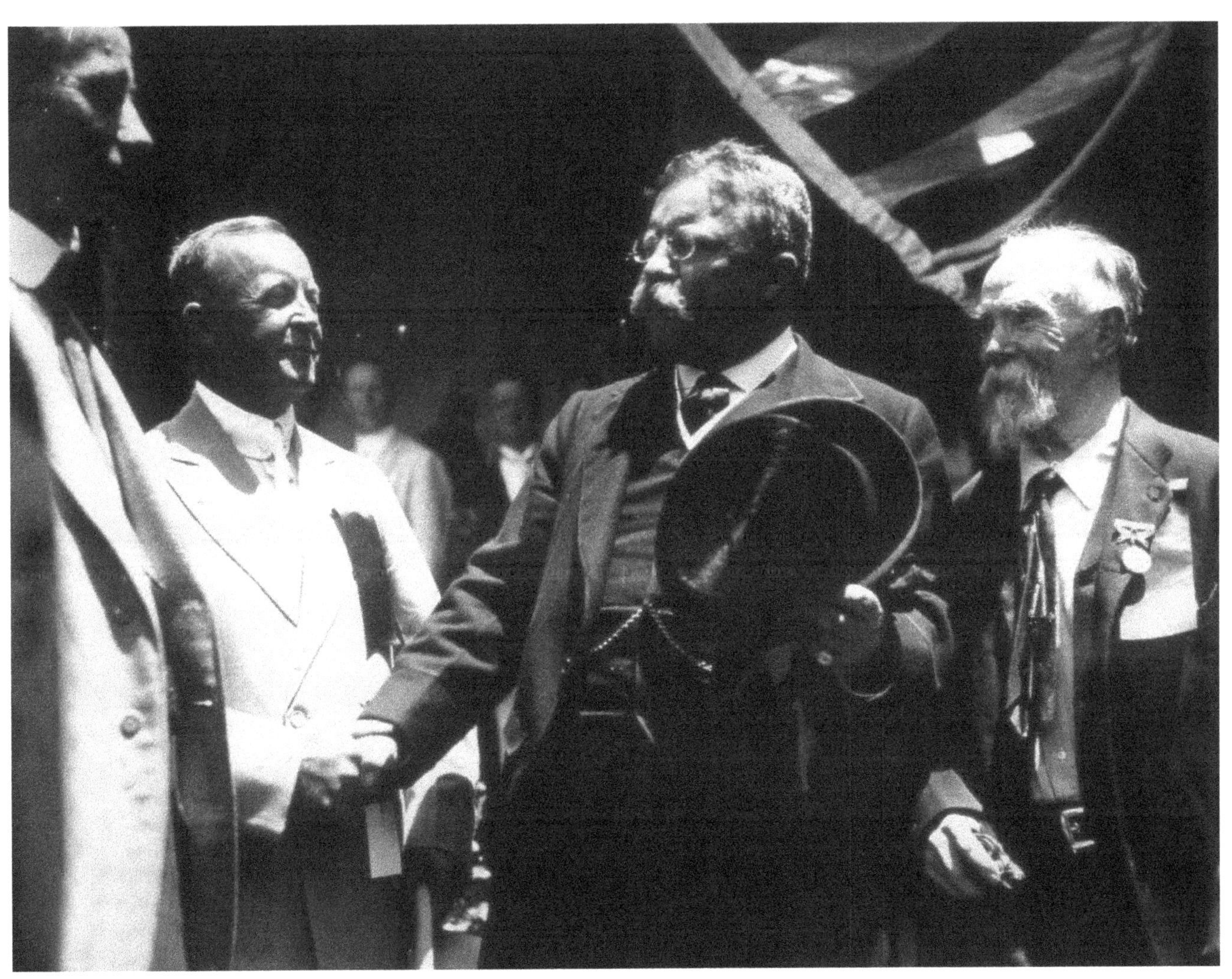

Roosevelt greeting Rough Riders at the Panama-Pacific Exposition, July 26, 1915.

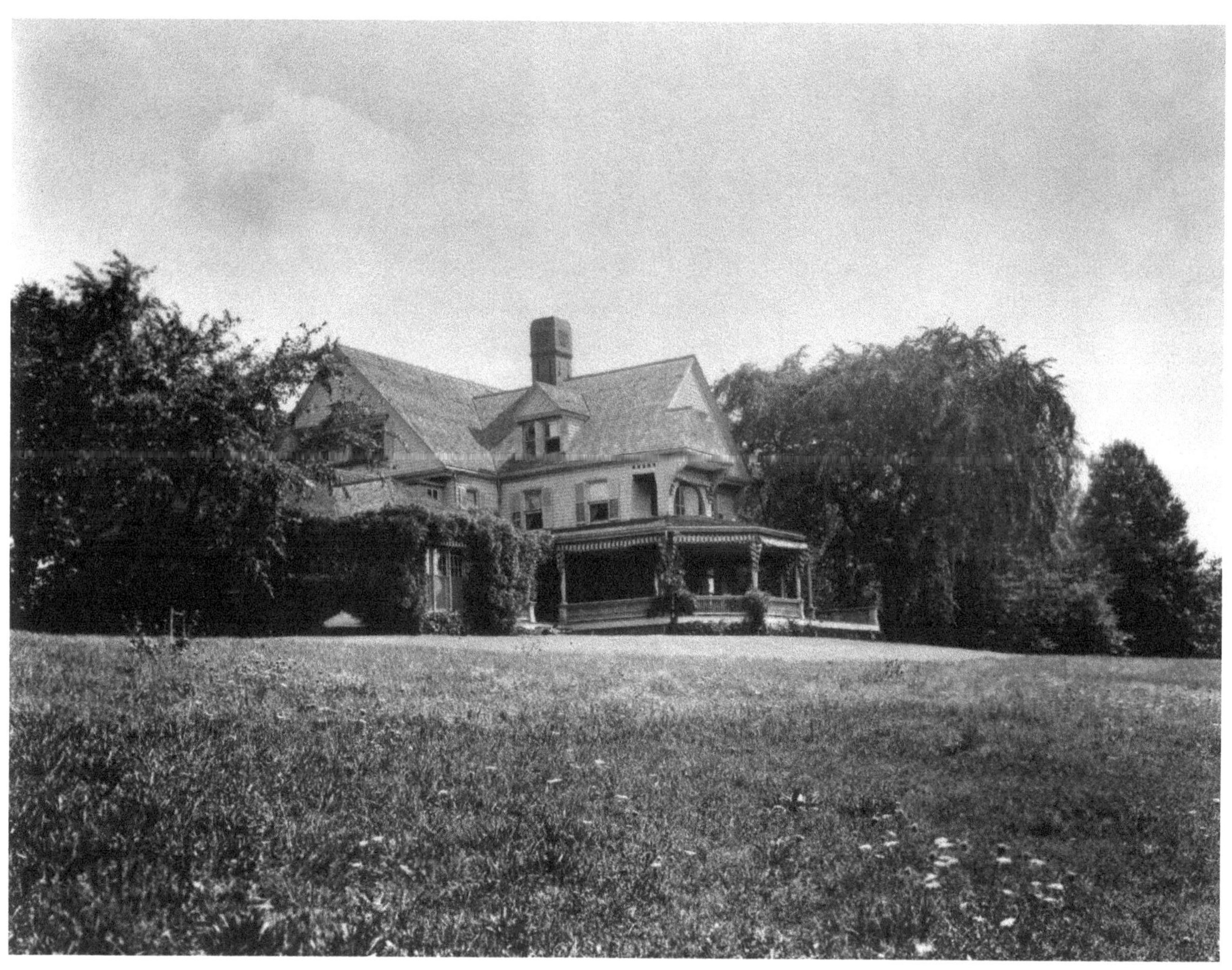

A view of Sagamore Hill, the home the Roosevelts loved.

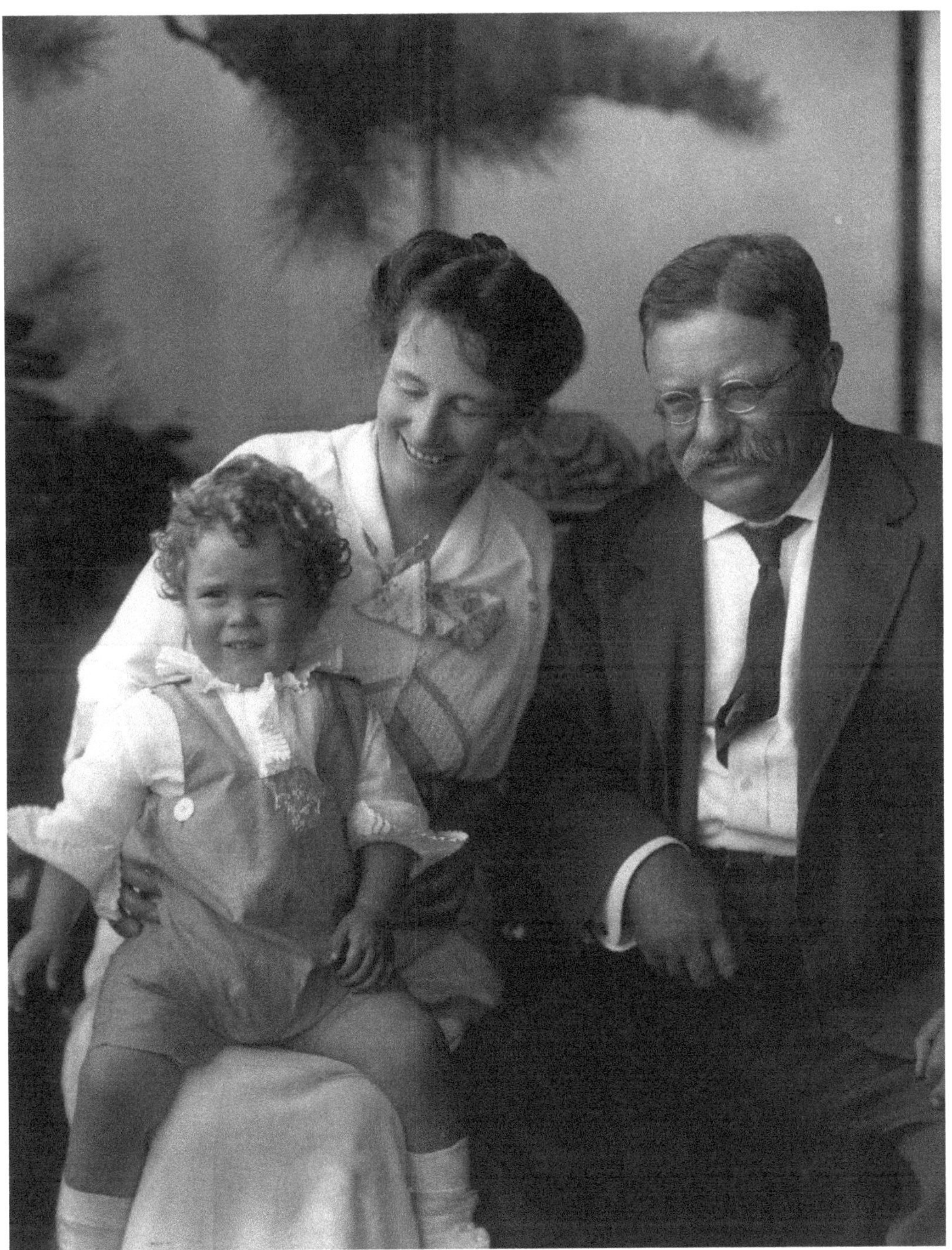

Theodore and Edith with grandson Richard Derby, Jr., in 1915.

The well-known chopping motion Roosevelt made with his hands to press a point home, here to Yale University's Professor Hiram Bingham. Bingham was credited with the discovery, in 1911, of Machu Picchu, a part of the ancient Incan Empire, and the author of *Inca Land: Explorations in the Highlands of Peru.*

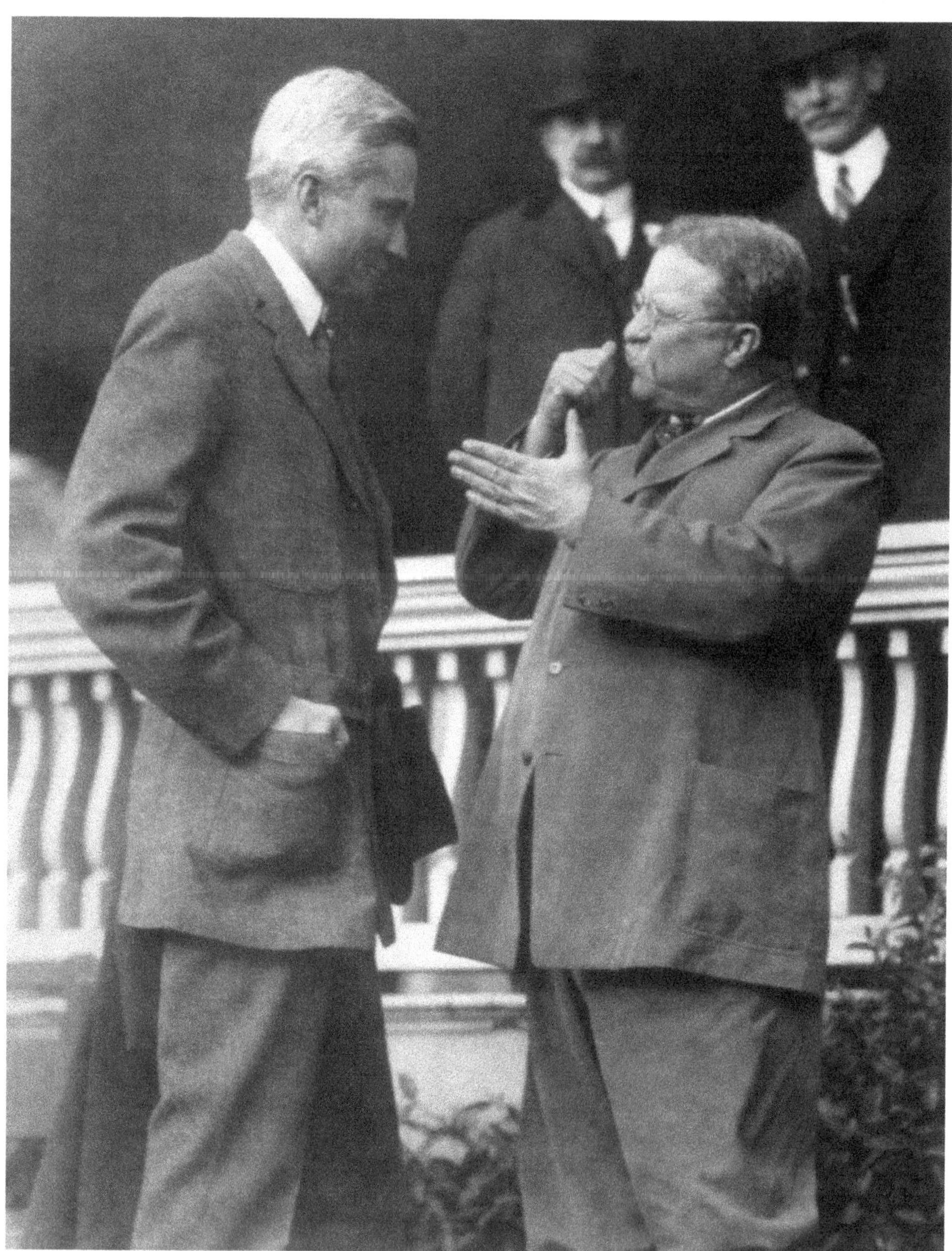

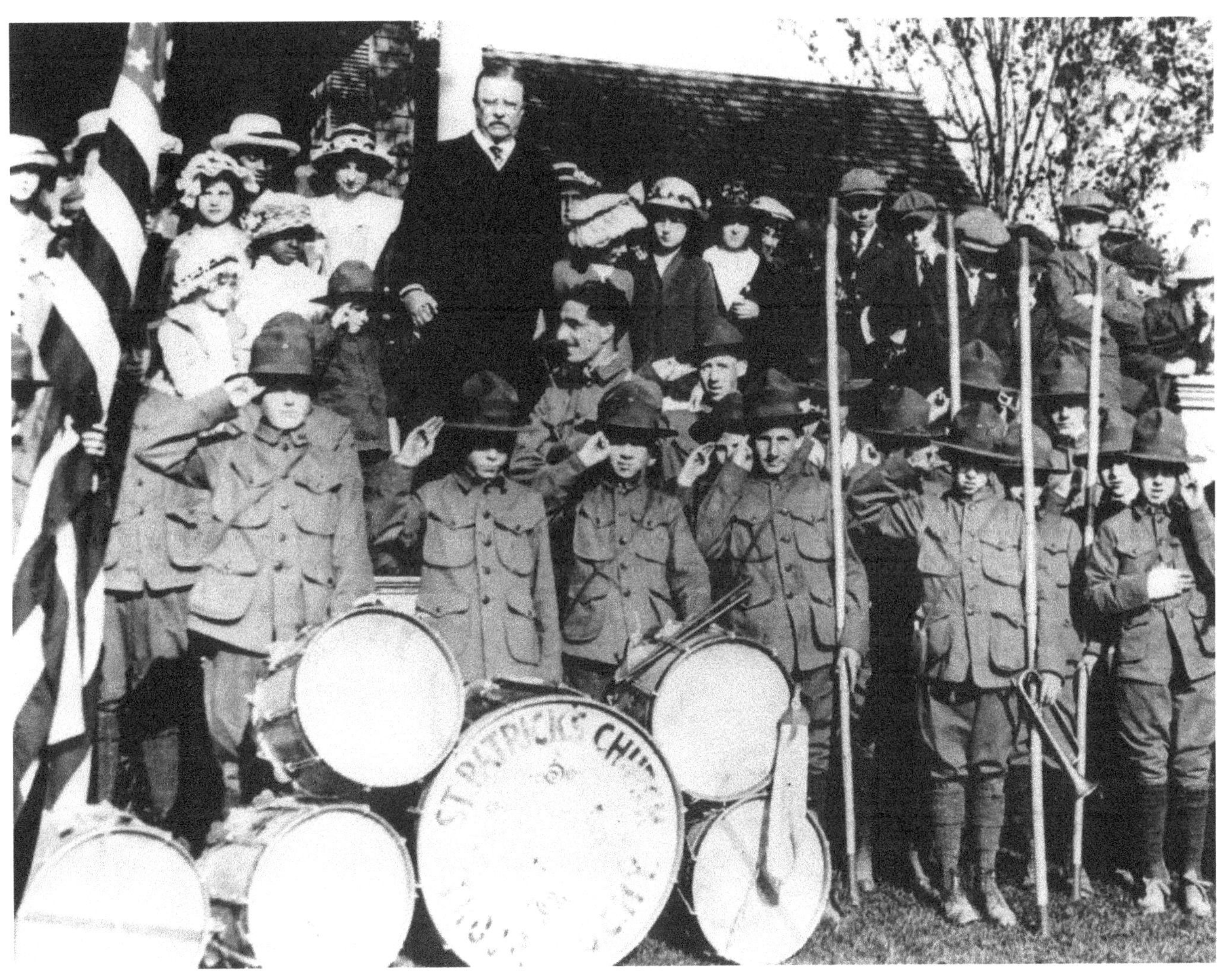

The former president receiving the Oyster Bay Boy Scouts with suitable pomp and circumstance, May 13, 1916.

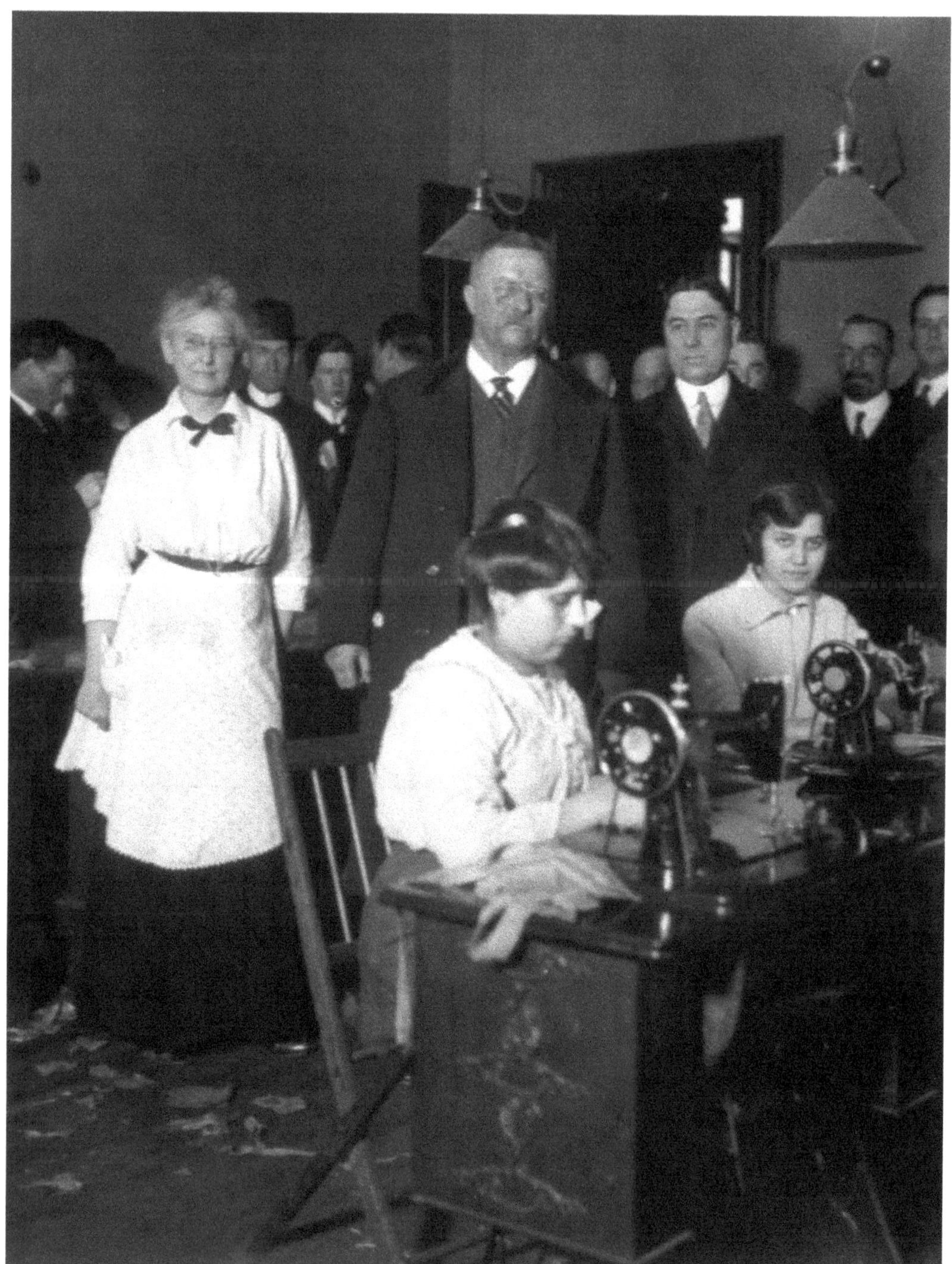

Roosevelt stands behind women at their sewing machines in the election year of 1916. Although Roosevelt's Progressive ideals remained undimmed, the party he founded died when he refused their nomination for president that year. Roosevelt was more concerned about the war that had broken out in Europe in 1914—a terrible war, but not wholly unexpected to TR, who had seen militarism on the rise as he toured the continent after the safari.

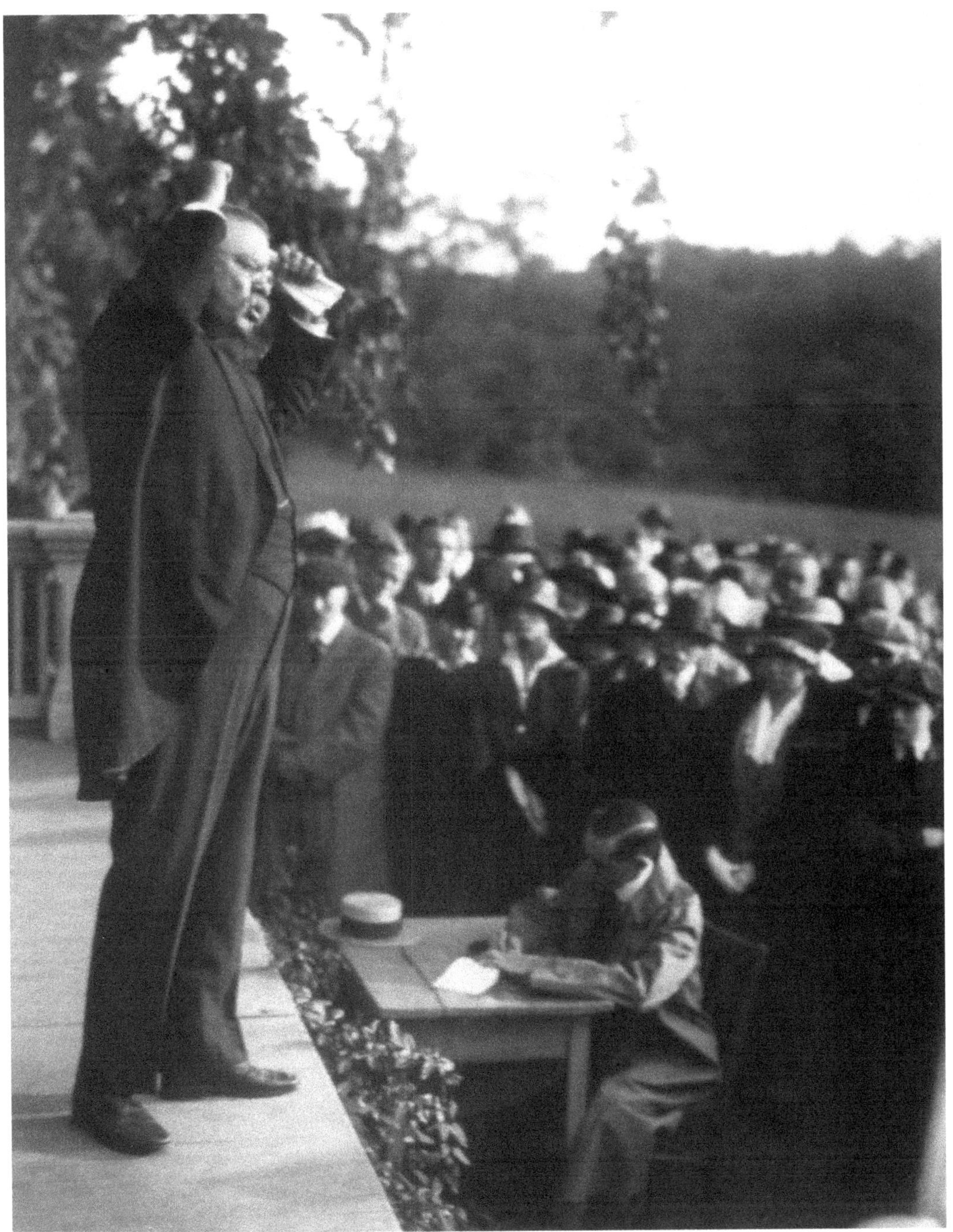

Theodore Roosevelt supported national women's suffrage, but the newly re-elected president, Democrat Woodrow Wilson, believed suffrage was for the states to decide. Here Roosevelt speaks in favor of suffrage at the opening of the New York state suffrage campaign. New York women gained the vote in 1918.

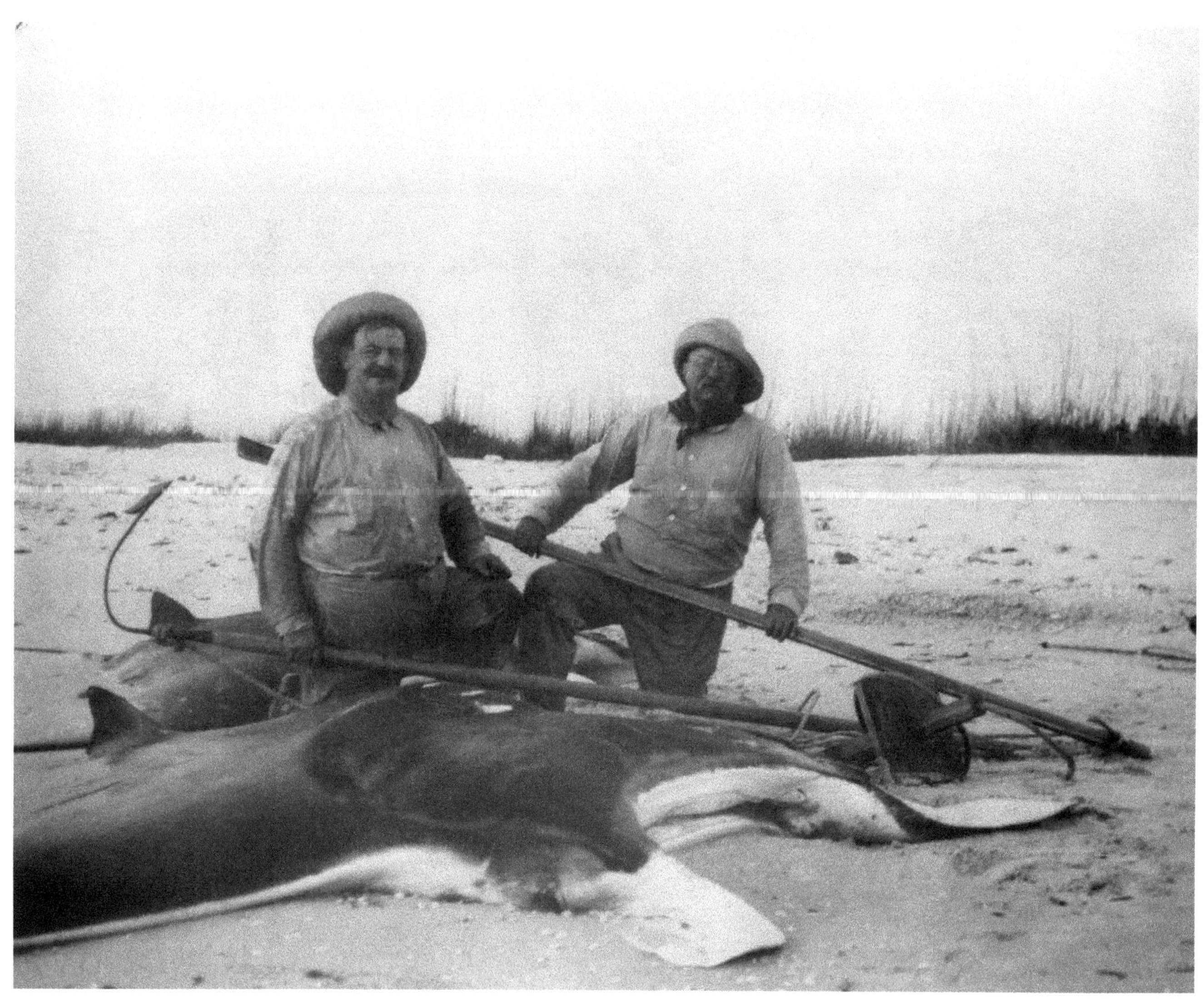

Roosevelt in Punta Gorda, Florida, with Russell J. Coles and manta rays on March 26, 1917. Coles was one of the earliest naturalists to observe and catalog sharks and their behavior.

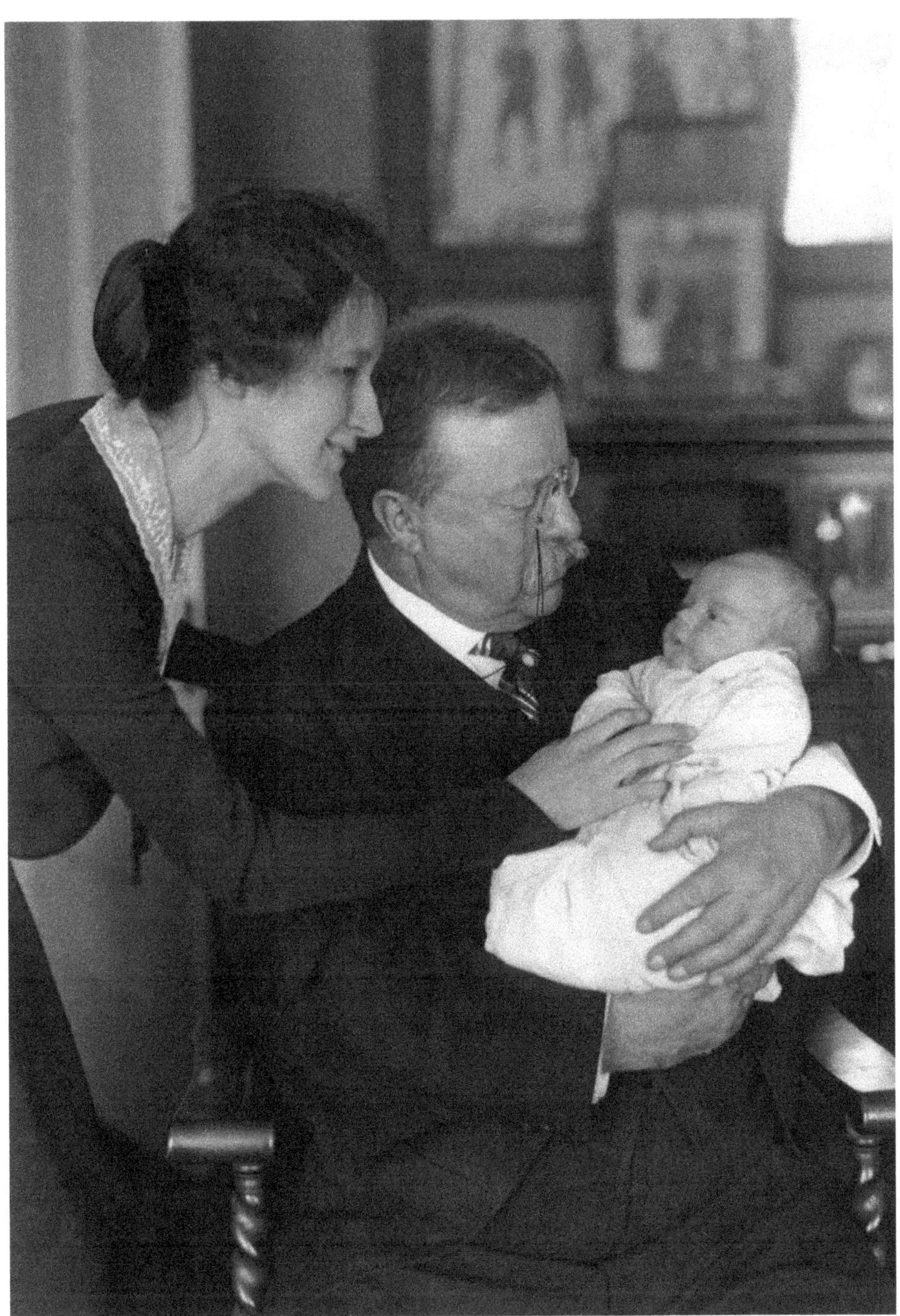

Proud grandfather Theodore Roosevelt with his daughter-in-law Grace Lockwood Roosevelt and her son Archibald Bulloch Roosevelt, Jr., March 29, 1918.

Edith Roosevelt was the steadying force in TR's life. "Whenever a man thinks," Roosevelt wrote in his memoir, "that he has outgrown the woman who is his mate, he will do well carefully to consider whether his growth has not been downward instead of upward, whether the facts are not merely that he has fallen away from his wife's standard of refinement and of duty."

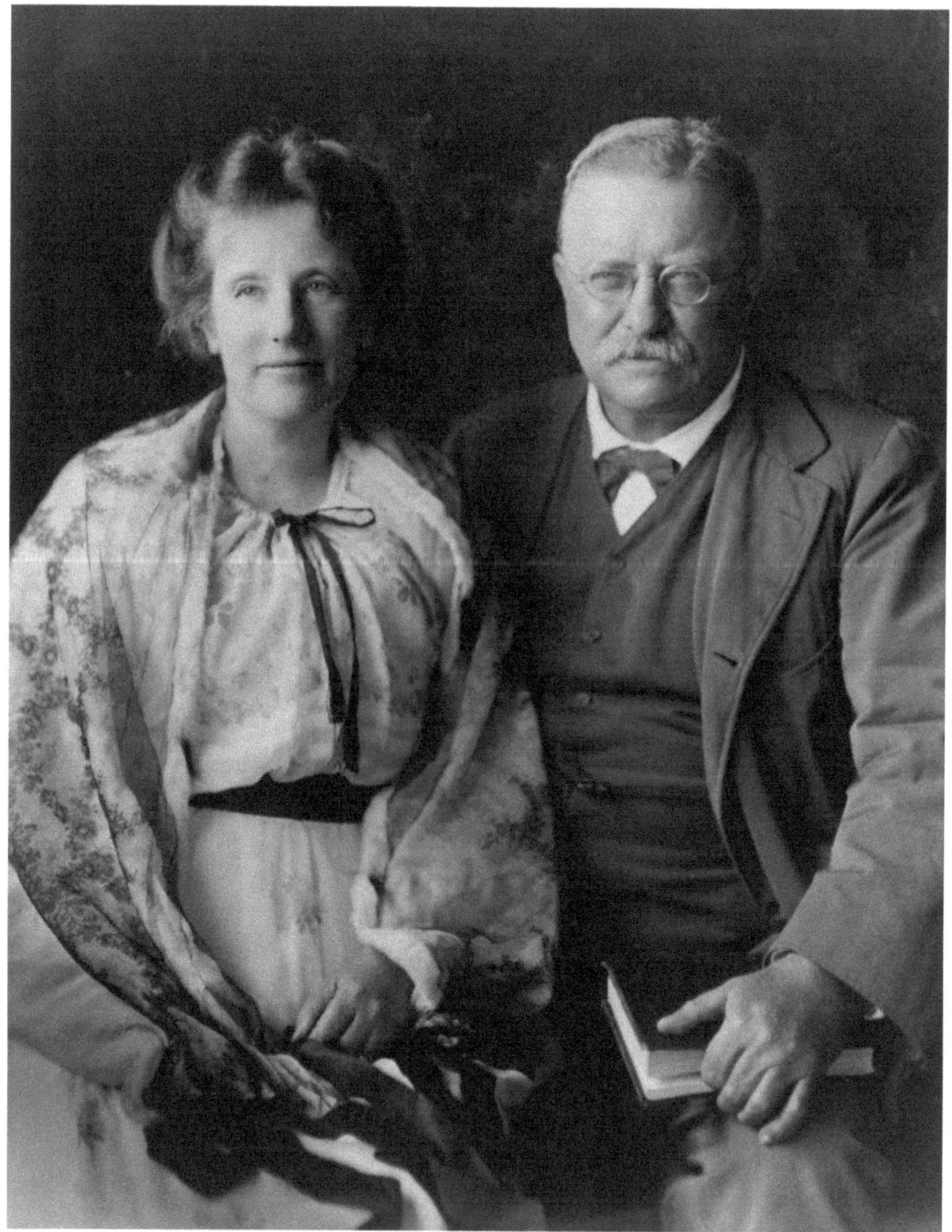

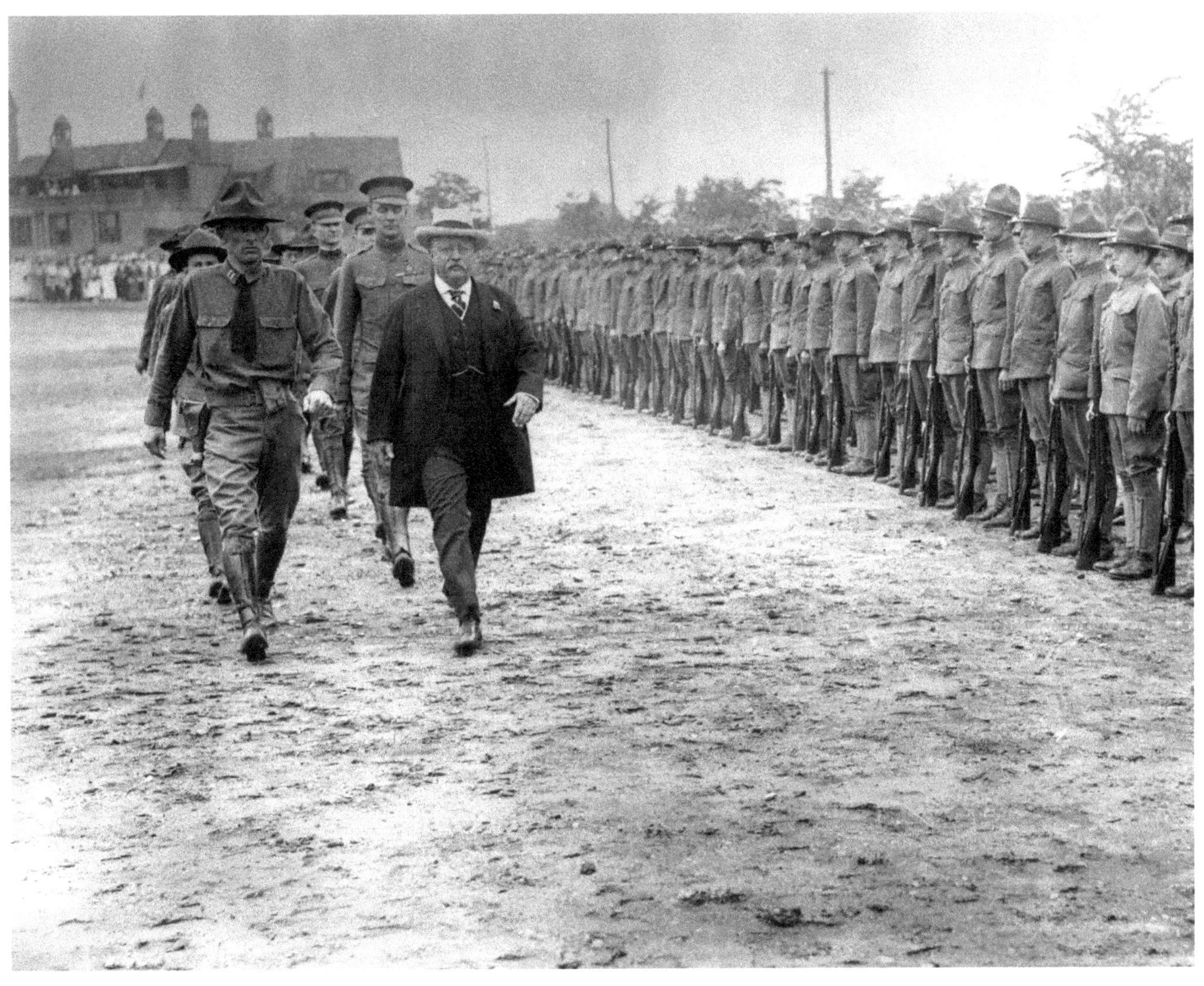

World War I began in Europe in 1914, and TR was soon convinced that Germany should be punished for the international crimes it committed, among them the invasion of neutral Belgium. As a former chief executive Roosevelt made headlines as he sounded the tocsin of preparedness and urged Wilson to enter the fighting. TR's good friend Leonard Wood opened a military training camp at Plattsburg, New York, and TR toured it as well as this camp at New York's Forest Hills Rifle Club urging American involvement.

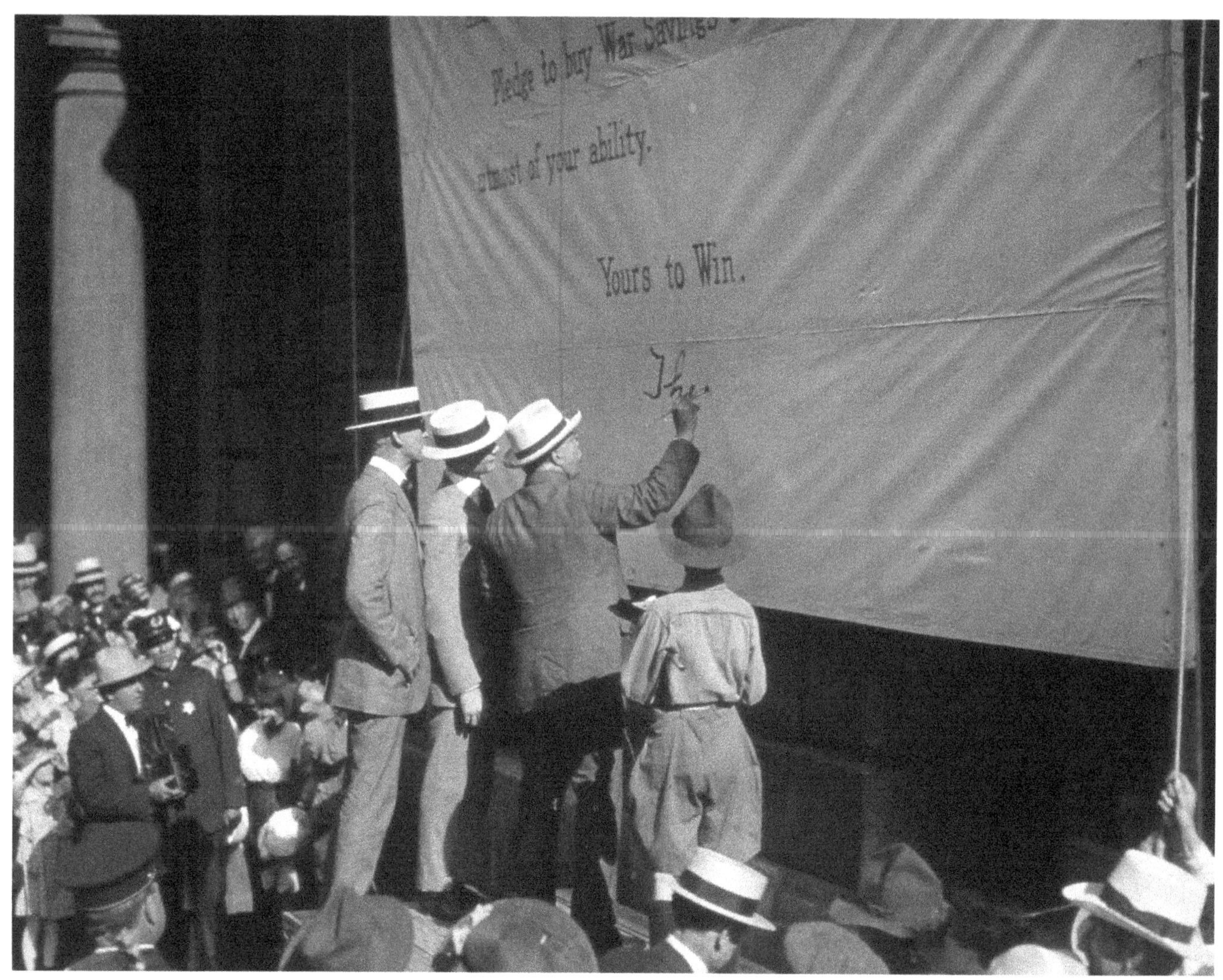

All four Roosevelt sons, and his son-in-law Richard Derby, served in World War I. Ethel went to France to work alongside her physician husband. Nick Longworth worked toward preparedness in the House of Representatives, while Alice did some traditional war work and kept her political salon running. Edith was a member of the Needlework Guild. TR gave speeches, wrote articles, and published three books chastising pacifists and cowards in strident tones. He asked Wilson's permission to raise a volunteer fighting unit. It was denied.

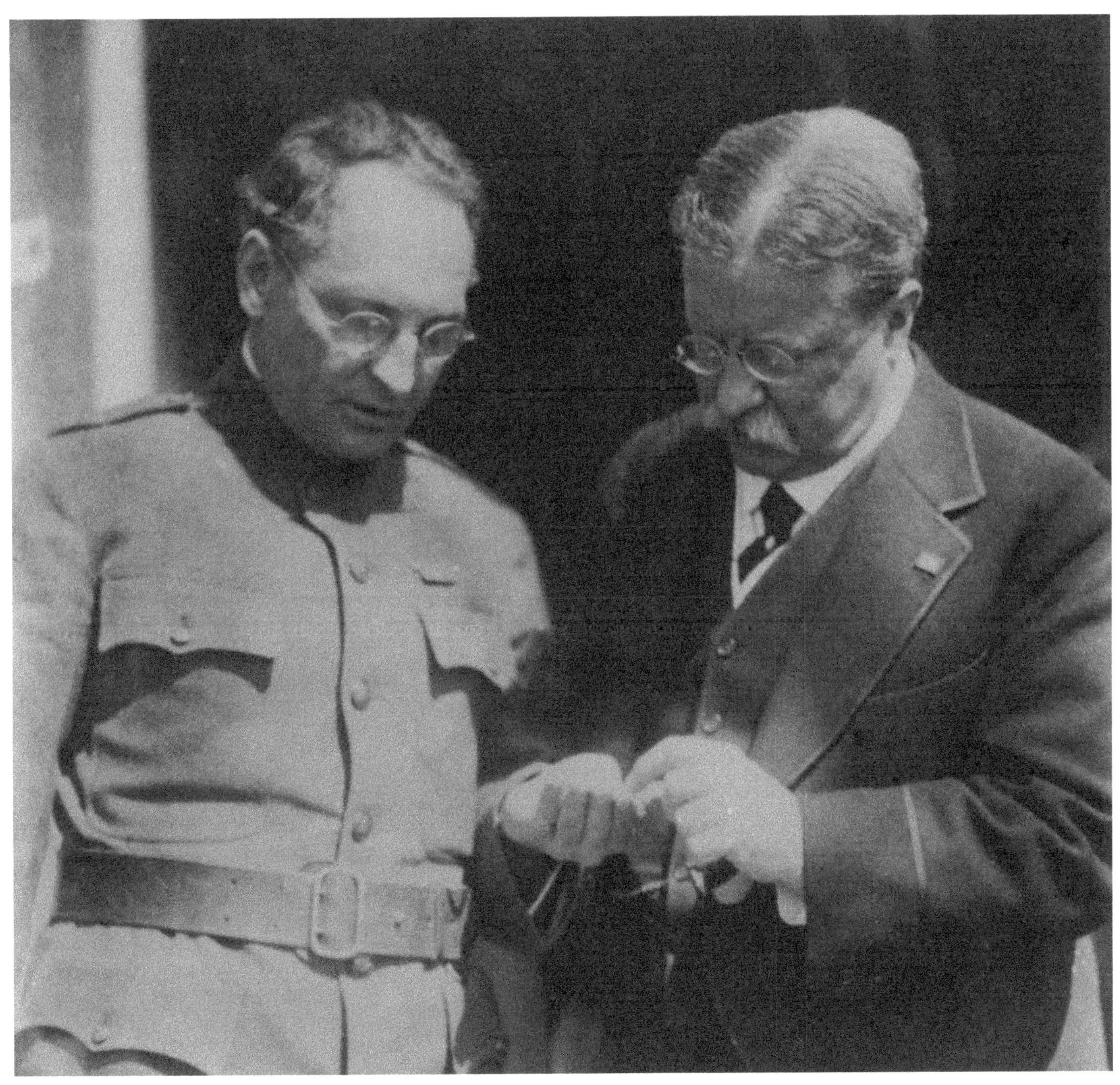

Roosevelt inspects a bullet that wounded his son Archie in France, April 14, 1918. Archie would recover, but Quentin, age 20, was killed when his airplane was shot down in a dogfight over France on July 14, 1918. The family was devastated.

Roosevelt never stopped working, but his family always gave him great joy, too. "Children," he wrote once, "are better than books." He is shown here hugging his infant granddaughter Edith Roosevelt Derby on April 12, 1918.

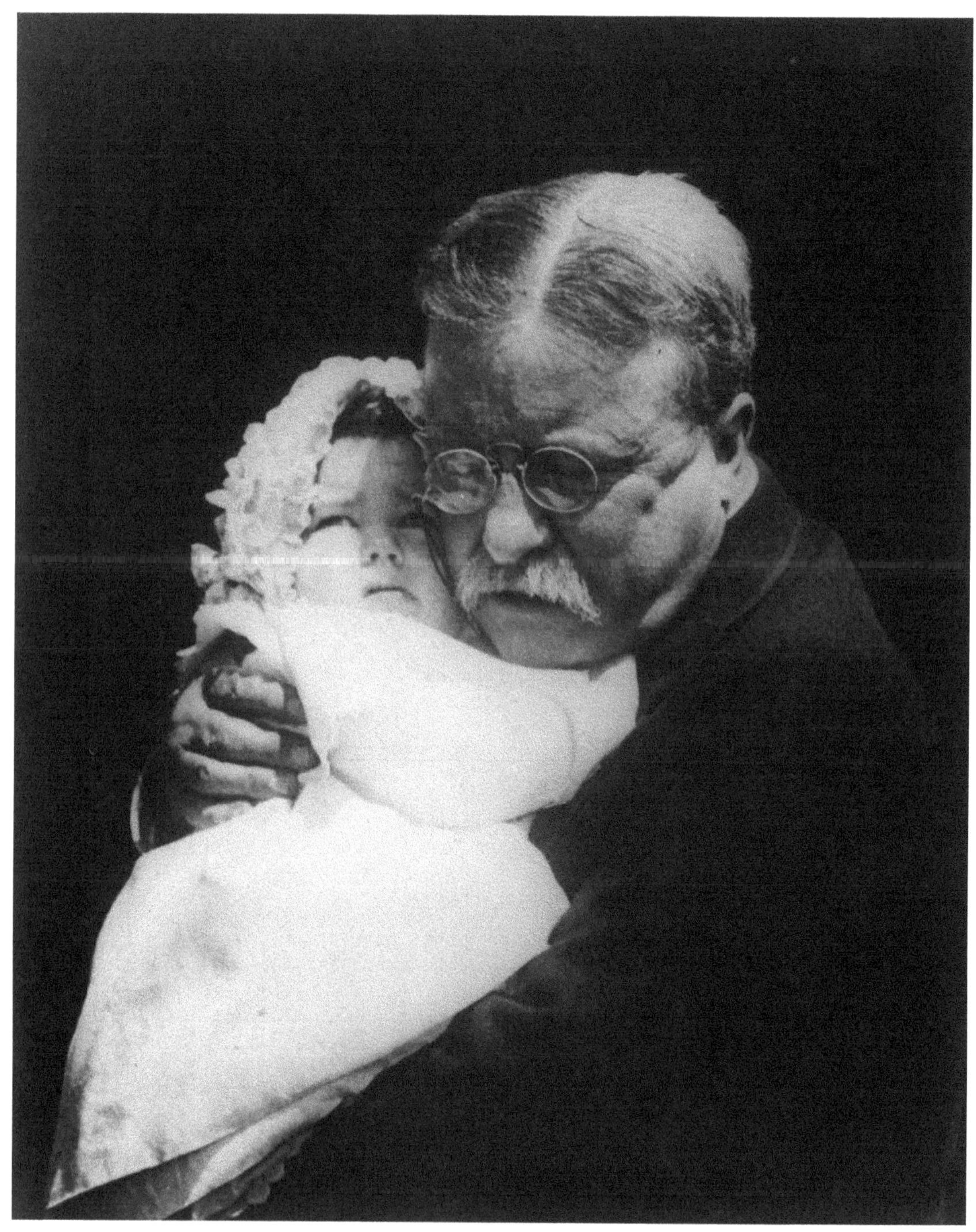

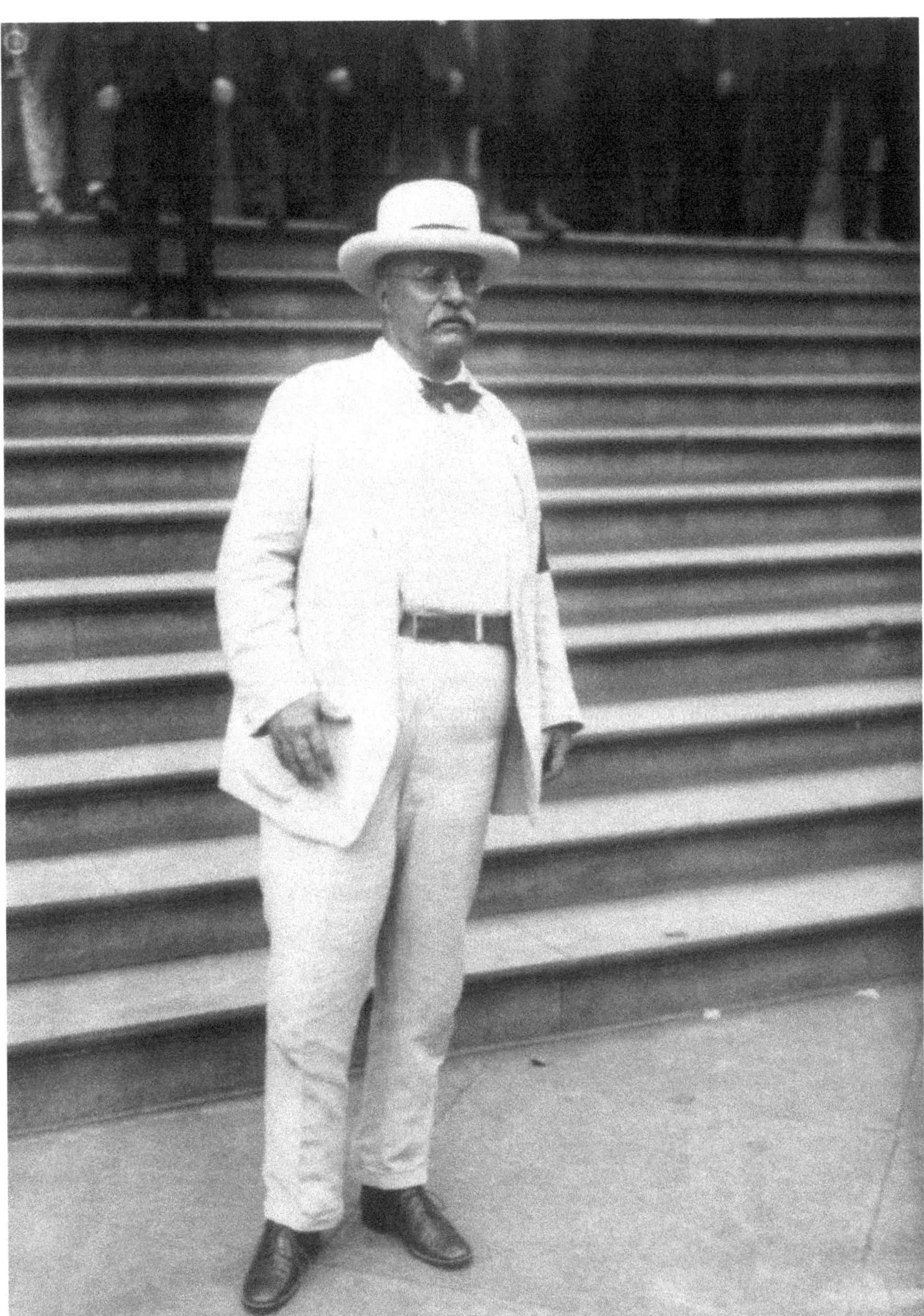

Roosevelt in September 1918. He suffered from bouts of malaria, blindness in one eye, a bad leg, and painful rheumatism—among other ailments—but was troubled most, his family maintained, by his broken heart. Less than half a year after his youngest son's death, TR died in his sleep at Sagamore Hill on January 6, 1919.

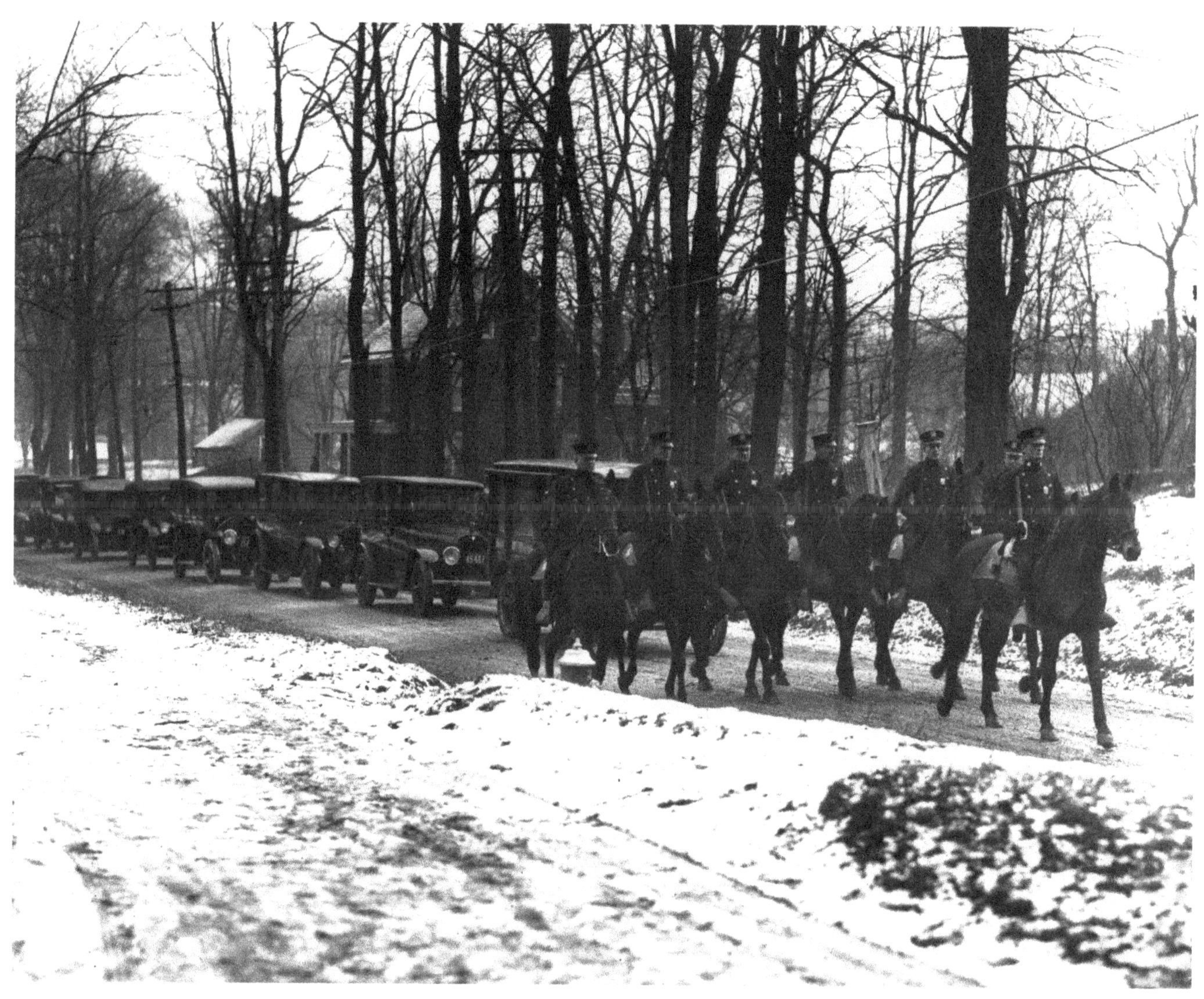

"The old lion is dead," Archie cabled distant family members. Ted and Kermit were still overseas, but everyone else returned for Roosevelt's funeral, held at Oyster Bay on January 8, 1919. Five hundred people crowded into Christ Episcopal Church, and thousands of mourners stood outside.

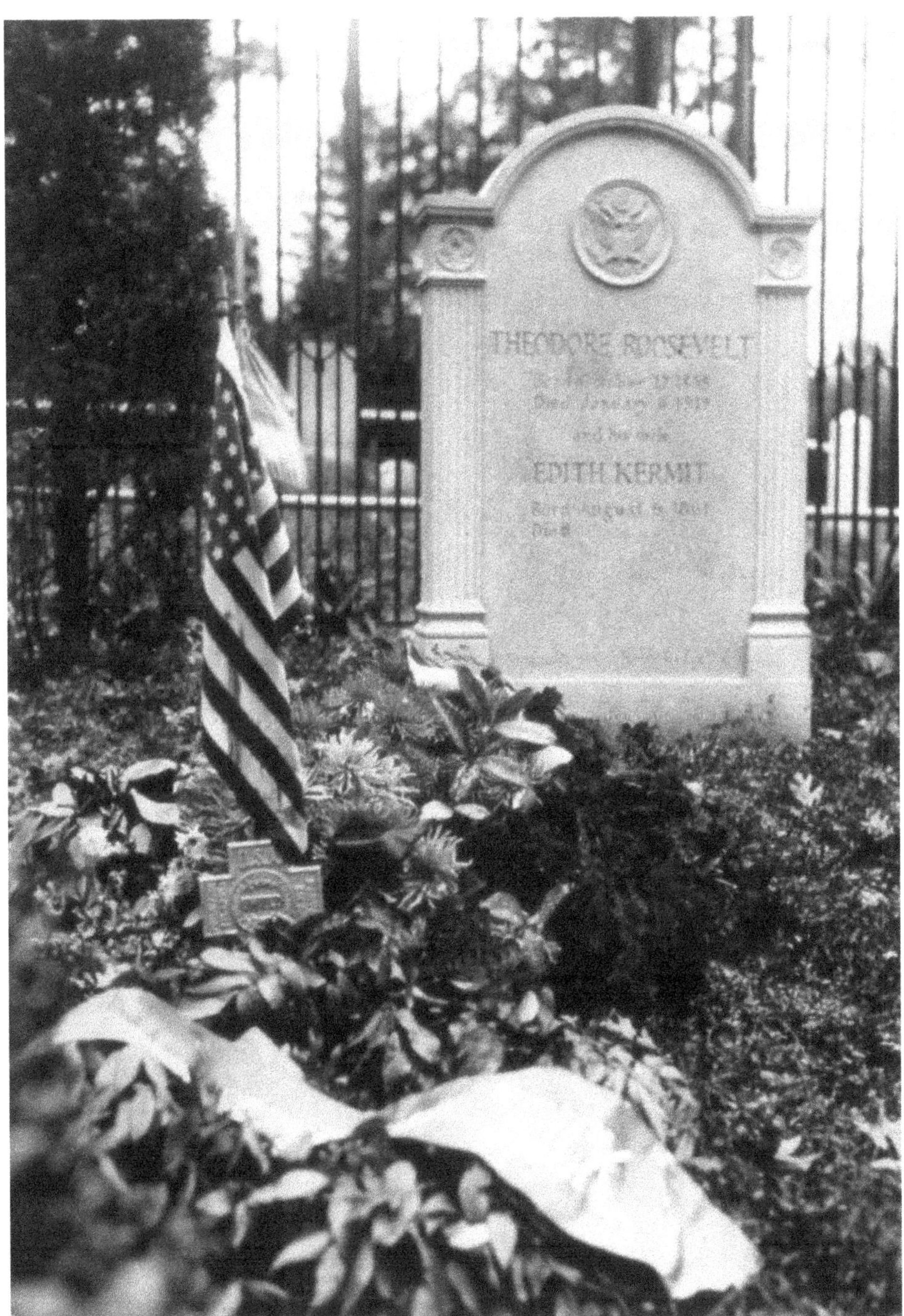

Theodore Roosevelt's gravestone, on October 26, 1919. The wreath was from King Albert of Belgium. Edith was buried beside him, after her death on September 30, 1948.

"There are many forms of success, many forms of triumph. But there is no other success that in any shape or way approaches that which is open to most of the many, many men and women who have the right ideals. These are the men and women who see that it is the intimate and homely things that count most. They are the men and women who have the courage to strive for the happiness which comes only with labor and effort and self-sacrifice, and only to those whose joy in life springs in part from power of work and sense of duty." Theodore Roosevelt, from his autobiography.

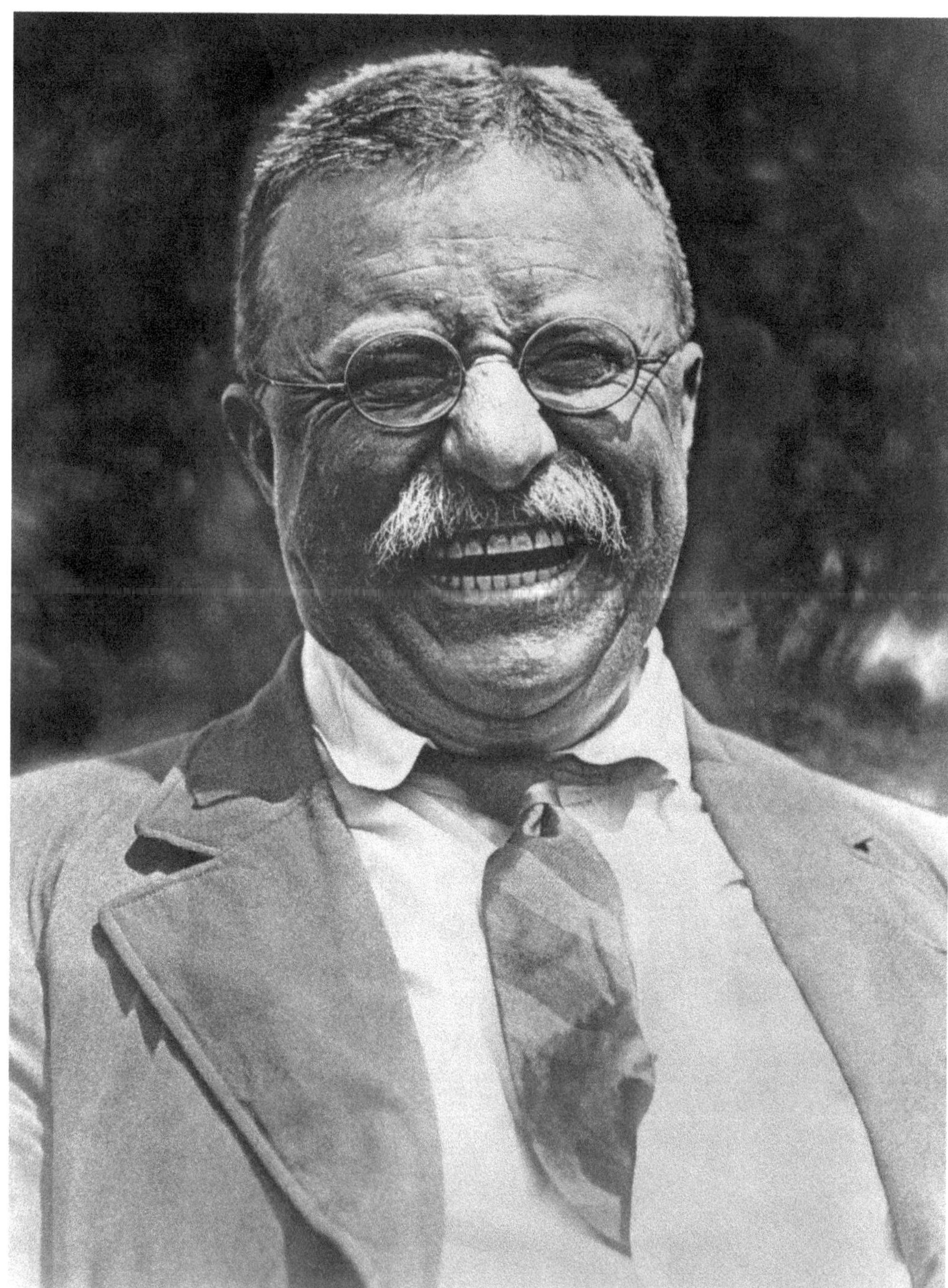

Notes on the Photographs

These notes, listed by page number, attempt to include all aspects known of the photographs. Each of the photographs is identified by the page number, photograph's title or description, photographer and collection, and archive. Call or box numbers and identifying phrases, to a maximum of 30 characters, are added when applicable. Although every attempt was made to collect all data, in some cases complete data may have been unavailable due to the age and condition of some of the photographs and records.

ii **Theodore Roosevelt**
Library of Congress
LC-USZ62-117454

vi **Roosevelt in Buckskin**
Library of Congress
LC-USZ62-23232

x **Bright Angel Trail**
Library of Congress
LC-USZ62-128069

2 **Collage**
Theodore Roosevelt Collection
Harvard College Library
Photographer: Underwood & Underwood, New York
529

3 **Roosevelt, 1858**
Theodore Roosevelt Collection
Harvard College Library
Photographer: Rockwood, New York
520.11

4 **Cornelius Van Schaak Roosevelt's Home**
Theodore Roosevelt Collection
Harvard College Library
570.1.R67c

5 **President Abraham Lincoln's Funeral**
Theodore Roosevelt Collection
Harvard College Library
570.1.R67c

6 **The Roosevelt Family**
Theodore Roosevelt Collection
Harvard College Library
520.11

7 **Age 17**
Theodore Roosevelt Collection
Harvard College Library
520.11

8 **Roosevelt Sr.**
Theodore Roosevelt Collection
Harvard College Library
From: *Theodore Roosevelt, Sr., a Tribute* (New York, 1902)

9 **Family**
Theodore Roosevelt Collection
Harvard College Library
520.11

10 **Roosevelt, 1876**
Theodore Roosevelt Collection
Harvard College Library
520.12

11 **With Alice H. Lee**
Theodore Roosevelt Collection
Harvard College Library
Photographer: Allen & Rowell, Boston
By permission of the Houghton Library, Harvard University
bMS Am 1541.9 (136)

12 **Winthrop Street**
Theodore Roosevelt Collection
Harvard College Library
Photographer: Morrison
560.12

13 **Roosevelt, 1880**
Theodore Roosevelt Collection
Harvard College Library
520.12

14 **Hunting Trip**
Theodore Roosevelt Collection
Harvard College Library
Photographer: H. Rocher, Chicago
520.12

15 **Wilderness Guides**
Theodore Roosevelt Collection
Harvard College Library
520.12

16 **New York's Youngest Assemblyman**
Theodore Roosevelt Collection
Harvard College Library
Photographer: Falk, New York
520.13

17 **Dakota Territory**
Theodore Roosevelt Collection
Harvard College Library
520.14

18 **Roosevelt, 1886**
Theodore Roosevelt Collection
Harvard College Library
R500.R67-003

20 **Board of Police Commissioners**
Theodore Roosevelt Collection
Harvard College Library
Photographer: J. Imhoff
520.22

21 **High Chair Lunch Room**
Theodore Roosevelt Collection
Harvard College Library
Photographer: Kay C. Lenskold
560.22

22 **Roosevelt Playing with Children**
Theodore Roosevelt Collection
Harvard College Library
541.21

23 **Ethel on Piggyback**
Theodore Roosevelt Collection
Harvard College Library
R500.R67-037

24 **Office at the State, War, and Navy Building**
Theodore Roosevelt Collection
Harvard College Library
Photographer: Clinedinst, Washington
520.23

25 **Roosevelt in Rough Rider Uniform**
Library of Congress
cph 3c33866

26 **The First United States Volunteer Cavalry**
Library of Congress
LC-USZ62-127283

27 **The Rough Riders in San Antonio, May 1898**
Theodore Roosevelt Collection
Harvard College Library
Photographer: Barr, San Antonio
560.3

28 **Theodore Roosevelt and Leonard Wood in San Antonio, May 1898**
Theodore Roosevelt Collection
Harvard College Library
Photographer: Barr, San Antonio
560.3

29 **The Rough Riders' Last Dinner**
Theodore Roosevelt Collection
Harvard College Library
560.3

30 **The Embarkation at Tampa**
Theodore Roosevelt Collection
Harvard College Library
R560.3.Em3-085

31 **Theodore Roosevelt as Colonel**
Library of Congress
LC-USZ62-39935

32 **Colonel Roosevelt and His Rough Riders**
Library of Congress
LC-USZC4-7934

33 **Boneyard of the Cabanas Military Prison**
Theodore Roosevelt Collection
Harvard College Library
Photographer: S. A. Cohner
560.3

34 **Montauk, Long Island**
Theodore Roosevelt Collection
Harvard College Library
Photographer: D. L. Elmendorf
R560.3.EL61-027

35 **TR and Rough Rider Officers**
Theodore Roosevelt Collection
Harvard College Library
Photographer: D. L. Elmendorf
R560.3.EL61-003a

36 **Parade**
Theodore Roosevelt Collection
Harvard College Library
560.3

37 **Governor of New York in 1898**
Theodore Roosevelt Collection
Harvard College Library
From: *Theodore Roosevelt and His Time,* Joseph Bucklin Bishop (New York, 1920)

38 **New York State National Guard Association Speech**
Theodore Roosevelt Collection
Harvard College Library
Photographer: Paul Thompson
560.41

39 **Republican Party's Choice**
Theodore Roosevelt Collection
Harvard College Library
Photographer: International
560.41

40 **Governor of New York**
Library of Congress
LC-USZC2-6201

41 **President William McKinley and Roosevelt**
Library of Congress
LC-USZ62-91482

42 **The 1900 Vice-Presidential Campaign**
Theodore Roosevelt Collection
Harvard College Library
560.41

43 **Roosevelt's Vice-Presidential Campaign**
Theodore Roosevelt Collection
Harvard College Library
Photographer: Underwood & Underwood, New York
560.41

44 **Theodore Roosevelt Campaigning in Freeport**
Library of Congress
LC-USZ62-95887

45 **Theodore Roosevelt Campaigning**
Theodore Roosevelt Collection
Harvard College Library
Photographer: H. O. Langley
560.41

46 **The 1900 Election**
Theodore Roosevelt Collection
Harvard College Library
560.42

48 **Honoring McKinley**
Library of Congress
LC-USZ62-96529

49 **In Buffalo**
Library of Congress
LC-USZ62-96530

50 **A Dreadful Thing**
Theodore Roosevelt Collection
Harvard College Library
Photographer: Underwood & Underwood, New York
560.51 1902

51 **Carriage Accident**
Theodore Roosevelt Collection
Harvard College Library
560.51 1902

52 **President Roosevelt Emphasizes the Point**
Theodore Roosevelt Collection
Harvard College Library
Photographer: Underwood & Underwood, New York
560.51 1902

53 **Eighteen-year-old Alice Roosevelt**
Theodore Roosevelt Collection
Harvard College Library
R500.P69a-057

54 **In Asheville, North Carolina, 1902**
Theodore Roosevelt Collection
Harvard College Library
Photographer: Underwood & Underwood, New York
560.51 1902

55 **Roosevelt Surrounded by Luminaries**
Theodore Roosevelt Collection
Harvard College Library
Photographer: Underwood & Underwood, New York
560.51 1902

56 **Students in Summerville**
Theodore Roosevelt Collection
Harvard College Library
Photographer: Underwood & Underwood, New York
560.51 1902

57 **Annapolis**
Library of Congress
LC-USZ62-127778

58 **The Office in the White House**
Theodore Roosevelt Collection
Harvard College Library
Photographer: Leet Brothers, Washington
558

59 **Jumping Rails**
Library of Congress
LC-USZ62-4698

60 **Sagamore Hill in 1902**
Library of Congress
LC-USZ62-94011

61 **Hunting in Mississippi**
Theodore Roosevelt Collection
Harvard College Library
Photographer: A. L. Blanks, Vicksburg, Miss.
560.51 1902

62 **Deck of the Mayflower**
Library of Congress
LC-USZ62-97317

63 **Prince Henry of Prussia, President Roosevelt, and Their Attendants**
Library of Congress
LC USZ62 100080

64 **Hannibal, Missouri, 1903**
Theodore Roosevelt Collection
Harvard College Library
Photographer: Underwood & Underwood, New York
560.51 1903

65 **Roosevelt Speaking**
Library of Congress
LC-USZ62-116512

66 **President Roosevelt Stresses a Point**
Theodore Roosevelt Collection
Harvard College Library
Photographer: Underwood & Underwood, New York
560.51 1903

67 **The Newlands Act**
Theodore Roosevelt Collection
Harvard College Library
Photographer: Underwood & Underwood, New York
560.51 1903

68 **President Roosevelt on Horseback**
Library of Congress
LC-USZ62-6231

69 **Yellowstone National Park**
Theodore Roosevelt Collection
Harvard College Library
Photographer: Underwood & Underwood, New York
560.51 1903

70 **John Burroughs at Home**
Theodore Roosevelt Collection
Harvard College Library
Photographer: Underwood & Underwood, New York
560.51 1903

71 **Camping and Tramping**
Theodore Roosevelt Collection
Harvard College Library
Photographer: Illustrated Sporting News
560.51 1903

72 **Roosevelt at Inspiration Point**
Library of Congress
LC-USZ62-40981

73 **Yosemite Valley**
Theodore Roosevelt Collection
Harvard College Library
Photographer: Underwood & Underwood, New York
560.51 1903

74 **Theodore Roosevelt at Glacier Point**
Theodore Roosevelt Collection
Harvard College Library
Photographer: Underwood & Underwood, New York
560.51 1903

75 **Wielding a Shovel**
Theodore Roosevelt Collection
Harvard College Library
Photographer: Avery Edwin Field
560.51 1903

76 **At the University of California, Berkeley**
Theodore Roosevelt Collection
Harvard College Library
Photographer: Underwood & Underwood, New York
560.51 1903

77 **The House Atop Cove Neck**
Library of Congress
LC-USZ62-93845

78 **Roosevelt Family, 1903**
Library of Congress
LC-USZ62-113665

79 **Roosevelt and His Sons**
Theodore Roosevelt Collection
Harvard College Library
Photographer: Arthur Hewitt
541.51

80 **Inaugural Oath, 1905**
Library of Congress
LC-USZ62-231

81 **Roosevelt's Inaugural Address**
Library of Congress
LC-USZ62-5069

82 **Inaugural Parade**
Library of Congress
LC-USZ62-56009

83 **Roosevelt in Carriage**
Library of Congress
LC-USZ62-135043

84 **With His Cabinet**
Library of Congress
LC-H25-5450

85 **Lawn Party**
Library of Congress
LC-USZ62-126408

86 **Greeting "the Boys"**
Library of Congress
LC-USZ62-97687

87 **Speech in Chicago, 1905**
Library of Congress
pan 6a24998

88 **In Durant, 1905**
Library of Congress
LC-USZ62-102528

89 **Coyote Hunt**
Theodore Roosevelt Collection
Harvard College Library
560.52 1905

90 **Rifle, Colorado, 1905**
Library of Congress
LC-USZ62-93046

92 **Twenty Days Hunting Bear and Bobcat**
Theodore Roosevelt Collection
Harvard College Library
Photographer: Underwood & Underwood, New York
560.52 1905

93 **Bear Hunt**
Library of Congress
LC-USZ62-11866

94 West Divide Creek in Colorado
Theodore Roosevelt Collection
Harvard College Library
Photographer: Philip B. Stewart
R560.52.Em3s-073

95 Victory Supper
Theodore Roosevelt Collection
Harvard College Library
Photographer: Philip B. Stewart
R560.52.Em3s-018

96 Roosevelt and Skip, the Terrier
Theodore Roosevelt Collection
Harvard College Library
560.52 1905

97 John Avery McIlhenny, TR, John C. Greenway
Theodore Roosevelt Collection
Harvard College Library
Photographer: Underwood & Underwood, New York
560.52 1905

98 Tuskegee Institute
Theodore Roosevelt Collection
Harvard College Library
Photographer: American Press Association
560.52 1905

99 Roosevelt with His Saint Bernard, Rollo
Theodore Roosevelt Collection
Harvard College Library
Photographer: Charles L. Ritzmann, New York
560.52

100 Roosevelt at Work
Library of Congress
LC-USZ62-107365

101 Chopping Wood
Theodore Roosevelt Collection
Harvard College Library
Photographer: J. Horace McFarland
560.52 1905

102 Rowing
Theodore Roosevelt Collection
Harvard College Library
Photographer: J. Horace McFarland
560.52 1905

103 Mediator of Treaty
Theodore Roosevelt Collection
Harvard College Library
Photographer: Underwood & Underwood, New York
560.52 1905

104 La Boca, Panama
Library of Congress
LC-USZ62-124257

105 The Panama Canal
Theodore Roosevelt Collection
Harvard College Library
Photographer: Underwood & Underwood, New York
560.52 1906

106 The Presidential Party at Culebra Cut
Theodore Roosevelt Collection
Harvard College Library
Photographer: Underwood & Underwood, New York
560.52 1906

107 Shuttle Car at the Panama Canal Site
Theodore Roosevelt Collection
Harvard College Library
560.52 1906

108 President and First Lady Aboard the Bolivar
Theodore Roosevelt Collection
Harvard College Library
Photographer: Underwood & Underwood, New York
560.52 1906

109 Roosevelt in Rio Piedras, Puerto Rico, 1906
Library of Congress
LC-USZ62-108296

110 Official Portrait Photograph
Library of Congress
LC-USZ62-90057

111 With Vice-president Charles W. Fairbanks
Theodore Roosevelt Collection
Harvard College Library
Photographer: C. F. Bretzman, Indianapolis
560.52 1907

112 Portrait of the Roosevelt Family and Dog
Theodore Roosevelt Collection
Harvard College Library
Photographer: Pach Brothers, New York
541.52

113 Parade in Canton, Ohio
Theodore Roosevelt Collection
Harvard College Library
Photographer: Underwood & Underwood, New York
560.52 1907

114 On the USS Mississippi
Theodore Roosevelt Collection
Harvard College Library
Photographer: Underwood & Underwood, New York
560.52 1907

115 Hunting in Tenesas Bayou, Louisiana
Theodore Roosevelt Collection
Harvard College Library
Photographer: Alexander Lambert
560.52 1907

116 Leaving St. Louis, Missouri
Library of Congress
LC-USZ62-91666

117 On the Mayflower
Theodore Roosevelt Collection
Harvard College Library
Photographer: Underwood & Underwood, New York
560.52 1907

118 Roosevelt and the 1908 U.S. Olympic Team
Library of Congress
LC-USZ62-133049

119 Roosevelt and Commodore Robert Perry
Theodore Roosevelt Collection
Harvard College Library
Photographer: Underwood & Underwood, New York
560.52 1908

120 With Group of Advisors
Theodore Roosevelt Collection
Harvard College Library
560.52 1909

121 Leaving the White House
Theodore Roosevelt Collection
Harvard College Library
Photographer: Harris & Ewing
541.52

122 Taft and Roosevelt
Library of Congress
LC-USZ62-32737

124 Packing for Africa
Theodore Roosevelt Collection
Harvard College Library
Photographer: Abercrombie & Fitch
560.61

125 Winchester Rifles
Theodore Roosevelt Collection
Harvard College Library
Photographer: Paul Thompson
560.61

126 The Azores
Theodore Roosevelt Collection
Harvard College Library
560.61

127 On Safari
Library of Congress
LC-USZ62-106033

128 African Bearers
Library of Congress
LC-USZC2-6210

129 With Elephant Kill
Library of Congress
LC-USZ62-131443

130 First Lion Kill
Theodore Roosevelt Collection
Harvard College Library
560.61

131 St. Mary's Convent
Theodore Roosevelt Collection
Harvard College Library
560.61

132 Luxor, Egypt
Library of Congress
LC-USZ62-113664

133 Camelback in Kerrei
Theodore Roosevelt Collection
Harvard College Library
Photographer: Underwood & Underwood, New York
560.61

134 Watching a Horse Show
Theodore Roosevelt Collection
Harvard College Library
560.61

135 Standing in Carriage
Library of Congress
LC-USZ62-95742

136 In Europe
Theodore Roosevelt Collection
Harvard College Library
560.62 Italy

137 International Peace
Theodore Roosevelt Collection
Harvard College Library
Photographer: Rol
560.62 France

138 Stockholm
Theodore Roosevelt Collection
Harvard College Library
Photographer: C. Trampus
560.62 Sweden

139 Roosevelt and Kaiser Wilhelm
Theodore Roosevelt Collection
Harvard College Library
Photographer: Franz Tellgman, Berlin
560.62 Germany

140 Funeral of England's King Edward VII
Theodore Roosevelt Collection
Harvard College Library
Photographer: M. E. Berner
560.62 England

141 Biological Analogies in History
Theodore Roosevelt Collection
Harvard College Library
Photographer: C. Roberson
560.62 England

142 Arriving in New York
Library of Congress
LC-USZC2-6236

143 **Edith and Theodore Roosevelt, 1910**
Theodore Roosevelt Collection
Harvard College Library
Photographer: Paul Thompson
560.6

144 **Sagamore Hill Inside**
Theodore Roosevelt Collection
Harvard College Library
Photographer: Paul Thompson
559

145 **Doing His Part**
Theodore Roosevelt Collection
Harvard College Library
560.6

146 **First President Ever to Fly in Airplane**
Theodore Roosevelt Collection
Harvard College Library
Photographer: E. W. Loos, St. Louis
560.6

147 **North River Ferry, New York, September 11**
Theodore Roosevelt Collection
Harvard College Library
Photographer: American Press Association
560.6

148 **The National Child Labor Committee Address**
Library of Congress
LC-DIG-nclc-04725

149 **Spokane, Washington, April 1911**
Theodore Roosevelt Collection
Harvard College Library
560.6

150 **Roosevelt's Announcement**
Library of Congress
LC-USZ62-90405

151 **Progressive Party Platform**
Theodore Roosevelt Collection
Harvard College Library
Photographer: International
560.7

152 **Steel Eyeglasses Case**
Theodore Roosevelt Collection
Harvard College Library
Photographer: International
560.7

153 **Bloodied Shirt**
Theodore Roosevelt Collection
Harvard College Library
Photographer: International
560.7

154 **Mercy Hospital**
Theodore Roosevelt Collection
Harvard College Library
560.7

155 **The 1912 Campaign**
Theodore Roosevelt Collection
Harvard College Library
560.7

156 **Flowers**
Theodore Roosevelt Collection
Harvard College Library
Photographer: International
560.7

157 **In Library at Sagamore Hill**
Library of Congress
LC-USZC2-6234

158 **With Leonard Wood**
Library of Congress
LC-USZC4-11865

159 **At His Sister's Home**
Theodore Roosevelt Collection
Harvard College Library
Photographer: Paul Thompson
560.8

160 **On the North Rim of the Grand Canyon**
Theodore Roosevelt Collection
Harvard College Library
Photographer: H. S. Stephenson
560.8

161 **After New Mexico and Arizona**
Theodore Roosevelt Collection
Harvard College Library
560.8

162 **First Grandchild**
Theodore Roosevelt Collection
Harvard College Library
Photographer: W. Burden Stage
541.8

163 **Ethel Roosevelt Weds Richard Derby**
Theodore Roosevelt Collection
Harvard College Library
Photographer: Underwood & Underwood, New York
560.8

164 **Buenos Aires**
Theodore Roosevelt Collection
Harvard College Library
560.81

165 **Colonel Candido Mariano da Silva Rondon**
Theodore Roosevelt Collection
Harvard College Library
Photographer: Kermit Roosevelt
560.81

166 **Encamped**
Theodore Roosevelt Collection
Harvard College Library
560.81

167 Near Rio Taquary in Brazil
Theodore Roosevelt Collection
Harvard College Library
Photographer: Frank Harper
560.81

168 The River of Doubt
Theodore Roosevelt Collection
Harvard College Library
Photographer: Leo Miller
560.81

169 Roosevelt Writing
Theodore Roosevelt Collection
Harvard College Library
Photographer: Anthony Fiala
560.81

170 Roosevelt and Rondon with Bush Deer
Theodore Roosevelt Collection
Harvard College Library
Photographer: Anthony Fiala
560.81

171 Poling up the River
Theodore Roosevelt Collection
Harvard College Library
560.81

172 River Injury
Theodore Roosevelt Collection
Harvard College Library
Photographer: George Cherrie
560.81

173 Swimming with Piranhas
Theodore Roosevelt Collection
Harvard College Library
Photographer: Kermit Roosevelt
560.81

174 Portaging the Boats
Theodore Roosevelt Collection
Harvard College Library
Photographer: George Cherrie
560.81

175 Writing Under Mosquito Netting
Theodore Roosevelt Collection
Harvard College Library
560.81

176 Sharing Discoveries
Theodore Roosevelt Collection
Harvard College Library
560.81

177 Poetry and Novels
Theodore Roosevelt Collection
Harvard College Library
560.8

178 Friends of the Roosevelts
Theodore Roosevelt Collection
Harvard College Library
560.8

179 Houdini with Roosevelt
Library of Congress
LC-USZ62-112437

180 The Honor of a Cherry Tree
Theodore Roosevelt Collection
Harvard College Library
By permission of the Houghton Library, Harvard University
*87M-100: Notebook of Edith Kermit Roosevelt

181 On Board the Daisy
Theodore Roosevelt Collection
Harvard College Library
560.8

182 Roosevelt with Arthur Roy "Art" Smith
Theodore Roosevelt Collection
Harvard College Library
Photographer: Press Illustrated Service
560.8

183 Greeting Rough Riders
Theodore Roosevelt Collection
Harvard College Library
560.8

184 Sagamore Hill
Theodore Roosevelt Collection
Harvard College Library
Photographer: Underwood & Underwood, New York
559

185 With Grandson
Theodore Roosevelt Collection
Harvard College Library
Photographer: Campbell Studios
541.8

186 Pressing a Point
Theodore Roosevelt Collection
Harvard College Library
Photographer: Cosmopolitan Photo Service
560.9

187 Oyster Bay Boy Scouts
Theodore Roosevelt Collection
Harvard College Library
Photographer: American Photo Service
560.9

188 Women Sewing
Theodore Roosevelt Collection
Harvard College Library
Photographer: Underwood & Underwood, New York
560.9

189 In Favor of Suffrage
Theodore Roosevelt Collection
Harvard College Library
Photographer: Cosmopolitan Photo Service
560.9

190 Punta Gorda, Florida
Theodore Roosevelt Collection
Harvard College Library
560.9

191 Grandson Archibald Bulloch Roosevelt
Theodore Roosevelt Collection
Harvard College Library
Photographer: International
541.9

192 Edith Roosevelt, a Steadying Force
Theodore Roosevelt Collection
Harvard College Library
541.9

193 World War I
Theodore Roosevelt Collection
Harvard College Library
Photographer: Underwood & Underwood, New York
560.92

194 World War Efforts
Theodore Roosevelt Collection
Harvard College Library
Photographer: Bretzman Studio, Indianapolis
560.92

195 Archie's Bullet Wound
Theodore Roosevelt Collection
Harvard College Library
560.92

196 Granddaughter Edith Roosevelt Derby
Theodore Roosevelt Collection
Harvard College Library
Photographer: Clarence LeGendre
541.9

197 Roosevelt in September 1918
Theodore Roosevelt Collection
Harvard College Library
Photographer: Underwood & Underwood, New York
560.9

198 The Old Lion Is Dead
Theodore Roosevelt Collection
Harvard College Library
Photographer: Paul Thompson
560.98

199 Roosevelt's Gravestone
Theodore Roosevelt Collection
Harvard College Library
Photographer: International
560.98

200 Theodore Roosevelt Laughing
Library of Congress
LC-USZ62-134760

HISTORIC PHOTOS OF
THEODORE ROOSEVELT

Following the assassination of President McKinley, Theodore Roosevelt charged into the limelight and the twentieth century as the 26th president of the United States. Charismatic, fiercely energetic, and adored by Americans everywhere, TR would champion a host of causes to bring the nation into the new century brimming with optimism and onto the international scene as a world power.

From his youth in New York City to his declining years during World War I, *Historic Photos of Theodore Roosevelt* captures the greatest exploits of one of the nation's greatest Americans. As soldier and explorer, as conservationist and big game hunter, as governor, vice-president, and president, as scientist and writer, and as family man, TR's life in pictures blazes a path sure to enthrall every reader, from the student of history to the history buff.

TR became and remains an American icon. The hundreds of photographs in *Historic Photos of Theodore Roosevelt,* many of them unusual and rarely seen, and all published in vivid black-and-white, help Americans a hundred years later to understand why.

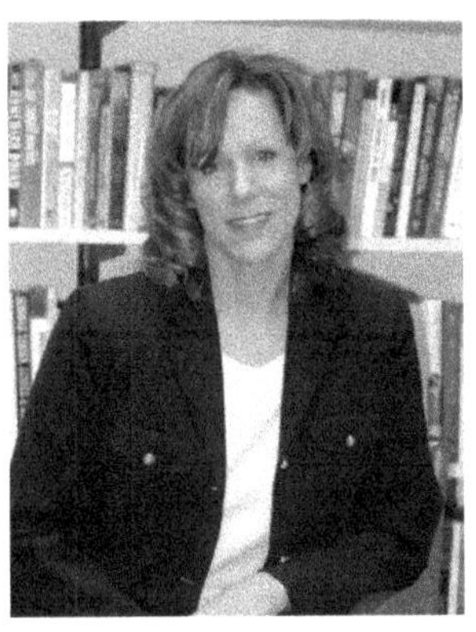

Stacy A. Cordery is the author of *Alice: Alice Roosevelt Longworth, from White House Princess to Washington Power Broker* (Viking, 2007) and *Theodore Roosevelt: In the Vanguard of the Modern* (Thompson/Wadsworth, 2003). Since 2001 she has been the web bibliographer for the National First Ladies Library in Canton, Ohio. Cordery earned her doctorate in history at the University of Texas. She is a professor of history at Monmouth College in Monmouth, Illinois, where she has earned several teaching awards.

WWW.TURNERPUBLISHING.COM